Modern Critical Views

Edward Albee
African American Poets Volume I
American and Canadian Women Poets, 1930–present
American Women Poets, 1650–1950
Maya Angelou
Asian-American Writers
Margaret Atwood
Jane Austen
James Baldwin
Samuel Beckett
Saul Bellow
The Bible
William Blake
Jorge Luis Borges
Ray Bradbury
The Brontës
Gwendolyn Brooks
Elizabeth Barrett Browning
Robert Browning
Italo Calvino
Albert Camus
Lewis Carroll
Willa Cather
Cervantes
Geoffrey Chaucer
Anton Chekhov
Kate Chopin
Agatha Christie
Samuel Taylor Coleridge
Joseph Conrad
Contemporary Poets
Stephen Crane
Dante
Daniel Defoe
Charles Dickens
Emily Dickinson
John Donne and the 17th-Century Poets
Fyodor Dostoevsky
W.E.B. Du Bois
George Eliot
T. S. Eliot
Ralph Ellison
Ralph Waldo Emerson
William Faulkner
F. Scott Fitzgerald
Sigmund Freud
Robert Frost
George Gordon, Lord Byron
Graham Greene
Thomas Hardy
Nathaniel Hawthorne
Ernest Hemingway
Hispanic-American Writers
Homer
Langston Hughes
Zora Neale Hurston
Henrik Ibsen
John Irving
Henry James
James Joyce
Franz Kafka
John Keats
Jamaica Kincaid
Stephen King
Rudyard Kipling
D. H. Lawrence
Ursula K. Le Guin
Sinclair Lewis
Bernard Malamud
Christopher Marlowe
Gabriel García Márquez
Cormac McCarthy
Carson McCullers
Herman Melville
Molière
Arthur Miller
John Milton
Molière
Toni Morrison
Native-American Writers
Joyce Carol Oates
Flannery O'Connor
Eugene O'Neill
George Orwell
Octavio Paz
Sylvia Plath
Edgar Allan Poe
Katherine Anne Porter
J. D. Salinger
Jean-Paul Sartre
William Shakespeare: Histories and Poems
William Shakespeare: Romances
William Shakespeare: The Comedies
William Shakespeare: The Tragedies
George Bernard Shaw
Mary Wollstonecraft Shelley
Percy Bysshe Shelley
Alexander Solzhenitsyn
Sophocles
John Steinbeck
Tom Stoppard
Jonathan Swift
Amy Tan
Alfred, Lord Tennyson
Henry David Thoreau
J. R. R. Tolkien
Leo Tolstoy
Mark Twain
John Updike

Modern Critical Views

Kurt Vonnegut
Alice Walker
Robert Penn Warren
Eudora Welty
Edith Wharton
Walt Whitman
Oscar Wilde
Tennessee Williams
Thomas Wolfe
Tom Wolfe
Virginia Woolf
William Wordsworth
Richard Wright
William Butler Yeats

Modern Critical Views

AFRICAN-AMERICAN POETS

PHILLIS WHEATLEY THROUGH MELVIN B. TOLSON

Edited and with an introduction by
Harold Bloom
Sterling Professor of the Humanities
Yale University

CHELSEA HOUSE
PUBLISHERS
An imprint of Infobase Publishing

Bloom's Modern Critical Views: African-American Poets: Phillis Wheatley through Melvin B. Tolson

Chelsea House
An imprint of Infobase Publishing
132 West 31st Street
New York NY 10001

ISBN-10: 0-7910-6332-1
ISBN-13: 978-0-7910-6332-3

Library of Congress Cataloging-in-Publication Data
African-American Poets : Phillis Wheatley through Melvin B. Tolson /
Harold Bloom, ed.
p. cm. — (Modern critical views)
Includes bibliographical references and index.
ISBN 0-7910-6332-1
1. American poetry—African-American authors—History and criticism.
2. African Americans in literature. I. Bloom, Harold. II. Series.
PS310.N4 A69 2002
811.009'896073—dc21 2002006352

Contributing Editor: Janyce Marson

Printed in the United States of America

IBT EJB 10 9 8 7 6 5 4

This book is printed on acid-free paper.

Contents

Editor's Note

My Introduction provides brief critical overviews of six poets: Paul Laurence Dunbar, Claude McKay, Jean Toomer, Sterling A. Brown, Langston Hughes, and Countee Callen.

Marcellus Blount traces the influence of African-American sermons upon the poets of the same tradition, while Leo Hamalian indicates the effect of D. H. Lawrence's "dark gods" upon McKay, Toomer, and Hughes.

The eighteenth century slave poet Phillis Wheatley is studied by Julian D. Mason, Jr. and Sandra O'Neale, after which Patricia Liggins Hall considers the nineteenth century Frances Harper, Abolitionist and early Feminist.

Paul Laurence Dunbar's dialect verse is examined by John Keeling, while Ralph Story takes into account historical limitations imposed upon Dunbar.

Richard A. Long praises James Weldon Johnson's prophetic intensity, after which the Jamaican poet Claude McKay is accurately seen by Geta J. LeSeur as a High Romantic.

Walt Whitman's legacy in regard to Jean Toomer is studied by George B. Hutchinson, while Sterling Brown's extension of black folk traditions is analyzed by John S. Wright.

Langston Hughes is usefully judged by Anita Patterson to be imbued with the spirit of jazz, after which Countee Cullen is seen in public perspective by Peter Powers, and in relation to William Blake by Ronald E. Sheasby.

M. B. Tolson is studied in his stylistic development by Mariann B. Russell, and as a sonneteer by Gary Smith.

Introduction

This Introduction will comment briefly upon six poets: Paul Laurence Dunbar, Claude McKay, Jean Toomer, Sterling A. Brown, Langston Hughes, and Countee Cullen.

1

Paul Laurence Dunbar was the first major African-American poet, and in my judgment remains one of the truly authentic poets of his American generation, which included Edwin Arlington Robinson, Trumbull Stickney, Edgar Lee Masters, James Weldon Johnson, and the earlier work of Robert Frost. Dead at thirty-five (tuberculosis augmented by alcoholism), Dunbar essentially wrote in the skeptical strain of Shelley, except in dialect poems. He inherited from Shelley an agonistic spirit, expressed strongly in "The Mystery," one of his undervalued poems, where he deliberately echoes "To a Skylark": "I fain would look before/ and after, but can neither do." Caught in an unhappy present for a black poet, Dunbar concludes "The Mystery" with memorable eloquence:

> I question of th'eternal bending skies
> That seem to neighbor with the novice earth;
> But they roll on and daily shut their eyes
> On me, as I one day shall do on them,
> And tell me not the secret that I ask.

The secret is the mystery of being an eternal novice, a kind of Promethean complaint, which leads to what may be Dunbar's best poem, "'Ere Sleep Comes Down to Soothe the Weary Eyes." The fifth of the six stanzas is an epitome of how intensely Dunbar can transcend his situation and its limitations:

> Ere sleep comes down to soothe the weary eyes,
> How questioneth the soul that other soul,—
> The inner sense which neither cheats nor lies,
> But self exposes unto self, a scroll
> Full writ with all life's acts unwise or wise,
> In characters indelible and known;
> So, trembling with the shock of sad surprise,
> The soul doth view its awful self alone,
> Ere sleep comes down to soothe the weary eyes.

"That other soul" or "awful self" is what the early African American Baptists called "the little me inside the big me," a spark or breath that is no part of nature or history. After eleven repetitions of: "Ere sleep comes down to soothe the weary eyes," we are startled by the poem's closing line, where "seal" replaces "soothe." In his perpetual struggle between bitterness and the Shelleyan wisdom of casting out personal remorse, Dunbar most frequently yields to a bitterness that transcends his personal sorrows.

One of the lucid voicings of that bitterness is Dunbar's memorial sonnet to Robert Gould Shaw, the Harvard College colonel who commanded the black 54th Massachusetts Regiment in its suicidal attack upon Fort Wagner (near Charleston) in July 1863. The sonnet's sestet laments the sacrifice of Shaw and his African American recruits, in a skepticism still relevant in 2001:

> Far better the slow blaze of Learning's light,
> The cool and quiet of her dearer fane,
> Than this hot terror of a hopeless fight,
> This cold endurance of the final pain,—
> Since thou and those who with thee died for right
> Have died, the Present teaches, but in vain!

Dunbar's emblematic poem remains "Sympathy," popularized by Maya Angelou's autobiographical appropriation of "I know why the caged bird sings!" Though Dunbar's High Romantic lyricism has long been unfashionable, his achievement in it remains considerable.

2

The Jamaican Claude McKay, who went from Marxism to Roman Catholicism, was a fierce spirit, whose sonnets have a formalist, baroque intensity that is also now undervalued, as here in "Saint Isaac's Church, Petrograd":

> Bow down my soul in worship very low
> And in the holy silences be lost.
> Bow down before the marble man of woe,
> Bow down before the singing angel host.
>
> What jewelled glory fills my spirit's eye!
> What golden grandeur moves the depths of me!
> The soaring arches lift me up on high
> Taking my breath with their rare symmetry.
>
> Bow down my soul and let the wondrous light
> Of Beauty bathe thee from her lofty throne
> Bow down before the wonder of man's might.
> Bow down in worship, humble and alone;
> Bow lowly down before the sacred sight
> Of man's divinity alive in stone.

This is still the admirer of Leon Trotsky, but the poem's complexity arises out of McKay's repressed awareness that something in his spirit is moving towards conversion. The sestet retreats from the octave's spirituality, and overtly hymns an aesthetic humanism. And yet "The marble man of woe," a representation of the Russian Christ, is not wholly consonant with "man's divinity alive in stone."

The most rugged of McKay's poems is "The Desolate City," a Romantic lament for the lost innocence of the spirit, and another indication of this poet's road to Rome. It may be that McKay, poetically speaking, was born at the wrong time, but too late rather than too early. For all his political anger, which has an authority difficult to withstand, he would have been culturally at home in the Catholicism of Gerard Manley Hopkins and Francis Thompson, a generation earlier than his own.

3

Jean Toomer's remarkable *Cane* (1923), a subtly interwoven medley of prose-poem and verse, was never matched by him again in the more than forty years remaining. *The Blue Meridian* (1929) fades away in contrast with Hart Crane's *The Bridge* (1930), though Toomer and Crane were friends, and some mutual influence was involved. Toomer's immersion in quack spiritualities was fatal both to his work and his sense of identity. And yet, in his brief flowering, he became the authentic poet of what would have to be called black pastoral, as in his marvelous "November Cotton Flower":

> Boll-weevil's coming, and the winter's cold,
> Made cotton-stalks look rusty, seasons old,
> And cotton, scarce as any southern snow,
> Was vanishing; the branch, so pinched and slow,
> Failed in its function as the autumn rake;
> Drouth fighting soil had caused the soil to take
> All water from the streams; dead birds were found
> In wells a hundred feet below the ground—
> Such was the season when the flower bloomed.
> Old folks were startled, and it soon assumed
> Significance. Superstition saw
> Something it had never seen before:
> Brown eyes that loved without a trace of fear,
> Beauty so sudden for that time of year.

This extraordinary lyric is both beautifully wrought and humanly profound. The late blooming of the flower becomes emblematic of a freedom from psychic dearth, the freedom to love.

4

Sterling Brown, at his frequent best, was able to assimilate the strong influences of A.E. Housman, Thomas Hardy, and Robert Frost, and to fuse them in a mode of his own. I should say "modes," for this eclectic poet had several voices, very much his own. The Frostian "Idyll" juxtaposes a sheltered woodland cranny with an intrusive hawk, and sees the deep peace return after the hawk's kill, giving the reader the burden of the final irony: "The stream purred listlessly along, / And all grew quite as peaceful as before."

In another mode developed from Hardy, Brown gives us the poignant "Rain," a remarkable transformation of the sonnet form:

Outside the cold, cold night; the dripping rain. . .
The water gurgles loosely in the eaves,
The savage lashes stripe the rattling pane
And beat a tattoo on November leaves.
The lamp wick gutters, and the last log steams
Upon the ash-filled hearth. Chill grows the room.
The ancient clock ticks creakily and seems
A fitting portent of the gathering gloom.

This is a night we planned. This place is where
One day, we would be happy; where the light
Should tint your shoulders and your wild flung hair.—
Whence we would—oh, we planned a merry morrow—
Recklessly part ways with the old hag, Sorrow. . .

Outside dripping rain; the cold, cold night.

After that wonderfully gloomy octave, there is the fine poetic shock of "This is a night we planned." The speaker is solitary, erotic loss is overwhelming, and yet everything proceeds by indirection. Thomas Hardy, with his acute sense of life's ironies, might have admired Sterling Brown's "Rain," which precedes Robert Penn Warren in reviving Hardy's spirit.

5

Langston Hughes, still the best-known African-American poet, was a considerable ironist, who nevertheless transformed himself into a populist of the imagination, somewhat influenced by the example of the now largely forgotten Carl Sandburg. His fame is securely founded upon his sophisticated variations on the blues form, as in the justly admired "The Weary Blues," with its shrewdly managed close:

In a deep song voice with a melancholy tone
I heard that Negro sing, that old piano moan—
    "Ain't got nobody in all this world,
    Ain't got nobody but ma self.

I's gwine to quit ma frownin'
And put ma troubles on the shelf."
Thump, thump, thump, went his foot on the floor.
He played a few chords then he sang some more—
"I got the Weary Blues
And I can't be satisfied.
Got the Weary Blues
And can't be satisfied—
I ain't happy no mo'
And I wish that I had died."
And far into the night he crooned that tune.
The stars went out and so did the moon.
The singer stopped playing and went to bed
While the Weary Blues echoed through his head.
He slept like a rock or a man that's dead.

The singer-pianist performs for all of us, as who does *not* suffer from the weary blues? At seventy-one, a lifelong bad sleeper, I envy Hughes's bluesman, whose art sublimates exhaustion and sorrow into comedy and rest. It is this ability to touch the universal that distinguishes Langston Hughes.

6

I have a particular fondness for Countee Cullen, as I do for Edwin Arlington Robinson, who was a benign influence upon Cullen's art, showing him how to be at once Keatsian and oneself. Like Robinson and Keats, Cullen was a highly self-conscious artist who knew that moral concerns could sink a poem without trace. Answering those who would make him only a "protest poet," Cullen eloquently prophesied for the best African American poets after him in his "To Certain Critics":

No radical option narrows grief,
Pain is no patriot,
And sorrow plaits her dismal leaf
For all as lief as not.

That wry pun upon "leaf" and "lief" is wonderfully typical of Countee Cullen, and is part of his legacy.

MARCELLUS BLOUNT

The Preacherly Text: African American Poetry and Vernacular Performance

> Nothing is more material, physical, corporeal than the exercise of power.
>
> —*Michel Foucault*

> When it comes to handling the Bible, I knocks down verbs, breaks up prepositions, and jumps over adjectives.
>
> —*Nineteenth-century vernacular preacher*

Even though African American critical theory has finally come into its own, theorists have yet to give black poets their proper voice in constructing an African American literary tradition. With few exceptions, recent scholars in the field have focused attention on a canon of fiction and autobiography to the exclusion of poetry.[1] While the ground-breaking work done in the early 1970s by Bernard Bell, Stephen Henderson, Blyden Jackson and Louis D. Rubin, Eugene Redmond, and Joan Sherman remains important today, surprisingly few studies of the diversity of African American poetry have been published in the last decade. A notable exception is Vera Kutzinski's treatment of comparative New World poetics in *Against the American Grain*;

while moving outside the boundaries of the strictly African American texts, her discussion encourages us to rethink the concepts—such as race, geography, and national identity—that have defined our sense of the African American poetic canon.[2] Fortunately, the most important single-author studies from the 1970s, including the work of Kimberly Benston (*Baraka*), J. Lee Greene, Onwuchekwa Jemie, and Wemer Sollors, have been joined by more recent volumes—for example, those by Rudolph P. Byrd, Wayne F. Cooper, Robert M. Farnsworth, William J. Harris, D. H. Melhem, and Arnold Rampersad. Scholars know more about individual African American poets now than they ever did before. In many ways, however, black critical theory has yet to respond to the rich voices of black poets from the past.

One indication of poetry's place in the current construction of African American critical theory is revealing. In *The Signifying Monkey*, Henry Louis Gates, Jr., proposes a compelling way of tracing the lines of continuity among major African American texts. With consummate skill, he teaches us to read this literature through the paradigms of vernacular culture as a way of chronicling a common African American struggle for authority and voice.[3] Taking off from Roland Barthes, Gates defines Hurston's *Their Eyes Were Watching God* as the first instance in our written tradition of a "speakerly" text—that is, a text "oriented toward imitating one of the numer-ous forms of oral narration to be found in classical Afro-American vernacular literature" (181). Gates's characteristic reinvention of literary theory, grounded in the language and rituals of African American culture, is insightful, yet this particular moment in his revisionary strategy raises an important concern. By slighting poetry in his newly constructed canon, Gates neglects such "speakerly" nineteenth-century texts as Paul Laurence Dunbar's seminal poem "An Ante-bellum Sermon" (1895). Elsewhere, Gates has written instructively about Dunbar and African American poetry. His early essay "Dis and Dat: Dialect and the Descent" remains crucial to our understanding of the conventions of "dialect" and vernacular poetry. My point here is simply that his exclusion of poetry from *The Signifying Monkey*, given the ensuing authority of that work, reenacts what has become a familiar pattern in African American literary history. The effect of such omissions in our most influential readings of African American literature may well serve to lessen the perspective of poetry in current revisions of black critical theory and the African American canon.

In his essay "Performing Blackness," Kimberly Benston surmises that it may be the "relative susceptibility" of African American poetry "to discrete analyses [that] resists theoretical efforts that move toward totalization, toward recuperation and ideological closure" (184). He confronts the risks involved in theorizing about the lines of continuity between disparate poetic works only to underscore the necessity of defining the shared themes, literary forms, and rhetorical strategies that constitute a distinctive poetic tradition. In particular, he entreats us to recognize that seemingly discrete, fragmented expression—enacted as a mode of performance—characterizes African American discourse. Black utterance, like other counterdiscourses, masks its own continuity as a way of veiling its challenges to the legitimacy of dominant political institutions and cultural traditions. In theorizing about African American poetry, critics might be guided by what Richard Terdiman describes, in a different context, as the "capacity [of counterdiscourses] to *situate*: to relativize the authority and stability of a dominant system of utterances which cannot even countenance their existence," as a way of enacting a new realm of subjectivity (15–16). When black writers turn to African American vernacular performance, they call into question the authority of the literary conventions and racial ideologies of the dominant society. Critics should neglect neither the insistence of African American poets on challenging the authority of dominant American institutions nor the individual black poet's struggle for recuperation and wholeness. Their individual texts make up an ongoing tradition of black poetic subjectivity.

While the term *performance* can be applied variously to a range of cultural and literary phenomena, I use it to designate verbal performance viewed as a cultural event. In revising the boundaries of what has traditionally constituted the folklore text, recent scholars, especially Roger D. Abrahams and Richard Bauman, have reconceptualized the distinctions between textual representations and what Robert Georges calls "complex communicative events" (313). Such scholars often associate the term *vernacular* with the modern concept of folklore as an intricate interaction between performer and audience that relies on linguistic, paralinguistic, kinesic, and thoroughly contextual codes and conventions.[4] This implied notion of performance has become a model for how to discuss formal literary texts. In written texts that draw on the aesthetics of vernacular performance, the relations of orality and literacy are continuous. The tensions between repetition and improvisation that operate in a verbal performance are translated into competing structures of creation and recollection for literary artists and their audiences.

Construing performance in this way, I argue that Paul Laurence Dunbar's early poem "An Ante-bellum Sermon" is an instructive example of an African American "preacherly text." The poetic heritage to which this poem belongs stretches back at least to the eighteenth- and nineteenth-century sermons of African American religious leaders, even as it looks forward to the preacherly performances of James Weldon Johnson, Langston Hughes, Robert Hayden, and Gwendolyn Brooks. In scaling what Hughes calls the "racial mountain," Dunbar's vernacular performance illustrates the solid ground of African American poetic traditions.

I

For black poets of the nineteenth and twentieth centuries, the challenge has been to establish the grounds of their literate and poetic authority without sacrificing the distinctiveness of their experiences in the New World. These poets have often relieved the disruptions resulting from different aspects of themselves by locating their work in a continuum of African American expressive culture. In their search for poetic voice, they have struggled to define their experiences as African Americans through tropes of indigenous and communal subjectivity. Many of them, including Dunbar, Hughes, Hayden, and Brooks, have made vernacular sermonic performance of their heritage a primary site of cultural authority and artistic creativity.[5] The narratives, rhetorical strategies, and rituals of performance of the vernacular sermon have helped shape the recurring aesthetic and ideological tendencies of African American poetry. The relations of preachers and their congregations have provided these poets with a model for what Barbara Bowen has called "untroubled voice": the performance of perfect continuity between artist and audience. By performing these sermons, black poets have mended the divisions in their artistic voices and the contradictory expectations of their various audiences, thereby recovering for themselves and their communities the privileges of vernacular eloquence.

To explicate the cultural status of the vernacular sermon, I begin with the historians of the American slave—including John Blassingame, Eugene Genovese, Lawrence Levine, and Al Raboteau—who have drawn on "folklore," interviews, autobiographies, and various other kinds of texts to suggest that slaves were able to survive their oppression by evolving sustaining forms of cultural expression. The early black sermonic performance was one of the rituals that defined for slaves and free African Americans their participation in a unique religious fellowship.[6] According to the available evidence, slave preachers were esteemed as exemplary figures in the black community, whether they preached in church, in the quarters, or in the fields, whether they preached out of the Bible or from the depths of their hearts. While many slaves were required to listen to white preachers, some of whom were well educated and well trained, they clearly preferred to hear black preachers deliver messages from God. As Nancy Williams, an ex-slave from Virginia, put it: "Dat ole white preachin' wasn't nothin'. Ole white preachers used to talk wid dey tongues widdout sayin' nothin' but Jesus told us slaves to talk wid our hearts" (Yetman 13).

The slave preachers did not necessarily derive their cultural authority from their ability to read or their facility in speaking standard English. Often the important issue was whether they could perform sermons that moved their congregations toward freedom. One former slave, Clara Young, told her interviewer that it did not matter that her favorite preacher, Mathew Ewing, was illiterate; what she cared about most in judging his sermons was his style and his message. "He never learned no readin' and writin'," she reminisced, "but he sure knowed his Bible and would hold his hand out and make like he was readin' and preach de purtiest preachin' you ever heard" (Yetman 335). She must have been impressed with his wit in reenacting the gestures of white preachers who read Scripture to their congregations, but not as much as she was stirred by his eloquence. Judging from his vast experience with slave congregations, the white minister Charles C. Jones could say that they were natural judges of a "good sermon," even though such a sermon might corrupt Christian theology and the English language (14–15). While recognizing that the slaves preferred to hear black preachers, he was not willing to admit that these preachers were evolving their own style of address. Jones championed the use of religion among slaves as a means of social control without ever realizing that slaves would use their religion as a way of fighting oppression.

Many black congregations expected their preachers to be vigorous, dramatic, and instructive in language, theme, and gesture. The textual accuracy of their preachers' readings of the Bible may not have been a consideration, but the dynamics of performance were essential. Even if the preachers had to create the biblical references in their sermons, their congregations demanded that they breathe life into those creations. In her *Letters from New York*, Lydia Maria Child, the well-known abolitionist, describes an especially dramatic sermon that Rev. Julia Pell, a black itinerant preacher, delivered to a Methodist congregation in 1841.[7] Although the regular minister of this church felt compelled to apologize to the congregation for Pell's misquotations of Scripture, her performance must have been remarkable. Even the skeptical Lydia Child admitted that this "dusky priestess of eloquence" made her shout and cry with religious fervor (67). Child offers a rare early description of the rhythmic pacing of a black sermon, noting that Pell "began with great moderation, gradually rising in her tones, until she arrived at the shouting pitch . . . [that] she sustained for an incredible time, without taking breath, and with a huskiness of effort." This rhythm of performance, and the physical effort it required, undoubtedly reinforced the effect of the sermon's thematic climax and encouraged the enthusiastic response of the congregation. The section of this climax that Child records can be transcribed as lines of poetry:

Silence in Heaven!
The Lord said to Gabriel,
bid all the angels keep silence.
Go up into the third heavens,
and tell the archangels to hush their golden harps.
Let the sea stop its roaring,
and the earth be still.
What's the matter now?
Why, man has sinned,
and who shall save him?
Let there be silence,
while God makes search for a Messiah.
Go down to the earth;
make haste, Gabriel,
and inquire if any there are worthy;
make haste, Gabriel;
and Gabriel returned and said,
No, not one.
But don't be discouraged.
Don't be discouraged, fellow sinners.
God arose in his majesty,
and he pointed to his own right hand,
and said to Gabriel,
Behold the Lion of the tribe of Judah;
he alone is worthy.
He shall redeem my people. (65)

While the members of the church congregation could not have found this conversation in their Bibles, they would have understood that the invented narrative testified to the possibility of redemption. Although Child cannot record the sound of the sermon, one can discern a pattern of rising and falling intonations and perceive the shrillness of Pell's dynamic "shouting pitch." As the black preachers tell us at the beginning of their sermons, they preach as God's instruments. Here Pell literally creates music with her voice. She provides the congregation with proof that she is one of "God's trombones."

Pell could neither read nor write, Child reports, yet this preacher's "illiteracy" does not limit her talents as an artist. Without "book learning," she nonetheless reads and performs the cultural conventions of the black vernacular sermon. While societies define and use *literacy* differently, "literacy is always connected with power" (Pattison viii).[8] The sermon quoted above demonstrates that Pell is literate in the rituals of African American culture, and it measures the extent to which she exploits her power as a prophet. Unable to read the Bible, Pell still knows what sermons her congregation needs to hear. Such knowledge is communal. It is *shared* by preacher and audience.

Knowing the tacit rules of performance, many of the blacks in Pell's audience would have recognized her skill in drawing on the conventions of delivering a vernacular sermon: the conspicuous patterns of repetition; the Old Testament imagery and diction; the allusions to the spirituals; the preacher's freedom to assume the identity of a biblical character; her dwelling on the inadequacies of language in the face of divine revelation; her own version of a biblical character's conversion, narrated through the devices of vernacular storytelling. Even though partly improvised, her sermon was probably constructed out of four key parts: the invocation of God's authority, indicating that he provides the sermon text; the identification of the sermon's theme with a quotation from Scripture; the interpretation of that passage through the construction of what Gerald Davis calls "independent narrative units" and "theme-related bridges" that reveal a sacred–secular tension; and, finally, the open-ended conclusion (56).[9] When confronted with the recurring typologies of these early black sermons, the white observers who generously used the phrase "natural eloquence" to account for the rhetorical force of what they heard appear now to have betrayed the biases and limitations of their own, seemingly more authoritative, modes of cultural literacy.

II

In famous review of Dunbar's second volume of poetry, *Majors and Minors*, William Dean Howells argues that Dunbar finds his true voice as a writer in his "dialect" poems. When Howells revised this review as the preface to Dunbar's *Lyrics of Lowly Life*, he introduced the poet to a national and enduring audience. However unwittingly, Howells's brief essay bears all the trappings of the authenticating preface to the typical slave narrative: the white writer testifies that Dunbar is black, that his Negro ancestry is pure, and that the volume is, as the expression would have it, "written by himself."[10] After asserting that Dunbar's poems in standard English, while competent, are "not distinctively his contribution to the body of American poetry," Howells proceeds to define Dunbar's dialect pieces as "delightful personal attempts and failures for the written and spoken language." He insists on arguing that Dunbar's dialect poems are humorous evidence of the "negro's limitations" (xvii–xviii). As a celebrated white writer, Howells was eager to help this young black poet. Yet Dunbar would later declare, perhaps unfairly, that Howells's support had done him "irrevocable harm" ("Unpublished Letters" 73). He came to resent the preface for suggesting that readers could enjoy his work most by ignoring the poems in standard English and not taking the dialect poems seriously. Given the potentially negative connotations of the term *dialect*, especially those relating to the concerns expressed by Dunbar and other black writers, present-day scholars tend to avoid it and to refer to faithfully rendered black speech as "black English," "black vernacular," or "black English vernacular" (see Dillard; Labov; Smitherman). Even at the turn of the century, Dunbar's response to Howells suggests that the issue of using dialect to represent black voices in literature was fraught with complexity.

Although some white writers of dialect, especially Joel Chandler Harris and Thomas Nelson Page, claimed to represent African American speech accurately, they appear to have paid more attention to accepted literary conventions than to the remembered speech of blacks in the nineteenth century.[11] Steeped in regional and racial bias, the authors of such conventions worked to undermine the authority of their black speakers by casting them as objects of cultural distortion and ridicule. Some black writers, like Daniel Webster Davis, merely submitted to these ideologies of objectification. In "An Ante-bellum Sermon" Dunbar reverses this tendency by writing a poem that straddles the boundary between literary convention and African American vernacular culture in ways that emphasize their mutual exclusivity.

In writing in the vernacular, black poets like Dunbar donned their stereotypical guises as a way of deceiving white audiences. During the Harlem Renaissance, James Weldon Johnson, himself a writer of dialect poetry, urged black poets to move from behind this veil of literary convention.[12] Yet in the 1890s, Dunbar challenged his audience's assumptions by revealing that the use of such language, depending on the rhetorical and ideological contexts, could be liberating. In "An Ante-bellum Sermon," Dunbar adopts dialect as a mask to demonstrate for his black audience and his informed white readers that the vernacular could serve to subvert the constraints of literary convention. Claiming authority by revealing the ideological complexities of the forms of discourse that part of his audience expected him to choose, Dunbar helped to wrestle the vernacular sermon, as a mode of privileged subjectivity, from the assumed authority of American racism. Instead of turning to dialect to represent the "negro's limitations" within American popular culture, Dunbar performs the agenda of black selfhood in the feral terrain of the vernacular. In the process, he makes it possible for us to theorize about the rhetoric of African American poetry.[13]

Dunbar realized that the early-nineteenth-century slave preachers evolved strategies of representation that would enable them to educate and inform their black congregations without arousing the suspicions of the slaves' owners and censors. He also recognized that the postbellum conditions of cultural servitude with which he struggled posed similar rhetorical constraints. Dunbar needed to create literary strategies to come to terms with his own fractured audience of 1895. While his poem is qualitatively different from the masking essential for survival in the real-life experience of slaves, it requires the same kind of participation from his implied readers that black preachers sought from their congregations early in the century. Those of his contemporaries who understood the poem within the traditions of many antebellum vernacular sermons would have savored the various levels of desire and representation it encodes. Thus Dunbar's apparent deference to the patronizing expectations of his unenlightened white audience can be seen as a self-conscious strategy for educating discerning readers in the subversive tactics of these performances. In short, "An Ante-bellum Sermon" offers us a pattern for reinscribing the politics of racial discourse in the conventions of nineteenth-century American popular culture. By undercutting American racisms, Dunbar's "preacherly text" represents a crucial dimension of the African American struggle for freedom.

Recognizing the artistic and cultural significance of Dunbar's attempts to translate the rhetorical strategies of the sermon into a model for literary performance depends, in part, on some familiarity with the place of the black sermon in American minstrelsy. After Daniel Emmett's Virginia Minstrels; debuted in New York in 1843, the minstrel show became an enduring American cultural institution.[14] Emmett, best known for his 1859 song, "Dixie," was instrumental in establishing the conventions of this form of American entertainment. His specialty was delivering "black" sermons as the so-called stump speech that climaxed the variety-act segment of the typical minstrel performance. Listen to one of Emmett's parodies of the black preacher:

> Bredren, de text am foun' in de inside ob Job whar Paul draw'd him pistol on 'Feesians, lebenteenth chapter, an' no 'ticklar verse: "*Bressed am dem, dat 'spects nuttin, kase dey aint gwine to git nuttin*"!
> (Hans 410)

The humor of this passage is obvious. If Emmett's preacher can read at all, he is quite confused in his understanding of the Bible. He turns Paul into an Old Testament figure and manages somehow to make a gun out of the apostle's letter to the Ephesians, addressed to the churches Paul founded in Asia Minor. Emmett entertains his minstrel audiences by drawing on cultural misconceptions about the black sermon. The simple-minded errors, like the substitution of the word *pistol* for *epistle*, suggest the preacher's ignorance. Unfortunately, for black readers and, subsequently, for "liberal" white ones, the minstrel's popularity with white Northern audiences may well have diminished the viability of the black sermon as a vernacular model for African American poetry.

Even though the opening of "An Ante-bellum Sermon" can be located within the shared conventions of black vernacular practices and American cultural representations of blacks, the poem as a whole works to sever the connections between these two traditions. Dunbar's preacher begins:

> We is gathahed hyeah, my brothahs
>   In dis howlin' wildaness,
> Fu' to speak some words of comfo't
>   To each othah in distress.
> An' we chooses fu' ouah subjic'
>   Dis—we'll 'splain it by an' by;
> "An' de Lawd said, 'Moses, Moses,'
>   An'de man said, 'Hyeah am I.'
> (*Lyrics* 26)[15]

Dunbar uses the first-person plural *we* to represent the shared identities of his poem's speaker and audience. The poem's call thus appears to be democratic, yet Dunbar suggests that both the preacher and his congregation are black. While the greeting "my brothahs"—if we disregard, for the moment, its sexist implications—could merely connote their fellowship in a religious community, the strategies of indirection that shape, and are revealed in, the entire poem suggest that Dunbar's preacher uses the term to signify his fellow blacks in such a community. Dunbar works to establish perfect continuity between poet and speaker, speaker and silent auditor, silent auditor and the poet's imagined audience, the poet and that audience.[16] In his sensitivity to the American racial climate of the 1890s, Dunbar recognized the difficulty of this endeavor. His faith in his preacher's authority risks the ridicule of his white audience. Whatever the preacher and his black flock might share, they must come to terms with what the white audience expects of them. That audience would never imagine identifying with the responses of the black congregation. Seemingly, Dunbar would have been compelled to define himself as a minstrel figure to earn his white audience's complicity, but then he would have to distance himself from the clarity of his preacher's sentiments. In having the preacher speak in dialect, Dunbar appears to forgo his belief both in his preacher's authority as a speaker and in this figure's claims to any audience other than his own congregation. Yet Dunbar's sense of rhetorical coherence insists on a community divided. He solves the problems involved in his ideal of communication by silencing his antagonistic audiences, both within and outside the poem. By clarifying, at least for some, that the "we" of his speaker's address calls to the black community that the poet imagines as his own ideal audience, Dunbar undermines the minstrel traditions that he might appear to engage in the poem's opening line. In "An Ante-bellum Sermon," blacks are no longer the objects of cultural misinterpretation. They—or, rather, "we"—have become the subject and the medium of his performed black representations. This rhetoric of community signals the poem's search for an untroubled voice for blacks. Yet, as the gendered appellation "brothahs" calls into question the extent to which Dunbar's preacher hails the black women in his congregation, "we" have every reason to protest Dunbar's silence about their role in his newly empowered slave community.[17]

Unlike the parodic figures whom many of his readers might have expected, Dunbar's preacher is a careful reader of Scripture and its potential relations to everyday life. Instead of ridiculously conflating biblical passages as Emmett does, Dunbar's preacher brings disparate texts together to intensify his own. Taking as his basic text the flight of the Israelites from their enslavement in Egypt, he borrows the image of "dis howlin' wildaness" from Moses's narration of the Hebrew god's rescue of Jacob in Deuteronomy (32.10). By using biblical language, albeit cloaked in dialect, to describe the performance situation of his sermon, Dunbar's preacher locates the lives of the members of his congregation within the context of biblical exegesis, reinforcing the parallels between the slaves and the chosen people that the sermon seeks to establish in a decidedly African American typology.

If Dunbar's preacher were a traditional white minister, he might proceed to discuss the significance of God's appearance before Moses and then explain how it could point his own congregation in the right Christian path. As an antebellum black preacher, he moves in a different direction, and the ensuing narrative calls on a dual source of authority. Although he relies on the general movements of the Exodus story, he earns his right to speak to his congregation by relating that biblical myth to the details of the slaves' own lives. As a result, he appropriates the scriptural text only as a point of reference for another text that he and his congregation share:

Now ole Pher'oh, down in Egypt,
    Was de wuss man evah bo'n,
An' he had de Hebrew chillun
    Down dah wukin' in his co'n;
'T well de Lawd got tiahed o' his foolin',
    An' sez he: "I'll let him know—
Look hyeah, Moses, go tell Pher'oh
    Fu' to let dem chillun go." (26)

The preacher locates his scene in Egypt, yet he transposes the geography of the slave South onto the physical setting of the narrative, translating the terms of Hebrew slavery into the realities of antebellum enforced black labor. If he corrupts the biblical text through this method of reading, he does so only to interpret the particular significance of the Exodus narrative for his congregation. Instead of separating his tasks of narrating and interpreting, he binds the two processes into a single coherent text.

His listeners' faith in his authority as a speaker depends on how convincingly he can narrate their own desire for freedom. To this end, he talks about Exodus as a way of reminding them that their enslavement is temporary. Representing Moses as a type, not merely as the biblical character, the preacher entreats them to believe that someone like Moses—"some Moses" figure—will lead them away from their "chains an' shackles." Like Moses, this figure will base his authority on divine instruction. Dunbar's preacher uses the Bible to justify the violence and destruction of the impending battle for freedom, and he earns the right to speak to the members of his congregation by speaking for them. He assuages their fears even as he incites their anger.

Like the historical antebellum preacher whose rhetoric he imitates, Dunbar's speaker must hide his real message under the guise of what is acceptable. The performance context of the antebellum sermon required that the preacher take into account the expectations of whites and of the fearful slaves in his audience. Listen to how Dunbar's preacher sets up the terms of their misinterpretation of his text:

But fu' feah some one mistakes me,
    I will pause right hyeah to say,
Dat I'm still a-preachin' ancient,
    I ain't talkin' 'bout to-day. (27)

Of course, he is talking about "to-day," but he pretends to lie to the faithful slaves to deceive whites and disloyal slaves. The dissimilarity between the details of the Exodus narrative and the plot of his sermon reveals that he is not "a-preachin' ancient." He pretends to consign his sermon to the task of biblical exegesis to dupe those listeners who might be threatened by his real text. Though he invites two kinds of audience to participate in his sermon, he works to keep his enemies at a distance from his narrative to ensure that he can bring his accomplices even closer. He manages to stabilize his relations to his audiences by insisting on the split in their responses and expectations. The implicit contradictions between these two voices are risky, but the double and antagonistic voices allow him the freedom to console his black listeners and the discerning whites.

Dunbar's preacher recognizes that his sermon has both "addressees" and "hearers," and here I am drawing on the work by Herbert Clark and Thomas Carlson, two speech-act theorists who distinguish different types of audience (333). While directing his sermon to the other faithful black slaves, the preacher is aware that auditory predators may be lurking about the area of his performance. They are hearers, and although Dunbar never speaks directly to them, he is aware that they prey upon his message. His sermon turns on the conflict between these two audiences. In the one direction, he moves to ensure his addressees that deliverance is at hand; he tells them, "Now, de Lawd done dis fu' Isrul, / An' his ways don't nevah change." In the other, he pretends to check that progress by feigning deference to the slave owner. He tells the slaves, but not for their benefit, "Now don't run an' tell yo' mastahs / Dat I's preachin' discontent." He offers another version of this disclaimer before the poem's end, declaring that he is talking about "freedom / In a Bibleistic way." Yet in emphasizing that it is "ouah freedom," he reveals his intimate relations with the addressees in his audience as he directs the poem toward them:

> But when Moses wif his powah
>   Comes an' sets us chillun free,
> We will praise de gracious Mastah
>   Dat has gin us liberty;
> An' we'll shout ouah halleluyahs,
>   On dat mighty reck'nin' day,
> When we'se reco'nised ez citiz'—
>   Huh uh! Chillun, let us pray! (29–30)

By the poem's end, the speaker has discarded at least one of his masks. He prophesies that Moses will come to set "us chillun" free, both the preacher and his congregation. Even in the present of the poem's time frame, he has substituted the authority of God, "de gracious Mastah," for that of the slave owner. Furthermore, Judgment Day is imagined not merely as the occasion for their escape from slavery but as the time when the ex-slaves are granted citizenship, when indeed they will no longer be seen as ex-slaves but as fully empowered participants in the decisions that govern their lives. In their shared challenge to the institutions of slavery and legal oppression, the preacher invites these blacks to signal their community in a prayer for freedom. The abrupt ending of the poem is itself a subversive strategy. Only Dunbar knows what these folks will do when their meeting is over.

Finally, it should be clear that the preacher's initial use of the pronoun "we" indicates both the inclusion of some and the exclusion of others. While his two audiences in the poem are silent, he obviously speaks only for the oppressed. Although the poem, throughout, exploits the rhetoric of the black sermon, at the end Dunbar self-consciously betrays the duplicity of that rhetoric. The repetition of the narrative digressions—disclaimers intended for some white hearers' ears—shows that Dunbar wants these auditors to understand the codes of his deceptions, as he reveals the veiled purpose of sermonic rhetoric to those who would normally misunderstand it. By overemphasizing his denials, he exposes their falsehood. It is difficult for anyone, no matter how unsuspecting, to miss the implied aggression that complicates Dunbar's humor. Within the context of the poem, he subverts his culturally ascribed status as minstrel figure.

The political dimensions of the poem emerge most fully when we recognize that Dunbar throws his double voice in yet another direction. His preacherly text is certainly an antebellum sermon to be understood, in part, within the context of legalized slavery. Yet it is crucial to see that Dunbar is also addressing the issues of the political and economic oppression of blacks at the time he is writing. Dunbar witnessed the promise of Reconstruction become the specter of the repressive 1880s and 1890s. Historians have carefully documented the pervasive patterns of "disfranchisement, segregation, and racial subordination" (Meier and Rudwick 186). The preacher's emphasis on citizenship reflects Dunbar's dismay that late-nineteenth-century blacks were systematically denied the rights they had gained under the Thirteenth, Fourteenth, and Fifteenth Amendments. Even though many of Dunbar's contemporaries would have understood that his poem flaunts the hidden aggression of antebellum sermons, they might well have missed his criticism of race relations in their own time. Readers who did appreciate the complexity of the poem's protestations would realize that the joke was on readers who resisted admitting that the poem unravels its critique of slavery only to register the same complaint about realities of the present. This perceptive audience could laugh—with Dunbar—at readers who missed the irony beneath the humor and refused to acknowledge that the poem, along with the cultural traditions it performs, is also serious. Dunbar's preacher does exploit the rhetoric of entertainment, yet as Ralph Ellison might put it, when black folks live with their heads in the mouth of American racism, the game is *always* serious.[18]

However bent and twisted by the unrelenting cultural and political authority of white America, "An Ante-bellum Sermon" is self-consciously angled and refracted as Dunbar risks rhetorical instability. To the extent to which Dunbar can master and manipulate the expectations of his various audiences, this 1895 poem serves as a guide for translating oral vernacular performance into black poetic subjectivity. "An Ante-bellum Sermon" *performs* the devious agenda of African American cultural practices and invites us to theorize about the revisionary impulses of African American poetry. It also compels us to conceptualize the patterns of representation that resonate throughout this poetic tradition—whether they are the strategies of authentication of James Weldon Johnson's sermons in *God's Trombones*, Langston Hughes's wonderful parody of preacherly performance in poems like "Sunday Morning Prophecy," or the "preachment" poems that helped Gwendolyn Brooks stabilize her sense of poetic identity when she embraced the new "congregation" of the Black Arts Movement. In teaching us how to read this crucial aspect of African American poetics, Dunbar posits a useful challenge to the work of contemporary theorists. To the extent to which Dunbar represents the possibilities, real or imagined, of black men and women at the end of the nineteenth century, Dunbar's preacher offers himself as a model of what it means to be free.[19]

Notes

1. For major theoretical volumes that include discussions of African American poetry, see Baker and Redmond; Fisher and Stepto; Gates, *Black Literature*; and Wall.
2. For two other recent composite studies of African American poetics, see Baker, *Afro-American Poetics*, and Hull.
3. Although Hemenway's work predates the widespread use of the term *vernacular*, his 1979 study is a useful guide for analyzing the relations of written and folk literature. Baker's *Blues, Ideology, and Afro-American Literature* (1984) is the first sustained theoretical reading of the vernacular within the context of African American literary history.
4. In the last twenty years the study of folklore has undergone so striking a metamorphosis that some scholars now call the discipline "folkloristics," to indicate its new directions. For a useful discussion of this term, see Jackson. For two recent attempts to master the difficulties of translating

verbal folklore into written and notational texts, see Tedlock and Fine.

5. I use such multivalent labels as "African American vernacular sermon" and "black sermonic performance" throughout this discussion to define those verbal performances of blacks in the United States that abide by a set of conventions the black preachers and their congregations would consider characteristically African American. Although many sermons by white Americans participate in these conventions, I focus my attention exclusively on oral sermons by black Americans. Davis, Mitchell, Raboteau, and many other scholars have presented persuasive evidence for the emergence and continuity of a distinctive African American sermonic experience. The most notable dissenter is Rosenberg, who reads those sermons as a decidedly American art form that blacks merely helped to fashion.
6. Both Berlin and George discuss the rise of independent black churches that parallel the Baptist, Methodist, Presbyterian, and Episcopalian denominations. Though affected by such factors as geographical location, legal status, and socioeconomic station, the religious practices of early African Americans tended to transcend these boundaries. As a group, blacks shared a distinctive religious style that, while heavily influenced by white institutions, bore the stamp of their African cultural heritage.
7. The best-known rendition of an antebellum African American vernacular sermon can be found in Frederick Law Olmsted's description of a service at an independent black church he visited in New Orleans in 1854 (241–47). See also Watson 98–104.
8. In this regard, Robert Pattison's critique of Western notions of literacy is instructive: "We have produced two literacies, one of formal language as encoded in grammars and dictionaries, another of the living language found in daily intercourse and in popular art. To some degree every culture faces this split between formal and informal discourse, between the language of power and the language of the streets. But with us the split has assumed troubling dimensions" (84). These divisions structure our characteristic misreadings of vernacular culture.
9. Davis defines an African American sermon as a "performed verbal mold based in one stated theme, developed through four or more independent subthematic formulaic units unified by thematic bridges, or free-clause formulas. Each component of the verbal mold and the verbal mold itself must be subordinated to a larger concern for a concretized secular and an abstracted sacred balance" (60–61).
10. For a cogent analysis of the use of such authenticating documents in African American texts, see Robert Stepto's ground-breaking work, *From Behind the Veil*, esp. 3–31.

11. For an excellent discussion of the sentimental white poets whose nostalgia for the plantation South became a popular form of late-nineteenth-century American poetry, see Wagner 48–72.
12. In his 1922 preface to the first edition of *The Book of American Negro Poetry*, Johnson urges other black writers to reform and complicate their use of dialect. By 1931, in the preface to the second edition of his anthology, he surmises that "the passing of traditional dialect as a medium for Negro poets is complete" (3). The following year, however, the black author Sterling Brown published a collection of poems, *Southern Road*, that proved Johnson's eulogy premature.
13. For a useful discussion of the technique of "masking" in black dialect poetry, see Gates, "Dis and Dat" 88–97; for excellent reinterpretations of Dunbar's work in this form, see Martin. Bruce's essay in that collection provides the best sustained reading of "An Ante–bellum Sermon" (99-106).
14. The two most useful general studies of the American minstrel show are those by Hans and by Toll. More recently, both Lott and Mahar have considered the discursive and political racisms of this form of American popular culture.
15. Even though "An Ante-bellum Sermon" was first published in *Majors and Minors* (102–05), I have used the slightly revised version that appears in *Lyrics of Lowly Life*.
16. For two fascinating discussions of such complex rhetorical relations, see Mermin and Jauss.
17. The larger issue here, one that goes beyond the scope of this essay, is the position of black women within the conventions of vernacular performance. The gender implications of the construction of race in the use of the vernacular are both complex and open to question. When black men use the vernacular to constrain black women, they do not liberate themselves; they simply choose to perform for a different master.
18. I have in mind a passage from the dying grandfather's speech in *Invisible Man*: "Live with your head in the lion's mouth. I want you to overcome 'em with yeses, undermine 'em with grins, agree 'em to death and destruction, let 'em swoller you till they vomit or bust wide open" (16). For readings of the grandfather's speech as Ellison's artistic philosophy, see Blount, "'Certain Eloquence,'" and Petesch.
19. I wish to thank Houston A. Baker, Jr., for his invaluable comments on an earlier draft of this essay. The final version is for him.

Works Cited

Abrahams, Roger D. *The Man-of-Words in the West Indies: Performance and the Emergence of Creole Culture*. Baltimore: Johns Hopkins UP, 1983.

Baker, Houston A., Jr. *Afro-American Poetics: Revisions of Harlem and the Black Aesthetic*. Madison: U of Wisconsin P, 1988.

———. *Blues, Ideology, and Afro-American Literature: A Vernacular Theory*. Chicago: U of Chicago P, 1984.

Baker, Houston A., Jr., and Patricia Redmond, eds. *Afro-American Literary Study in the 1990s*. Chicago: U of Chicago P, 1989.

Bauman, Richard. *Story, Performance, and Event: Contextual Studies of Oral Narrative*. Cambridge: Cambridge UP, 1986.

Bell, Bernard W. *The Folk Roots of Contemporary Afro-American Poetry*. Detroit: Broadside, 1974.

Benston, Kimberly W. *Baraka: The Renegade and the Mask*. New Haven: Yale UP, 1976.

———. "Performing Blackness: Re/Placing Afro-American Poetry." Baker and Redmond 164–93.

Berlin, Ira. *Slaves without Masters: The Free Negro in the Antebellum South*. New York: Vintage-Random, 1976.

Blassingame, John. *The Slave Community: Plantation Life in the Antebellum South*. New York: Oxford UP, 1972.

Blount, Marcellus. "'A Certain Eloquence': Ralph Ellison and the Afro-American Artist." *American Literary History* 1 (1989): 675–88.

Bowen, Barbara. "Untroubled Voice: Call and Response in *Cane*." Gates, *Black Literature* 187–203.

Brooks, Gwendolyn. *The World of Gwendolyn Brooks*. New York: Harper, 1971.

Brown, Sterling A. *Southern Road*. New York: Harcourt, 1932.

Bruce, Dickson, Jr. "On Dunbar's 'Jingles in a Broken Tongue': Dunbar's Dialect Poetry and the Afro-American Folk Tradition." Martin 94–113.

Byrd, Rudolph P. *Jean Toomer's Years with Gurdjieff: Portrait of an Artist, 1923–1936*. Athens: U of Georgia P, 1990.

Child, L[ydia] Maria. *Letters from New York*. New York, 1843.

Clark, Herbert H., and Thomas H. Carlson. "Hearers and Speech Acts." *Language* 58 (1982): 332–73.

Cooper, Wayne F. *Claude McKay: Rebel Sojourner in the Harlem Renaissance*. Baton Rouge: Louisiana State UP, 1987.

Davis, Gerald L. *I Got the Word in Me and I Can Sing It, You Know: A Study of the Performed African-American Sermon*. Philadelphia: U of Pennsylvania P, 1985.

Dillard, J. L. *Black English: Its History and Usage in the United States*. New York: Random, 1972.

Dunbar, Paul Laurence. *The Complete Poems of Paul Laurence Dunbar*. 1913. New York: Dodd, 1980.

———. *Lyrics of Lowly Life*. New York: Dodd, 1896.

———. *Majors and Minors*. Toledo: Hadley, 1895.

———. "Unpublished Letters of Paul Laurence Dunbar to a Friend." *Crisis* 20 (1920): 73–76.

Ellison, Ralph. *Invisible Man*. New York: Vintage-Random, 1972.

Farnsworth, Robert M. *Melvin B. Tolson: Plain Talk and Poetic Prophecy*. Columbia: U of Missouri P, 1984.

Fine, Elizabeth C. *The Folklore Text: From Performance to Print*. Bloomington: Indiana UP, 1984.

Fisher, Dexter, and Robert B. Stepto, eds. *Afro-American Literature: The Reconstruction of Instruction*. New York: MLA, 1979.

Gates, Henry Louis, Jr., ed. *Black Literature and Literary Theory*. New York: Methuen, 1984.

———. "Dis and Dat: Dialect and the Descent." Fisher and Stepto 88–119.

———. *The Signifying Monkey: A Theory of Afro-American Literary Criticism*. New York: Oxford UP, 1988.

Genovese, Eugene D. *Roll, Jordan, Roll: The World the Slaves Made*. New York: Pantheon-Random, 1974.

George, Carol V. R. *Segregated Sabbaths: Richard Allen and the Emergence of Independent Black Churches, 1760–1840*. New York: Oxford UP, 1974.

Georges, Robert. "Toward an Understanding of Storytelling Events." *Journal of American Folklore* 82 (1969): 313–28.

Greene, J. Lee. *Time's Unfading Garden: Anne Spencer's Life and Poetry*. Baton Rouge: Louisiana State UP, 1977.

Hans, Nathan. *Dan Emmett and the Rise of Early Negro Minstrelsy*. Norman: U of Oklahoma P, 1962.

Harris, William J. *The Poetry and Poetics of Amiri Baraka: The Jazz Aesthetic.* Columbia: U of Missouri P, 1985.

Hayden, Robert. *Collected Poems*. Ed. Frederick Glaysher. New York: Liveright, 1985.

Hemenway, Robert. "Are You a Flying Lark or a Setting Dove?" Fisher and Stepto 122–52.

Henderson, Stephen, ed. *Understanding the New Black Poetry, Black Speech and Black Music as Poetic References*. New York: Morrow, 1973.

Howells, W[illiam] D[ean]. "Life and Letters." *Harper's Weekly* 27 June 1896: 121–22.

Hughes, Langston. "The Negro Artist and the Racial Mountain." *Voices from the Harlem Renaissance*. Ed. Nathan Huggins. New York: Oxford UP, 1976.

———. *Selected Poems of Langston Hughes*. New York: Vintage-Random, 1974.

Hull, Gloria T. *Color, Sex, and Poetry: Three Women Writers of the Harlem Renaissance*. Bloomington: Indiana UP, 1987.

Jackson, Blyden, and Louis D. Rubin, Jr. *Black Poetry in America: Two Essays in Historical Interpretation*. Baton Rouge: Louisiana State UP, 1974.

Jackson, Bruce "Folkloristics." *Journal of American Folklore* 98 (1985): 95–101.

Jauss, Hans Robert. "Levels of Identification of Hero and Audience." *New Literary History* 5 (1974): 283–317.

Jemie, Onwuchekwa. *Langston Hughes: An Introduction to the Poetry*. New York: Columbia UP, 1976.

Johnson, James Weldon, ed. *The Book of American Negro Poetry*. 1922. New York: Harcourt, 1931.

———. *God's Trombones: Seven Negro Sermons in Verse*. New York: Viking, 1927.

Jones, Charles Colcock. *Suggestions for the Religious Instruction of the Negroes in the Southern States*. Philadelphia: Presbyterian Board of Pubs., 1847.

Kutzinski, Vera. *Against the American Grain: Myth and History in William Carlos Williams, Jay Wright, and Nicolas Guillen*. Baltimore: Johns Hopkins UP, 1987.

Labov, William. *Language in the Inner City: Studies in Black English Vernacular*. Philadelphia: U of Pennsylvania P, 1972.

Levine, Lawrence. *Black Culture and Black Consciousness: Afro-American Folk Thought from Slavery to Freedom*. New York: Oxford UP, 1977.

Lott, Eric. "'The Seeming Counterfeit': Racial Politics and Early Blackface Minstrelsy." *American Quarterly* 43 (1991): 223–54.

Mahar, William J. "Black English in Early Blackface Minstrelsy: A New Interpretation of the Sources of Minstrel Show Dialect." *American Quarterly* 37 (1985): 260–85.

Martin, Jay, ed. *A Singer in the Dawn: Reinterpretations of Paul Laurence Dunbar*. New York: Dodd, 1975.

Meier, August, and Elliot Rudwick. *From Plantation to Ghetto*. New York: Hill, 1970.

Melhem, D. H. *Gwendolyn Brooks: Poetry and the Heroic Voice*. Lexington: U of Kentucky P, 1987.

Mermin, Dorothy. *The Audience in the Poem: Five Victorian Poets*. New Brunswick: Rutgers UP, 1983.

Mitchell, Henry H. *Black Preaching*. Philadelphia: Lippincott, 1970.

Olmsted, Frederick Law. *The Cotton Kingdom*. Ed. Arthur Schlesinger. New York: Knopf, 1953.

Pattison, Robert. *On Literacy: The Politics of the Word from Homer to the Age of Rock*. Oxford: Oxford UP, 1982.

Petesch, Donald A. *A Spy in the Enemy's Country: The Emergence of Modern Black Literature*. Iowa City: U of Iowa P, 1989.

Raboteau, Albert J. *Slave Religion: The "Invisible Institution" in the Antebellum South*. New York: Oxford UP, 1978.

Rampersad, Arnold. *The Life of Langston Hughes*. 2 vols. New York: Oxford UP, 1986–88.

Redmond, Eugene B. *Drumvoices: The Mission of Afro-American Poetry*. Garden City: Anchor-Doubleday, 1976.

Rosenberg, Bruce. *The Art of the American Folk Preacher*. 1970. Rev. ed. New York: Oxford UP, 1988.

Sherman, Joan R. *Invisible Poets: Afro-Americans in the Nineteenth Century*. Urbana: U of Illinois P, 1974.

Smitherman, Geneva. *Talkin and Testifyin: The Language of Black America*. Boston: Houghton, 1977.

Sollors, Werner. *Amiri Baraka/LeRoi Jones: The Quest for a "Populist Modernism."* New York: Columbia UP, 1978.

Stepto, Robert B. *From Behind the Veil: A Study of Afro-American Narrative*. Urbana: U of Illinois P, 1979.

Tedlock, Dennis. *The Spoken Word and the Work of Interpretation*. Philadelphia: U of Pennsylvania P, 1983.

Terdiman, Richard. *Discourse/Counter-discourse: The Theory and Practice of Symbolic Resistance in Nineteenth-Century France*. Ithaca: Cornell UP, 1985.

Toll, Robert C. *Blacking Up: The Minstrel Show in Nineteenth-Century America*. New York: Oxford UP, 1974.

Wagner, Jean. *Black Poets of the United States: From Paul Laurence Dunbar to Langston Hughes*. Trans. Kenneth Douglas. Urbana: U of Illinois P, 1973.

Wall, Cheryl, ed. *Changing Our Own Words: Essays on Criticism, Theory, and Writing by Black Women*. New Brunswick: Rutgers UP, 1989.

Watson, James. *Tales and Takings, Sketches and Incidents, from the Itinerant and Editorial Budget*. New York, 1857.

Yetman, Norman P., ed. *Life under the "Peculiar Institution": Selections from the Slave Narrative Collection*. New York: Holt, 1970.

LEO HAMALIAN

D.H. Lawrence and Black Writers

> The Negro American writer is also an heir of the human experience which is literature, and this might well be more important to him than his living folk tradition.
>
> Ralph Ellison, *Shadow and Act*

AS UNLIKELY AS IT MAY SEEM at first, one of the important influences on black American poets and novelists of the 1940s and 1950s was D.H. Lawrence. We may wonder what there was in the work of this prickly, consumptive son of an English collier that could have appealed to the chief figures of this period: Claude McKay, Jean Toomer, Langston Hughes, Richard Wright, and Ralph Ellison, and why they found him so relevant to their concerns.[1]

To begin, Lawrence was a rebel and an unrelenting enemy of oppression and repression in whatever form he encountered them. He fought against a coercive bureaucracy in England which virtually blacklisted him in his profession. Langston Hughes understood the meaning of this act precisely. Speaking before the National Assembly of Authors and Dramatists Symposium on "The Writer's Position in America," he declared, "Negro writers, just by being black, have been on the blacklist all our lives."[2] For

From *Journal of Modern Literature* 16, no. 4 (Spring 1990).

aspiring black writers seeking affirmation of their own sense of outrage, Lawrence's refusal to yield to the injustice of such evil practices, and his combative, feisty character were both endearing and inspiring. ("Is life strife, is it the long combat? / Yes, it is true. I fight all the time. / I am forced to," Lawrence wrote in "The Battle of Life.")[3] Lawrence's hostility to the "iron machine"—his term for the modern industrialized world—as a weapon of ruthless capitalism opposed to the health of the "soul," was almost obsessive. He understood that the factory system was simply a scheme for extending the benefits of the slave system into the age of emancipation, and he expressed his sympathy for the factory workers in such poems as "City-Life":

> I, that am flesh of their flesh,
> when I see the iron hooked into their faces
> their poor, their fearful faces
> I scream in my soul . . . (*Poems*, 632).

Willie Struthers, the labor leader in *Kangaroo*, preaches rebellion against the upper classes and proposes an international union of workers which grants equality and "the tight grip of fellowship" to all workers, "brown, black, white, green, or whatever."[4] The gamekeeper Mellors remains a Marxist to the very end of *Lady Chatterley's Lover*, perhaps the first political hero of this persuasion in the modern English novel.

In the poem cycles of *Birds, Beasts and Flowers*, Lawrence formulates the myth of a dark Dionysian presence associated with "tendrilled avenues of wine and the otherworld."[5] In "Grapes" (*Poems*, 285), Lawrence describes the world prior to the flood, "When the vine was rose, Gods were dark-skinned" (286). At that time, even "God was all negroid / . . . man was dark and evasive / . . . And all in naked communication communicating as now our clothed vision can never communicate" (286). The sacreligious radicalism of these lines went unnoticed by most readers. In "The Revolutionary," Lawrence has his Samson say, "I am so weary of pale-face importance. / . . . See if I am not Lord of the dark and moving hosts / Before I die" (*Poems*, 287). The martyred Samson's sympathy for dark-skinned slaves would not be lost on a reader such as Hughes. In "The Evening Land," Lawrence seems almost possessed by the secret powers of dark people:

> Dark, elvish,
> Modern, unissued, uncanny America,
> Your nascent demon people
> Lurking among the deeps of your industrial thicket
> Allure me till I am beside myself,
> A nympholept (*Poems*, 289).

The myth of the dark god is also embodied in Lawrence's fiction, especially in the figure of Cipriano in *The Plumed Serpent* and the gypsy in *The Virgin and the Gypsy*. In *Etruscan Places*, Lawrence associates dusky people with the Etruscans whom the "white" Romans destroyed. Throughout *Studies in Classic American Literature*, Lawrence reveals a marked preference for the dark-skinned and a skeptical wariness of the white-skinned. In terms which he uses in all his works, the dark races are closer to "blood knowledge" and, with their sanity thus ensured, will finally triumph over the white "mind-conscious" civilization that has oppressed them for so long. ("The old consciousness has become a tight-fitting prison to us, in which we are going rotten.")[6] When he writes about the black Kanaka boy, Hope, in Dana's *Two Years Before the Mast*, he describes him as a "beautiful South Sea Islander sick of a white man's disease."[7] In his essay on *Moby Dick*, Lawrence remarks: "Melville knew. He knew his race was doomed. His white soul, doomed. His great white epoch, doomed." Summing up his creed, he declares, "My soul is a dark forest."[8]

* * *

While some readers may find Lawrence's vision too fanciful, its implications would not be lost on a black writer such as Claude McKay, often called *l'enfant terrible* of the Harlem Renaissance.[9] McKay spent the period between 1919 and 1921 in London. He had already written poetry that John Dewey would later say "expresses that identity of the self with the ever fresh always renewed wonders of living."[10] Nevertheless, at first he was accused of being a spy, and he was advised by George Bernard Shaw to become a pugilist. Although bothered by the snobbery of the English, he eventually gained entree to London literary circles in which he probably heard from other writers about the young Lawrence, whose star was just beginning to rise. But it was somewhat later, during his expatriate days in Paris in 1923, that McKay really discovered Lawrence. According to Wayne Cooper, "Only one great modern writer touched [McKay] profoundly, and he was not part of the Paris expatriate scene, though like McKay, he, too was a restless traveler. That writer was D.H. Lawrence, with whom McKay felt a psychic kinship and for whom he had a profound and lasting admiration."[11] Although McKay had also been reading James Joyce and recognized that *Ulysses* was "a bigger book than any one of Lawrence's books," he was drawn more powerfully to the English novelist: "No confusion, no doubt, no inquiry and speculation about the future in James Joyce." McKay acknowledges Lawrence as the writer who freed him into sensuality in his writing. In his autobiography, McKay says, "I thought that D.H. Lawrence was more modern than James Joyce. In . . . D.H. Lawrence I found confusion—all of the ferment and turmoil, the hesitation and hate and alarm, the sexual inquietude and the incertitude of this age, and the psychic and romantic groping for a way out."[12] His friends in Paris believed that McKay preferred Lawrence because of his dissident views, but Lawrence's appeal "lay instead in his compulsive and impassioned struggle to overcome the psychological traps that threatened to imprison and destroy man's direct appreciation of life and its mysteries in the modern age" and what he described as "the ripest and most voluptuous expression of English since Shakespeare."[13] In Lawrence, McKay found a constant personal struggle against those alien forces that inhibited the individual. McKay could relate on many levels to such a struggle. *Sons and Lovers*, in particular, articulated McKay's situation.

Although he came from a very different culture, Lawrence was a writer whose fundamental parental loyalties, social status, and young manhood resembled McKay's own. McKay, too, had a mother with whom he identified closely ("Mother" and "December, 1919" are no less touching than Lawrence's poems on the same subject) and an emotionally distant father with whom he felt limited kinship. McKay believed that Lawrence's distinguishing trait, mirroring his own, was a psychological restlessness that drove him steadily towards artistic achievement and away from the marginal existence of his natal community [i]n his own life."[14] Obviously, McKay faced the additional complication of his racial background as he entered the expatriate world of the white American artists and writers in Paris. Just as Lawrence hated the idea of returning to class-conscious England to live, McKay dreaded the prospect of facing the pervasive racial oppression of America, especially after he had been virtually lionized during his stay in the Soviet Union. But he was determined, as Eugene Jolas said of him when he first arrived in Paris, to capture in fiction, just as Lawrence had, the essence of his rich sensual experiences in exotic corners of the world. When Lawrence died in 1930, McKay wrote to his agent W.A. Bradley that "it was very sad to hear of D.H. Lawrence's death. Although I never met him, it was like losing a close friend."[15]

After returning to America, McKay worked increasingly in a new genre, and before he fell into undeserved oblivion, succeeded in writing five novels (two published posthumously) and a collection of short stories. in addition, he completed his autobiography and a historical study, *Harlem: Negro Metropolis*. Although the overt tension in these novels derives from McKay's identification with black militancy, we misjudge him if we assume that his rejection of bourgeois society was based solely on his experience as a black. His social realism reflects the naturalistic tradition of European writers; his sense of satire, his reading of Shaw and Ibsen; and his emphasis on sex, his admiration of Lawrence—all of them contributed to his flaming spirit of dissidence.

Among the stories in *Gingertown*, "Crazy Mary" most obviously shows the influence of Lawrence. It is a compact drama of "a pretty young yellow woman" who is destroyed by the sexual hysteria of her village and the forced repression of her strong sexuality.[16] In this story as elsewhere, McKay uses flowers as symbols of sexuality much as Lawrence does.[17] There are also tangible traces of Lawrence's presence in *Banjo: Story Without a Plot* (1927). A black American called Banjo leaves his boring job and goes to France hoping somehow to support himself as a musician (he eventually works as a coal-miner). He finds a mentor in a vagabond Haitian intellectual named Ray, who rescues him when he falls seriously ill. McKay uses the friendship to present two contrasting but complementary versions of his own reality.[18] By the end of the novel, both characters are left suspended on the verge of a new experience. The general outline of the plot and the nature of the relationship between Banjo and Ray have much in common with Lawrence's novel, *Aaron's Rod*, published five years earlier and no doubt familiar to McKay. Aaron Sisson, like Banjo, decides to leave his roots for a free life as a flautist in Europe, and through his relationship with the intellectual Rawdon Lilly (who nurses the ill Sisson back to health), Lawrence reveals the two sides of his own character.

To dramatize his theme in *Banana Bottom* (1933), the story of Bita Plant, a Jamaican girl who struggles to find her identity in a hostile world, McKay blends sexual passion with a rich nostalgia for the landscape of his youth, reminding us of how close he remained to Lawrence's conviction that sexual passion was compatible with spiritual quest. In all his fiction, McKay identifies "with the earthbound realism and forthright candor of his black folk heroes," while voicing his hostility toward "the mechanically regimented 'progress' of Western industrialism" for which, in his opinion as in Lawrence's, the working-class paid dearly.[19]

McKay never made it a secret that Tolstoy, Yessenin, Mayakovsky and, above all, Lawrence were his favorite writers. Even during his most militant period, he never felt that it was necessary for him to repudiate the great artistic tradition of Europe.[20] He drew freely upon his broader cultural heritage and participated widely in the intellectual currents of his day. In his mature work, McKay found fulfillment by creating out of this legacy what amounts to a new genre of fiction—the novel of West Indian life, with "its poverty and struggle, its simple dignity and qualified human happiness, against the backdrop of a tropical isle whose natural beauty cannot completely ease the hardship and pain."[21] The same theme that preoccupied

Lawrence—the value of the vitalizing instinctive life of the peasant as an antidote to the ills of civilization—helped to affirm McKay's imaginative and brilliant vision.

* * *

Jean Toomer, the author of *Cane*, and his wife, Margery Latimer, met Lawrence and Frieda through Mabel Dodge Luhan in New Mexico, probably in 1924. Toomer reviewed *Studies* for the *New Mexico Sentinel*, but, more important, he incorporated Lawrence's vision of a new race in America in one of his poems, "Blue Meridian," which appeared in *New Caravan* in 1933. Lawrence had asserted in his *Studies* that civilization on the "new" American continent suffered from the inherited Old World curse of "the maniacal fanaticism of our white mental consciousness," that is, modern civilization.[22] In order to restore health and sanity to society, the demise of the old ego-self, which is rooted in this false consciousness, must be accompanied by the resurrection of the bodily self. In "Blue Meridian," Toomer takes a similar tack: "modern civilization has been responsible for the chaotic condition of the present-day world,"[23] a situation which can be overcome only by a true communion among people achieved by eliminating racial barriers through "sensing, feeling and understanding / That we are beings, / Co-existing with others in an inhabited universe."[24]

But, even earlier, when he was writing his most important book, *Cane* (1923), Toomer had already come under the influence of Lawrence. Soon after, he began to absorb the ideas of the Eastern mystic George Gurdjieff as elaborated by P.D. Ouspensky. Although Toomer would eventually distrust the Gurdjieff system—convinced that there is no single way mapped out and never will be—Lawrence's ideas resembled those of the visionary Russian Armenian in espousing the principle of cosmic harmony and the importance of internal harmony, the achievement of which he made a central concept in his fiction from *Sons and Lovers* to *Lady Chatterley's Lover*. Toomer's *Cane* clearly shows the impress of Lawrence.

The leading character of *Cane* is named Paul. He and a colleague named Bona are, at the outset, examples of a life anathema to Lawrence: an external and artificial consciousness displacing the natural blood consciousness that creates sexual health and personal integration. Paul says to Bona, in words reminiscent of Paul Morel's to Miriam in *Sons and Lovers*, "Mental concepts rule you."[25] But Toomer's Paul will accept "mental concepts" so long as they are "flush" with his own. If Lawrence inspired Toomer with a reverence for wholeness and unity, for integration with nature, that aspiration is hardly the standard that directs Paul's behavior. He is mental when he should be physical, physical when he should be mental. His rhetoric about the "blood" rings false, and his denial of the "mental" is not believable."[26] If *Cane* fails in invention, it fails because Toomer is working too closely to Lawrence, too much in his shadow.

* * *

In 1932, ten years after McKay's Moscow success, Langston Hughes went to the Soviet Union as part of a group of black Americans who were engaged to work with the Russians on a film called *Black and White*. When the film project fell apart, most of the others in the group returned to the United States; Hughes stayed for a year and wrote many articles and poems in support of the revolution and the regime. By then he had written a novel, *Not Without Laughter* (1930) and five volumes of poetry, but no short fiction. During that long winter in Moscow, Hughes would discover the short story, the genre in which, many critics think, he excels. The British author, Marie Seton, who had written a biography of Sergei Eisenstein, gave Hughes a paperback copy of Lawrence's short stories, *The Lovely Lady*. He did not tell Marie Seton so, but he was particularly taken with "The Rocking Horse Winner" and the title story, both of which made his "hair stand on end."[27] A night or two after reading these stories, Hughes sat down to write an article about his travels in Tashkent for *Izvestia*. Instead, he found himself creating a short story under the spell of Lawrence. He had been saying to himself all day, "if D.H. Lawrence can write such psychologically powerful accounts of folks in England, that send shivers up and down my spine, maybe I could write stories like his about folks in America."[28] Hughes adds, "It was Marie Seton's loan of D.H. Lawrence that started me off writing short stories. . . . I had had no thought of doing so. But I am glad it happened that way because I sent my first three stories from Russia to an agent in New York, and by the time I got back to America he had sold all three." By then, "he was overwhelmingly influenced by D.H. Lawrence and "the whirlwind of fiction that had started in Moscow with his reading of Lawrence carried Hughes through long sessions on his typewriter during the fall [of 1933] in Carmel."[29] Using Lawrence as a general model, he wrote *The Ways of White Folks* (1934).

There was much in Lawrence's stories that affected Hughes. "The Lovely Lady," for example, is a tale of murder that mocks the mechanics of that genre (apparently Hughes missed that aspect of it), but the horror was real enough for anyone who had to live with a domineering, hateful parent, as Hughes did. The story presents two murders and one foiled attempt: Pauline Attenborough smothers her first son, Henry, with her own will and personality and attempts to do the same to her younger son, Robert; her niece retaliates, causing Pauline's death. For Lawrence, nothing was worse than the destruction of another person in order to possess and enslave that person's essence—-for him, the ultimate act of cannibalism. Growing up in a racist America, Hughes was all too familiar with destructive power relationships and their subtle capacity to terrorize their target.

"The Rocking-Horse Winner" opens as a fairy-tale about power and money. Undercutting this fairy tale, however, is another—a grotesque shadow, a nightmare counter to the wish fulfillment narrative. The boy's cruel, demanding mother recalls Hughes' own father: "He was interested only in making money," Hughes wrote in *The Big Sea*.[30] Hughes may have been most impressed by Lawrence's suggestion that our revered authority figures, representing a society run on a money ethic, can best educate the younger generation in violation and murder.

Hughes now began to think about some of the people in his own life and some of the stories he had heard that had affected him much as did the mothers in Lawrence's two stories. He recalled a story that a young lawyer in California had told him: in the small Kansas town where he had grown up, there had been a very pretty black girl who attracted the amorous eye of the town's only black doctor, the town's only black undertaker, and the town's black minister. All three enjoyed her favors. The girl became pregnant, although the father was uncertain. At any rate, the doctor performed an abortion on her, and she died. The undertaker took charge of her body. The minister preached her funeral, which was uneventful, and she was buried, an innocent victim of adult abuse.

When Hughes sat down to write his first story, "Cora Unashamed," these facts became little more than framework. The black girl Hughes turned into a white girl of a middle-class family with materialistic values not unlike those of Paul's family in "The Rocking-Horse Winner." The tactics of her domineering and self-centered parents, who do not want her to fall in love with an immigrant Greek boy whose father runs an ice-cream stand, bring to mind Pauline Attenborough in "The Lovely Lady." The story centers on what happens after the girl dies as a result of an abortion forced upon her. The mother is clearly the destructive force in the life of the young victim. At the funeral, Cora, the black maid, condemns the family's compulsive drive for false status and accuses the neurotic adults of killing their child. Thus, what Lawrence suggests in his two stories Hughes applies bluntly to these people: motivated by racist attitudes that prove to be deadly, these upward-bound Americans have behaved like Lawrence's morally bankrupt English gentry.

After Hughes returned to Harlem, his "great dark city," he turned his attention to the oral tradition of his people and developed an original technique for making it into an instrument of political militancy. That, however, did not mean that he was finished with the English writer. One of the chapters in his autobiography is called "D.H. Lawrence Between Us." Faith Berry thinks that Lawrence's "reactionary political views"[31] probably limited Lawrence's influence on Hughes, but clearly Hughes could not have read Lawrence without believing that his spirit was radical. It is more plausible to suggest that Lawrence's poems calling for revolution may have imprinted themselves on Hughes' psyche and inspired his own poems of revolution. More certainly, Hughes learned from Lawrence that poetry could be written in simple, plain yet personal language with its own music. He also learned that indignation before injustice could be expressed in that same simple phrasing and that poetry could be an act of resistance, a public stance against tyranny of any kind. The poem "Ph.D" has a controlled savagery that matches Lawrence at his satirical best. In short, Hughes gained from Lawrence the confidence to try his own most intimate voice in verse. We hear it, briefly, with imagery reminiscent of Lawrence's "Pansies," in such poems as "Lament for Dark Peoples":

> Now they've caged me
> In the circus of civilization.
> Now I herd with the many—
> Caged in the circus of civilization.[32]

We hear it again in "A House in Taos," which Hughes wrote in 1926. Although he had never been to Taos, the poem, Faith Berry speculates, may have been indirectly inspired by stories that Carl Van Vechten and others told Hughes about Mabel Dodge and Tony Luhan. Hughes had also heard gossip about an affair between Mabel and Jean Toomer. "And if stories about them," asks Faith Berry, "why not stories about Mrs. Luhan and D.H. Lawrence, whose liaison in Taos was equally well-known to the New York *literati* through the writer-critic Witter Bynner, who lived in nearby Santa Fe, and had housed Lawrence and his wife, Frieda, during their first night in New Mexico."[33] Although Lawrence probably never conducted a liaison with Mrs. Luhan, it is likely that Hughes had in mind that rumor—as well as her house—when he wrote "A House in Taos." It was by his own admission "a strange poem [for him] to be writing in a period when [he] was writing mostly blues and spirituals":[34]

That there should be a barren garden
About the house in Taos
Is not so strange.
But that there should be three barren hearts
In this one house in Taos—
Who carries ugly things to show the sun?[35]

(When Mabel Dodge Luhan later met Hughes in Carmel, her first remark to him was, "My house is not a bit like that.")

In the final stanza of the poem, the speaker may be Frieda (her first volume of memoirs is called *Not I, But the Wind*), speaking through the voice of the third person mentioned in the opening stanza. Whoever it is, the open form, the phrasing, and the use of nature imagery to suggest other meanings, distinctly bear the stamp of Lawrence in "The Song of a Man Who Has Come Through":

Touch our bodies, wind.
Our bodies are separate, indirect things.
Touch our bodies, wind,
But blow quickly
Through red, white, yellow skies
Of our bodies
To the terrible snarl,
Not mine,
Not yours,
Not hers,
But all one snarl of souls.[36]

Hughes took certain cues from Lawrence during a short but significant period of his career. To paraphrase Etheridge Knight, I don't think the Mythmaker meant for him to do that but at the time, he didn't know what else to do. For the young Hughes, the connection was creative, one that got him started and then left him free to pursue his own direction once he found it. Lawrence "challenged Hughes to new endeavors as a literary practitioner and enriched his literary perspective."[37] Perhaps his relationship with Lawrence is best summed up by one of his own lines from "Theme for English B":—"You are white— / yet a part of me."[38] Had Lawrence remained in America and read Hughes, he might have responded in like language.

* * *

At first glance, Lawrence seems too remote to be an influence on an aspiring writer from an impoverished family of Mississippi share-croppers. However, during the early stages of his literary development in Chicago, when Richard Wright read the English writers omnivorously, he "preferred D.H. Lawrence, especially after absorbing the mother–son relationship in *Sons and Lovers*."[39] Margaret Walker, for whom Wright acted as an affectionate mentor, says that among all Lawrence novels he was fondest of *Sons and Lovers*[40] and that Wright's reading of Lawrence and others led to discussions of Freud, Jung, and Adler.

All this reading would fructify in his early attempts to exorcise the demons of his own adolescence en route to creating his own great chronicle of a poor, gifted boy growing into his vocation as a writer. Before *Black Boy* appeared, Wright had composed "The Man Who Was Almost a Man," a short story about a black youth in Mississippi who lights out for the north in order to escape his domineering father. In Wright's imagination, there must have echoed not only Paul Morel's decision to leave Eastwood, but the words of Gudrun as well: "'One must be free, above all, one must be free,'" followed by Ursula's response, "'We've had one home—that's enough for me.'"[41]

Soon afterwards, Wright added to his meager library *Lady Chatterley's Lover* and used to recommend it, along with the other great novels of Lawrence, to his friends.[42] Lawrence's drama of sexual repression and the psychic damage which it causes became the central theme of Wright's *Savage Holiday*, a novel which introduced to black literature a new candor in the treatment of sexual issues. The novel met with little success, partly because readers were not ready for a highly sexual black protagonist driven to violence by his repressive environment.

Margaret Walker thinks that it may have been Henry James who first interested Wright in the long short story or the short novel form, which he correctly called by the Italian name, the novella, but she believes that he could have just as well been led in that direction by Joyce, Mann, or Lawrence. According to Walker, Wright was very familiar with Lawrence's short fiction.[43] When he began to develop a style suitable for his own fiction, he learned by copying. He tried to incorporate into his own writing the periodic structure and word combinations of Gertrude Stein, using the sound and repetition of the words to create a state of mind that would prolong the meaning of the words themselves. He also seems to have imitated the technique of Lawrence's great purple passages:

> My purpose was to capture a physical state or movement that carried a strong subjective impression, an accomplishment that seemed supremely worth struggling for. If I could fasten the mind of the reader upon words so firmly that he would forget

> words and be conscious only of his response, I felt that I would be in sight of knowing how to write narrative.[44]

Native Son reveals how well Wright mastered this difficult style while thoroughly absorbing Lawrence. Through the end of Book Two, the career of Bigger Thomas is a radical criticism of the dominant American attitude which elevates a person's individual needs over the social. Lawrence's claim that the essential American soul was "hard, isolate, stoic, and a killer"[45] is in effect illustrated in the first two books. But Bigger, although he acts out the deepest destructive meaning of his culture, possesses the human capacity to transcend its limits.

Like Lawrence, Wright was drawn to the dark-skinned people of Mexico. He spent a shorter period of time there (three months) than did Lawrence, but he responded to its ambience much as Lawrence had. He felt comfortable if not at home among the Mexican peasants. While living in Vera Cruz, he received visits from American neighbors such as Mabel Dodge Luhan and took part reluctantly in the social life of the colony. However, just as Lawrence had done fifteen years earlier, Wright showed a real desire to understand the country and its native population. He emphasized the dignity of the Indians even as they sold their goods and their children scratched around in the garbage. In spite of the poverty, Wright discovered a new kind of peace in Mexico, reacting much as Lawrence did to that scene. He also admired the sense of independence and distinct identity of the native Mexican. In "I Bite the Hand That Feeds Me," he said:

> Whites and Indians live and work and die here, always resisting the attempts of Anglo-Saxon tourists and industrialists to introduce social hate and racial discrimination.[46]

As Lawrence did (especially in *Mornings in Mexico*), Wright deplored the intrusions of Western mentality on the consciousness of the American Indian. Before his death, he was planning a novel about the Aztecs to be called *When the World Was Red*.[47] We know little about it, but apparently it would have been a story about Montezuma's rejection of his Spanish conqueror's Christianity as inappropriate for Mexico, suggesting that Wright had been reading *The Plumed Serpent*.

Wright not only survived his youth but transformed his dehumanizing experiences into the very stuff of art. This was a triumph of the will and spirit even more remarkable than the similar achievement of the English coal-miner's son. In many unexpected ways his strange and tormented genius is akin to Lawrence's, and it is to his credit, as it is to Lawrence's, that he remained profoundly concerned with the psychological effects of industrialism on people whose rural or peasant backgrounds ill prepared them for the pressures of city and factory life. He kept the faith.

* * *

Ralph Ellison came up just behind Richard Wright—he is five years younger—and for a few years in the 1930s they both moved in Communist circles. Unlike Wright, Ellison showed almost no interest in Africa, and his work does not derive from those roots. His own comments have led us to believe that Dostoevsky's *Notes from Underground* was the initial inspiration for his *Invisible Man*, but Tony Tanner in *City of Words* speculates that Ellison may have drawn the idea for his masterpiece from Lawrence. The Invisible Man, seeking a new way of being in reality, finds himself falling into a pattern that leaves him dangerously sealed off from all contact with reality—"like those people D.H. Lawrence describes as living under an umbrella."[48] Ellison begins, "I am an invisible man . . . I am a man of substance, of flesh and bone, fiber and liquids—and I might even be said to possess a mind. I am invisible, understand, simply because people refuse to see me"[49] (hence making it dubious that H.G. Wells may have been his source). Tanner cites a passage from Lawrence as being crucial for Ellison:

> Man must wrap himself in a vision, make a house of apparent form and stability, fixity. In his terror of chaos he begins by putting up an umbrella between himself and the everlasting whirl. Then he paints the underside of the umbrella, like a firmament. . . . Man fixes some wonderful erection of his own between himself and the wild chaos, and radically goes bleached and stifled under his parasol. Then comes a poet, enemy of convention, and makes a slit in the umbrella; and lo! the glimpse of chaos is a vision, a window to the sun.[50]

Tanner points out that Ellison's protagonist recognizes that his narrative, like any work of art, is a "fixity" of "apparent form." To achieve any sense of ongoing identity, man needs that umbrella. Consciousness depends on "some wonderful erection of his own," whether it be a corner of Italy or a cellar in Harlem. What is important is not to forget the fluidity in which it stands. For Lawrence, living within the paintings we put on the underside of our umbrellas is a suffocation, a deprivation, and he considered it the job of the creative individual to slash a gap in the protective umbrella and let in reality. Thus, says Tanner, the Invisible Man's highest aspiration is not to allow himself to be trapped in any one plan, while recognizing that to achieve any identity he must be involved in plans. His final comment is that he is sloughing off his old skin. Skin here is an important metaphor, inevitably recalling Lawrence's dominant imagery of skin-shedding in *Studies*. "For skin," Tanner urges, "read plan of any kind" and appreciate the fact that just as the narrator sheds skins when he needs to, Ellison himself sheds styles as the moment requires.[51]

Tanner has sniffed out one possible source of Ellison's inspiration but has overlooked another, a passage which has a more direct bearing on *Invisible Man*. In *Aaron's Rod*, when Aaron Sisson, a musician, first reaches Italy, he is overwhelmed by an existential sense of Nothingness:

> His mask, his idea of himself dropped and was broken to bits. There he sat now maskless and invisible. That was how he strictly felt: invisible and undefined, rather like Wells's *Invisible Man*. He had no longer a mask to present to people: *he was present and invisible* [italics added] they could not really think anything about him, because they could not really see him. What did they see when they looked at him? He neither knew nor cared. He only knew he was invisible to himself and everybody.[52]

Symbolic rather than literal, invisibility can be the metaphor for either liberation or limitation. Shaken by his recognition of the limits that upper-class English society places on an individual, Aaron is rendered impotent while he is in Novarra visiting the affluent Franks. When he recovers his visibility and strength (that is, his self-identity) in Florence, he does so interestingly enough through the energy of his "black rod of power."[53] That episode ends with his "phoenix [rising] in fire again, out of the ashes."[54] The Invisible Man's "black rod of power" may also rise again when he chooses to leave his sanctuary. Neither Ellison's nor Lawrence's protagonist has discovered his identity at the conclusion of his narrative.

Each is left dangling between hope and despair. The old love-ethic no longer works, and *via negativa* beckons to both. Finally free of his past in the closing chapter, Aaron says, "'There's probably more hate than love in me.'"[55] Rinehart wonders, preparing to declare his visibility, whether one has to hate in order to be free. Whatever he borrowed from Lawrence for his metaphor (and *Aaron's Rod* rather than H.G. Wells' novel does appear to have been its source), Ellison transformed and expanded it into a powerful and original statement about human oppression. Like Lawrence's Aaron Sisson, the Invisible Man senses intuitively that the only healthy response to an oppressive society is to reject those aspects of it that threaten his own possibilities for self-respect and self-expression. Few writers were equipped to observe the world of black people with Ellison's degree of bitterness, intensity, and precision. The next expression of that truth would be left to a younger compatriot, James Baldwin.

In a recent letter to me, James Emanuel observed that because black literary criticism has such a curious history, the study of influences is just beginning to emerge from its infancy. D.H. Lawrence's impact on the early careers of five major black writers suggests that a sense of spiritual kinship was possible between writers of very different milieus and very distinctive cultures.

Lawrence's superb spontaneous style exerted a liberating influence on black writers seeking new forms of expression; his skill as a storyteller opened new vistas; and his relentless opposition to industrial civilization and its enslaving effects—coupled with the conviction that modern humanity had to choose a simpler, more sensual and instinctive way of life in order to survive as a species—reinforced a similar feeling among black writers who feared the same dilemma. Since then, the shift in political climate has made such interaction more problematical

Notes

1. Obviously Leroi Jones was not thinking of Lawrence when he wrote in "The Myth of Black Literature" that all black writers were committed to mediocrity because "The literary and artistic models were always those that could be socially acceptable to the white middle class, which automatically limited them to the most spiritually debilitated imitation of literature available." Leroi Jones, "The Myth of Black Literature," in *Black Expression*, ed. Addison Gayle (Weybright and Talley, 1969), p. 192.
2. Langston Hughes, "The Writer's Position in America," *Mainstream* X (July 1957), 47.
3. D.H. Lawrence, "The Battle of Life," in *The Collected Poems* (London: Heinemann, 1964), p. 606. Hereafter cited within the text as *Poems*.
4. D.H. Lawrence, *Kangaroo* (London: Heinemann, 1955), pp. 319–320.
5. D.H. Lawrence, "Birds, Beasts and Flowers," in *Poems*, p. 287.
6. D.H. Lawrence, *Studies in Classic American Literature* (Penguin, 1977), pp. 57–58. Hereafter cited as *Studies*.
7. *Studies*, p. 180.
8. *Studies*, pp. 238, 224.
9. Wyndam Lewis, in "D.H. Lawrence," in *Enemy Salvoes: Selected Literary Criticism*, ed. C.J. Fox (London: Vision Press, 1975), p. 125.
10. John Dewey, Introduction, *The Selected Poems of Claude McKay* (Bookman Associates, 1953), p. 8.

11. Wayne Cooper, *Claude McKay: Rebel Sojourner in the Harlem Renaissance* (Louisiana State University Press, 1987), p. 208. Hereafter cited as *Sojourner*.
12. Claude McKay, *A Long Way From Home* (Lee Furman, 1937), p. 247, as quoted in *The Passion of Claude McKay*, ed. Wayne Cooper (Schocken Books, 1973), p. 31. Hereafter cited as Passion.
13. Sojourner, p. 208; *A Long Way From Home*, p. 248.
14. Sojourner, p. 208.
15. As quoted in *Passion*, p. 31.
16. Claude McKay, "Crazy Mary," in *Gingertown* (Harper, 1932), p. 192.
17. James R. Giles, *Claude McKay* (Hall, 1976), p. 119. Hereafter cited as Giles.
18. *Passion*, p. 31.
19. *Passion*, p. 31.
20. Giles, p. 139.
21. Sister M. James Conroy, *Claude McKay: Negro Poet and Novelist* (Dissertation: University of Notre Dame, 1968), p. 10.
22. *Studies*, p. 169.
23. Jean Toomer, "Blue Meridian," in Brian Benson and Mabel Dilliard, *Jean Toomer* (Twayne Publishers, 1980), p. 126.
24. Jean Toomer, in *The New American Caravan* (Macauley, 1929), p. 645.
25. Jean Toomer, *Cane* (Boni & Liveright, 1923) p. 151.
26. Michael G. Cooke, *Afro-American Literature in the Twentieth Century* (Yale University Press, 1984), p. 181.
27. Langston Hughes, *I Wonder As I Wander* (Rinehart, 1956), p. 213. Hereafter cited as *Wonder*.
28. *Wonder*, pp. 213, 214.
29. Faith Berry, *Langston Hughes: Before and Beyond Harlem* (Lawrence Hill & Co., 1983), p. 18. Hereafter cited as Berry. Arnold Rampersad, *The Life of Langston Hughes Vol. 1: 1902–1946* (Oxford University Press, 1986), p. 282. Hereafter cited as Rampersad.
30. Langston Hughes, *The Big Sea* (Alfred Knopf, 1940), p. 39.
31. Berry, p. 188.
32. Langston Hughes, "Lament for Dark Peoples," in *The Weary Blues* (Alfred Knopf, 1926), p. 100.
33. Berry, p. 80.
34. Berry, 80.
35. Rampersad, p. 120.
36. Rampersad, p. 121.
37. Richard Barksdale, *Langston Hughes: The Poet and His Critics* (American Library Association, 1977), p. 11.

38. Langston Hughes, *Montage of a Dream Deferred* (Henry Holt, 1951), p. 34.
39. Michael Fabre, *The Unfinished Quest of Richard Wright* (William Morrow, 1973), p. 85. Hereafter cited as *Quest.*
40. As quoted in David Ray and Robert M, Farnsworth eds., *Richard Wright: Impressions and Perspectives* (University of Michigan Press, 1971), p. 531.Hereafter cited as *Impressions.*
41. D.H. Lawrence, *Women in Love* (Heinemann, 1921), p. 366.
42. Quest, p. 112.
43. *Impressions*, p. 54.
44. Richard Wright, *American Hunger* (Harper & Row, 1977), p. 22.
45. *Studies*, p. 68.
46. Richard Wright, "I Bite the Hand That Feeds Me" *Atlantic Monthly*, CLXV (June 1940), 826–828.
47. Constance Webb, *Richard Wright: A Biography* (G.P. Putnam's, 1968), p. 357.
48. Tony Tanner, *City of Words* (Harper & Row, 1971), p. 61; hereafter cited in the text as *City*.
49. Ralph Ellison, *Invisible Man* (Random House, 1952), p. 3.
50. D.H. Lawrence, as quoted in *City*, p. 61.
51. D.H. Lawrence, as quoted in *City*, p. 61.

52 D.H. Lawrence, *Aaron's Rod* (London: Heinemann, 1954), p. 159–160.

53. *Aaron's Rod*, p. 250.
54. *Aaron's Rod*, p. 251.
55. *Aaron's Rod*, p. 285.

JULIAN D. MASON, JR.

Introduction to The Poems of Phillis Wheatley

When the first edition of this book was published in 1966, it appropriately spoke of the need to make readily available once more Phillis Wheatley's poems, which had become difficult to obtain despite various printings of them over the decades. Since 1966 her poems have become much more widely available through that edition and also through the work of a respectable body of scholars and critics over only a little more than two decades since that first edition was prepared. Various factors have contributed to increased interest in Phillis Wheatley and her poetry during that time, including the country's bicentennial (focusing on the period when she flourished) and a general heightening of awareness of past and continuing contributions by blacks to American culture as a whole. Another of the catalysts and aids in this interest (as had been intended) was the first edition of this book, making most of her work readily available once more and in context in a scholarly edition. Now, thanks mostly to a handful of persistent scholars whose contributions are obvious in the pages of this new edition, we know of more poems, more variants of poems, and more letters by her, and we know a good bit more about her life and its contexts. Also, much more aesthetic, cultural, and intentional critical attention has been paid to her writings.

Therefore, it is time to enlarge and revise the 1966 book accordingly and to make it even better than it was before by including the additional works and an index and by correcting the first edition's errors (and some of those by others) in text and in facts, while cutting away both some contexts and some suppositions that were appropriate for what was known in 1966 but now have been proven wrong or are no longer needed or no longer appropriate, often superseded by clearer or fuller information or interpretation. Also (to be found primarily in the notes) for this new edition I have been able to add some things that have not been published before. For example, see some new information concerning her personal library which adds a southern connection, in this introduction; two more books she owned, in the notes to her poem to Thomas Amory and her letter to David Wooster; a new way to understand her poem on George Washington, in the note for it; a corrected transcription of a letter from John Andrews, which letter has been used by others to interpret partially incorrectly what happened in response to her 1772 Proposals, in the note for them; and two of her manuscripts previously unnoticed by scholars, with the variants of her poems to Mr. Pitkin and on Samuel Marshall. By providing this new edition, we again offer honor and respect to her and her works, through a much better book, collecting her now available works and putting them in even better contexts; and it is hoped that this new edition will help even more readers find it easier to own and to know her poetry and to understand and appreciate it in context. Written by a young black slave of Boston in the last third of the eighteenth century, her poems, though as a whole not exceptional in quality, are almost as good as any that were published by Americans at that time, even though they are the work of one who had been brought from Africa as a child and who knew no English when she arrived on these shores.

Even though by far we still do not know all we would like to know about Phillis Wheatley, and there are some things concerning her that yet are subject to interpretation, we do know a good bit more than was the case in 1966.[1] She was brought from west Africa[2] to Boston on the slave-trade schooner *Phillis* (owned by Timothy Fitch and captained by Peter Gwin), arriving on July 11, 1761. Later that month the frail child, apparently about eight years old, was personally selected for purchase, through the Boston slave dealer John Avery, by Susanna Wheatley (1709–74), wife of a prominent Boston merchant, John Wheatley (1703–78), for the purpose of assisting Mrs. Wheatley during the remaining years of her life. The child was taken to the Wheatley home on King Street (in the heart of Boston's political, social, book-selling, printing and publishing, and other business activities), into a household of Mr. and Mrs. Wheatley, their eighteen-year-old twins, Mary and Nathaniel, and a few other slaves. Certainly this home and Boston were quite different from the world from which she had been taken. Boston's population was something over fifteen thousand, of which about one thousand were slaves and only about twenty were free blacks. The Wheatley family were members of the New South Congregational Church and firm Christian believers, and Susanna Wheatley was a quite active Christian. She became a great admirer of the Calvinist Methodist evangelist George Whitefield and engaged in missions work by correspondence, encouragement, accommodating visiting ministers in her home, and (at least occasionally) donations of money. John Wheatley's wholesale business was good and expanding, and he owned some residential real estate, some dockside warehouses, some wharfage, and the three-masted schooner *London Packet*, on which Phillis in 1773 would go to London and return. Increasingly, Nathaniel Wheatley (1743–83) became effective and active in the family business, gradually undertaking more and more responsibility in it. (Sometimes in the years ahead he would call upon the intelligence and good handwriting of Phillis to help him, dictating letters to her.)

Mary Wheatley (1743–78) became Phillis's friend and her tutor in religion and language, and Phillis proved to be an apt pupil with a quick mind, studying the Bible, English (language and literature), Latin (language and literature), history, geography, and Christian principles. Indeed, she gained as good an education as (and probably a better one than) most Boston women had, and her learning and abilities gradually gained the interest of a wider and wider segment of the community, especially after she began writing poetry at about the age of twelve, after having been in Boston only about four years. Apparently she became well acquainted with the Bible and with works of Horace, Vergil, Ovid Terence and various contemporary English poets, especially Pope (and through his translations, Homer), and probably Milton. Apparently, hers was an education that would have been prized in many a Boston family, even among its elite; and it was supplemented by contact with persons of status and education, both townspeople and visitors, particularly ministers, who tended to encourage her religious, intellectual, and literary development, apparently sometimes sharing their books with her[3] and occasionally even giving her books to be her own.[4] In her 1767 poem to the students at Harvard College, in nearby Cambridge, she made quite clear her ideas about the purposes for and the value of education (especially in relation to the strong Christian beliefs she had adopted), and the Wheatleys continued to aid and encourage her.

The location of the Wheatley home also provided another education, one about much that was going on in Boston, certainly a leading cultural and business center, experiencing growing friction with the British. From this house she would witness or easily hear much about many of the significant prerevolutionary actions of patriot protest and rebellion (and British response) taking place nearby, and to some of them she responded with early poems. However, despite various evidence in her poems and letters of her sympathy and friendliness (for philosophical and personal reasons, as well as because of local pride and business factors) with the patriots and with the Revolution as it developed, she also maintained loyalist and British friendships and contacts (for both personal and religious reasons). She was young, black, female, a slave, a pious Christian, clever, talented, and astute; and she understood the various aspects of her position in society and the need to be alert, decorous, open, careful, and nimble of mind. She also seems, above party and strife, to have been a loyal friend and a sincere Christian. She was proud to be American in such trying times, but for her there were many types of Americans—and, even more important, there were many types of Christians, all of them children of God, worthy of concern and help, and often capable of giving, and willing to give, help to her. Her principal loyalties were to God, herself, and the Wheatleys, in that order.

Once Phillis began writing poetry, apparently it was Susanna Wheatley who, in addition to providing Phillis social awareness and decorum, encouraged her publication in every way she could, including useful contacts, financial backing, and helping to publicize and distribute her works through letters and in information given to the newspapers and magazines. It is not strange, then, that in such a favorable context (despite her legal slavery) Phillis should have been able to develop her talent for and her inclinations toward poetry. She came to be treated almost as a member of the family and was assigned only very light housekeeping tasks, with permission and encouragement to ignore even these duties when she felt poetically inclined. It is to her credit that such preferential treatment did not make her haughty, but rather fostered in her a strong attachment, respect, and concern for the members of the Wheatley family. However, her fortunate circumstances apparently did not alienate the respect of her fellow slaves, even though she was accepted as a guest in the homes of some of the Wheatleys' friends and was allowed the unusual privilege of having both heat and light in her own room in the Wheatley home at night in deference to her relatively frail health and a memory apparently so untrustworthy as to make it desirable for her to commit her ideas and poems to paper as quickly as possible.

The first poem listed in her 1772 Proposals is dated there 1765, and apparently her earliest poem to be published was "On Messrs Hussey and Coffin" in December 1767 in Newport, Rhode Island. Her literary career can be traced through the poems, letters, and proposals for book publication (and here the notes for them) which give this book its reason for being, for they are why we are interested in knowing about Phillis Wheatley. After she had published a few more poems, including the 1770 poem on the death of George Whitefield which had given her some wide reputation, an attempt was made in 1772 to publish a volume of her poems in Boston. When it did not succeed, efforts for publication of a book of her poems were shifted to England. Meanwhile, Phillis's respiratory problems and generally frail health, which plagued her all of her life and sometimes bad caused her to be sent to the country for awhile, were serious enough that a medical decision was made that she needed sea air. In 1771—the same year in which Mary Wheatley had married the Reverend John Lathrop (1740–1816) and Phillis on August 18 had become a member of the Congregationalist Old South Church (not the church of which the Wheatley family had been and still were members)—John Wheatley had retired and Nathaniel had bought his father's business holdings and part ownership of the family home. Now Nathaniel planned a trip to London in the spring of 1773 to expand certain aspects of the family business, and it was decided that Phillis would accompany him. They sailed from Boston in the family's ship *London Packet* on May 8 and arrived in London on June 17.

As plans for a London publication of her book had begun, the contents of the book had been altered by deletion of poems (particularly anti-British ones), addition of poems, and changing the titles and contents of some poems to be more appropriate for an English audience. (Her poem on leaving Boston, "A Farewel to America," was added after she reached London, and perhaps others were added then also.) Captain Robert Calef of the Wheatley-owned *London*, which made regular runs between Boston and London, had already served as the family's representative in first having the manuscript accepted for publication by Archibald Bell, a London bookseller emphasizing religious works (after the book's authenticity had been attested by John Wheatley and by prominent Boston citizens), and then in securing (through Bell) permission to dedicate the book to the Countess of Huntingdon, thereby elevating its status, the notice given of it, and its sales. The Samson Occom Papers at the Connecticut Historical Society contain a letter of March 29, 1773, from Susanna Wheatley to Occom that sheds some light not only on the progress of Phillis's book during this period but also on the state of affairs in the Wheatley household. The letter, which appears to be in Phillis's hand, indicates that she was not the only one with physical problems:

> Rev'd Sir Boston March 29. 1773
> I have rec'd both your Letters, and was glad to hear you was so kindly entertain'd upon the Road. & got Safe home. I am glad to

embrace this oppy by Dr. Downer [an insertion above this phrase reads: a particular acquaintance of mine & I wish you cou'd See him] who says he Shall come within 5 miles of you to buy Cattle. I importun'd him much to proceed the other 5 miles, but he says he can't go So far but would take care to forward the Letter. I wrote you before of the Sad accident which befel Mr. Wheatley from a fall, who remains in such a Situation, that he has never been able to get out of his Bed without the assistance of 5 or 6 men: and it is now near 5 weeks Since it happen'd.

I am very weak and low, my old indispositions returning upon me, and to Such a degree, as makes me doubtful whether I shall live to See you once more in this World. I must beg your earnest prayers to God for Mr. Wheatley and Me, that when Death comes he may not be a terror, but as the Outward Man decays the inward may be strong in Faith. Don't forget the injunctions upon you to pray for my Son, for when we are gone, I believe You'll be the only praying Freind he will have left.

I have rec'd a Letter from Capt Calef, he had waited upon Mr. Thornton but could not see him, therefore could not write anything upon our affairs; we expect him [Calef] every Day: My Son intends to go home [to England] with him. You Said you'd give him Letters to your freinds when he went. He would be glad as the roads are good and People will be travelling down this way You would Send them as Soon as a convenient opportunity presents. I have wrote to Mrs. Pierce but have not an Oppy to send it. I hope you'll not forget to write to the revd Mr. Moorhead. He is very kind to Mr. Wheatley & visits him almost every Day.—

The following is an Extract from Capt Calef's Letter dated Jan 7th. "Mr. Bell (the printer) Acquaints me that about 5 weeks ago he waited upon the Countess of Huntingdon with the Poems, who was greatly pleas'd with them, and pray'd him to Read them; and often would break in upon him and Say, "is not this, or that, very fine? do read another," and then expressd herself, She found her heart to knit with her and Questiond him much, whether She was Real without a deception? He then Convinc'd her by bringing my Name [Calef] in question. She is expected in Town in a Short time when we are both to wait upon her. I had like to forget to mention to you She is fond of having the Book Dedicated to her; but one thing She desir'd which She Said She hardly tho't would be denied her, that was to have

> Phillis' picture in the frontispiece. So, that, if you would get it done it can be Engrav'd here, I do imagine it can be Easily done, and think would contribute greatly to the Sale of the Book. I am impatient to hear what the Old Countess Says upon the Occasion, & shall take the Earliest Opp,y of waiting upon her when She comes to Town!"
>
> My Husband, Sister and Son join me in their Sincere love to you and your wife. Shall be glad to hear from you pr. first Oppy and remain your affectionate Friend. Susanna Wheatley[5]

A picture of Phillis was provided and was added to the book (and even was available for separate purchase).

Preparations for the book's publication continued while Phillis was in London, but it did not appear while she was there because a message that Mrs. Wheatley was seriously ill led to her returning to Boston earlier than she had intended. This change in plans also made her have to refuse an invitation to visit the Countess of Huntingdon in Wales and also forgo any chance of seeing the king. Nevertheless, she had met many people of interest and seen many sights while in London. She sailed near the end of July and arrived back in Boston on September 13. (Nathaniel stayed in England and in November married Mary Enderby, a member of a thriving mercantile family.) Phillis's *Poems on Various Subjects, Religious and Moral* was published in early September, received a good bit of attention in the London press via ads and notices, and was for sale in at least six places in London. It also was noticed and reviewed elsewhere in England and in Scotland. At some point between September 13 and October 18 Phillis Wheatley was freed by her master and legally was a slave no more.[6] It would be early January 1774 before she would receive copies of her book. When she did receive them she immediately began to market them in letters and in person (as she would for some years to come), a free person now and aware of the necessity to be more responsible for herself in every way. On March 3, 1774, Mrs. Wheatley died. Phillis apparently was allowed to remain in the Wheatley home with Mr. Wheatley as long as he was able to stay there.

While Phillis was in London, she had acquired a number of handsome books,[7] each of which (as far as we know) she inscribed and treasured. Later most of these books would be owned by the Pickman family of Salem, Massachusetts, who over the decades preserved them well. The Pickmans also owned two volumes of the works of William Shenstone, which now are at the Schomburg Center in New York. The inscriptions in them say that they were given to Phillis by Mary Eveleigh on September 24, 1774; and in the rare book collection of Duke University there is a copy of Wheatley's

Poems given to Mary Eveleigh by Wheatley, perhaps in a face-to-face exchange, since Mary Eveleigh was in New England that summer. Earlier that year Mary Shubrick of Charleston, South Carolina, had married Nicholas Eveleigh of South Carolina, who became the first comptroller of the United States Treasury. When he died, Mary married Edward Rutledge of Charleston, a member of the first and second Continental Congresses, a signer of the Declaration of Independence, and a governor of South Carolina (his brother John was a member of the first and second Continental Congresses, a signer of the Constitution, and a member of the United States Supreme Court). The book of her poems which Wheatley had given to Mary Eveleigh also bears the bookplate of Edward Rutledge's law partner, Charles Cotesworth Pinckney of Charleston, another signer of the Constitution and an important figure in many facets of the government of the new nation, including being the Federalist candidate for president in 1804 and 1808. This is a heretofore unanticipated southern connection. Wheatley's poems were indeed known among the prominent families of Charleston during and after the Revolution, as well as among those of Boston, elsewhere in New England, New York, and Philadelphia.

During the British occupation of Boston, John Wheatley apparently left the city and its many difficulties and great confusion and went to Chelsea, to the north. John and Mary Lathrop went to Providence, Rhode Island. Apparently, Phillis joined them there, temporarily a refugee when she sent her poem about George Washington to him from Providence in October 1775, which eventually led to her visiting Washington at his headquarters in Cambridge the following year just before the British left Boston. The publication by others of her poem about Washington in the spring of 1776 gave her some continued visibility and notoriety. But when the war unsettled her residence and her life in general, though she continued writing, this woman, who had been exchanging poems with Royal Navy personnel as late as December 1774, would publish no more poems over the nine years before 1784, during which period her life departed further and further from the encouragement and security she had known during most of the time since her arrival in Boston as a child slave in 1761.

Eventually John Wheatley, Phillis, and the Lathrops returned to Boston, but life would never be the same for them again. John Wheatley died in March 1778 and Mary on September 24 of the same year. Nathaniel had become a permanent resident of London in 1773 (he would die there in 1783). Phillis's British friends and many of her Tory friends had left, and by 1778 almost half of those who had signed the letter "To the PUBLICK" at the front of her book were dead. However, on April 1, 1778, Phillis married John Peters, about whom the surviving bits and pieces provide no clear picture except that he was free, thought well of himself, tried various occupations, often had financial difficulties, and remains an enigma. It appears that what began as a marriage which was financially and otherwise comfortable gradually deteriorated. She bore three children, and if a prayer that is said to have been found in her Bible is indeed hers, it is in part an expression of concern by her in June 1779 about childbirth.[8] During the early 1780s the Peters family lived for some time in the small town of Wilmington, Massachusetts, north-northwest of Boston. In the fall of 1779 and again in September 1784, proposals for a second book of Phillis's poems appeared in Boston periodicals, but in the difficult financial conditions following the war, the proposals failed.

As circumstances worsened, Phillis seems to have written little until 1784, after the family's return to Boston. Perhaps during these difficult years she sometimes even wondered whether she should have acquiesced to earlier suggestions that she go to Africa as a missionary, which she had rejected as impractical and not suited to one from the contexts to which she had become accustomed.[9] The reports of her circumstances in the period before her death on Sunday, December 5, 1784, seem to agree that her life was then at least one of hardships, personal, financial, and familial. Her children did not survive her; the last surviving one was buried with her. The year had begun with the funeral of Samuel Cooper, who had baptized her in 1771 as a girl of eighteen, and his death had started her publishing, again after a nine-year hiatus. The year ended with her own death and her burial in a now lost grave. Her husband apparently later secured her manuscripts and books and disposed of them to pay debts. At least that is what is written inside of and about the copy of *Paradise Lost* that had been given to her in London and now is at Harvard.)

The last of her poems to be published during her lifetime had been another of the many poems about death which she had written over the almost two decades of her career as a poet (we have the poems; the titles of at least nine others appear in her Proposals; of such poems in her first Proposals, only one was not included in her book, which included fourteen in its thirty-eight poems by her; her 1779 Proposals include at least nine poems on death [of which we have only one] among the thirty-three titles listed; of the forty-six poems we know were published during her lifetime twenty were on death). Apparently her first poem dealt with death, and her last one may have also; certainly she felt that she needed to write a poem on Cooper's death that last year—it was expected of her, especially for him. She may even have been asked to write it, for people had certainly come to think of her in an elegiac context; and those who had read her last published poem (on death), in the September *Boston Magazine*, probably thought of it when they read of her death in the same magazine for December and found there also an "Elegy on the Death of a Late-Celebrated Poetess," twenty-seven couplets memorializing her, by "Horatio." Like so many of her own poems, Horatio's had to have been written quickly, for the occasion, with little, if any, advance notice. Her community now once again thought of her in relation to death, but this time her own. Of course, one of the reasons for her many elegies was the prevalence of the genre in her place and time, and she was good at writing it. However, I suspect that the combination of her firm and forthright religious faith and a lively, pleasing, and gentle personality also contributed to her being called on so much for this and accepted it; in fact, one of her poems on death had been chosen as the example poem for yet another try for a second book of her poems only three months before her death. In her elegies, hope and love and faith usually firmly triumph over death—there can be no doubt about that. She knew what was wanted and needed in such circumstances. Her last poem published during her lifetime began:

> O DEATH! whose sceptre, trembling realms obey,
> And weeping millions mourn thy savage sway;
> Say, shall we call thee by the name of friend,
> Who blasts our joys, and bids our glories end?

but it ended with the admonition to the grieving parents of the child: "suppress the clouds of grief that roll, / Invading peace, and dark'ning all the soul." Such suppression of grief should be possible because of the consoling picture of heavenly happiness, free from earthly sin, which the poet presents as the dead infant's present experience.

In her short life, like most of her contemporaries, she had seen death much and thought of it often (in Africa, on the slave ship, in often harsh New England); even if it were not always welcome, it was no stranger and a part of life, readily available as a subject. Now her time had come. According to the obituaries, she was buried on Thursday, December 9: "Phillis Peters formerly Phillis Wheatley aged 31, known to the literary world by her celebrated miscellaneous poems. Her funeral is to be this afternoon, at 4 o'clock, from the house lately repaired by Mr. Todd, nearly opposite Dr. Bullfinch's at West Boston, where her friends and acquaintances are desired to attend" (from the *Boston Independent Chronicle and Universal Advertiser*). Periodicals across New England carried notices of her death, usually identifying her as "known to the literary world by her celebrated miscellaneous poems." At the end, she was to be known to all only for her writing, not as a former slave or in any other context, and I suspect that she would have liked Horatio's poem, which said in part:

As if by heaven inspir'd, did she relate,
The souls grand entrance at the sacred gate!
And shall the honour, which she oft apply'd,
To other's reliques, be to hers deny'd?
  O that the muse, dear spirit! own'd thy art,
To soften grief and captivate the heart,
Then should these lines in numbers soft array'd
Preserve thy mem'ry from oblivion's shade;
But O! how vain the wish that friendship pays,
Since her own volumes are her greatest praise.[10]

As a poet she would have been pleased with such last praise from another poet, who could best understand what the most important part of her life had been and why. She had published at least forty-six poems during her lifetime (not counting variants) and had written a good many more (of which nine have now been published). They and her book had been generally well received at home and abroad, and from various quarters she had been praised as a poet. In this regard, in her brief life of thirty-one years she had accomplished a great deal, despite circumstances that would have suggested that she either could not or would not be able to do so. Perhaps if she had lived longer or in more stable times, she would have accomplished even more.

* * *

Phillis Wheatley was not the first black American to publish. For example, Briton Hammon preceded her with a fourteen-page pamphlet in 1760 (his only publication); and Jupiter Hammon published an eighty-eight-line broadside poem that same year but would not publish again until 1778 with a poem praising Wheatley after she was already well established as a poet. Certainly she was the first truly significant black American writer, and her 1773 book of poems was probably the first book—and certainly the first book of poetry—published by a black American. Her progress and development as a writer can be followed in her works in this volume, which are arranged with a chronological emphasis. There is no doubt that her 1773 book was her most significant publication. Though she also published poems as pamphlets and broadsides and in newspapers and magazines on both sides of the Atlantic, her book contains the core, the majority, and most of the best of the poems by her which we have. The printing and reprinting history of her book and individual poems and her letters is best followed in Robinson's *Phillis Wheatley: A Bio-Bibliography*, though much of that history is also found in this volume, especially in its notes and in "A Note on Text."

Phillis Wheatley is important historically, and her works are of importance and interest in their own right, especially in the contexts of her time and place—though some of them easily transcend both. Phillis Wheatley, however, was not a great poet. She was not really a poet in the classical Greek sense of maker, seer, creator, nor were her concerns really much with Ralph Waldo Emerson's meter-making argument or Edgar Allan Poe's rhythmical creation of beauty. She had aspirations, but she also knew her shortcomings; and her concerns usually were not very august or pretentious. Her primary endeavor was to put into rhythmical, poetic forms thoughts that came to her, or were brought to her attention by the crises and significant experiences of the people of Boston as they met life, death, and change, from day to day and, year to year. Much of what she wrote of was not noted by the world outside of that place, though she occasionally did treat more general topics, particularly relating to the American Revolution, and did try for general pertinence while treating local particulars. While most successful writers strive for such pertinence, in her case it seems too often to have been a secondary goal that emerged most obviously when she revised a poem for a secondary audience, as in her revisions to make some of her Boston or American poems more acceptable, meaningful, or attractive to an English audience. Mostly, first of all she wrote for local audiences and local publication. When she occasionally did turn to more general emphases, she produced some of her best work, as in her hymns to morning and evening.

Nevertheless, on the basis of the poems that have survived her short career, she must be labeled as primarily an occasional poet, one interested in the clever crafting of verse. Such a craftsman is less concerned with selecting topics and creating patterns than with taking a given or obvious topic and fitting it skillfully to an existing pattern. If she is a good craftsman, she is distinctive in her own right and possesses a gift that is worthy of the world's attention, if not its lasting praise. Such was Phillis Wheatley's gift and her concern, and she was a better craftsman of verse than most of the others attempting the same type of thing in America in the 1770s, a time and place that certainly produced more craftsmen than true poets. Her reward was in immediate praise—not that which echoes through the ages, but which appropriately sounds again from time to time.

Yet some of her poems reveal an exceptional being producing exceptional poetry. Most of her best work is in her nonoccasional poems, certainly in her more philosophic ones. In this regard it is interesting that various commentators have chosen different ones of her small body of poems to praise as the best,[11] and almost all writers on this subject favor to some degree "An Hymn to the Morning" and "An Hymn to the Evening." One would be amiss not to place in this company "On Virtue" and "Goliath of

Gath," and each reader might wish to include yet others; for in certain complete poems and in parts of others, Wheatley was able to surpass to a great degree what was at once both her great asset and her great liability—a favor for and a remarkable spontaneous ability to recreate the neoclassical poetic mode of Alexander Pope and his followers, in diction, meter, rhyme, and syntax. In such happy instances she avoided ordinary subject matter and clichés, using instead striking, appropriate poetic figures in pleasing form, which attracted both the mind and the ear. In these she was more than just an imitator, and she reflected a fortunate influence of the best neoclassism. Unfortunately, she could not write this well consistently enough for such good poetry to dominate her work, leaving her to be known primarily as a prodigious imitator. For the same poet who wrote the exceptional poems mentioned above also wrote too many run-of-the-mill elegies.

Wheatley seems to have been fascinated with the device of invocation, and her mixing of Christian and classical in the many invocations in her poems (as well as in other parts of the poems) reflects the two greatest influences on her work, religion and neoclassicism. Indeed, this device and a few others remind one of Milton, she certainly does not use them with his skill. For example, one can see the mixing of the Christian and the neoclassic in "To Mæcenas" and "On Recollection," and she apparently attempts the Miltonic device of vague exactness in measurement in "Thoughts on the Works of Providence" when she says of the sun's distance from the earth, "Of miles twice forty millions is his height." Vernon Loggins has pointed to the influence of English writers on her poems dealing with imagination, recollection, and virtue and to the influence of Milton on her hymns to the morning and evening and her poem about General Lee. He also suggests the specific influence of Gray on her poem on Whitefield's death and of Addison and Watts on "Ode to Neptune" and "Hymn to Humanity."[12]

The strongest influences on her work definitely were religion (including the Bible) and neoclassicism. Wheatley has been called a typical New Englander of the eighteenth century in her pious religious views, which seem to crop up everywhere. She is constantly aware of God, His Son, His beneficence, and His power; and she intends that her readers be aware of them too. Almost every poem produces a moral at some point, and the mood and message of her poem to the University of Cambridge sound as if it might have been issued from the pulpit. She had definite, if stereotyped, ideas that Heaven is a place of halos, angels, and reunion with God and His beloved; and she used these ideas with the same seriousness of purpose that surrounds her classical material. It is not at all strange that one who attended Boston's Old South Meeting House should show such firm Christian convictions and concern with the soul, and these facets of her personality, made it very appropriate for friends to turn to her for elegies. In this vein we should not overlook her embellishment of biblical accounts in her poems based on Isaiah and on the encounter of David and Goliath (following in an old New England tradition and beginning a long tradition of black writers' embellishing the Bible). In both of these poems she adds to the biblical narrative and couches it in the neoclassical form that was familiar to her from the poems she read most—iambic pentameter couplets, opening invocation of the muse, panoramic view, attempted elevation of language (especially in the august speeches of the characters) eye-catching details, and hyperbole. It is clear that Wheatley read as much as possible. Her favorite volumes are reported to have been the Bible, a collection of tales from mythology, and Pope's Homer; and we also know that she read at least some of the Latin authors in the original. Although some of her subject matter can be traced to classical origins outside of Pope's translations and although it is difficult to pinpoint clearly indisputable instances of his influence on her, it still is held by most who study her poems that Pope's translation of Homer was the single most important influence on her work. To that view I too subscribe.

Certainly Pope's relatively fixed formulas for neoclassical poetic music found a ready response in this young African girl's natural imitative ability. However, I suspect that what led her back to Pope time and time again was really Homer's grand narrative, which had retained its greatness of concept even when encased in a neoclassic gait. Wheatley was content to take the form she found because she could use it with ease, but it seems that in choosing Snider, Niobe, David and Goliath, Lee, and Washington, she was also feeling the tug of Homer's heroes on her impressionable young mind. I believe it was the classical world which kindled her talent and interest, though she used the neoclassical approach because of its vogue, its availability to her, and her ability to employ it. Her best-treated subject matter tends to support this view. There has been conjecture about what the rising romanticism would have done to her work if she had lived either later or longer. One may with more pertinence wonder what her poems would have been like had she been immersed in Milton sooner, for what he had done seems to suit her basic interests more. Phillis Wheatley was not the wasp that Pope was, but tended to be more compatible with Milton's Christian classicism and its view of life. It is interesting to note that in a poem dated December 5, 1774, she acknowledges her proper place to be but at the feet of such men as Newton and Milton and reserves for Milton, the grand creator—not for Pope, the translator—the title "British Homer."

On the other hand, even in the face of these facts and of the fact that her best poems seem to be those that depart most from neoclassical imitation, the strong influence of neoclassicism on her in her first, formative years as a poet may not have been a bad thing. It certainly gave her a respect for regularity (which even Wordsworth recognized as necessary), happened to be something she had a natural talent to reproduce (thus probably encouraging her in her own eyes and in the eyes of those who made Pope so popular), was readily available, and was usually not too deep philosophically. The pity is that events and her short career did not give her talent time enough to discover if it could broaden, mature, and diversify more.

The neoclassical influence also may have been responsible for the lack of much about Wheatley herself in her poems. She certainly leaves the reader of her poems only here and there aware of her being black and a slave. Saunders Redding has pointed out, "The Wheatleys had adopted her, but she had adopted their terrific New England conscience."[13] She was conscious of her color, but the degree to which she became a New Englander helped moderate this awareness during her most formative years. For her, Heaven was more to be desired than earthly toil, not so much for the physical rewards which many later slaves would emphasize, but rather for its spiritual rewards. Some seem to chide her for her apparent unconcern over slavery in a Boston where it was obviously much discussed, but it was probably better for her poetry that whatever feelings she had about this subject were sublimated in most of her poetry (it emerges more in her letters).

The few thoughts on Africa and slavery's effect on her that are included in her poems are interesting. Her individual situation did not equip her for abolitionism—indeed, her real and necessary poetic patron was the Wheatleys, particularly Susanna Wheatley. She came to America too young for that hard experience not to be modified by her being part of the Wheatley household. But she clearly was not entirely unmindful of blacks' delegated place in the popular mind of the time. She makes good use of this knowledge in her poems to the Earl of Dartmouth, to the University at Cambridge, and on Wooster's death, almost turning it to advantage to strengthen her points. She surely was aware that much of her own notoriety was the result of her work's being usually labeled as that of an African (and she is careful to so call herself in several poems and to entitle one poem "To S. M., A Young African Painter, On Seeing His Works").

In her particular case, she seems to have viewed the captivity that brought her to Boston and to the Wheatleys as not entirely unfortunate. Her poem to Dartmouth speaks of "seeming cruel fate" which snatched her "from Afric's fancied happy seat," and she shows concern primarily for the sorrow of her parents. But she immediately makes it clear that she does not endorse slavers, slavery, or the usual results of slavery. Her poem "On Being Brought from Africa to America" sees the event as fortunate because it allowed her to be a Christian, and the poem almost sounds like the product of missionary propaganda (though she specifically refused to be a missionary to Africa). In this same vein she speaks to the students at the University at Cambridge of her not enjoying the advantages they have because of her having so recently come from a land of "errors" and "gloom," brought forth to safety by the "gracious hand" of God. However, in her poem dated December 5, 1774, to the "Gentleman in the Navy," she seems quite taken with western Africa as a place of peace, beauty, and plenty, but this may be simply a reaction to his poem to which this is a reply. At any rate, in "To Mæcenas" she makes it clear that she thinks the muses ought to come to her aid and not give Terence alone claim to being an inspired African poet. (Of course, here is reflected the narrowness of her knowledge.) Incidentally, this also affords us one of the few instances when we learn anything of Phillis herself from her poems.

Although she did not write much of slavery, certain of her poems do reflect an awareness of current events affecting the society in which she lived. For example, see her poems to the king and to the Earl of Dartmouth and her poems on Snider, Lee, Wooster, and Washington and the poems *Liberty and Peace* and "America."

In her worst poems, Wheatley falls prey to the clichés of neoclassical poetic diction, to wrenched syntax, to trite devices, to runaway rhythm, and to an overemphasis on religion. These appear most frequently in her occasional verses. Over one-third of her extant poems are elegies. Loggins points out the long tradition of elegies in Boston and that hers too are impersonal and artificial in feeling, with much use of hyperbole, overuse of personification, and pompousness of ornamentation.[14] Not only is neoclassical tradition to blame here, but also the fact that most of these were written for the occasion, to console loved ones and embellish the memory of the departed. Yet sometimes a genuine note of understanding and concern is found in her elegies, especially for persons who had played a part in her own life, at which times one feels even more the strain resulting from her poetic form. Sometimes her good product is found close by her poor one in the same poem. In "To a Lady and Her Children, On the Death of Her Son and Their Brother," she speaks of the mother's realization of the death: "Th' unhappy mother sees the sanguine rill / Forget to flow, and nature's wheels stand still." However, later in the same poem we are rudely accosted by the cliché and the wrenched syntax of the following: "No more in briny show'rs, ye friends around, / Or bathe his clay, or waste them on the ground." In her better work, she is much more in control of the syntax and rhythm and employs them with unobjectionable diction and figures, if not always fresh or new ones. An example is found in "Thoughts on the Works of Providence," in which she speaks of dawn and sunset: "Or when the morning glows with rosy charms, / Or the sun slumbers in the ocean's arms," and speaks of God

"Which round the sun revolves this vast machine, / Though to his eye its mass a point appears," and of the moon, which "True to her course th' impetuous storm derides, / Triumphant o'er the winds, and surging tides." Or note the opening lines of "An Hymn to the Evening": "Soon as the sun forsook the eastern main / The pealing thunder shook the heav'nly plain; / Majestic grandeur! From the zephyr's wing, / Exhales the incense of the blooming spring. / Soft purl the streams, the birds renew their notes, / And through the air their mingled music floats." These are not great lines, but they are good ones.

Of course, her favorite poetic form was the heroic couplet of English neoclassicism. All of her extant poems employ this form, with six exceptions.[15] There are occasional interspersed three-line rhyme sequences, and "An Answer to the Rebus" departs from the heroic couplet in its last four lines to employ iambic tetrameter. She attempted her most complicated formal poetic pattern in "An Hymn to Humanity," a poor poem; but her one use of ballad stanza was quite successful. However, she apparently found that the heroic couplet came easier, and she did not abandon it in her later poems.

Wheatley only occasionally used such devices as alliteration and onomatopoeia, and they were not significant in her poetic method. However, as with good neoclassicism, the caesura was important as she constantly attempted not just iambic pentameter couplets but the heroic couplet employed by Alexander Pope. Unfortunately, her work was subject to the uncertainties and irregularities of eighteenth-century English spelling and punctuation, and she was too dependent on elision for regulating her meter. She also rhymes in the eighteenth-century manner—for example, "join" with "divine." Nevertheless, the ear will not excuse her occasional lack of consistency in tense, especially noticeable in her poem on Goliath. If she were responsible for the order of the poems in the 1773 edition (which is somewhat chronological in relation to date of composition), we might note that that order is basically a good one. She seems to have preferred the medium-length poem of from forty to fifty lines, with the eight-line poems "On Friendship" and "On Being Brought from Africa to America" being her shortest and her two narrative poems on Goliath and on Niobe being her longest, each having 224 lines. Wheatley seldom employed her talents in narrative; but she was fairly good at it, sustaining the reader's interest with a good mixture of details, action, speech, and pacing.

For a good number of her poems we have variant versions (sometimes more than one) which show that she could improve the diction, poetic figures, syntax, rhythm, tone, rhyme, and general quality of her work through both changes and deletions, sometimes for different audiences. However, basically Wheatley was a spontaneous poet, not a laborious one.

Therefore, the general regularity of her meter is striking.

Her poetic career began early in her life and was sporadic, brief, and in its later stages apparently difficult. Nevertheless, in the community where she lived, Wheatley practiced the art of poetry and was known there for that practice; and Boston in the years before and after the American Revolution was still the literary capital of America, as well qualified to produce, cultivate, encourage, and judge a poet as any community in the land. In part because she was young, in part because she was female, and in part because she was black and nominally a slave, her work has too often been overpraised. On the other hand, she also has been too often dealt with unfairly or not at all because of this overpraising and the reasons for it. The proper position lies somewhere between these extremes, for her work definitely does have some literary merit, despite its obvious shortcomings. It becomes even more significant in any literary-historical or cultural consideration of it.

Her poems are certainly as good as or better than those of most of the poets usually included and afforded fair treatment in a discussion of American poetry before 1800, and this same evaluation holds true when she is compared with most of the minor English poets of the eighteenth century who wrote in the neoclassical tradition. Finding our early literary soil generally unfit for real poetry, Moses Coit Tyler in his *A History of American Literature, 1607–1765* and *The Literary History of the American Revolution* does, however, treat many "verse-writers," especially those of New England. In comparing his appraisals of these writers, as frank and blunt as the statements are, one still cannot help but conclude that his harsh treatment of Phillis Wheatley in the latter volume is unjust. For she certainly deserves as much praise, or as little blame (depending on whether one is measuring by a relative standard or by an absolute one, as Tyler was), as such early poets as Thomas Morton, Benjamin Tompson, Thomas Godfrey, Nathaniel Evans, Nathaniel Niles, Jonathan Odell, Joseph Stansbury, Michael Wigglesworth, Ebenezer Cook, Mather Byles,[16] and perhaps Francis Hopkinson, John Trumbull, Timothy Dwight, Joel Barlow, and Anne Bradstreet (though Wheatley is not as sustained and consistent as these latter five, her best work certainly is worthy of inclusion with their best). There is no doubt whatever that she was the best black American author before 1800 and the best black American poet until Frances Ellen Watkins Harper in the middle of the nineteenth century.

As I have said, she was not a great poet; but in her way, in her time, and in her locale, she was a fairly good writer of poems generally in imitation of the neoclassical mode made popular by Alexander Pope. She deserves our consideration by either absolute or relative standards—and not just because of her youth, her sex, or her race. As Perry Miller and countless others have reminded us and shown us, it is indeed a mistake to think there is nothing worth reading in American literature before Washington Irving—and this applies to black authors as well, for there stands Phillis Wheatley of Boston, not one of the very best, but far from one of the worst of the many who, in spite of the struggles of establishment, felt the influence of the muses in colonial America.

The reader who wishes to pursue further critical approaches to and evaluations of Wheatley's poems is referred to the list of works near the end of this volume. (Note Robinson's edition of *Critical Essays* and his "On Wheatley's Poetry" in his *Her Writings*.) For various aesthetic emphases (both theoretical and applied) especially see some works by Barksdale, Cook, Holder, Isani, Rigsby, Scruggs, Shields, and Sistrunk. For critical focuses on other than aesthetic concerns in her poems (including some racial, religious, and feminist emphases) especially see some works by Burroughs, Collins, Gates, Huddleston, Isani, Jordan, Levernier, Mason, Matson, O'Neale, Rogal, Smith, and Stetson.

Notes

1. This very brief biographical sketch is distilled from almost twenty-five years of scholarly work on Phillis Wheatley. Some of it is indebted to my own research, in both primary and secondary sources; but the major part of it is indebted (for clues, sources, information, and clarification) to so many sources hither and yon that it would not be feasible to try to list them all here. Some of them are mentioned in the section on her reputation, but more important is the work of numerous scholars whose efforts have now taken us far beyond most of the older biographical sources about her, and whose contributions appear in the list of works near the end of this volume, especially Mukhtar Ali Isani and William H. Robinson. Indeed, special mention should be made of Robinson's very full and helpful essay "On Phillis Wheatley and Her Boston" in his *Phillis Wheatley and Her Writings* (pp. 3–69, hereafter cited as *Her Writings*) and the many notes to that volume.

   This brief essay gives only an overview of the broad pattern and important aspects and events of Wheatley's life, as an introduction. In deciding what not to include, it was presumed that the reader will also read the rest of this volume and especially her works themselves and the notes to them. Therefore, an effort has been made to avoid repetition among the various parts of this volume, but also to provide adequate access and awareness at any given point through cross-reference and an index. Therefore, to know all that this book can provide about her life one must go beyond this sketch to the other sections of the book, particularly the chronologically arranged sections of her works and the notes to them, both for supplementing what is in this sketch and for what is not in it. All of that will provide a great deal of information about her and her works, but by no means all there is to know, which one can pursue further with the help of the list of works near the end of this volume (and what will appear in this active field after this book is published).

Further notes will be given with this sketch when the directly pertinent complementary or supplementary information in this volume is not otherwise obvious (in poem titles, letter recipients, dates, and so on), or for what is not said elsewhere in this volume.

2. Although there has been some reference to her as a native of the Senegal–Gambia region, that cannot be substantiated. See her poem "To a Gentleman of the Navy" and note 37.
3. For example, see Shields, "Phillis Wheatley and Mather Byles."
4. See the note to her poem to Thomas Amory.
5. I believe that this is the first time that this letter has been published in full, though part of the third paragraph and all of the fifth paragraph have been published several times previously. See the note to her 1772 Proposals. Robert Calef was the captain of the Wheatley-owned *London Packet*, which made regular runs between Boston and London. If Occom did provide letters to his English friends they would have been useful for meeting various important people engaged in the interests supported by the Countess of Huntingdon and John Thornton, both of whom helped support Occom's efforts, as did Lord Dartmouth. See Wheatley's letter to David Wooster, her poem to Mary Moorhead, and "A Note on the Text."
6. See her 1773 letter to David Wooster.
7. See her 1773 letter to David Wooster.
8. The prayer is at the Schomburg Center in New York and is very fragile and torn. Its provenance apparently is unknown, and it is not possible to tell whether Phillis composed it, copied it, or even wrote down what is there. The note above the prayer telling where it was found appears to be in the same handwriting as the prayer itself. It does seem to be from her period. (The prayer is printed in Robinson, *Her Writings*, p. 346, and Shields, *Collected Works*, p. 194.)
9. See her letters to Samuel Hopkins of May 6, 1774, and to John Thornton of October 30, 1774. Samson Occom also had favored such a possibility for her.

10. The *Boston Magazine*, December 1784, p. 630. The poem is reprinted in full in the 1966 edition of this volume, pp. xvii–xviii; and Kaplan, *Black Presence*, p. 169, has a photograph of the original printing of it.
11. For example, Loggins, *Negro Author*, p. 373 n. 75, calls "A Farewell to America" "perhaps her most graceful achievement in versification"; Benjamin Brawley, *The Negro in Literature and Art in the United States* (New York, 1934), p. 35, calls "On Imagination" her best poem; Redding, *To Make a Poet Black*, p. 12, favors "Thoughts on the Works of Providence."
12. Loggins, *Negro Author*, pp. 24, 27, 373 n. 75. Also see the work of John Shields for other suggestions of possible influences on her poems by various English and classical writers.
13. Redding, *To Make a Poet Black*, p. 9.
14. Loggins, *Negro Author*, p. 22.
15. The exceptions are "On Virtue," which is free verse (although she may have intended it for blank verse) ending with a heroic couplet; "To the University of Cambridge," which is primarily blank verse; "Ode to Neptune," which has two sections of six lines each, with each section having four lines of iambic tetrameter couplets, followed by one heroic couplet—with a third six-line section that is mostly iambic tetrameter and has rhyme of ababcc; "An Hymn to Humanity," which has six sections of six lines each, with each section having first an iambic tetrameter couplet, followed by an iambic trimeter line, followed by an iambic tetrameter couplet, followed by an iambic trimeter line that rhymes with the third line of the section; "A Farewel to America," which is in ballad stanza (but the newspaper version, perhaps because of space considerations, is not separated into the usual four-line sections—this is the only one of these six poems that saw newspaper publication); and "An Elegy on leaving," which has seven sections, with iambic pentameter lines, with rhyme of abab in each section (with second and fourth lines indented).
16. Because Byles offers such an apt comparison with Wheatley, one becomes especially impatient with the treatment given him by various authors and editors. (See the Facsimile Text Society edition of Mather Byles, *Poems on Several Occasions*, with introduction by C. Lennart Carlson [New York, 1940].) Similarities extend to volume title, preface, general subject matter, age, and place (Boston, where his volume appeared in 1744). One has only to compare the poem of each on the subject of David and Goliath to note Wheatley's superior imagination, sophistication, and general poetic ability. She is in command of her subject and is not just adapting a biblical account. Yet most general

accounts or collections of early American poetry do not acknowledge the superiority of her poetry to that of Byles. (Shields's "Phillis Wheatley and Mather Byles" has appeared since the first publication of this note in 1966.)

SONDRA O'NEALE

A Slave's Subtle War: Phillis Wheatley's Use of Biblical Myth and Symbol

Any evaluation of Phillis Wheatley must consider her status as a slave. Wheatley was one of only three Americans who were able to publish poetry and prose while they were still in bondage. (The other two were Jupiter Hammon [1711–179?] and George Moses Horton [1797–1883].) Speaking out against one's "owners" or the society which either condoned or ignored the owners' action—while held in their joint "possession"—was a monumental task. Most of Wheatley's critics have not considered these factors when assessing her work. Nor have many modern critics of Black American literature been kind to Wheatley. James Weldon Johnson, Benjamin Brawley, Darwin Turner, Benjamin Mays, and J. Saunders Redding have castigated her as an unfeeling woman foolishly immersed in colonial refinements, oblivious to her own status as a slave and to that of her African peers. A recent and more stinging comment is from Eleanor Smith, who put Wheatley among those "Blacks who are taught to think white and to divorce themselves from who they are. When they direct their energies, be they creative or otherwise, towards Whites, they are never consciously contributing to their own liberation or the liberation of Black people. Phillis Wheatley did not help herself by following all the dictates of Whites nor did she contribute to the well-being of black people of her time" (407). Although Arthur P. Davis, Lynn Matson, John C. Shields, William H. Robinson, Jr.,

From *Early American Literature* 21, no. 2 (Fall 1986).

Mukhtar Ali Isani and others have recently begun to correct this one-sided picture by showing that Wheatley was not unmindful of racial concerns, their works still overlook biblical terminology and its implications for slavery.

Horton and Frederick Douglass explain in their autobiographies that a slave who wanted to tell the truth about the oppressive system first had to acquire the requisite language skills, usually surreptitiously. While Hammon was probably schooled with his master's children, both Douglass and Horton tell of tricking other youngsters into teaching them how to spell. A slave all of his life, Hammon managed to publish several poems and some essays and sermons; Horton published two books of poetry while he was still a slave, but he produced his most radical volume after he found refuge among officers in the Union Army. However, Douglass did not publish his famous autobiography until after he had escaped from slavery and was a prominent spokesman in the abolition movement.

In addition, appropriate whites had to authenticate the writer's mental and moral capacity, and then the slave's master had to agree that the slave could publish the work.[1] Moreover, the slave's offering was carefully censored to ensure that it was in no way incendiary. While Wheatley did not have to acquire the language skills stealthily, she was subject to authentication for proper classical and evangelical content. Within such constraints Wheatley—as did Hammon, Horton and Douglass—found the biblical myth, language and symbol to be the most conducive vehicles for making subtle, yet effective, statements against slavery.[2]

The writings of these enslaved authors resemble the Southern plantation hymns of the nineteenth century, which the slaves sung on one level with intense religious commitment and on another level as a code language to protest slavery and to plan for escape.[3] In a more formal tactic, Wheatley challenged eighteenth-century evangelicals in their cherished religious arena by redeploying the same language and doctrine that whites had used to define the African, thereby undercutting conventional colonial assumptions about race and skin color. Simultaneously, she gave her African-American readers enhanced self-esteem with new and respected ethnic identity, and thus created a strong foundation for their inclusion as equals within the Christian community. Because critics have failed to consider her status as a slave; to read her work in light of the social, political and religious culture of the eighteenth century; and to interpret her use of biblical symbolism, Wheatley has been undervalued as a poet and as an abolitionist.

First, Wheatley manipulated the connotations of the color black by placing them in a widened, more authentic Christian context for her readers. (And here I define even slaves who could not read as "readers," as it was the usual practice in the North for sympathetic slavemasters to read Wheatley's and Hammon's works to their slaves; in fact, many whites used both writers as tools for evangelism among their servants.) For Calvinist Puritans and for the later Methodist Arminians, among whom Wheatley lived, the color black was the most ominous of signs. As Roger Bastide notes:

> The "frontier complex" or restricted-group feeling rests . . . upon the Calvinist idea of predestination and visible signs of divine election.
>
> In this way, dark skin came to symbolize, both in Africa and in America, the voluntary and stubborn abandonment of a race in sin. Contact with this race endangered the white person's soul and the whiteness of his spirit. The symbolism of color thus took on one of the most complicated and subtle forms . . . through which darkness of color became associated with evil itself. (44–45)[4]

From such logic evolved simplified colonial definitions of white and black: white became associated with light, purity, safety, understanding, God and heaven; black, in turn, represented insecurity, sin, self-loathing, fear, ignorance, eternal death, Satan and hell.[5] Such dichotomies were particularly convenient for slaveholders, who used them to explain the African's assumed heathenism and thus to justify his enslavement. Eulalio R. Baltazar emphasizes that it was the twisting of biblical imagery rather than the biblical text itself that was used as early as the sixteenth century to support the slave trade. He points out that black often functions as a positive symbol in the Bible. For instance, the female persona in Song of Solomon 1:5–6 twice identifies herself as Black, as in "I am black, but comely. . . ." Moreover, the Bible itself does not refer to sin as blackness; the usual association is with scarlet.[6] But for centuries theologians in England and in New England had failed to teach these contexts. Thus Wheatley wrote for an audience that had inherited the traditionally denigrating associations for the color black.[7] With a system of diction and imagery that was well understood in the age (but was still subtle enough to satisfy those in the society—masters, publishers and readers—who insisted that a slave's writings had to be both harmless and docile), she attempted to change her readers' perceptions about color. Although she sometimes mirrored usual linguistic assumptions by using "dark" and "black" to denote evil or a state of damnation, she was careful to differentiate these associations from human skin color. To a fellow slave, Arbour Tanner, she wrote:

> . . . let us rejoice in and adore the wonders of God's infinite Love in bringing us from a land semblant of darkness itself, and where the divine light of revelation (being obscur'd) is as darkness. Here the knowledge of the true God and eternal life are made manifest; but there, profound ignorance overshadows the land. (*Poems and Letters* 23–24)[8]

In this quotation Wheatley seems to be using the language of the slave culture, yet she is covertly undermining its definitions of race by equating blackness with a spiritual illumination rather than with a condition of physical pigmentation.

In "On Being Brought from Africa to America," one of her best known poems, Wheatley not only illustrates her conscious manipulation of prevailing associations of blackness but also uses biblical myth to make some of her most comprehensive comments on slavery:

> 'Twas mercy brought me from my *Pagan* land,
> Taught my benighted soul to understand
> That there's a God, that there's a *Saviour* too:
> Once I redemption neither sought nor knew.
> Some view our sable race with scornful eye,
> "Their colour is a diabolic die."
> Remember, *Christians, Negroes*, black as *Cain*,
> May be refin'd, and join th' angelic train.
> (*Poems* 7)

Using biblical typology and the traditionally antagonistic black and white color imagery to symbolize societal assumptions about race and election, Wheatley constructs several contrasting configurations, including: 1) "my benighted soul" as a state of the persona's spiritual condition, versus "Their colour is a diabolic die," which alludes to the skin color of the slave; 2) "God" as an impersonal designation of deity, a nomenclature for the unseen world that would be familiar to any religious heathen, versus "*Saviour*," the intimate and personal title through which the "born again" Christian refers to Christ as the only sovereign God and the One who has rescued the speaker from a situation of great peril; 3) "redemption" into the privileged class of the elect, versus the preordained state of a non-elect "pagan"; 4) white "Christians," versus Black and enslaved "Negroes"; and 5) "black as *Cain*," indicating the ultimate and egregious sin for which whites claimed the slaves must suffer, versus the (white) "angelic train," symbolizing the purity that evangelicals assumed for themselves both in time and in eternity.

As in her letter to Arbour, when the poet writes "benighted soul" she is referring to her spiritual innocence before salvation and conversion. She further points out in this poem that white Christians regard black skin as an indication of an inherent relationship with Satan, hence a "diabolic die," regardless of the African's renewed spirituality. This thesis creates a vortex from which Wheatley positions tensions of ambiguity between the multiple opposites listed above. In several other poems, Wheatley discusses the soul, as opposed to the skin, as the repository of sin. When, in "An Address to the Deist," she chastens the students at Cambridge for their lack of faith, she chides, ". . . must an Ethiopian be employed for you?"—i.e., Must a person of darker skin have to tell you of your sins? Although some scholars have been quick to blame Wheatley for rejecting her native Africa with such phrases as "my Pagan land," she neither denies her African blood nor agrees with contemporary views of the predetermined inferiority of her race.[9] Instead she moves her images of the darkness and the "diabolic die" from dark skin (or a literary expression of psychological depression) to a heightened and totally spiritual and evangelical world view whereby anyone who has not heard and received the gospel (i.e., "in whose heart the divine light of revelation" is obscured) is in darkness.

Wheatley's affirmation "that there's a God, that there's a *Saviour* too" is not simply empty repetition to create rhyme. Colonists who believed that they were chosen before birth as God's elite in racial, religious and societal standing did not approach Christianity in the desperate or penitent state of persons needing help or seeking deliverance from oppression, exterior forces against which the victims' were powerless. To the Calvinists, the Being objectified in Christian affection was simply, on a subliminal level, "a God," One who had chosen them to rule and whom they served often through fear and loyalty, rather than because of personal affection. However, to those believers who were rejected, labeled as non-elect by the society—as were all Africans, slaves and otherwise indentured persons—He was not just "a God" but "a *Saviour*." The poet's constituency, avid Bible readers, knew that the term *Saviour* was used in the Old Testament in conjunction with God's deliverance of Israel from slavery in Egypt. Various dictionaries and commentaries on the eighteenth-century usage of the word *Saviour* define it as "a deliverer, preserver, who saves from danger or destruction, and brings into a state of prosperity and happiness."[10] Colonial Christians would encounter the term often in a discussion of Israel's slavery in Egypt: "They forgat God their saviour, which had done great things in Egypt" (Ps. 106:21); "And it shall be for a sign and for a witness unto the Lord of hosts in the land of Egypt: for they shall cry unto the Lord because of the oppressors, and he shall send them a saviour, and a great one, and he shall deliver them" (Isa.

19:20). In a text reprinted and read in the colonies throughout the eighteenth century, William Burkitt, a seventeenth-century Anglican theologian, spoke of Christ as "that Saviour, not a particular Saviour to the Jews only, but an universal Saviour, whose *salvation is to the ends of the earth*" (1: 266). As a Black woman and a community pariah (i.e., still enslaved despite her popularity), Wheatley expected the Saviour's power to be just as applicable to the African in America as to the Jew in Egypt.

A deific title of even more social and biblical significance than "Saviour" was "Redeemer." The terms "redeem," "redemptioneer," and "redeemer" were quite familiar in eighteenth-century America as they applied to the system of temporary indentured servitude for European servants. While a few lower-class British and European servants were kidnapped for the Atlantic passage, most willingly sold themselves to a ship captain or to a specific colonist in order to pay the travel expenses. If not part of the original transaction, a new "purchaser" entered the financial arrangement between the worker and the ship captain when the boat landed. The settled colonist would pay the travel bill and indenture the servant. When the worker had fulfilled the work agreement, or even when someone else purchased his freedom, then the servant was said to have been "redeemed."[11] (This option was not available to most Africans. They were considered to be slaves for life with no hope of emancipation or redemption.) As long as the European servant was indentured, he was called a "redemptioneer."

The redemption concept and its terminology originated in the Old Testament book of Leviticus. If a Hebrew had to sell himself into bondage to pay off his debts, a member of his family was obligated to "redeem" him:

> If thy brother be waxen poor, and hath sold away some of his possession, and if any of his kin come to redeem it, then shall he redeem that which his brother sold. And if the man have none to redeem it, and himself be able to redeem it. . . . And if a sojourner or a stranger wax rich by thee, and thy brother that dwelleth by him wax poor, and sell himself unto the stranger or sojourner by thee, or to the stock of the stranger's family: After that he is sold he may be redeemed again; one of his brethren may redeem him. . . . And if there remain but few years unto the year of jubilee, then he shall count with him, and according unto his years shall he give him again the price of his redemption. (Lev. 25:25–26, 47–48, 52)[12]

Again, as with "Saviour," when "redemption" is used in the Old Testament it is usually in connection with Israel's exodus from slavery in Egypt. Venture

Smith, an ex-slave and one of Wheatley's contemporaries, managed to discuss his extraordinary self-redemption in writing. When he wrote his narrative in 1798 at the age of sixty-nine, Venture constantly used the language of redemption to relate the purchase of his own freedom and that of his wife and children:

> As Miner [one of his owners in Stonington, Connecticut] did not appear to redeem me I went, and called at my old master Stanton's first to see my wife, who was then owned by him. . . . I never had an opportunity of redeeming myself whilst I was owned by Miner. . . . By cultivating this land with the greatest diligence and economy, at times when my master did not require my labor, in two years I laid up ten pounds. This my friend tendered my master for myself. . . . Being encouraged by the success which I met in redeeming myself, I again solicited my master for a further chance of completing it. . . . This left only thirteen pounds eighteen shillings to make up the full sum for my redemption. . . . I had already redeemed from slavery myself, my wife and three children, besides three negro men. (551–55)

Clearly, when Wheatley writes, "Once I redemption neither sought nor knew," some of her immediate readers would have understood that she was not only speaking of religious salvation but implying redemption from slavery as well.

In the phrase "black as *Cain*," Wheatley again subverts prevailing racial attitudes. Any reference to Cain, Adam's eldest son, would evoke complex religious and literary associations for Wheatley's readers. The biblical story of Cain was an appropriate narrative through which to confront national thinking on color and race. To ostracize Cain's descendants forever, God had marked them with a stain presumably reinforced eight generations later when Ham's children were cursed with perpetual servitude (Gen. 4:9–15 and 9:18–27). The Cain and Ham myths were curiously misapplied in Western culture to explain racial differences. New World Christians connected Cain's mark with black skin and Ham's curse with eternal servitude for Ham and his offspring; white Westerners believed that the offspring were Africans.[13] Again Wheatley's phraseology "black as *Cain*" had multiple applications: first to Cain's sin because he murdered his brother and second to those whites who assumed that Blacks were Cain's descendants. If, in the opinion of whites, Cain's act was the most heinous sin and if black skin was the inherited demarcation of that sin, Wheatley—although the poem does not say that she agrees with the hypothesis, hence the qualification "even"—insists that

Christ's sacrifice was the sufficient atonement for Cain's sin. If white colonists wished to deny her claim, they would be likewise denying the efficacious power of the Blood of Christ, which was at that time a foundational tenet of Christian belief.

Wheatley's wisdom in choosing Cain as the central archetype in slave philology, rather than Ham, can be seen in the various connective allusions between Adam's son and the American slave: 1) the Cain symbol established the slave as a primal member of the human race instead of a quasi-animal, as some thinkers of the time posited; 2) Cain's suffering was irrevocably tied to guilt over an "elected" righteous brother (an analogy to the tension between "chosen" Whites and rejected Blacks); 3) his relationship to the earth was cursed: he could work the land but would not profit from the fruits of his labor (no different from the unrequited labor of the American slave); 4) his relationship to nature made him the prototype of the nonspiritual man: fleshly and lustful (characteristics which whites applied to the slaves); 5) there was a visible mark placed upon Cain to expose his guilt and curse to the world (whites claimed black skin accomplished the same stigma); 6) Cain's curse, his mark, his enmity with the land rendered him a vagabond and a fugitive (just like the homeless and alienated African-American); 7) yet God promised Cain mercy and protection, thus establishing a dualistic relationship that was no different from the negative deterministic gospel of servitude as expiated payment for possible receipt of God's love and mercy, which was the alternative gospel so often preached to eighteenth-century slaves. Detoxifying both an ancient biblical curse and a pervasive theory of race that was employed in support of the slave system, Wheatley insisted that the Cross of Jesus Christ could make even a "black Cain" a fit citizen for heaven *and* earth.

Paramount among these factors is the poet's inclusion of Africans as full-fledged members of the human family, a privilege denied them by John Augustine Smith, Edward Long, and other thinkers of that era, who viewed them as beasts rather than as humans. Once the slave was seen as human, any discussion of inherited or innate sin could be dealt with on the basis of Christ's atonement, but displacement from the human race precluded Christian equality in both temporal and eternal spheres. Further connotations of extreme wickedness were correlated with these theories of animality. Although Jefferson published his attempts to define Africans' characteristics and personality in 1787 and Long issued his even more damaging discussion in 1788, the interpretations of African identity which they codified had always been undercurrents in eighteenth-century colonial thought (Jordan, *Negro Versus Equality* 15–23, 28–32, 41–43). Long's *History of Jamaica* articulates a pervasive attitude:

> They are represented by all authors as the vilest of the human kind, to which they have little more pretension of resemblance than what arises from their exterior form. . . . When we reflect on the nature of these men, and their dissimilarity to the rest of mankind, must we not conclude, that they are a different species of the same *genus*? Of other animals, it is well known, there are many kinds, each kind having its proper species subordinate thereto. . . . (2: 353, 356)

To countermand such thinking, Wheatley argued that even those labeled the animalist sons of Cain could be refined through salvation in Christ. If slaves were animalistic because they descended from Cain, then Adam, Cain's father, was animalistic, and advocates of slavery who claimed that whites were sons of Adam through Seth (Adam's third son) must be animalistic, too. Conversely, if whites were both human and godlike with many divine qualities remaining after the Fall—this is a particular tenet of Wesleyan-Arminianism, which had captured center stage in the Great Awakening by the time Wheatley was grown—Blacks such as Cain and Adam's descendants would possess the same traits.[14] In another poem, "Phillis's Reply to the Answer in our last by the Gentleman in the Navy," one can see that she was aware of the conjecture that Africa was the seat of Eden:

> And pleasing Gambia on my soul returns,
> With native grace in spring's luxuriant reign,
> Smiles the gay mead, and Eden blooms again. (86)

This geographical reference further correlates Black people with the dawn of mankind, as does Wheatley's repeated use of the term *Ethiopian*.

By insisting on refinement for her race, Wheatley attacked another negative conception of blackness. Her reference to "their diabolic die" mirrors folkloric tradition rooted in the New England witchcraft trials: that black-skinned persons were the direst offspring or re-embodiment of Satan. Several defendants and witnesses testifying at these trials claimed to have met with Satan and described him as a Black man. Cotton Mather in *Memorable Providences* reported that a "possessed" woman, Mary Short, saw the devil as this sort of spectral figure:

> There exhibited himself unto her a Divel having the Figure of A Short and a Black Man; and it was remarkable that altho' shee had no sort of Acquaintance with Histories of what has happened elsewhere, to make any Impressions upon her Imagination, yett

> the Divel that visited her was just of the same Stature, Feature, and complexion with what the Histories of the Witchcrafts beyond-sea ascribe unto him; he was a wretch no taller than an ordinary Walking-Staff; hee was not of a Negro, but of a Tawney, or an Indian colour; hee wore an high crowned Hat, with strait Hair; and had one Cloven-Foot. (261)

Another trial judge, John Hale, said that one defendant, William Barker, confessed to "giving the Devil advantage over me appearing to me like a Black." Hale said that "this he [Barker] had before explained to be like a Black man" (419, 420).[15] Taylor, tracing this superstition from medieval England to eighteenth-century Connecticut, says that whole communities were afraid because "the Devil starteth himself up in the pulpit, like a meikle black man. . ." (5). Eichhorn, studying historical interpretations of spiritual phenomena, collapses speculation about Cain, Satan, animalism and blackness into a theory on the procreative process called "superfecundation," whereby Eve was said to have produced two ova and then received sperm from both Adam and Satan; Adam's son's Seth and Abel were "sons of light" and Satan's son Cain was a "son of darkness" (24–29).

Although enamoured with neoclassical ideals of Americanism (she was the first to refer to the nation as "Columbia"), Wheatley never calls herself or her fellow slaves "Americans."[16] Instead she used the racial and biblical term *Ethiopian*, indicating not only that Blacks were separate racially but also that they still did not have a nation that they could claim as their own. Other eighteenth-century spokesmen also took this position, as have major Black American leaders in the nineteenth and twentieth centuries.[17] In a newly discovered poem, "America," Wheatley lauds the nation but maintains her African ethnicity:

> New England first a wilderness was found
> Till for a continent 'twas destin'd round
> From feild to feild the savage monsters run
> E'r yet Brittania had her work begun
> Thy Power, O Liberty, makes strong the weak
> And (wond'rous instinct) Ethiopians speak. . . . (Kuncio 293)

This strategy of identifying herself and her personae as "Ethiopian" allowed Wheatley to mask her protest, for how could a Christian society object to such a noble biblical identity? Conversely she calls white slaveholders the "Egyptians" (as in her letter to Samson Occom discussed below), identifying them with those who had oppressed the Jews.

Through juxtaposition of these ancient concepts on the origin of race, Wheatley clearly implies that because Americans were ignoring Africa's superior status in biblical interpretations of "chosen" nations, the slaves—denied knowledge of their inclusion in God's promises—were held in a psychological bondage even more demeaning than their physical enslavement. But if, on biblical grounds, she could prove their lineage to be superior to that of Europeans, then both slave and slaveholder would be forced to consider the biblical ramifications of American slavery. The term *Ethiopian* might compel eighteenth-century Christians to consider that they had enslaved the heirs of biblical patriarchs: descendants of Moses and his Ethiopian wife (Num. 12:1); of King Solomon and the Queen of Sheba—Sheba is an Old Testament term for Ethiopia, 1 Kings 10:1–13 (2 Chron. 9:1–12); of Ebed-Melech, the Ethiopian who rescued the prophet Jeremiah (Jer. 38 and 39); or of the Ethiopian eunuch whose conversion comprises a chapter in Acts and who, as the first Gentile convert, took the gospel to Africa long before it was taken to Europe (Acts 8: 26–39).

Eighteenth-century evangelical churchmen read the Bible every day and memorized as much of it as possible. Ullendorff lists some twenty-one scriptural references that Wheatley's readers would have read in daily devotionals, discovered in group or family Bible study, or heard in Sunday sermons. The piety and royalty of the Ethiopians is particularly noted in most of these instances. Ullendorff explains that the reference in Psalms 68:31 to "Ethiopia stretching out her hands to God"—a verse which Wheatley repeats in one of her letters—became "a symbol of the country's [Ethiopia's] passionate adherence to the orthodox faith" (5–8).

In several other poems, Wheatley uses the Christian historicity vested in the term *Ethiopian* to convince white Americans of their need to repent. In the last stanza of "To the University of Cambridge, in New-England," she writes:

> Let sin, that baneful evil to the soul,
> By you be shunn'd, nor once remit your guard;
> Suppress the deadly serpent in its egg.
> Ye blooming plants of human race devine,
> An Ethiop tells you 'tis your greatest foe. . . . (*Poems* 6)

Here she deploys her biblical references to the Ethiopian to counter the eighteenth-century colonists' arguments that Blacks were soulless animals. In this work it is whites who are akin to the Edenic animal and its master, Satan. In addition, *Ethiopian* gave Wheatley's contemporary African-American readers a sense of ethnicity related to Israel and antiquity that Europeans could not have.

Wheatley also uses biblical allusion to indict her white enslavers in "An Address to the Deist." She contrasts the position of white nonbelievers—whom she depicts as Satan's children, doomed to Hell unless they repent—with her own status as a Black Christian who is among the elect:

> Must Ethiopians be employ'd for you?
> Much I rejoice if any good I do.
> I ask O unbeliever, Satan's child
> Hath not thy Saviour been too much revil'd . . . ?
> (*Black Beginnings* 79–80)

Indeed, in her poetic eulogy to General David Wooster, she boldly castigates Christian patriots who oppress her people:

> But how presumptuous shall we hope to find
> Divine acceptance with the Almighty mind
> While yet o deed ungenerous they disgrace
> And hold in bondage Afric: blameless race
> Let virtue reign and then accord our prayers
> Be victory ours and generous freedom theirs[18]

The most caustic example of just how ironically bitter Wheatley could be about slavery is her letter to the famed American Indian preacher, Samson Occom, with whom she shared camaraderie because of his embitterment against some evangelicals for perceived racial discrimination and financial neglect. In this correspondence, written after she was free, she responds:

> Rev'd and honor'd Sir, I have this Day received your obliging kind Epistle, and am greatly satisfied with your Reasons respecting the Negroes, and think highly reasonable what you offer in Vindication of their natural Rights: Those that invade them cannot be insensible that the divine Light is chasing away the thick Darkness which broods over the Land of Africa; and the Chaos which has reign'd so long. . . . Otherwise, perhaps, the Israelites had been less solicitous for their Freedom from Egyptian Slavery; . . . . [I]n every human Breast, God has implanted a Principle, which we call Love of Freedom; it is impatient of Oppression, and pants for Deliverence; and by the Leave of our modern Egyptians I will assert that the same Principle lives in us. (Bruns 306–08)

Wheatley asserts that Blacks have as much right to seek God for freedom from slavery as had the Old Testament Israelites whom eighteenth-century Christians held in such esteem.[19] Moreover, she emphasizes the irony of eighteenth-century patriots who pray for freedom while oppressing Africans.[20] The letter also shows her constant tendency to think and write in those biblical metaphors most applicable to American slavery.

On one occasion Wheatley's use of scriptural idiom is even more ingenious and complex than her control of "blackness," "Cain," and "Ethiopia." In 1771, she sent a letter and a poem to the Earl of Dartmouth, who had recently been appointed Secretary of State for the Colonies and President of the Board of Trade and Foreign Plantations. The letter itself appears to be innocent: Wheatley commends his success and closes with hopes that "the united blessings of Heaven & Earth may attend you here and the endless Felicity of the invisible State in the presence of the divine Benefactor may be your portion hereafter. . ." (*Poems* 111). However, in light of the poem and of its biblical meaning, the gravity of this statement becomes clear. She is subtly but insistently warning Dartmouth of the eternal judgment that awaits him if he does not use his influence to intercede for the slaves.

In the last eight lines of the accompanying poem, entitled "To the Right Honourable William, Earl of Dartmouth, His Majesty's Principal Secretary of State for North-America, etc." Wheatley achieves full ironic resonance through biblical allusion:

> May heav'nly grace the sacred sanction give
> To all thy works, and thou for ever live
> Not only on the wings of fleeting *Fame*,
> Though praise immortal crowns the patriot's name,
> But to conduct to heav'ns refulgent fane,
> May fiery coursers sweep th' ethereal plain,
> And bear thee upwards to that blest abode,
> Where, like the prophet, thou shalt find thy God.

She reminds Dartmouth that, in contrast to brief earthly fame, he should seek "sacred sanctions" for his political actions. Earlier in the poem she mentioned New England's hope that Dartmouth would end English tyranny over the colonies. She also expresses the African slaves' hope that the Earl would end the colonists' tyranny over them:

> Such, such my case. And can I then but pray
> Others may never feel tyrannic sway?

For favours past, great Sir, our thanks are due,
And thee we ask thy favours to renew,
Since in thy pow'r, as in thy will before,
To sooth the griefs, which thou did'st once deplore.

She writes of herself as one who "young in life, by seeming cruel fate / Was snatch'd from Afric's fancy'd happy seat." There are perhaps no more moving lines in the entire Wheatley canon than:

What pangs excruciating must molest,
What sorrows labour in my parent's breast?
Steel'd was that soul and by no misery mov'd
That from a father seiz'd his babe belov'd. (*Poems* 34, 35)

With this deeply emotional appeal, she prepares Dartmouth for her final challenge: to stand up against the wickedness of the slavery system, just as the Prophet Elijah stood against the wickedness of Jezebel's prophets in Old Testament times. The phrases "to conduct to heav'ns refulgent fane," "fiery coursers sweep th' ethereal plain," and "bear thee upwards to that blest abode, / Where, *like the prophet*" (emphasis added) refer to Elijah's ascension in a fiery chariot after he had slain eight hundred and fifty prophets of Baal by calling down fire from heaven and had turned the whole nation of Israel back to the worship of Jehovah. Elijah had confronted not only the religious system but the political system as well. The false prophets had subverted the nation at the invitation of the apostate King Ahab and his Canaanite wife, Jezebel. Wheatley reminds Dartmouth that God was Elijah's strength who rewarded the prophet with eternal honor far more splendid than that any earthly king could bestow. Elisha, Elijah's successor, said that the leader of the fiery procession that came from heaven to receive Elijah was none other than God himself (I Kings 7: 18–19). Wheatley suggests that Dartmouth can have a similar triumphal entrance to heaven if he confronts the political and religious forces supporting slavery. No stronger challenge could have been given by an enslaved Christian poet to a national leader of a Christian people. Dartmouth had considerable influence in the colonies that he could have used as a contributing force to abolish slavery. Wheatley was demanding that he follow the example set in what he confessed was his highest moral authority—the Bible. She was further admonishing Dartmouth, along with other proponents of the slave system, that temporal arrangements were "fleeting" and that God's eternal judgment would avenge the slave.[21]

Wheatley's effectiveness as an eighteenth-century poet and as a writer in the Black American protest tradition has been largely misunderstood. She was more than just an occasional poet who employed neoclassical images and phraseology to flatter her patrons. Having garnered some of her fame from such works, she used her talents and her success to wage a subtle war against slavery. Her methodology included biblical language and allusions that were much more comprehensible to readers in the eighteenth-century revivalist era than to those in this more secular age. She believed that citizens in her biblically knowledgeable society would recognize the scriptural allusions and symbols she used so well, that they would realize the implications of such references and turn from the practice of slavery. Recent scholarship shows that Phillis Wheatley wrote perhaps one hundred and forty-five poems (most of which would have been published if the "encouragers" she solicited had come forth to support the second volume, but much of this artistic heritage is now lost), and that she continued a proliferation of national and international correspondence with political and religious leaders, of which some two dozen notes and letters are extant (Robinson, *Essays* 10).

Wheatley's contemporary reception was phenomenal. As an example of superior African intellect—with talents that were exploited by Enlightenment intellectuals for "scientific" commentary, by evangelical Christians to promote a Christian witness among Blacks, and by others in the budding abolitionist movement to prove that Blacks were not merely dumb semi-animals—she was perhaps recognized even more in England and Europe than in America. In the past ten years Wheatley scholars have uncovered poems, letters, and more facts about her life and her association with eighteenth-century abolitionists, and they have charted her notable use of classicism.[22]

Some of these findings have proven Wheatley's disdain for the institution of slavery and her use of art to undermine its practice. The time has come for scholars to recognize the consummate art with which Phillis Wheatley solved two problems: how to write poetry and prose in protest of slavery while being a slave, and how to find an authentic language that could offer consolation to fellow slaves while prodding the consciences of their enslavers. Before the end of this century the full aesthetic, political, and religious implications of Wheatley's art and even more salient facts about her life and works will surely be known and celebrated by all who study the eighteenth century and by all who revere her as an important poet in the American canon.

Notes

1. For an excellent discussion of this authentication process, see Stepto.
2. Slaveholders feared the effects of the Bible in the hands of literate slaves just as much as they dreaded the potential volatility of abolitionist tracts and blank travel passes. For more discussion of Blacks' interpretation of the scriptures, their preaching, and slave owners' hesitancy to keep literate slaves, see Genovese 161–184, 561–66; Blassingame 59–76, 523–56.
3. Examples of such hymns having double meanings include "Go Down, Moses," "Steal Away," "Swing Low, Sweet Chariot," "O Canaan," and "Cheer the Weary Traveller." Discussion of these songs as subtle forms of protest can be found in Thurman.
4. Poole's *Annotations Upon the Holy Bible*, a standard eighteenth-century reference work in two volumes, indicates that the light and dark imagery was translated into spiritual realities. This transmutation is particularly evident in Poole's commentary upon a line from Eph. 5:8 ("For ye were sometimes darkness, but now are ye light in the Lord: walk as children of light. . . ."):

   > And because the night is the time of darkness, and the day of light, he therefore hereby describes the present state positively, "ye are all children of the light, and the children of the day," which is an Hebraisme: Ye are partakers of a Spiritual Light, and this light is not the darker Light of Nature, or the Light of Prophesy which the Jews had, compared to a Lamp, II Peter 1:19. but ye are children of the day, as the time of the Gospel is called day, Romans 13:12, II Corinthians 6:2. Negatively, Ye are not of the night, nor of darkness, your state is exceeding different from other Gentiles, and from what it once was, as the light is from the darkness, and day from night, not as if there was no ignorance remaining in them, for the best men see but through a glass darkly, I Corinthians 13:12. But the Apostle compares them with their former estate when they were Gentiles, and with Jews, under the Law, and with respect to their state in Christ, they were not Children of the night, or as to their state of the night, but "children of the Light, and the Day."

5. For additional reading on the implications of the colors white and black for eighteenth-century slaves and slaveholders see two of Jordan's works: *White Over Black*, particularly 216–59, and *The White Man's Burden*, 3–15. Other helpful sources include Burr 285–86, 308–12, 391, 420; Heather; Kobrin; Taylor.

6. For example, Isa. 1:18 says "though your sins be as scarlet, they shall be as white as snow; though they be red like crimson, they shall be as wool." See also Baltazar 42–45, 169.
7. A good example is Cotton Mather's *Memorable Providences*. While he does not use the term *black* outright, nevertheless he clearly associates that color with the very roots of *evil* itself, Satan and his minions. In an exhortation condemning witchcraft, the minister warns:

> Go tell Mankind, that there are Devils and Witches; and that tho those night-birds least appear where the Day-Light of the Gospel comes, yet New Engl. has had Exemples of their Esistence and Operation; and that not only the Wigwams of Indians, where the pagan Powaws often raise their masters, in the shapes of Bears and Snakes and Fires, but the Houses of Christians, where our God has had His constant Worship, have undergone the Annoyance of Evil spirits. (Burr 99)

   Jonathan Edwards also correlates "black" with the satanic in his writings. In "The Future Punishment of the Wicked: Unavoidable and Intolerable" (1741) he warns the sinners of his congregation against "the blackness of darkness; this [Hell] is it. . . . this is to lose the soul: they that are the subjects of this are utterly lost" (8: 459–60). Similarly, Michael Wigglesworth's *Day of Doom* (1653) frightens its listeners with bleak descriptions of the blackness of hell. Wigglesworth describes the place as a crowded, miserable pit where "souls are now reserved in Iron Chains, / Under thick darkness to eternal pains" (81).
8. Similarly, in her "Letter to the Rev. Mr. Samuel Hopkins of New Port, Rhode Island, May 6, 1775," Wheatley was cautious to use light and dark imagery in a way that suggested the soul's search for goodness rather than evil in the epidermis. In imploring Hopkins to garner aid for a fellow African who wanted to do Christian missionary work, Wheatley wrote of her hope that God would turn "the African 'from darkness to light' (Robinson, *Black American Beginnings* 67, 92).
9. One such scholar who castigates the poet for displaying an insensitive stance towards her native land is Dathorne.
10. *Concise Dictionary of the Holy Bible* 417. Another contemporary text, *Dictionary of the Holy Bible*, explains "Saviour" to mean an all-inclusive Deliverer, a Protector from any evil, whether trouble created by the Devil and his followers on the spiritual plane or the worries and catastrophes that shadow mortals on earth (513–14).
11. For more on the indentured system in the colonies and "redemption" as its legal terminology, see Herrick 1–26, McKee 89–113, and Smith 3–86.

12. Other examples of biblical uses of the term in the Old Testament in its connotation of "buying back" kinsmen: "What day thou buyest the field of the hand of Naomi, thou must buy it also of Ruth the Moabitess, the wife of the dead, to raise up the name of the dead upon his inheritance. And the kinsman said, I cannot redeem it for myself, lest I mar mine own inheritance: redeem thou my right to myself. . ." (Ruth 4:5–6); ". . .and, lo, we bring into bondage our sons and our daughters to be servants, and some of our daughters are brought unto bondage already: neither is it in our power to redeem them . . ." (Neh. 5:5); "They that trust in their wealth, and boast themselves in the multitude of their riches; none of them can by any means redeem his brother, nor give to God a ransom for him. . ." (Ps. 49:6–7).
13. For example, John Woolman writes of a conversation with a Quaker Friend who vehemently defended slavery:

 > . . . a Friend in company began to talk in support of the slave trade, and said the Negroes were understood to be the offspring of Cain, their blackness being the mark God set upon him after he murdered Abel his brother, that it was the design of providence they should be slaves, as a condition proper to the race of so wicked a man as Cain was.

 Similarly, Woolman's colleague linked the Ham incident to the Black race as justification for enslavement:

 > . . . after the flood Ham went to the land of Nod and took a wife, that Nod was a land far distant, inhabited by Cain's race, and that the flood did not reach it, and as Ham was sentenced to be a servant of servants to his brethren, these two families being thus joined were undoubtedly fit only for slaves. (62–63)

 For more on theologians who, like Woolman's colleague here, supported the view of Blacks as inheritors of the maledictions of Cain and Ham, see Hopkins 153–59 and 175–87. On the other hand, earlier in "A Testimony Against the Antichristian Practice of Making Slaves of Men" (1733), Elihu Coleman questions the use of the Cain–Ham arguments to label Blacks as cursed and to justify slavery. For another offensive against this proslavery tactic, this made by a former slave, see Cugoano 32–36.
14. For more on the roots of Wesleyan-Arminianism, the debates that this religious sentiment stirred, and its influence during the Great Awakening, consult Goodwin.
15. Other studies of the witchcraft trials that mention testimony of the devil and his witches to be black mortals or preternatural creatures include Levin 169, MacFarlane 83, Remi 17 and 40–43, and Spalding 51–52.

16. Moore has noted that Wheatley probably first used this word in reference to America in her poem addressed to General George Washington. Applauding her nation's fight for liberty, she writes:

> One century scarce perform'd its destined round,
> When Gallic powers Columbia's fury found;
> And so may you, whoever dares disgrace
> The land of freedom's heaven-defended race!
> Fix'd are the eyes of nations on the scales,
> For in their hopes Columbia's arm prevails.
> Anon Britannia droops the pensive head,
> While round increase the rising hills of dead.
> Ah! cruet blindness to Columbia's state!
> Lament thy thirst of boundless power too late.
> (*Poems* 90)

17. DuBois describes Blacks' feelings of alienation in what they must of necessity claim to be their new homeland:

> After the Egyptian and Indian, the Greek and Roman, the Teuton and Mongolian, the Negro is a sort of seventh son, born with a veil, and gifted with second-sight in this American world,—a world which yields him no true self-consciousness, but only lets him see himself through the revelation of the other world. It is a peculiar sensation, this double-consciousness, this sense of always looking at one's self through the eyes of others, of measuring one's soul by the tape of a world that looks on in amused contempt and pity. One ever feels his twoness,—an American, a Negro; two souls, two thoughts, two unreconciled strivings; two warring ideals in one dark body, whose dogged strength alone keeps it from being torn asunder. (16–17)

Similarly, in his "Evening's Improvement" Jupiter Hammon, the first published Black poet and essayist, in recognition of the outcast status of his people among the inhabitants of America, identifies the Black slaves as "Africans" or "Ethiopians" (*Works* 91–94). See also Crummell on the Black race's assimilation and acceptance into this country's mainstream as compared to that of European groups.

18. Bruns quotes this portion of a 1788 poem of Wheatley's which is not printed in any other modern collection (306).
19. See Hammon's mention of the Israelites in his "Winter Piece" (73). In his discussion of the Israelites' deliverance from Egypt, Hammon, the first Black Christian of his nation to do so, compares their enslavement to the servitude of his own people. That Blacks paralleled their bondage

to the oppression of the Israelites in Egypt is apparent in the works of many eighteenth-century Black writers. In his autobiography, for example, Olaudah Equiano tells of a fellow slave who complains how, after snatching a few hours for fishing, he would return home only to have his master confiscate his catch:

> 'I can't go to anybody to be righted; 'then' said the poor man, looking up above 'I must look up to God Mighty' in the top for right.' This artless tale moved Me Much, and I could not help feeling the just cause Moses had in redressing his brother against the Egyptian. (1: 222)

See also the former slave Ottobah Cugoano's discussion of the deliverance of Israel from Egypt as a rescue from sin, in his abolitionist treatise (49).

20. See Davis (773–84) for more of the verbal and ideological juggling that many eighteenth-century colonists performed in their desire to be free from Britain's rule yet maintain a chattel race system. See also Bruns, particularly the letter of Roger Pleasants to George Washington (508–09) and records from the Constitutional Convention of 1787 (522–26), and Hopkins.
21. History seems to indicate that Wheatley's admonitions were fruitless. During his tenure Dartmouth did nothing to end slavery nor to ameliorate the conditions of Africans by law, edict or example.
22. See Bridenbaugh, Isam, Jackson, Shields, Silverman, Sistrunk.

Works Cited

Baltazar, Eulalio R. *The Dark Center: A Process Theology of Blackness*. New York: Paulist Press, 1973.

Bastide, Roger. "Color, Racism and Christianity." *Color and Race*. Ed. John Hope Franklin. Boston: Houghton Mifflin, 1968.

Blassingame, John W. *The Slave Community: Plantation Life in the Antebellum South*. New York: Oxford Univ. Press, 1971.

Brawley, Benjamin Griffith. *Early Negro American Writers*. New York: Dover Publications, 1970.

———. *The Negro in Literature and Art in the United States*. New York: Duffield & Company, 1930

Bridenbaugh, Carl. "The Earliest Published Poem of Phillis Wheatley." *New England Quarterly* 42 (1969): 583–84.

Brown, John. *A Dictionary of the Holy Bible*. Berwick, England, 178–.

Bruns, Roger, ed. *Am I Not a Man and a Brother: The Antislavery Crusade of Revolutionary America, 1688–1788*. New York: Chelsea House, 1977.

Burkitt, William. *Expository Notes, with Practical Observations, on the New Testament of Our Lord and Saviour Jesus Christ, Vol. 1*. Philadelphia: Sorin and Ball, 1844.

Burr, George Lincoln. *Narratives of the Witchcraft Cases: 1648–1706*. New York: Charles Scribner's Sons, 1914.

Coleman, Elihu. "A Testimony Against that Anti-Christian Practice of Making Slaves of Men." *Friends Review* 5 (Oct. 25, 1851): 84–85.

Covel, James J. *A Concise Dictionary of the Holy Bible*. New York: Lane and Scott, 1852.

Crummell, Alexander. *Africa and America: Addresses and Discourses*. 1891; rpt. Miami: Mnemosyne Publishing, Inc., 1969.

Cugoano, Ottobah. *Thoughts and Sentiments on the Evil of Slavery*. 1787; rpt. London: Dawsons of Pall Mall, 1969.

Dathorne, O. R. "Africa Their Africa." *Neo-African Literature and Culture*. Eds. Bernth Lindfors and Ulla Schild. Weisbanden: B. Heymann, 1976.

Davis, Arthur P. "Personal Elements in the Poetry of Phillis Wheatley." *Phylon* 113 (1953): 192.

Davis, David Brion. *The Problem of Slavery in the Age of Revolution, 1770–1823*. Ithaca: Cornell Univ. Press, 1975.

Douglass, Frederick. *Narrative of the Life of Frederick Douglass, An American Slave*. 1845; rpt. New York: Anchor Books, 1973.

DuBois, W. E. B. *The Souls of Black Folk; Essays and Sketches*. 1903; rpt. Greenwich, Conn.: Fawcett, 1961.

Edwards, Jonathan. *The Works of President Edwards*. Ed. Edward Williams and Edward Parsons. Vol. 7. London, 1817; rpt. New York: Burt Franklin, 1968.

Eichhorn, David Max. *Cain: Son of the Serpent: A Midrach of Homiletical Narration of the Fourth Chapter of the Book of Genesis*. New York: Whittier, 1975.

Equiano, Olaudah. *The Life of Olaudah Equiano: or, Gustavas Vassa the African. Written by Himself*. 1789; rpt. London: Dawsons of Pall Mall, 1969.

Fisher, Miles Mark. *Negro Slave Songs in the United States*. New York: Cornell Univ. Press for the American Historical Association, 1953.

Genovese, Eugene D. *Roll, Jordan, Roll: The World the Slaves Made*. New York: Pantheon Books, 1972.

Goodwin, Gerald J. "The Myth of 'Arminian-Calvinism' in Eighteenth-Century New England." *New England Quarterly* 41 (1968): 113–37.

Hammon, Jupiter. *America's First Negro Poet: The Complete Works of Jupiter Hammon of Long Island*. Ed. Stanley Austin Ransom. Port Washington, N.Y.: Kennikat Press, 1970.

Heather, P. J. "Colour Symbolism: Part I." *Folk-Lore: A Quarterly Review of Myth, Tradition, Institution, and Custom Being the Transactions of the Folk-Lore Society* 59 (1948): 1683–85.

Hopkins, John Henry. *A Scriptural, Ecclesiastical, and Historical View of Slavery, from the Days of the Patriarch Abraham to the Nineteenth Century*. 1864; rpt. New York: Negro Univ. Press, 1969.

Hopkins, Samuel. "A Dialogue Concerning the Slavery of the Africans." *The Anti-Slavery Crusade in America*. Eds. James M. McPherson and William Loren Katz. 1785; rpt. New York: Arno Press, 1968.

Horton, George Moses. *The Poetical Works of George M. Horton, the Colored Bard of North-Carolina, to Which is Prefixed the Life of the Author, Written by Himself*. Hillsborough, N.C.: D. Heartt, 1845.

Isani, Mukhtar Ali. "Early Versions of Some Works of Phillis Wheatley." *Early American Literature* 14 (1979): 119–35

Jackson, Sarah Dunlap. "Letters of Phillis and Susanna Wheatley." *Journal of Negro History* 57 (1972): 211–15.

Johnson, James Weldon, ed. *The Book of American Negro Poetry*. New York: Harcourt, Brace and Company, 1922.

Jordan, Winthrop D. *The Negro Versus Equality, 1782–1826*. Chicago: Rand McNally, 1969.

———. *The White Man's Burden: Historical Origins of Racism in the United States*. New York: Oxford Univ. Press, 1974.

———. *White Over Black: American Attitudes Toward the Negro: 1550–1812*. New York: Norton, 1968.

Katz, Bernard. *The Social Implications of Early Negro Music in the United States*. New York: Arno Press, 1969.

Kobrin, David. *The Black Minority in Early New York*. Albany: The State Univ. of New York Press, 1971.

Kuncio, Robert C. "Some Unpublished Poems of Phillis Wheatley." *New England Quarterly* 43 (1970): 293.

Levin, David. *What Happened in Salem*? New York: Harcourt, Brace and World, 1960.

Levine, Lawrence W. "Slave Songs and Slave Consciousness: An Exploration in Neglected Sources." *Anonymous Americans: Explorations in Nineteenth-Century Social History*. Ed. Tamara K. Haraven. Englewood Cliffs: Prentice Hall, 1971.

Loggins, Vernon. *The Negro Author: His Development in America to 1900*. Port Washington, N.Y.: Kennikat Press, 1964.

Long, Edward. *The History of Jamaica; or, General Survey of the Antient [sic] and Modern State of that Island, Vol. 11*. 1774; rpt. London: Frank Cass and Company, Ltd., 1970.

Macfarlane, Alan. *Witchcraft in Tudor and Stuart England: A Regional and Comparative Study*. New York: Harper & Row, 1970.

Mather, Cotton. *Memorable Providences, Relating to Witchcrafts and Possessions*. Boston, 1689.

———. *On Witchcraft, Being the Wonders of the invisible World*. 1692; rpt. Mount Vernon, N.Y.: Peter Pauper Press, 1950.

Matson, Lynn R. "Phillis Wheatley—Soul Sister?" *Phylon* 33 (1971): 222–30.

Mays, Benjamin. *The Negro's God, as Reflected in His Literature*. New York: Russell and Russell, 1968.

McKee, Samuel. *Labor in Colonial New York: 1664–1776*. New York: Columbia Univ. Press, 1935.

Moore, George H. "The Name 'Columbia.'" *Proceedings of the Massachusetts Historical Society*, 2nd Series, 1 (1855–1886): 1963.

Poole, Matthew. *Annotations Upon the Holy Bible*. 2 vols. London, 1685

Redding, J. Saunders. *To Make A Poet Black*. 1939; rpt. College Park, Md.: McGrath Publishing Co., 1968.

Remi, Nicolas. *Demonolatry*. London: John Rodker, 1930.

Richmond, M. A. *Bid the Vassal Soar: Interpretive Essays on the Life and Poetry of Phillis Wheatley and George Moses Horton*. Washington, D.C.: Howard Univ. Press, 1974.

Robinson, William H., ed. *Critical Essays on Phillis Wheatley*. Boston: G. K. Hall & Co., 1982.

———. *Phillis Wheatley in the Black American Beginnings*. Detroit: Broadside Press, 1975.

Shields, John C. "Phillis Wheatley and Mather Byles: A Study in Literary Relationships." *CLA Journal* 23 (1980): 377–89.

———. "Phillis Wheatley's Use of Classicism." *American Literature* 52 (1980): 97–111.

Silverman, Kenneth. "Four New Letters by Phillis Wheatley." *Early American Literature* 8 (1974): 157–71.

Sistrunk, Albertha. "The Influence of Alexander Pope on the Writing Style of Phillis Wheatley." *Critical Essays on Phillis Wheatley*. Boston: G. K. Hall & Co., 1982.

Smith, Abbot Emerson. *Colonists in Bondage: White Servitude and Convict Labor in America, 1607–1776*. Chapel Hill: Univ. of North Carolina Press, 1947.

Smith, Eleanor. "Phillis Wheatley: A Black Perspective." *The Journal of Negro Education* 43 (1974): 401–07.

Smith, Venture. *A Narrative of the Life and Adventures of Venture, A Native of Africa: But Resident Above Sixty Years in the United States of America. Early Negro Writing, 1760–1837*. Ed. Dorothy Porter. Boston: Beacon Press, 1971.

Spalding, Thomas Alfred. *Elizabethan Demonology*. London: Chatto and Windus, 1880.

Steele, David N., and Curtis C. Thomas, eds. *The Five Points of Calvinism: Defined, Defended, Documented*. Philadelphia: Presbyterian and Reformed Publishing Co., 1963.

Stepto, Robert E. *From Behind the Veil: A Study of Afro-American Narrative*. Urbana: Univ. of Illinois Press, 1979.

Taylor, John M. *The Witchcraft Delusion in Colonial Connecticut, 1647–1697*. New York: The Grafton Press, 1908.

Thurman, Howard. *Deep River*. 1945; rpt. Mount Vernon, N.Y.: Kennikat Press.

Turner, Darwin T., ed. *Black American Literature: Essays, Poetry, Fiction, Drama*. Columbus, O.: Merrill Publishing Co., 1970.

Ullendorff, Edward. *Ethiopia and the Bible*. London: Oxford Univ. Press, 1968.

Wheatley, Phillis. *Phillis Wheatley (Phillis Peters): Poems and Letters*. Ed. Charles Frederick Heartman. Miami: Mnemosyne Publishing, Inc., 1969.

———. *The Poems of Phillis Wheatley*. Ed. Julian D. Mason, Jr. Chapel Hill: Univ. of North Carolina Press, 1966.

Wigglesworth, Michael. *The Day of Doom; or, A Poetical Description of the Great and Last Judgment: With Other Poems*. 6th ed. 1715; rpt. New York: American News Co., 1867.

Woolman, John. *The Journal and Major Essays of John Woolman*. Ed. Phillips P. Moulton. New York: Oxford Univ. Press, 1971.

PATRICIA LIGGINS HILL

"Let Me Make the Songs for the People": A Study of Frances Watkins Harper's Poetry

I

Very little has been written about Frances Watkins Harper, the major black female literary figure and "the most popular nineteenth-century poet before Dunbar."[1] As a poet and a public lecturer for various social reform causes, the Abolitionist Movement, the Underground Railroad, the Women's Suffrage Movement, and the Women's Christian Temperance Union, Harper has been hailed as "the Bronze Muse"[2] of the ante-bellum period. She has been described by S. Elizabeth Frazier as "having attracted more attention by her poetic productions than any Negro woman since Phyllis Wheatley."[3]

Harper's popularity, unlike Phyllis Wheatley's however, is not based on conventional notions of poetic excellence. In her handling of poetic forms and her major subject matter—race (abolition in particular), religion, and women's rights—she is considered generally to be less a technician than either of her contemporary abolitionist poets, James Whitfield and George Moses Horton. According to Benjamin Brawley, Harper's earlier poems, especially *Poems on Miscellaneous Subjects* (1854) and *Poems* (1871), in which she relies primarily on the ballad stanza and rhymed tetrameter, reveal the heavy influences of Henry Wadsworth Longfellow, John Greenleaf Whittier, and Felicia Dorothea Hemans.[4] With the exception of *Moses: A Story of the*

From *Black American Literature Forum* 15, no. 2 (Summer 1981).

Nile (1869) and *Sketches of Southern Life* (1872), Harper's poetry varies little in form, language, and poetic technique.

Harper's fame as a poet, instead, rests on her excellent skills in oral poetry delivery. Her oratorical talents have been attested to by her contemporaries and modern critics alike. For instance, in the *Zion's Herald* (1870?), a Boston periodical which reviewed her delivery of *Moses*, she is praised for her "captivating eloquence that held her audience in rapt attention from the beginning to the close" (*TUR*, p. 811). Phebe A. Hansford speaks of her "clear, plaintive, melodious voice" and "the flow of her musical speech in her logical presentation of truth."[5] William Robinson makes clear that Harper read her poems with "her disarmingly dramatic voice and gestures and sighs and tears."[6] Such histrionics Harper used effectively to move large masses of people throughout the country towards her social/political sentiments. As Gloria Hull in "Black Women Poets from Wheatley to Walker" has astutely observed, Harper's

> popularity stemmed from the fact that she took her poetry to the people just as did the young black poets of the 1960's and 70's. As a widely traveling lecturer of the Anti-Slavery Society, who spoke to packed churches and meeting halls, giving dramatic readings of her abolitionist poems which were so effective that she sold over fifty thousand copies—an unheard figure—of her first two books.[7]

Indeed, there are similarities between Frances Harper's poetry and the verse of the new black poets—Imamu Baraka (LeRoi Jones), Madhubuti (Don L. Lee), Nikki Giovanni, Latia Mannan (Sonia Sanchez), and others. Just as these latter-day poets base their oral protest poetry primarily on direct imagery, simple diction, and the rhythmic language of the street to reach the masses of black people, Harper relies on vivid, striking imagery, simplistic language, and the musical quality and form of the ballad to appeal to large masses of people, black and white, for her social protest. Moreover, she, like the new black poets, embraces an "art for people's sake" aesthetic, rather than a Western Caucasian aesthetic assumption, "an art for art's sake" principle. In her "Songs for the People" which is her closest statement on aesthetics, Harper makes this point clear:

> Let me make the songs for the people,
>   Songs for the old and young;
> Songs to stir like a battle cry
>   Whenever they are sung.

Let me make the songs for the weary,
Amid life's fever and fret,
Till hearts shall relax their tension
And careworn brows forget.

I will sing for the poor and aged,
When shadows dim their sight,
Of the bright and restful mansions,
Where there shall be no right.

Our world, so worn and weary
Needs music, pure and strong
To hush the jangle and discords
Of sorrow, pain and wrong.[8]

Clearly, in this poem and in her other works, Harper assumes the stance of a poet-priestess whose "pure and strong" songs serve to uplift the oppressed in particular and humanity as a whole. The corpus of her poetry indicates that she, like the new black poets, however, is primarily concerned with uplifting the masses of black people. According to William Still the question as to how Harper could best serve her race lay at the very core of her literary and professional career (*TUR*, p. 786). She answers this question early in her career when she writes to Still in 1853 that she decided to devote her life to the liberation of her people. As she expresses to him, "It may be that God Himself has written upon both my heart and brain a commissary to use time, talent, and energy in the cause of freedom" (*TUR*, p. 803). This intrinsic concern for black liberation led her to envision herself as a race-builder, the black shepherd who will provide leadership for her flock of sheep (the black masses). In her February 1870 letter to Still, Harper states, "I am standing with my race on the threshhold of a new era . . . and yet today, with my limited and fragmented knowledge, I may help my race forward a little. Some of our people remind me of sheep without a shepherd" (*TUR*, p. 786).

Harper's poetry is essentially a product of this vision. In this regard, she focuses the majority of her poems on abolition and postwar appeals for freedmen's rights, suffrage, and racial equality. Even her major religious poetry such as *Moses: A Story of the Nile* reflects her concern for the liberation of blacks. Also, as a race-architect, Harper undertakes the black woman's cause and women's rights as a whole. As Larsen Scruggs points out, Harper reminds the Southern freedwomen who had been victims of physical abuse that "they had rights which all men should regard and that a free people could be a moral people only when the women were respected."[9] Thus, in several of her poems she champions the cause of women's rights and stresses the important roles that women must play in the black liberation struggle.

II

The major theme of Harper's abolitionist poems is the evils of slavery. Even though she was born free in Baltimore, Maryland, in 1825, and was educated in the North in Pennsylvania and Ohio, she identifies readily with the brutalities of the Southern slavery system. As Linda Riggins makes clear, because Harper herself was orphaned at the age of three and was in constant contact with slaves while working in the Underground Railroad, she "easily identifies with the emotional loss accompanying the break up of a family."[10] Consequently, most of her abolitionist verse deals with the tragic impact of the slavery system upon the black nuclear family.

In "The Slave Auction" from *Poems* (p. 55), for instance, Harper uses harsh, graphic imagery to bring attention to this tragic emotional loss. In this poem, she portrays the anguish of the slave mothers who are standing defenselessly watching their children sold away:

> And mothers stood with streaming eyes,
>   And saw their dearest children sold;
> Unheeded rose their bitter cries,
>   While tyrants bartered them for gold . . .

She concludes her poem by insisting that only those who are slaves themselves can fully understand the deep sense of loss:

> Ye who have laid your love to rest,
>   And wept above their lifeless clay,
> Know not the anguish of that breast,
>   Whose lov'd are rudely turned away.
> Ye may not know how desolate
>   Are bosoms rudely forced to part,
> And how dull and heavy weight
>   Will press the life-drops of the heart.

Again, using emotionally charged language and imagery, Harper depicts the break up of the black slave family in two other abolitionist poems, "The Slave Mother I" and "The Fugitive's Wife" from *Poems on Miscellaneous Subjects*. "The Slave Mother I" (p. 49), which is very similar to "The Slave

Auction," tells of a mother's parting from her son who is to be sold to a slave trader:

She is a mother, pale with fear,
  Her boy clings to her side,
And in her kirtle vainly tries
  His trembling form to hide.

He is not hers, for cruel hands
  May rudely tear apart
The only wreath of household love
  That binds her breaking heart.

In "The Fugitive's Wife" (p. 65), Harper varies her theme slightly. This poem depicts the agony of a slave woman whose husband is planning to escape. Even though she is suffering because he must leave her, she encourages him to escape to freedom:

"Bear not," I cried, "unto your grave,
  The yoke, you've borne from birth
No longer live a helpless slave
  The meanest thing on earth!"

Unlike "The Fugitive's Wife," the slave woman in Harper's "Eliza Harris" (p. 51) shares the fortune of not being totally separated from her family. In this poem, which Vernon Loggins postulates the ballad influence of both Longfellow and Whittier,[11] the poet tells of the experiences of Harriett Beecher Stowe's character Eliza who escapes to the North with bloodhounds at her heels:

But she's free!—yes, free from the land where the slave
From the band of oppression must rest in the grave;
Where bondage and torture, where scourges and chains
Have plac'd on our banner indelible stains.

However, Harper portrays in another poem, "Slave Mother II" (p. 76), the ill fate of a slave mother who attempts to escape with her children. In this ballad, the poet reflects a theme that was prevalent in the nineteenth-century slave narratives—that death is preferable to slavery. Realizing that she and her children will be caught in Ohio, she decides to kill them:

But Ohio had no sacred fane,
  To human rights so consecrated,
Where thou mayst shield thy hapless ones
  From their darkly gathering fate.

Then said the mournful mother,
  If Ohio cannot save,
I will do a deed for the freedom
  Shall find each child a grave.

Harper repeats the "death is preferable to slavery" theme in "The Tennessee Hero" (p. 70). As she relates in the introduction to the poem, this work tells of a black male slave who "heard his comrades plotting to obtain their liberty and, rather than betray them, he received 750 lashes and died." As the hero tells the slave beaters,

"I know the men who would be free;
  They are the heroes of your land;
But death and torture I defy,
  Ere I betray that band.

And what! oh! what is life to me,
  Beneath your base control?
Nay! do your worst—ye have no chains
  To bind my free-born soul!"

Indeed, to Harper, the worst evil that has befallen the black race is that of slavery. In one of her best abolitionist poems, "Bury Me in A Free Land" (p. 127), in which her own poetic voice is clearly heard, she expresses that the worst fate that she could suffer would be to be buried in a land of slaves:

Make me a grave where'ere you will
In a lowly plain, or lofty hill;
Make it among earth's humblest graves,
But not in a land where men are slaves.

I'd shutter and start if I heard the bay
Of bloodhounds seizing their human prey,
And I heard the captive plead in vain
As they bound afresh his galling chain.

Harper's abolitionist poems only marked the beginning of her struggle for black liberation. Her postwar appeals for freedmen's rights can be found in her many lectures, her novel *Iola Le Roy* (1892), and her several volumes of poems, *Moses: A Story of the Nile* (1869), *Poems* (1871), *Sketches of Southern Life* (1872), *The Martyr of Alabama and Other Poems* (1894), *The Sparrow's Fall and Other Poems* (n.d.), *Atlanta Offering Poems* (1895), *Poems* (1898), and *Light Beyond the Darkness* (n.d.). Her post–Civil War literature stems primarily from her extensive travels throughout the country. As Theodora Daniel points out, she toured and lectured in the South from 1867 to 1871 and visited every state except Texas and Arkansas (*TWD*, p. 20). According to the *Anti Slavery Standard*, Harper traveled throughout the South, speaking and reading her poems on plantations, in schools, churches, courthouses, and legislative halls where she witnessed firsthand that blacks had not been receiving just treatment under the law (*TWD*, p. 22). She observed the violations of voting privileges, the lack of education and educational facilities, and the physical abuse of black people (*TWD*, p. 21).

These concerns are reflected in her postwar poetry. For instance, in "Word for the Hour" (p. 136), she appeals to the "Men of the North" to help to uplift the Southern black in terms of education and voting rights:

'Tis yours to banish from the land
   Oppression's iron rule;
And oer the ruined auction-block
   Erect the common school.
To wipe from labor's branded brow
   The curse that shamed the land;
And teach the Freedmen how to wield
   The ballot in his hand.

In "An Appeal to the American People" (p. 116), Harper calls on white America to improve the conditions of the black soldiers who fought side by side with the white infantry during the Civil War:

With your soldiers side by side,
Helped we turn the battle's tide,
Till oer ocean stream and shore,
Waved the rebel flag no more
And above the rescued sod
Praises rose to freedom's God.

Harper appeals to their manhood and Christian ideals to see that justice is served to all American people:

To your manhood we appeal,
Lest the traitors iron heel
Grind and trample in the dust
All our new-born hope and trust
And the name of freedom be
Linked with bitter mockery.

The continued physical abuse of blacks also lies heavily on Harper's mind. In another poem, "The Martyr of Alabama" (p. 177), she protests the actual death of Tim Thompson, a black Alabama boy, who was killed because he refused to dance for some Southern white males (*TWD*, p. 176). The poet uses vivid, descriptive imagery to unfold this horrifying event:

Then recklessly a man arose
   And dealt a fearful blow.
He crushed the portals of that life,
   And laid the brave child low.

And trampled on his prostrate form
   As on a broken toy;
Then danced with careless, brutal feet,
   Upon the murdered boy.

Even though Harper realizes the wrongs and crimes committed by white Americans to blacks, she advocates interracial brotherhood, rather than black separatism as the solution to the black liberation problem. Her poem, "The Present Age" (p. 194), expresses her optimism for racial equality:

Say not the age is hard and cold—
   I think it brave and grand:
When men of diverse sects and creeds
   Are clasping hand in hand.

The age to brighten every path
   By sin and sorrow trod,
For loving hearts to usher in
   The commonwealth of God.

Much of Harper's optimism about the black liberation struggle stems from her strong religious beliefs in Christian brotherhood and social equality. In this respect, her major religious poems deal also with the black liberation cause. One such poem is *Moses* (pp. 80–88), a forty-page blank verse narrative on this religious leader's life and death, which Joan R. Sherman considers to be Harper's best poem and one of considerable power.[12] This work was obviously inspired by the Emancipation and the death of Abraham Lincoln. As Still has observed, Harper frequently praises Moses and compares black people to the Israelites in bondage (*TUR*, p. 796). In addition, in her April 19, 1869, correspondence to him, Harper compares Moses to Lincoln:

> Moses, the meekest man on earth, led the children of Israel over the Red Sea, but was not permitted to see them settled in Canaan. Mr. Lincoln had led us through another Red Sea to the table land of a triumphant victory, and God has seen fit to summon for the new era another man. It is ours then to bow to the Chastener and let our honored and loved Chieftain go.
> (*TUR*, p. 796–97)

Just as Harper believes that Lincoln has been summoned by God to free her people, she portrays Moses, in this moving poem, as the great Liberator of the Israelites. In Moses' dramatic dialogue to his mother, Egypt's princess, for example, he tells her that he has been commissioned by God to free his people:

> Let me tell them, gracious princess: 'tis no
> Sudden freak nor impulse wild that moves my mind
> I feel an earnest purpose binding all
> My soul into a strong resolve, which bid
> Me put aside all other ends and aims
> Until the hour shall come when God—the God
> Our fathers loved and worshipped—shall break our chains,
> And lead our willing feet to freedom. (p. 81)

Then, in the following lines in which Moses tells his mother of the Hebrew story passed down from generation to generation, Harper's optimism about the black liberation struggle is also heard:

> That God, the God our Fathers loved and worshipped
> would break our chains and bring to us a great
> Deliverance: that we should dwell in peace
> Beneath our vines and palms, our flocks and herds
> Increase and joyful children crowd our streets. (p. 85)

That God of the Israelites will free her people, Harper expresses also in her religious poem "Ethiopia" (p. 53):

> The tyrant's yoke from off her neck,
> His fetters from her soul,
> The mighty hand of God shall break,
> And spurn the base control.
>
> Then, Ethiopia, stretch, O stretch,
> Thy bleeding hands abroad!
> The cry of agony shall reach
> And find redress from God.

The God of Moses is evoked again by Harper in "Retribution" (p. 142). He appears as the scourge of men and nations who "trample on his children." Here, Moses' words serve

> As a warning to the nations
> Bathed in blood and swathed in fire
> Lay the once oppressing nation
> Smitten by God's fearful ire.

On the whole, Frances Harper's postwar appeals for freedmen's rights are more effective than her abolitionist verse. Essentially, the former are less emotional, more objective than the latter. For instance, in *Moses* there is less moralizing than in her earlier verse. In addition, such poems as "An Appeal to American People" and "The Present Age" give a more balanced, optimistic view of the race problem than her early poems.

Besides her strong religious convictions in Christian brotherhood and social equality, Harper draws much of her optimism about the race problem from her postwar tour of the South. "Instead of the lash," Still tells us, "she saw school books, and over the ruins of slavery, education and free speech sprang up" (*TUR*, p. 799). Thus, she expresses to him in her June 17, 1867, letter her favorable view of the black's future in the South. She maintains "the South is to be a great theater for the colored man's development and progress. There is brain power here" (*TUR*, p. 798). Furthermore, she states in *The Anti Slavery Standard*:

> So far as the colored man is concerned, I do not feel particularly uneasy about his future. With his breadth of physical organization, his fundamental endurance and his former

> discipline in the school of toil and private, I think he will be able to force his way upward and win recognition even in the South.
> (*TWD*, p. 24)

In spite of this buoyant optimism, Harper realized that much more work and dedication were needed to insure the black race's continual growth and progress. Therefore, for several years, while she continued to assist the freedmen to obtain their rights and equality under the law, she turned much of her attention to the specific social problems of black women as well.

III

During her postwar Southern tour, Harper took the opportunity to assist many Southern black women who had been the objects of abuse in slavery and had been in a state of subjugation and ignorance since Emancipation. For instance she gave public lectures to many of them "about their daughters and about things connected with the welfare of the race" (*TUR*, p. 803). She taught others about the cultivation of the home life and the sanctity of the marriage state (*TUR*, p. 807). Furthermore, she gave private lectures to women who had been victims of physical abuse. On one occasion, she informs Still:

> The condition of the women is not very enviable in some cases. They have had, some of them, a terribly hard time in Slavery and their subjugation has not ceased in freedom. One man said of some women, that a man must leave them or whip them.
> (TUR, p. 810)

In her private lectures, she advises these women to demand their rights and respect from their husbands/male counterparts.[13] She adds in her March 29, 1870, correspondence to Still, "Now is the time for our women to begin to try to lift up their heads and plant the roots of progress under the hearthstone" (*TUR*, p. 803). Their efforts, Harper maintains, are important for the race's development. She continues, "Oh, if some more of our young women would consecrate their lives to the work of upbuilding the race" (*TUR*, p. 810).

Harper's Southern experiences convinced her that her social purpose concerning women must be two-fold: on the one hand, she must champion the cause of women's rights, while on the other hand, she must appeal to the women of both races, black and white, to become actively involved in the uplifting of the black race. After her 1867–1871 Southern tour, Harper spent a substantial portion of the last forty years of her life attempting to accomplish this purpose. Harper championed the women's rights cause as a lecturer and member of the National Association of Colored Women and the National Council of Women in the United States. In the latter organization, May Wright Sewall, Susan B. Anthony, and Harper were the most active members.[14] On February 22, 1891, for example, Harper delivered an eloquent, moving speech, "Our Duty to Dependent Races," in which she represented the black race, not as a dependent race, "but as a member of the body politic who asks simple justice under the law, the protection of human life, education and complete citizenship" (*TWD*, p. 28). Throughout her discourse, she urged also black and white women to improve the social/political status of the black race as well as their own social conditions.[15]

These passionate pleas are apparent in Harper's poetry as well. Above all, her women's poetry stresses that woman/womanhood must be respected by man and society as a whole. In her poem, "A Double Standard" (p. 203), which Eugene Redmond observes has "the stirrings of feminism,"[16] Harper makes the point clear. Her protagonist, a seduced woman, scorns society for excusing the male's social behavior in the affairs of love while holding the female responsible for hers:

Crime has no sex and yet today
  I wear the brand of shame
Whilst he amid the gay and proud
  Still bears an honored name.

Can you blame me if I've learned to think
  Your hate of vice and sham,
When you so coldly crushed me down
  And then excused the man.

She insists, in her concluding stanza, that the same moral standards which apply to woman should apply to man:

That I who fell, and he who sinned
  Shall reap as we have sown,
That each the burden of his loss
  Must bear and bear alone.
No golden weights can turn the scale
  Of justice in His sight;

And what is wrong in woman's life
In man's cannot be right.

The "respect for womanhood" theme is also evident in Harper's "Vashti" (p. 132). In this poem, her biblical heroine Vashti, Queen of Persia, falls victim to her husband's male pride. Her tyrant-husband commands her to unveil her face which, in return, will bring shame to her womanhood. Harper projects her own moral strength and courage into Vashti, who decides instead to give up her throne rather than shame herself and all other Persian women as well. Vashti replies:

"A queen unveil'd before the crowd'—
Upon each lip my name!—
Why, Persia's women all would blush
And weep for Vashti's shame!"

"Go back!" she cried and waved her hand,
And grief was in her eye:
"Go, tell the King," she sadly said,
"That I would rather die."

And, as the narrator tells us, even though the King dethrones her, she leaves her crown "strong in her earnest womanhood . . . a woman who could bend to grief / But would not bow to shame."

While such poems as "Vashti" and "A Double Standard" help to advance the women's rights cause, other poems point out the significant roles that Harper feels both black and white women must play in the black liberation struggle. Her Aunt Chloe poems from *Sketches of Southern Life*, which form a new idiom in black poetry that ripens into the dialect verse of Campbell, Davis, and Dunbar,[17] emphasize Harper's views on how the black woman can best serve her race during the ante-bellum period.

As with Vashti, Harper projects her own moral strength, courage, and social/political statements into Aunt Chloe, her charming, witty black protagonist, who has survived slavery and the separation from her two sons, and who has dedicated the remainder of her life to race-building during the Reconstruction era. In this regard, Aunt Chloe functions much like Harper herself: she exhorts the freedmen to gain education, to be independent, responsible, voting citizens, and to build strong black communities based on mutual cooperation and Christian morality.

In order to serve as an inspiration for other blacks in her small Southern town community to obtain their education, Aunt Chloe teaches herself to read. Even though others feel that she is too old to learn, Aunt Chloe, in the poem "Learning to Read" (p. 157), informs us:

> But as I was rising sixty,
> I had no time to wait
> So I got a pair of glasses
> And straight to work I went
> And never stopped till I could read
> The hymns and testament.

And now that slavery is over, Aunt Chloe maintains that Southern blacks will have the opportunity to be educated. The school teachers from the North have arrived to help them:

> Very soon the Yankee teachers
> Came down and set up school
> But Oh! how the Rebs did hate it
> It was agin' their rule.

Besides emphasizing the need for the Southern blacks to obtain an education, Aunt Chloe appeals to the freedmen to become responsible, voting citizens. In "The Deliverance" (p. 155), she chides several of the black males for selling their votes. She reveals that some of them sold their votes for "three sticks of candy," while others such as David Rand "sold out for flour and sugar / The sugar was mixed with sand." Yet, Aunt Chloe is quick to point out that the David Rands are exceptions to the rule:

> And yet I would not have you think
> That all our men are shabby
> But tis said in every flock of sheep
> There will be one that's scabby.

She makes clear that most of the freedmen understood "their freedom cost too much / For them to fool away their votes / For profit or for pleasure." However, until more freedmen vote responsibly, Aunt Chloe maintains that black female activists like herself must continue to intervene in the political process on behalf of the race. For instance, in a local election, she insists that the females made the difference in the outcome:

> I think that Curnel Johnson said
> His side had won the day
> Had not we women radicals
> Just got right in his way.

Above all, Aunt Chloe stresses that black males and females must work together for the betterment of the race. In "Church Building" (p. 158), for example, she tells that her male confidante and companion, Uncle Jacob, advises the black community after Emancipation "all to come together / And build a meeting place." The church is eventually built because the people "pinched and scratched and spared / little here and there."

While, in the Aunt Chloe poems, Harper emphasizes how the black woman can help uplift her race, she addresses white American women in her poem "An Appeal to My Countrywomen" (pp. 219–20) to help advance the black freedom cause. She reminds them that while they are praying for "the sad-eyed Armenian[s], the exile[s] of Russia and others who are suffering throughout the world, black men and women are suffering in this country:

> But hark! from our Southland are floating
> Sobs of anguish, murmurs of pain,
> And women heart-stricken are weeping
> Over their tortured and their slain.

In order to persuade them to take up the black liberation cause, Harper appeals to them as women, sisters, and mothers. First of all, she asks them to pity men who are the ones who cause wars:

> You can pity the men who have woven
> From passion and appetite chains
> To coil with a terrible tension
> Around their heartstrings and brains.

Then, she calls them as sisters of black women to have compassion for and to identify with the freedwomen who are still suffering throughout the South:

> Have ye not, oh, my favored sisters,
> Just a plea, a prayer or a tear
> For mothers who dwell 'neath the shadows
> Of agony, hatred and fear?

And, finally, Harper appeals to their motherhood, insisting that they pray not only for the black race but also for their own sons who must pay for their fathers' sins:

> Weep not, oh my well-sheltered sisters,
> Weep not for the Negro alone,

But weep for your sons who must gather
  The crops which their fathers have sown.

There are feminist overtones in her women's poetry as a whole. In this poem, Harper appeals to white females to form a bond of sisterhood with black females to help to correct the social ills of white males. And, in the Aunt Chloe series, the protagonist and other black women radicals are seen rectifying the political mistakes committed by black males. In addition, her poem "A Double Standard" establishes her clearly as the first black feminist poet. However, these poems, like Harper's other works, are essentially a product of her concern for social equality. In "A Double Standard," she wishes simply for males and females to be judged on equal terms, by the same moral standards. Furthermore, her intention in such poems as the Aunt Chloe series and "An Appeal to My Countrywomen" is to draw from women the leadership qualities and talents necessary to insure the rights of the freedmen. As an example, in "The Deliverance," she champions the black suffrage rather than women's suffrage cause. This poem, like her other works, reveals that her major concern remains that of black race-building. In this regard, Harper effectively uses both her black and feminine consciousness and her special literary talents as a black female artist to accomplish this end. As one of her contemporary critics, Phebe A. Hansford, says of Harper:

> She is one of the colored women of whom white women may be proud and to whom the abolitionists can point and declare that a race which can hold such women ought never to have been held in bondage.[18]

For her poetic and other literary achievements, Frances Watkins Harper deserves honor as a major healer and race-builder of nineteenth-century America. Her own words express the contributions she has made to black America and to America as a whole. In her essay "Our Greatest Want", she declares:

> We [black people] need men and women whose hearts are the homes of a high and lofty enthusiasm and a noble devotion to the cause of emancipation, who are ready and willing to lay time, talent and money on the altar of universal freedom.[19]

No words more aptly describe Harper who devoted unselfishly most of her adult life and literary talents for this cause. Her numerous poems and other works attest to this complete devotion. Her abolitionist verse and postwar appeals for freedmen's rights are effective propaganda: these "songs stir like a battle cry / Wherever they are sung." Her poem *Moses*, that has rhythms which liberate the minds and spirits of her readers, audiences, and her people as a whole, is the most natural and original verse that she produced. And her Aunt Chloe poems, which put her a century ahead of other black feminist poets, have a colloquial naturalness of speech and truth to black characterization achieved by no other poet before Dunbar. In essence, as Sherman makes clear, Harper's total output "is the most valuable single poetic record we have of the race whose fortunes shaped the tumultuous years of her career, 1850-1900."[20]

However, in spite of Harper's literary achievements, she is relatively unknown today. Like many other black literary artists and race-builders, her deeds and achievements, for the most part, have been forgotten. Soon after her death in 1911, her volumes of poetry disappeared from print and only occasional mention of her works appears in major black literature anthologies.

Whatever may be the reason for her present obscurity, Frances Watkins Harper and her poetry deserve serious literary/critical attention. As the editor of *Crisis* reminds us: "It is however for her serious attempts to forward literature among colored people that Frances Harper deserves to be remembered. She was a worthy member of that dynasty beginning with dark Phyllis in 1773. . . ."[21] Like Wheatley, Harper, the Black Muse of her age, has made significant contributions to black poetry. As the "Bronze Muse," an early black social protest poet, and the major black female poet of the nineteenth century, Harper has helped to lay a sound aesthetic foundation upon which much of contemporary black poetry is based.

Notes

1. Eugene B. Redmond, *Drumvoices: The Mission of Afro-American Poetry* (Garden City: Anchor Books, 1976), p. 75.
2. William Still, *The Underground Railroad* (1871; rpt. Chicago: Ebony Classics, 1970), p. 812. This was a major source on Harper for this study and includes several of Harper's correspondences, lectures, and essays. Subsequent references to this collection are noted parenthetically in the text as *TUR*.
3. "Some Afro-American Women of Mark," *A.M.E. Church Review*, 8 (April 1892), 378.
4. "Three Negro Poets," *Journal of Negro History*, 2 (1917), 386.

5. *Daughters of America* (Augusta, ME: True and Company, 1882), p. 302.
6. William Robinson, Jr., ed., *Early Black American Poets* (Dubuque: William C. Brown, 1971), p. 27.
7. "Black Women Poets from Wheatley to Walker," *Sturdy Black Bridges: Visions of Black Women in Literature*, ed. Roseann P. Bell et al. (Garden City: Anchor Books, 1979), p. 72.
8. Theodora Williams Daniel, "The Poems of Frances E. W. Harper," M.A. Thesis, Howard University, 1937, p. 189. This is basically a collection of Harper's poems with comments by Daniel. All poems cited are from this collection and are noted parenthetically in the text. All references to Daniel's comments are noted as *TWD*.
9. *Women of Distinction* (Raleigh, NC: published by the author, 1893), p. 12.
10. "The Works of Frances E. W. Harper," *Black World*, 22, No. 2 (1972), 31.
11. *The Negro Author in America to 1900* (1931; rpt. New York: Kennikot Press, Inc., 1964), p. 246.
12. *Invisible Poets: Afro-Americans of the Nineteenth Century* (Urbana: Univ. of Illinois Press, 1974), p. 67. Sherman devotes a chapter in her book to Harper's poetry.
13. *Women of Distinction*, p. 12.
14. Rachel Foster Avery, ed., *Transactions of the National Council of Women of the United States* (Philadelphia: J. B. Lippincott Company, 1891), p. 87.
15. Ibid.
16. Redmond, p. 76.
17. *Invisible Poets*, p. 71.
18. *Daughters of America*, p. 302.
19. "Our Greatest Want," *Anglo-Saxon Magazine*, 1 (May 1859), 160.
20. *Invisible Poets*, p. 74.
21. Editorial, *Crisis*, 1 (April 1911), 20.

JOHN KEELING

Paul Dunbar and the Mask of Dialect

Why should the world be overwise,
In counting our tears and sighs?
Nay, let them only see us, while
   We wear the mask.
—Dunbar, "We Wear the Mask"

He sang of life, serenely sweet,
with, now and then, a deeper note.
From some high peak, nigh yet remote,
He voiced the world's absorbing beat.

He sang of love when earth was young,
And love, itself, was in his lays.
But ah, the world, it turned to praise
A jingle in a broken tongue.
—Dunbar, "The Poet"

In these lines we may glimpse the central paradox of Paul Dunbar's poetry. The "We," in "We Wear the Mask," are essentially dissemblers, hiding their "torn and bleeding hearts" behind a "smile." Of course, the "mask" has been lifted for the reader in this poem; our pathos is heightened, however, by our

From *The Southern Literary Journal* XXV, no. 2 (Spring 1993).

knowledge that such a lapse is temporary, that masked suffering continues: "But let the world dream otherwise / We wear the mask." Readers have generally considered "The Poet" as Dunbar's lament over the critical indifference to his poems written in standard English in relation to the rather dubious popularity of his dialect poetry. In such a reading of the poem, we perceive Dunbaras an artist frustrated with not being taken seriously; we see a poet who feels his most profound work has been ignored while what he considers to be his trivial efforts have been lauded. Further complicating the issue for Dunbar (and contemporary readers as well) is the comic and sentimental characterization of plantation life portrayed in the dialect poetry as opposed to the characteristic melancholy of his standard English poetry. To conceive of Dunbar in this light one must view his motivations as troublesome and paradoxical. How could the author of "We Wear The Mask" and "The Poet" have written nostalgic, pastoral dialect poetry?

On the other hand, I would suggest that "The Poet" can also be read as referring only to the dialect poems. From this perspective, the first two lines—"He sang of life serenely sweet / With, now and then, a deeper note"—both refer to poems written in dialect. The poet laments the world's misinterpretation of these poems, rather than the world's preference for the dialect poetry over his poetry in standard English. Thus, the poem's focus is on the trivialization of the type of self-denial described in "We Wear The Mask." The smile and song of the dialect poet is misinterpreted as "A jingle in a broken tongue," and the poet's distress is unrecognized. The paradox here lies between the necessity for abnegation, expressed in "We Wear the Mask," and the poet's frustration with being misunderstood, detailed in "The Poet." While both of these poems have evoked sympathy in Dunbar's readers, the same cannot be said for Dunbar's dialect poetry, in which, I might add, are poems where the mask is firmly in place.

To support my reading of "The Poet" we should first turn to another standard English poem which seems to address those who find fault with his dialect verse. In "Misapprehension" Dunbar writes:

Out of my heart, one day, I wrote a song,
With my heart's blood imb'ued,
Instinct with passion, tremulously
strong, With grief subdued;
Breathing a fortitude Pain-bought.
And one who claimed much love for what I wrought,
And spoke:
"Ay, brother,—it is well writ,
But where's the joke?"

In the first half of the poem, Dunbar creates a persona not unlike that of "We Wear The Mask." The poet suppresses suffering, "breathing a fortitude / Pain-bought." But Dunbar's wry inclusion of the "sympathetic" reader who, apparently, misinterprets the "song" subtly shifts the emphasis from the stoic martyrdom of "We Wear The Mask" to the reader's inability to see the "grief subdued" in this later poem. In contrast to the former poem, Dunbar implies here that readers should see through the "mask."

Still, critics, African-American and white, read the dialect poems in much the same way as the "world" in "The Poet." In other words, critics have tended to place these poems in the Plantation Tradition, which is, in effect, to say that these poems are not all "masked" and to suggest that they exploit, rather than subvert, the stereotypical notions of African-American character and speech that existed in Dunbar's culture. Due in part to a somewhat presumptuous conclusion that Dunbar's use of this medium is capable of only superficial expression,[1] and in part to the unfortunate critical response that followed the publication of his dialect poetry.[2] Dunbar's dialect verse has been viewed as distinct in aim and tone from his poetry written in standard English. I would suggest, however, that if we use poems such as "We Wear the Mask" and "The Poet" as a lens for our reading, we may roil the apparently smooth surface of Dunbar's dialect poetry. We may unlock what Houston Baker calls the "unlikely expressive spaces" in African-American literature that, nevertheless, are charged with "blues energies" (Baker 115).

As I see it, there are at least two ways in which we can consider Dunbar's dialect poetry that differ considerably from the critical responses we have already reviewed. First, we might propose that these poems are subversive, acting against the Plantation Tradition they seemed to mimic. Or, we might acknowledge the sentimentalized idealism that critics have found so disturbing, yet, as contemporary readers, look for gaps in the construction of this never-never land," which is so obviously at odds with "real" history. In either kind of reading, we take Dunbar's adaptation of dialect and Plantation Tradition conventions as a starting point for critical practice rather than as proof of the literature's dubious value. The distinction between this way of reading and the kind made by other critics is that it looks for contradictions between the "real" world and Dunbar's "fantasy" world within the poems themselves. In a sense, I'm arguing that the controversy that has surrounded Dunbar's dialect poetry is due not to critics' misrepresentation of African-American life but to their misrecognition of the "mask" that is never removed in these poems. I want to suggest that the "mask" should be important to critics whether Dunbar's intentions were subversive or whether he had some other intention. For if we can see the mask as a mask, if we can locate the limits of its construction, then we can discover the kind of suffering and frustration, so evident in Dunbar's standard English poems, in the dialect poetry as well.

But first let us return to Baker's idea of "blues energy." In *Blues, Ideology, and Afro-American Literature* Baker's seminal theory moves outward from the network of meaning he terms the "blues matrix." Borrowing from Derrida, Baker uses the metaphor of the blues singer to represent the African-American author:

> the blues singer and his performance serve as codifiers, absorbing and transforming discontinuous experience into formal expressive instances that bear only the trace of origins; refusing to be pinned down to any final, dualistic significance. Even as they speak of paralyzing absence and ineradicable desire, their instrumental rhythms suggest change, movement, action, continuance, unlimited and unending possibility. Like signification itself, blues are always nomadically wandering. (8)

Baker also acknowledges the influence of Marxism on his thinking, and, indeed, we should emphasize that although the blues artist functions as "codifier," he or she is already encoded by the driving force of history at work within the matrix itself. In this vein, we should note the subject matter of the singer in the passage above—"paralyzing absence and ineradicable desire"—which is obviously determined by (even as artists free it from) cultural experience. Significantly, Baker shifts his focus from the multiplicity of meaning in Derrida's semiotics, from the inscribing force of history in Marxism, and turns his attention to those spaces where human agency is operating, where authors act as enablers within the "blues matrix" whose functioning should lead to social change, Baker clearly states the reformative function of the artist in *Modernism and the Harlem Renaissance*:

> For I am interested in a definition of the mastery of form that renders it more than a strategy adopted for the aesthetic satisfaction of the individual artist. Indeed, I am interested in the strategy to precisely the extent that it ensures cognitive exploration and affective transformations leading to the growth and *survival* of a nation. (37)

Blues literature, then, acts as a transforming force displacing and reshaping the experiences of the blues artist. The reader is implicated in the narrative and invited to participate in the exploration, wandering, and re-envisioning of the text

Some readers might argue, as Baker does in *Modernism and the Harlem Renaissance*, that Dunbar's dialect poetry fails to operate within this kind of "blues matrix." In fact, Baker goes so far as to say that Dunbar "does not have as one of his goals the general progress of the Afro-American populace" (39). Baker might point to a poem such as "To The Eastern Shore" to suggest that Dunbar is, at times, regressive.

> Oh, de ol' plantation's callin'
> To me, Come, come back,
> Heah's de place fu' you to la-
> bough an' to res',
> 'Fu my sandy roads is gleam-
> in' w'ile de city ways
> is black;
> Come back, honey, case yo'
> country home is bes'.

For Baker, the appeal of the plantation is alienating; the poem's nostalgia places a barrier between reader and narrative, allowing the reader little or no empathetic participation. This static vision of harmony on the old plantation, which apparently ignores the reality of slavery, belies the flux of African-American culture and understanding, thus fixing its character at "home" on the plantation, retarding African-American exploration and improvement. A key to understanding Baker's criticism (and, later, to following my interpretation of Dunbar's dialect execution) is to follow the necessary transience of Baker's blues vision which resists at all costs the desire for fixity.

Dunbar's dialect verse, such as "To The Eastern Shore," glosses over atrocities of slavery, conjures a static image of reality from a past that never was, and, most damaging of all, reinforces the marginalization of readers by adopting a regressive politics. In short, is it not appropriate to insist that a blues artist must sing the blues? When Baker envisions an author experimenting with dialect in the "blues matrix," he has in mind someone like Langston Hughes. Hughes authority Arnold Rampersad argues that "Hughes boldly reclaimed the use of dialect by black poets after it had fallen into disrepute and disuse ["a jingle in a broken tongue," Dunbar had called his own dialect verses] as the language of hated stereotypes, stressing either a gross humor or maudlin sentimentality" (Rampersad 43).[3] Implied here is a rigid classification of dialect experimentation confined to two antithetical discourses. To speak in dialect, it seems, is either to aspire to aesthetic realism—to create a down home character (a blues singer) who must explicitly confront insufferable "lack" (Baker's term) and longing—or to appropriate the form for denigration, caricature, or stereotype. As I have already stated, I believe that blues forces do interrupt the pastoral portraits of Dunbar's dialect verse, but to recognize these "blues energies" we must make an attempt to define Dunbar's use of dialect in a way different than the two theories which emerge from Baker's "blues matrix." We must show how Dunbar's mask of dialect can be a powerful active force rather than a self-defeating retreat into a fantasy world.

To do so, it is useful to look at Henry Louis Gates's reading of Zora Neale Hurston to see how he situates her within a signifying system not unlike that of Baker's "blues matrix"; however, Gates takes a different approach to describe the use of dialect within this system[4] as he looks at how Hurston's theory of African-American oral strategies is at work in the narratology of *Their Eyes Were Watching God.* Gates differs from Baker in the sense that he does not focus on Hurston's explicit subject matter, nor on her social politics, as he details the text's process of communication. Rather, Gates locates both in the speech activity that occurs within the text. Gates cites the use of irony and mimicry by Hurston's characters to discuss urgent and private issues in public. That is to say, her characters air their differences in an indirect manner because they do not have the opportunity—nor, perhaps, the conventions—to do otherwise. Gates describes this phenomenon of appropriating the means at hand in terms of Hurston's theory. In summary, she argues that people with extensive vocabularies have words for abstract ideas; those who do not, or who for reasons of circumstance cannot express themselves with that vocabulary, communicate with highly descriptive language, describing one event in relation to another (Gates 197).[5] This kind of approach is, of course, central to Baker's thinking in *Blues* as well, yet when Baker criticizes Dunbar, in *Modernism and the Harlem Renaissance*, he refuses to see beyond the apparent subject matter (or lack of a politically correct subject matter) of Dunbar's dialect verse in order to explore the possibilities of Dunbar as a blues codifier. In other words, Baker denies Dunbar's dialect verse the capability of expressing sophisticated blues rhythms because of its nonblues-like themes. On the other hand, Gates considers how an author's rendering of verbal signification (often through dialogue) can create an indirect discourse quite distinct from the nominal subject.

Gates terms this kind of signification a "speakerly text" (198).[6] In doing so, Gates is signifying on Roland Barthes's binary of "readerly" and "writerly" texts. In the former there is a homogeneous, noncontradictory realism, while in the latter an infinite play of signification upon realities. In the "speakerly text," or oral narrative, there is a potential for homogeneity in contradiction—which for my purposes, I shall call irony. As in a "writerly text," the construction of signification (the meaning process) is foregrounded, and, as in a "readerly text," there is a limited perspective offered by the text. The oral narrative constantly calls itself into question through the dialogue between two characters (who are often opposed to each other), or invites readers to interrogate the perspective of a single character telling the tale, a character who is distinct from the author. The irony built into this "speakerly text" allows for the presence of an author's perspective that is very different from that of the narrative speaker, which serves as an invitation for the reader to participate in the signification, in effect, to join the conversation by "specify'n" on the "word pictures" of the narrator (Gates 199).[7] Thus, our understanding of a "speakerly text" should be facilitated by our analysis of the text as an oral event that can be challenged, that can contradict itself, that may have a political agenda it attempts to keep hidden or, conversely, have a hidden agenda it attempts to bring to light. I feel we can apply my reading of Gates to signify upon the binary classification of dialect usage I see coming out of Baker's blues theory. I believe there is a space in addition to the discourses of the Plantation Tradition (often a white readerly text) and of the blues protester/explorer (most often an African-American writerly text) where an author such as Dunbar can wear a mask that "grins and ties" in order to expose blues realities.

As I see it, then, the tension between the voice of the blues poet in "We Wear The Mask" and the expression of pastoral appeal in "To the Eastern Shore" exists within the dialect poems themselves. As with "speakerly texts," irony incorporates the voice of a blues poet with the pastoral voice of the poems to create a potentially dramatic effect. In fact, Dunbar often constructs a poetic form similar to that of a dramatic monologue, where an interlocutor or the dramatic situation subverts the speaker's narrative. In these dialect poems, such as "The Party" and "When Malindy Sings," we overhear a character speaking to a silent yet identifiable listener. The relation of these poems to dramatic monologue is important, I think, because, as Alan Sinfield argues in his study of the form, in this idiom "we are obliged to give consideration to attitudes which in other circumstances we would find repellent" (5).[8] And, certainly, the first poem we shall consider, "The Party," seems to be most firmly grounded in the Plantation Tradition. But if, as Sinfield argues, we consider the "ironic discrepancy between the speaker's view of himself and a larger judgment which the poet implies and the reader must *develop*" (7, my italics), then we may see evidence of disruptive rhythms which undermine the narrator's overdrawn vignette of African-American life. If we pay close attention to the distance between the poem's speaker and listener, and if we look at the narrative details which seem to contradict the speaker's portrait, then we shall find a much bleaker vision rupturing the surface of the poem.

We are made to recognize early in "The Party" that it is no ordinary social event our narrator is describing: "Dey had a great big party down to Tom's de othah night / Was I dah? You bet! I nevah in my life see sich a sight." This social gathering is a rather bawdy affair complete with romantic intrigue, reckless dancing, bodily injury, and good eating. Judging from this summary alone, it seems easy to view the poem as satirizing these revelers, with their "high-toned mannahs" and coarse behavior. But such a reading closes off for discussion, among other things, the curious relationship between speaker and listener. It is important to recognize that the listener, who is not the reader (since he or she is apparently an active participant in the conversation), was not present at the party. Our narrator tells the listener: "I cain't tell you nothin' bout it, y' ought to seen it fu' yo'se'f." In fact, the listener acts as a kind of interpreter for the reader, responding to the speaker's narrative. We can pinpoint at least two occasions where the listener interrupts speaker. The first interruption occurs when we can infer that the listener questions if "Young Scott Thomas" is injured from his fall into the fire:

> Y' ought to seen dat man a-scramblin' from de ashes an' de grime.
> *Did it bu'n him! Sich a question*, why he didn't give it time.
> [my italics]

The question, I think, is significant as it shifts the tone away from the narrator's obvious delight at the young man's accident and, perhaps, brings into question the speaker's reliability. The speaker has already told us that one hundred-year-old "ole man Johnson" has "swung" three-hundred-pound "Aunt Maria" around the dance floor; this, combined with the elaborate meal that is described later, and with the description of "Cripple Joe" throwing away his crutch in order to join in the dancing, should leave our speaker suspect at best.

Moreover, the listener's second interruption of the narrative confirms that, for him, reality is quite different from the atmosphere of the party:

> Look out! What's de matter wif you? Don't be fallin' on de flo';
> Ef it's go'n' to 'fect you dat way, I won't tell you nothin' mo'.
> Dah now—well, we had hot chittlin's—now you's tryin' ag'in to fall,
> Cain't you stan I to hyeah about it? S'pose you'd been an' seed it all. . . .

Indeed, the listener cannot bear to hear out the narrator's description of the bountiful supper, which is curiously, or ironically, contradicted by the hostess, Mandy: "you all mus' 'scuse me, d'wa'n't much upon my she'ves, / But I's done my bes' to suit you, so set down an' he'p you'se'ves." In any case, the meal is described as anything but modest, and the listener's reaction to the narrator's description suggests that such feasting is unheard of. And, if this is the case, then the narrator's frequent hyperboles—for instance, "I nevah in my life see sich a sight—take on an added ironic significance.

We might look even closer at the reality/fantasy theme, and in particular at the flying imagery which occurs twice in the poem, in order to search for more ruptures in the narrator's "mask".

> Jigs, cotillions, reels an' breakdowns, cordrills an' waltz er two;
> Bless yo' soul, dat music winged 'em an' dem people lak to flew.

As with ole man Johnson and Cripple Joe, the people in the dance seem to break free from their limitations and in this case fly. Initially, these images seem firmly woven into the fabric of the fantasy narrative; however, the Scott Thomas accident has a much more pitiful tone, one which casts a shadow on the narrator's exaggerations:

> . . . Young Scott Thomas, tryin' to be so awful smaht,
> You know wehn dey gits to singin' an' dey comes to dat ere paht:
> "In some lady's new brick house,
> In some lady's gyaliden.
> Ef you don't let me out, I will jump out,
> So fa'you well, my dahlin'."
> Den dey's go a circle I roun' you, an' you's got to break de line;
> Well, dat dahky was so anxious, lak to bust hisse'f a-tryin"
> Kep' on blund'rin 'roun' an' foolin' 'twell he giv' one gread big jump,
> Broke de line, an lit head-fo' most in de fiah-place right plump;
> Hit 'ad fiah in it, mind you. . . .

The flying imagery from the quoted song is associated not just with liberation but with escape, and in the game the people play Scott must break free from the crowd that encircles him. Although Scott's flight, his "one gread big jump," does gain him his freedom, the end result is anything but liberating. The pitiful figure of Scott Thomas, with his "face all full o' soot," looms almost as a specter over the poem—especially if one considers the "coon show" caricatures of "hapless darkies" put on by white actors with soot on their faces. While the narrator uses this anecdote for a humorous effect, we see how the listener does not laugh but, instead, interrupts the narrative, and, therefore, the humor, at this point. Furthermore, Scott Thomas's desperation can be extended to all of the characters at his rambunctious party—regardless of whether we trust our narrator—and even to the narrator, whose exaggerations become more and more embellished as the story unfolds.

We may view the poem, then, as a kind of attempt at escapism which unravels. Certainly the narrator intends only to entertain and impress his listener with the events of the party. But the listener's responses and interruptions, as well as the somewhat dubious details of the narrative itself, undermine the narrator's intentions and hint of a different reality. The poem almost invites the reader to act, with even more vigor than the listener, to question and subvert the speaker's narrative. And though the reality beneath the party can only be glimpsed at—through Scott Thomas' desperation, through the hungry listener—we should not be fooled by our narrator's mask."

Why Dunbar invokes stereotypes (the possum-eating preacher and coarse revelers) is unclear; certainly he could have portrayed "The Party" in a more "bluesy" light. The speaker, in any case, is not the dupe of the minstrel show emcee, and we must bear in mind the use of dramatic monologue; we must decide for ourselves the function of the listener and the dramatic situation. It is significant that the listener, in this poem and others, is never an insider to the speaker's fantasy world, rather he is an innocent who seems alienated by the speaker's narrative. If we consider that the listener's presence emphasizes simultaneously the speaker's perspective and the possibility of other, perhaps preferable, perspectives, then we may see Dunbar's dialect poems as affecting the overwrought comedy and pathos of the Plantation Tradition as a way to undermine their stereotypical effectiveness. In other words, Dunbar's use of irony turns the blues inside out: his overt theme in some ways mirrors that of the Plantation Tradition, but the listener distracts us from the narrative and, in effect, points us to another reality. If we accept this approach, then Dunbar's dialect poetry is fascinating. Dunbar himself becomes the blues man utilizing the materials at hand to sing his unique style of blues. We should note the consensus that Dunbar wrote in dialect because it was the only form for which he had an audience. Moreover, we might speculate that that audience brought to his texts a demand for the stereotypical caricatures of the Plantation Tradition. Dunbar need not connect himself in any way to the Plantation Tradition, although not to was probably to lose his audience, but he might also appropriate stereotypes for a blues effect.

The dramatic monologue may be somewhat limited in "The Party," and the blues subversion may not be entirely successful; however, I feel the second poem we shall examine performs this kind of irony with greater success. The speaker of "When Malindy Sings" is very similar to that of "The Party." We are told of Malindy's "nachel o'gans," and of how her "real melojous music" puts to shame that of any "edicated band." As in "The Party," the speaker builds on this stereotype and goes on to tell the listener:

> Fiddlin' man jes stop his fiddlin'.
>   Lay his fiddle on de she'f;
> Mockin'-bird quit tryin' to whistle,
>   'Cause he jes' so shamed hisse'f.
> Foks a'playin' on de banjo
>   Drap dey fingahs on de strings—
> Bless yo' soul—fu'gits to move em,
>   When Malindy sings.
>
> She jes' spreads huh mouf and hollahs,
>   "Come to Jesus," twell you hyeah
> Sinnahs' tremblin' steps and voices
>   Timid-lak a-drawin' neah;
> Den she tu'ns to "Rock of Ages,"
>   Simply to de cross she clings;
> An' you fin' yo' teahs a-droppin'
>   When Malindy sings.

But here too the listener is an outsider to the speaker's narrative having never heard Malindy sing:

> Ain't you nevah hyeahd Malindy?
>   Blessed soul, tek up de cross!

In both poems, the speakers take their audience's innocence as a license to embellish, although in "When Malindy Sings" the speaker's version of events is so thoroughly checked by the blues rhythms that break through that, as we come to the last stanza, his desperation is obvious.

While we may find it easy to be drawn into the speaker's point of view, the concrete details of the poem, those which interrupt the narrative, force us to call into question the speaker's excessive sentiment. We might note first that Malindy never appears in the poem; the only singing represented is that of Miss Lucy, whose song is described by the narrator as "dat noise." In fact, it is the futility of Lucy's dedication to singing—"Put dat music book away; / What's de use to keep on tryin'?"—that launches the speaker into his tribute to Malindy. In effect, the poem begins with the discord of Miss Lucy's song which the speaker attempts to restructure into harmony. Unfortunately for the speaker, just as his embellishment reaches its peak (with the "sinnahs" crying at Malindy's feet), he is interrupted by a blues voice of dissension. We can infer what the listener's comment was by the speaker's response:

> Who dat says dat humble praises
>   Wif de Master nevah counts?
> Heish yo' mouf, I hyeah dat music. . . .

In these lines not only is the efficacy of the gospel questioned but, perhaps, the very existence of Malindy as well. In the next stanza the speaker attempts to continue but is completely undermined as we reach the final stanza:

> Towsah, stop dat ba'kin', hyeah me!
>   Mandy, mek dat chile keep still';
> Don't you hyeah de echoes callin'
>   F'om de valley to de hill?
> Let me listen, I can hyeah it,
>   Th'oo de bresh of angles' wings,
> Sof' an' sweet, "Swing Low, Sweet Chariot,"
>   Ez Malindy sings.

Instead of Malindy we are introduced to Mandy, and, with the image of the crying child, harmony has once again fallen into discord. The speaker's failure to harmonize leaves him desperate—"Let me listen, I can hyeah it"—and somewhat alienated from Mandy and the rest. Yet there is a sense that in the last lines Malindy's song has taken on a more poignant, personal relevance for the speaker, in the sense that his narrative's fictiveness has been exposed. We might even imagine the speaker singing the final three lines (with all of those long vowel sounds), beginning a kind of blues song out of the narrative which fails. In such a reading, Dunbar undermines the stereotype of the gospel singer Malindy and, at the same time, affirms the power of blues creativity. The speaker's exaggeration is subverted, but his creativity, faith, and spirit are confirmed.

We should also note that in addition to poems such as "The Party" and "When Malindy Sings," Dunbar uses dialect verse directly to record traditional blues narratives. In one of the most famous, "An Ante-Bellum Sermon," Dunbar's preacher, speaking metaphorically through the story of Moses, addresses the subject of emancipation and the hypocrisy of slaveholders' appropriation of Christianity. In a humorous move we might expect from Dunbar, the preacher interrupts his own narrative to deny this revolutionary theme's relevance to his listeners:

But fu' feah some one mistakes me,
    I will pause right hyeah to say,
Dar I'm still a-preachin' ancient,
    I ain't talkin' 'bout to-day.

By doing so, of course, he reinforces their relation to his audience's circumstances. Once again Dunbar uses irony to expose the content behind the mask of the poem, and although the mask is easily seen through in this case, the humor would soften the political content for his white readers. Yet his message would still be clear:

But when Moses wif his powah
    Comes an' sets us chillun free,
We will praise de gracious Mastah
    Dat has gin us liberty;
An' we'll shout ouah halleluyahs,
    On dat mighty reck'nin'day,
When we'se reco'nised ez citiz'—
    Huh uh! Chillun, let us pray!

Similarly, Dunbar seems to speak to the aesthetic principle expressed in "We Wear The Mask" in the dialect poem "Philosophy." This speaker questions a preacher who advises his people to "keep dey faces / bright . . . Meetin' evahbody roun' us wid ouah very nicest smiles," countering with "you don't ketch folks a-grinnin'wid a misery / de back;" and "you don't fin' dem a-smilin' w'en dey's hongry ez kin / be." It is fitting that Dunbar questions the philosophy of "We Wear The Mask" in a dialect poem. In this poem Dunbar finally gives a voice to the listener who has been preached to both in dialect and standard English. The critique of this poem is the critique of a blues man:

But it's easy 'nough to titter w'en de stew is smokin' hot,
    But hit's mighty ha'd to giggle w'en dey's nuffin in de pot.

The large number of perspectives Dunbar demonstrates in his poetry truly creates a dramatic dialogue that suffuses his body of work. As a blues man, Dunbar's "wanderings" often go in contradictory directions that do not fit neatly into a single teleological or political perspective, unless that perspective is one of contradiction—a perspective which, perhaps, best suited his times. I have tried to tease out the blues forces I see at work in a variety of Dunbar's dialect verse, but for those who are alienated by those poems which seem associated with the Plantation Tradition—such as "To The Eastern Shore" and "The Party"—I would emphasize that the circles of irony in Dunbar's work extend beyond the margins of any single poem and function in a dialogical relationship with Dunbar's body of work (in standard English and dialect) and with the literary traditions of his contemporaries. I would also argue that since freedom brought little or no improvement to the lives of the formerly enslaved, and since some were, in fact, more oppressed in life after slavery, then the type of nostalgia expressed in "To The Eastern Shore" would not be an altogether uncommon sentiment. Nonetheless, if we view Dunbar as a practitioner of the dramatic monologue, then blues rhythms haunt and disturb any lure of "de ol' plantation." In addition, to return to the idea of Dunbar's poetry as dialogic, the collision of languages that emerges from Dunbar, the conversation between other times, other places, and other sensibilities forms an ironic blues-like decentering, which cannot be contextualized by any critical approach (post-structuralist or otherwise) that attempts to place it within a rigid, canonical framework of Right and Wrong. In other words, the castigation, by some critics, of Dunbar's dialect poetry (which is, of course, a criticism of the poet's political stance) speaks largely to critics' opinions about the relationship between art and politics—the utilitarian aspects of poetry. Instead, we should consider the diversity of masks in Dunbar's blues poetry and how the poet's deliberate "masking" incorporates protest as well as nostalgia, intellect as well as emotion.

NOTES

1. For instance, J. Saunders Redding writes, "Though such a bastard medium it was (and is) impossible to speak the whole heart of a people" (63). Also, Houston Baker, in *Modernism and the Harlem Renaissance*, considers in detail what he perceives to be the shortcomings of Dunbar's dialect verse.
2. William Dean Howells wrote: "The precious difference in temperament between the races is best preserved and most charmingly suggested by Dunbar in those pieces of his where he studies the moods and traits of his race in its own account of our English. . . . He reveals in these a finely ironical perception of the Negro's limitations. . ." Howells' remarks provide a generation of readers with a rather faulty set of reading glasses through which Dunbar's dialect poetry is almost indistinguishable from the literature of the Plantation Tradition.
3. See Rampersad's *The Life of Langston Hughes*, Volumes I and II, for a thorough treatment of the life and work of Langston Hughes.

4. See Gates's *The Signifying Monkey*, 197–99. While Gates is taking the approach of a linguist, he, like Baker, is interested in those spaces of resistance where an author is an active agent in the signifying process.
5. Here Gates draws on Hurston's essay "Characteristics of Negro Expression."
6. Gates also identifies the Afro-American trope of the Talking Book as central to an understanding of black oral narration.
7. "Word picture" is Hurston's term; she argues that "the Negro thinks in hieroglyphics," a highly metaphorical use of language that she defines as "work pictures," "thought pictures," "verbal-nouns," etc.
8. Sinfield studies the history of the form and suggests: ". . .dramatic monologue is a specially immediate way of presenting character, that it affords an oblique mode of self-expression and an unusually teasing reading experience." (76).

Works Cited

Baker, Houston, A., Jr. *Blues, Ideology, and Afro-American Literature*. Chicago: U of Chicago P, 1984.

Baker, Houston, A., Jr. *Modernism and the Harlem Renaissance*. Chicago: U of Chicago P, 1987.

Dunbar, Paul Lawrence. *Lyrics of Hearthside*. New York: Dodd, Mead, 1899.

———. *Lyrics of Love and Laughter*. New York: Dodd, Mead, 1903.

———. *Lyrics of Lowly Life*. New York: Dodd, Mead, 1896.

Gates, Henry Louis, Jr. *The Signifying Monkey*. New York: Oxford UP, 1988.

Hughes, Langston. Selected Poems. *Black Writers of America*. Ed. Richard Barksdale and Kenneth Kinnamon. New York: McMillan, 1972. 520–21.

Hurmence, Belinda. *Before Freedom, When I Just Can Remember*. Winston-Salem: John F. Blair, 1990.

Rampersad, Arnold. *The Life of Langston Hughes*. Vol. 1. New York: Oxford UP, 1986.

Redding, J. Saunders. *To Make a Poet Black*. Ithaca: Cornell UP, 1939. 60–67.

Revell, Peter. "Poetry in Dialect." *Paul Lawrence Dunbar*. Boston: Twayne, 1979. 94–106.

Sinfield, Alan. *Dramatic Monologue*. New York: Barnes and Noble, 1977.

RALPH STORY

Paul Laurence Dunbar: Master Player in a Fixed Game[1]

During Paul Laurence Dunbar's junior year in Dayton, Ohio's, Central High School (1890), a notable event was taking place miles away. The First Mohonk Conference brought together an assortment of influential politicos, educators, and clergymen whose joint mission was to define the modern "Negro Problem." Indeed, as Herbert Gutman points out:

> No more prestigious group of northern and southern whites had come together to discuss the Afro-American condition since the Civil War than those gathered in upstate New York. With rare but important exceptions speaker after speaker blamed the blacks' difficulties on the blacks themselves. The negro [sic] today is the product of his sad and dismal past: . . . He has no history and never has been a history maker.[2]

Typical of the times and the majority's opinion of Afro-Americans, "not a single black attended the conference."

These years—the 1890s—were some of the most difficult years for blacks in their struggle for equality; these years were marked by the pervading feeling that blacks needed "benevolent" guidance; these turbulent years were especially significant for the vigilante type of violence that sought

From *CLA Journal* XXVII, no. 1 (September 1983).

to permanently disenfranchise and severely limit the "place" and "space" of black folk—their role(s) and mobility in American society. Little did Dunbar know that even before he began his literary career, a wave of racist, retrogressionist beliefs had taken hold of popular opinion, literally determining the destiny of a people—sight unseen:

> The real world inhabited by poor rural and urban southern ex-slaves and their children between 1880 and the start of the vast northward migration after 1900 was invisible to nearly all observers. Partly that is explained by the increasing popularity in the 1880s and the 1890s of the belief that essential restraining influences on unchanging "Africans" had ended with the emancipation, causing a moral and social retrogression among the ex-slaves.[3]

Although little (definitively) was known about blacks at this time, a number of spokespersons—so-called authorities on black life—had gained a sizable audience and, in the process, created a vicious imagery and, subsequently, distorted history of blacks that pervaded the mass consciousness of the nation. But the proliferation of a vicious imagery, particularly associated with blacks as fictional characters in literature, was another matter; the symbolic destruction of the black image was well underway and virtually complete—this was the age of "Little Black Sambo."

In fiction a variety of black types had flourished both during and after the Civil War. The stage was dominated by minstrel shows with virulent titles like "Rufus Rastus," "All Coons Look Alike to Me," and "Go Way Back and Sit Down."[4] Newspapers carried ludicrous cartoons such as *Spare Ribs and Gravy* or had characters with names like "Asbestos" or "Smokey." Even film, in its infancy at the turn of the century, was reflective of the society's condescending attitude toward blacks. For instance, the great Thomas Alva Edison "proved to be a pioneer in the exploitation and exploration of this type ["coon"] when he . . . photographed some blacks as 'interesting side effects.'"[5]

Much of this ridiculous imagery had its roots in the earlier works of plantation writers like Joel Chandler Harris, Thomas Nelson Page, and A. C. Gordon, Southern regionalists who "almost always . . . used the genre [dialect] to parade the stock Negro, contentedly servile on the plantation or comic in his favorite pursuits."[6] Apparently, the fact that slavery had ended some three decades before was unimportant; the nation in the 1890s was torn between opposing currents: a pastoral, idealized past and a heavy-metal industrialized future. When given the choice, American readers decided in favor of sentiment, seeking a return to the "good old days" prior to the Civil War, before regional, cultural, and ethnic differences were accentuated, to coin a phrase, "when black folk 'knew their place.'"[7] Nevertheless, a sentimental escapade did little to obfuscate the truth chronicled in the newspapers, the fact that blacks struggled to assert themselves, and to survive, against tremendous odds in a nation seemingly resolved to return them to slavery:

> In the last sixteen years of the nineteenth century, there had been more than 2,500 lynchings, the great majority of which were Negroes, with Mississippi, Alabama, Georgia, and Louisiana leading the nation.
>
> Few regarded these manifestations of violence as an inherent part of the industrial imperialism to which America was committed, in the ideology of which the subjection of the black man to caste control and wage slavery was an integral part.[8]

It is understandable that by the time of Paul Laurence Dunbar's first work—*Oak and Ivy* (1893)—the black man's role, as artist, artistic subject, and as person, was extremely constrained by tons of propaganda and, eventually, institutionalized injustice. In more than one way Dunbar's poetry was received by the reading public as a novelty; his audience and the white forerunners of his genre had stoneset the conditions of his craft, placing restraining parameters on the substance and style of his work and on whatever popularity he accrued:

> When black writers tried to use dialect to reproduce sounds characteristic of our people, they were told that the only emotions dialect could convey were humor and pathos. We can either laugh at you or be maudlin over you. Our early writers accepted this two-valued orientation, apparently not realizing that this judgement on the possible uses of dialect had nothing to do with dialect, but rather with the only two feelings the arbiters of culture were willing either to show toward us themselves or to allow us to show.[9]

In addition to limiting the black writer's use of dialect to humor and sympathy, there were societal anxieties about the current status of blacks that had to be addressed indirectly. The black writer was obligated to be entertaining, to assure readers that although blacks had changed since the emancipation, they were still basically a "kind," "helpless," "lazy" lot with no thoughts of malice or, better still, retribution for past foul deeds. It is with these broader requirements that Dunbar launched his artistic career.

Dunbar wrote primarily for a white audience; consequently, satisfying an audience looking only for types necessitated compromise(s) and a willingness to withstand economic obstacles:

> There were, of course, practical problems which reinforced the exercise of such a sensibility; the expectations of a white audience who largely provided the cash (although Dunbar's celebrations of the simple delights of black life were enjoyed by a rather sizable black audience) and the expectations of publishers of magazines and books.[10]

In spite of the fact that Dunbar's books were read by a certain number of blacks, the vast majority could not "afford to spend a dollar for his book."[11] Even more pertinent to consider is the basic fact that Dunbar did not have the opportunity to submit work to black editors and publishers:

> During much of this time, middle-class black communities of some size and importance existed in only a few centers, such as Atlanta, Georgia, and Washington, D.C., and the audience for books by black authors was small indeed. There were no black owned trade-book publishing firms, and those books that black authors produced had to be acceptable to white publishers, few of whom were known for their sympathy for black people. Dunbar, though born and brought up in Ohio, deliberately chose to write in dialect partly because stories about black people were more readily accepted by both publishers and readers.[12]

In Dunbar's earliest work he clearly separated the two idioms, the "Oak" from the "Ivy," the standard verse from the dialect. Predictably, as Addison Gayle contends, Dunbar's intentions went overlooked; his niche in literature was achieved solely on the merit of his dialect pieces:

> Only later in life was he to learn that within this title he had planted the seeds of a truer metaphor; that of the ivy engulfing the oak, strangling the life out of it, so that in time what was first ornament replaced the dominant element, and was admired as if it had always been the more important of the two.[13]

Over the years an assumption about Dunbar's intent has outweighed the truth, the assumption that he relished his role as a dialect poet. Contrary to this assumption, Dunbar was conscious of his audience's preferences and expressed his dissatisfaction with these limitations more than once:

> You know of course that I didn't start as a dialect poet. I simply came to the conclusion that I could write it as well, if not better than anybody I knew of, and that by doing so I should gain a hearing, and now they don't want me to write anything but dialect.[14]

Evidently it was not important to readers or publishers that Dunbar's second book, *Majors and Minors* (1895), clearly demonstrated his desire to write most of his poetry in standard; of seventy-four poems, only twenty-six were in dialect: the title (again) reinforcing the intentional division of the two forms.[15] In contrast, Dunbar's biographers and critics have verified his desire to read his dialect poetry at every occasion, as if he had to make a choice, and that this decision, sadly, compromised his integrity. (Few, if any, of the analyses have speculated on the practical considerations inherent in a "live" performance.[16]) Notwithstanding the compromise, Dunbar was a skillful orator, one who was very adept at "delighting an audience,"[17] even when the work he cherished most, his standard poetry, received "condescending recognition."[18]

Lyrics of Lowly Life (1896), Dunbar's third work, is the book that catapults him from regionally recognized versifier into the role of nationally known poet. No less than America's prime literary mover of the day—William Dean Howells—wrote the introduction, giving Dunbar his largest "hearing." Howells' introduction is an entity unto itself, analyzed in retrospect it tells us much about the patronage system in general, so prevalent in Dunbar's age, and serves as a specific example of how white critics—both friend and foe alike-have been consistently ambivalent whenever the work of a black writer, or black writers, is placed "under a microscope."

First of all, with contradictory objectivism, Howells says he judges works of art regardless of the writer's background, race, etc., and then proceeds to delineate facts irrevocably tied to class and race, i.e., that Dunbar's parents had been slaves. Secondly, he does cursory damage to Dunbar's standard pieces by suggesting that they are comparable to the work "of most young poets." Third, he obliterates the existence of other black writers prior to Dunbar by uttering the following:

> So far as I could remember, Paul Dunbar was the only man of pure African blood and of American civilization to feel the Negro life aesthetically and express it lyrically.[19]

In this one sentence one can see the beginning of what eventuated in a trend—singling out one black writer for praise while simultaneously obfuscating the talent and life-work of others existing before (and sometimes after) the "chosen" artist. On the one hand, Howells is showering Dunbar with a complimentary remark; on the other hand, he tries to escape reaction, as if anticipating it, by saying at the outset, "So far as I could remember." By implication Howells is suggesting that if he cannot recall these writers, then they must not have been too significant. As a matter of fact, there were many black writers in print, and known, before Dunbar: Gustavas Vassa, Lucy Terry, Jupiter Hammon, Phyllis Wheatley, William Wells Brown, George M. Horton, Francis Harper, and the eminent Frederick Douglass. There were also many dialect writers in print prior to Dunbar, writers such as James Campbell, James Corrothers, Eliot Henderson, Daniel Davis, and J. Allen. But the most startling omission made by Howells is his failure to at least allude to Charles Chesnutt—a black writer he was definitely familiar with. Again he circumvents the mention of Chesnutt—a very light-skinned black man—by referring to Dunbar as "the only man of pure African blood."

The most telling comment that Howells makes is the slanderous description of Dunbar's dialect poetry. In this instance he undercuts and dismisses all previous compliments and performs a reduction through innuendo:

> We call such pieces dialect pieces for want of some closer phrase, but they are really not dialect so much as delightful personal attempts and failures for the written and spoken language.[20]

Howells' phrase, "for want of some closer phrase," is actually a euphemistic signal for the audience he is addressing. He then follows up the signal with explicit language. Dunbar's dialect pieces are "delightful" because they are "attempts and failures" representative of the general "errors" blacks make when using the written and spoken English language. There is no mistaking Howells' true intentions, for as Gayle contends, he goes on to "equate the souls of black people with dialect language."[21]

> In nothing is his essentially refined and delicate art so well shown as in these pieces, which as I ventured to say, described the range between appetite and emotion . . . which is the range of the race. He reveals in these a finely ironical perception of the Negro's limitations.[22]

One wonders how Dunbar coped with what had to be his extremely ambivalent reaction; how could he respond to such "beneficent" gamesmanship —

praising him, gaining him the hearing he desired, while in the same breath maligning his people and putting him into a traditional role: that of the "darky" entertainer? Dunbar knew that after Howells' critique it would be an uphill struggle to escape categorization, to garner a respect and appreciation for his standard verse equal to the curious praise extended his dialect work. For the most part, Dunbar's immediate reply to Howells was lukewarm, with the exception of one comment: "My greatest fear is that you may have been more kind to me than just." In this brief passage Dunbar indicates that he, too, had mastered the code of implications so much a part of the world inhabited by men of letters. He is thankful that a critic as highly regarded as Howells has praised his work, hence extending him an entry "pass" into the mainstream. Conversely, he lets Howells know that some of what he said was unfair. Dunbar was aware that all ports of entry to the world of success levy fees; it is the "price" he contemplates anxiously in the phrase, "my greatest fear." For Dunbar's eventual fame was without precedent, in that no other black poet before him had been given a national "stamp of approval." Certainly he was conscious of this fact.

It is more than coincidental that *Lyrics of Lowly Life* was the first of Dunbar's poetry collections without separate headings for standard and dialect. The line he wanted drawn had been obliterated. The game had begun and Dunbar had decided to play. He would have other opportunities throughout his career to voice his disdain for categorization; not once did he express his misgivings publicly.

It is hard, even today, to question Dunbar's motivation to remain silent, allowing editors, critics, and readers a free reign interpreting his work. His decision, when considered in today's light, was perhaps as valid as the contrasting moves made by his contemporaries, Charles Chesnutt (1858–1932) and Sutton Griggs (1872–1930). Kenny Williams provides an illuminating consideration and context:

> In the careers as novelists of Griggs, Chesnutt, and Dunbar is one of the best commentaries upon the American publishing scene at the turn of the century. Opting for a wide audience, Dunbar attempted to offer what that audience wanted to read. Griggs had a message, created his own audience, and provided his own publishing company to spread his word. Chesnutt refused to yield to popular pressure and insisted that his readers accept his unadorned portrait of race relations in this country. While he was perhaps better known among his people than either Dunbar or Chesnutt at the time, Griggs has become a literary statistic. Chesnutt ceased to use the novel as a means of

> expression when he ran into difficulty with his publisher. Only Dunbar survived the dilemma faced by the Negro author in the America of his day.[23]

Certainly all three writers—Chesnutt, Dunbar, and Griggs—were subject to multifaceted pressures, contradictory societal crosscurrents from without, and dual pangs of consciousness affecting them internally. One can only surmise that Dunbar needed an audience and desired a place in the national literature moreso than his fellow writers.

Principal among the external forces affecting black life when *Lyrics* made its debut were the consistent racist efforts in the South to disenfranchise Afro-Americans, rendering them politically impotent.[24] At the same time, the Supreme Court upheld segregation in the *Plessy v. Ferguson* decision, thus institutionalizing the separation of the races and solidifying the existence of two distinct (but sporadically conflicting) worlds—one black, one white—for fifty-seven years.[25] Significantly, 1896 was also the year the "first scientific historical monograph" by a black man was printed.[26]

The Suppression of the African Slave Trade, 1638–1870 was the first work in the Harvard Historical Studies Series. The writer of this work—W. E. B. Du Bois—would eventually activate the consciousness of black folk as never before. Seven years later, in his *Souls of Black Folk* (1903), Du Bois would pen a prophetic passage that not only addressed itself to America's treatment of black people, but also the ambivalent forces that eventuated psychologically within Afro-Americans as a result of this treatment.

In his description of "double-consciousness" Du Bois accurately delineated the inner struggle of all Afro-Americans; ironically this same passage can be read—explicitly—as a definitive understanding of Dunbar's work and the dichotomy so very characteristic of that work:

> One ever feels his two-ness—an American, a Negro; two souls, two thoughts, two unreconciled strivings; two warring ideals in one dark body, whose dogged strength alone keeps it from being torn asunder.[27]

Dunbar's dualism is manifested in a variety of ways: his dialect poetry and his standard verse being merely the initial example. A second dichotomy representative of Dunbar's creative efforts is the "success" of his poetry versus the "failure" of his novels.

Dunbar's critics are nearly unanimous in their assertion that his poetry, and specifically his dialect poetry, was his best work. His novels, on the other hand, reflect a kind of chaotic escapism, an idealistic, sentimental-journey-gone mind-set that is within the confines of double consciousness, but nevertheless indicative of a public–personal confusion.[28] One senses that Dunbar's novels were attempts to cater to an audience desirous of (and only willing to accept) the black stereotypes by now entrenched in the national psyche. Indeed, the reception of his first novel, *The Uncalled* (1898), seemed to drive home the point:

> *The Uncalled* was published in the same year as a collection of short fiction, *Folks from Dixie*. Most of the stories dealt with stereotypes; yet, *Folks from Dixie* received praise, whereas *The Uncalled* received disparagement. That Dunbar, a black man, could masquerade as a white youth, struck his audience as insincere, and they quickly showed their preference for the old image by pratting about the collection of short stories far in excess of its artistic merit.[29]

Dunbar had written most of *The Uncalled* the previous year while in England "as a public entertainer."[30] In practical terms this sojourn had provided Dunbar with a trying experience:

> His manager soon deserted him. At the very moment when Dunbar's recitals were about to bring him a few of the dollars of which he stood so surely in need, his erstwhile "manager" returned and showing a contract of which she had never consented to give the poet a copy—claimed all the proceeds! Thus he was left penniless in a strange land.[31]

(Moreover, Dunbar's manager was none other than the daughter of his first manager, Major Pond; it is apparent that the "games" played with black artists are perpetual.)

The Uncalled, a romantic tale of a preacher named Freddie Brent, was in actuality a thinly disguised delineation of Dunbar's rejection of a career in the ministry. In addition, this book exposed a facet of Dunbar's thinking that had not surfaced publicly before. It revealed Dunbar's idealistic desire to escape categorization by transcending race and its obvious attribute—black language—in one motion. In truth Dunbar had to know, at least intuitively, that his age and his audience would never allow a black writer such flexibility; what *The Uncalled* documents is Dunbar's ambivalent, torn, consciousness, his inner–outer struggle epitomized by the Du Bois phrase, "two warring ideals in one dark body." So it is that one can perceive *The Uncalled* and

Dunbar's other three novels as therapeutic exercise, symbolic leaps to freedom beyond rigid, but inescapable, limitations imposed from within and without:

> The truth, I believe, is that he lacked literary models from his own contemporaries and forerunners. In addition, he lacked literary tradition dedicated to validating the dignity and worth of the Afro-American. For a writer as sensitive as Dunbar, one so wracked by spiritual turmoil, such a lack produced, I believe, a schizophrenia, causing him to question whether he would see himself as black man as represented in the fiction of the Plantation School or as "the American Man" in general—he who had built the great cathedrals and railroads, created the enduring literature, and established the "official" institutions.[32]

Ultimately, Dunbar's novels evidence a writer in the throes of an identity crisis, a crisis which can (in part) be attributed to the times in which he lived:

> In Dunbar's time, however, black was not fashionable. The burden still rested upon the Negro to prove he could do what any other man could do, and in America that meant to use the white man's technique and meet the white man's standard of excellence. It was to this task that Dunbar addressed himself.[33]

Indeed, it was not only the times that contributed to Dunbar's ambivalence and, consequently, to his failure with the novel form; his perception of self—in this instance not a dualism but a triad—is both pertinent and necessary to the critique:

> Dunbar's conception of his art was based on his theory of life. He felt that he was first of all a man, then an American, and incidentally a Negro. To a world that looked upon him primarily as a Negro, he was thus a little difficult to understand. His position was debatable, of course, but that was the way he felt.[34]

Ironically Dunbar's novels follow this "theory" almost in order. *The Uncalled* is a book about a man—any man—rejecting the parochialism of a small town and criticizing the current religious obsession to relegate all sinners to hell without qualification—a real world conflict Dunbar felt would be perceived, and accepted, as universal; *Love of Landry* (1900) represents his American side metaphorically "going West," full of the sentiment and romanticism one usually associates with frontier fiction; *The Fanatics* (1901), set before and during the Civil War, is Dunbar's surrender to someone else's nostalgia. In this case Dunbar's "Negroness" is represented by a black type named "Nigger Ed." *The Sport of the Gods* (1902), Dunbar's last and best novel, finishes the sequence in that he returns exclusively to primary black characters. Yet, there is a progressive twist: he explores the impact of an urban-Northern environment on a rural-Southern black family during one of the largest migrational periods for blacks. This same exploration would eventually be put forth in naturalistic detail by Richard Wright and Ralph Ellison."[35]

Again one must turn to the Du Bois passage when appraising Dunbar's novels. The first three works constitute "unreconciled strivings" when compared to Dunbar's poetry, a genre he had worked with (and through) since adolescence. It is also rather obvious that Dunbar was quite prolific, producing a novel a year for four successive years—a phenomenal accomplishment when one considers the fact that he was very ill from 1898 until his death. Nevertheless, all but *The Sport of the Gods* lack the strength and power of a singular artistic intent. Without the benefit of a clear-cut controlling purpose, the artist (in general) is frequently haphazard or experimental; in Dunbar's case the former seems to be an adequate assessment. He was truly a man pulled in too many directions, too quickly, attempting to satisfy the whims of too many readers, as his biographers would submit. One of those biographers in particular deserves special consideration, dictating a departure from the chronology already established.

The Life and Works of Paul Laurence Dunbar by Lida Keck Wiggins not only tells us a great deal about Dunbar, but also (in much the same manner as the "celebrated" Howells introduction) illustrates the strange, masked forces characterized as "very liberal" in Dunbar's age. Surprisingly, none of Dunbar's critics or later biographers have passed judgement on this first biography. It would appear that *The Life and Works* has been spared criticism for merely existing, i.e., serving future scholars as a valuable, early resource.

As the first Dunbar biography, Mrs. Wiggins' book is definitely significant—but for all the wrong reasons. Here is a writer who knew Dunbar personally; a writer considered to be a friend; a writer who talked to Dunbar's mother, visited his home, and got her work into print (including much of Dunbar's) the year after his death (1907). The memory of the man, his creations, were still fresh in readers' minds. This was a timely opportunity to document Dunbar's trials, his happiness, his repeated attempts to escape categorization. Instead, we are given a great deal of information couched in rhetoric so condescending, so strange, that the reading experience is nauseating. There is page after page of reference to

Dunbar's health, perhaps owing much to the condition of Dunbar when he and Mrs. Wiggins met. Unfortunately, she gives us less than the "whole" we have come to expect from biographies.

Even more noteworthy are Mrs. Wiggins' repeated allusions to Dunbar as "the boy," or "the boy poet," or "Dunbar in his childlike way," or the incessant "poor Paul." (Keep in mind that Dunbar's first work was published when he was twenty-one—after his manhood was no longer a matter of dispute, and certainly before he had met Mrs. Wiggins.) Just as peculiar are the too frequent passages concentrating on Dunbar's benefactors, telling the reader (implicitly) that they are just as important as her subject. It is such a deliberately heavy-handed inclusion in her work that it diminishes her chronicle, almost consciously intruding at any given moment. Most curious of all are the few statements she makes about black folk; note the following comments, examples of "benevolent" racism:

> By this act [writing his first novel], he exhibited that desire to be provident which is so frequently lacking in members of his race. (p. 69)
>
> It is impossible for some of the race to realize the fact that there are exceptions to the rule. (p. 81)

The latter comment, made in reference to a black bus driver (whom Mrs. Wiggins calls a porter), is a tale within a tale.

The Wiggins' version of this incident differs drastically from the event covered by Dunbar's second biographer, Benjamin Brawley, and a more contemporary biography by Gayle. Compare these versions, beginning with the lead-in to the preceding quote (omitted intentionally):

> The negro [sic] porter is only a type. Having been held so long in the bonds of slavery, and having been taught from the cradle that the black man is the white brother's intellectual inferior . . . it is impossible. (p. 82)

(The next quoted passage reports a second encounter with a black waiter; Mrs. Wiggins' heated reaction follows, and afterwards, the Gayle chronicle of the same series.)

> He would not have dared say such words to a white person, regardless of his mental calibre, but here was one of the greatest geniuses that the world has known, insulted because of his color, by one of his own race! Blind, narrow, prejudiced humanity![36]

> The bus driver, a native of the city, was familiar with the town's customs. Repeatedly, he questioned the poet as to the nature of his business at the Kenmore. Once at the hotel, Dunbar became aware of the reasons for the driver's insistent questions. "Hold on! What are you going to do?" Dunbar remained calm. "To register, of course," he replied. "You can't register here," said the clerk. "We have no rooms for you in this hotel." However, rooms had been reserved in the name of Paul Laurence Dunbar. Having verified this astonishing fact, the clerk's rage became greater, and he scowled at the poet, gestured obscenely, and finally summoned the manager [who] said, "This Negro is crazy. Telephone to the police station and let them come up and get him."[37]

What Mrs. Wiggins had done with her version of the incident may seem very silly on the surface but, in retrospect, looms very important. She was an active participant in what is now a familiar, well-documented dissonance—an act of omission consciously designed to wipe out the existence of racism, obscuring a clear knowledge of the facts, and eventually obfuscating our present-day understanding of those facts in historical progression. Moreover, achieved just as intentionally, she accuses the black men of prejudice while simultaneously deleting the reactions of the hotel clerk and manager—both white males.

There are many other disparaging remarks that are necessary to this discourse. Peruse the statements that follow on a variety of subjects:

> [On Dunbar's mother]:
> Everyone wanted to meet the "little black Mammy" of the poet. (p. 60)
>
> [On Folks *from Dixie*]:
> No one can read these beautiful southern stories without realizing the sense of justice to each race which Mr. Dunbar inculcates. There are no bitter tirades against the masters; no exaggerated pen pictures of downtrodden negroes [sic]: he simply tells the truth. (p. 78)
>
> [On one of Dunbar's benefactors]:
> Later in that same good year of 1896 Paul Dunbar met a friend who was destined to be one of the stars of hope in his literary sky. (p. 55)

Of the three preceding quotes, only the interpretation of *Folks from Dixie* deserves comment. Apparently, Mrs. Wiggins had the same reaction to this book as Dunbar's mass audience, an audience who, as Gayle says, "pratted about the collection . . . far in excess of its artistic merit."

In general it is the overall tone of Mrs. Wiggins' biography that is most disturbing; it emphasizes the banality of forces both liberal and conservative operating manipulatively in Dunbar's time. Secondly, there are numerous events of an historical nature systematically deleted from her account, information pertinent to an understanding of Dunbar within a context that subsequent biographers like Brawley saw fit to include:

> As has been said, he lived at a time when his people were passing through one of the most crucial periods in their history in America . . . the terrible events of which he read daily—the burning of the home, and the death of a Negro postmaster in South Carolina; the election troubles in that state and Wilmington, N.C., in 1898; a gruesome lynching in Georgia, and a riot in New York tended to harden him."[38]

Conversely, even the condescending Mrs. Wiggins, and all future critics, biographers, scholars, et al., are in unanimous agreement on one matter: that a variety of editors and publishers were exclusively committed to printing Dunbar's dialect pieces, hence setting the terms of his career as he lived it and providing us a knowledge of the man that, until very recently, was less than complete—inadequate and imbalanced. It is no wonder that by 1904 Dunbar expressed the following resignation on the matter in a conversation with then associate Linda Wiggins:

> I am so tired, so tired of dialect. I sent out graceful little poems, suited for any of the magazines, but they are returned to me by editors who say, "We would be very glad to have a dialect poem, Mr. Dunbar, but we do not care for the language compositions."[39]

Turning to Brawley's *Poet of His People* (1936) we find Dunbar reiterating the same opinion to an interviewer at the Waldorf Astoria in 1898:

> I hope you are not one of those who would hold the Negro down to a certain kind of poetry—dialect and concerning only scenes of plantations in the South?[40]

Still later, the Gayle biography (1971) demonstrates Dunbar's disappointment with the literary establishment's resolution to limit his range—specifically William Dean Howells' introduction that led to that particular choice:

> "One critic," he wrote to a friend, "says a thing and the rest hasten to say the thing, in many cases using the identical words. I see now very clearly that Mr. Howells has done me irrevocable harm in the dictum he laid down regarding my dialect verse."[41]

Dunbar's choice of words is deliberate—particularly the words "irrevocable" and "dictum" indicate his awareness that dialect would be the primary and single expression allowed him during (and after) his career by mainstream critics; critics merely representative of the larger society, a society which, in the absence of a return to the real, physical enslavement of black folk, would settle for the symbolic recreation of that slavery by way of "quadrotypes." Further, there is reason to believe that these editors and publishers—individually or indirectly as a community—resisted accepting any of Dunbar's work that went against the broad national design initially promulgated by the Southern propagandists.

Work of Dunbar's that was courageous for its time, unmistakably black in point of view, work that would have had a decisive impact on how Dunbar was viewed in his time and, without a doubt, how most of us viewed him today, has until recently been denied us. Had it not been for the timely scholarship of Jay Martin and Gossie Hudson, an entire chapter of Dunbar's career—in nonfictional prose—would have gone, as it has for nearly seventy years, unnoticed. It is largely as a result of *The Paul Laurence Dunbar Reader*"[42] that yet another aspect of Dunbar's "twoness" comes to the surface—his black consciousness:

> Yet, though he was also the author of numerous essays, he is not now nearly so well known for these; his work as a journalist has been almost entirely neglected by historians and readers. The reasons for this neglect are clear. In the first place, much of his journalism was written for black papers. More important, wherever his essays appeared, they were all written from a black point of view.[43]

Dunbar's initial venture into journalism began when he was in high school, editing *Tattler*, a "newspaper established specifically to represent the black population of Ohio."[44] The most striking statement in one of his earlier editorials is his advocacy of activism instead of the empty rhetoric employed by spokespersons when addressing the topic of race:

> We do not counsel you, debaters, writers, and fellow editors, to throw away your opinions on this all important question [race]: on the contrary we deem it one worthy of constant thought. But the time has come when you should act your opinions out, rather than write them.[45]

The very next year, 1891, after he had graduated from high school, Dunbar applied for any number of white-collar jobs—including work with newspapers—only to be turned down in certain terms:

> Was there anything he could do, in an office, on a newspaper—anything of a clerical nature? No. There was no one who wanted a Negro youth in such capacity.[46]
>
> He tried factories, warehouses, and even newspapers, many of which had published his poems while he was still a student at Central High School (where he was editor of the school newspaper, The High School Times, president of his graduating class, and graduated with honors. He asked for positions such as clerk, accountant, or receptionist. At each place, the employer or a representative gave him the same answer, implied if not always spoken, "We have no jobs of this kind for Negroes."[47]

A number of years later, about the same time that his artistic career had taken shape, Dunbar assumed an editorial position with another black newspaper, the *Indianapolis World* (Martin, 1975). He continued to write articles, though his tenure at the *World* expired when the paper folded a few months later; by 1898 he was getting requests for essays by mainstream magazine editors. Yet, these invitations were substantively outnumbered by requests for his dialect poetry; for instance, the article titled "Recession Never," was published in the Chicago *Record*—after it had been rejected:

> "Recession Never" . . . was dispatched by Dunbar to a number of papers in response to the outbreak of lynchings and race riots in the fall of 1898, *after McClure's magazine, which had originally commissioned the article*, apparently *found it too strong to publish*.[48] (Emphasis added.)

Given the popularity of retrogressionist beliefs, the national mood concerning blacks, it is easy to concur with Martin's reasoning on McClure's.

In this article Dunbar's identification with black folk is blatantly obvious: his protest against the wanton violence directed against black people is specific and direct. Furthermore, "Recession Never" demonstrates an encompassing understanding of racism progressive for its time, in that he perceived the ill-treatment of black folk as a national malaise:

> It would be true in this instance, also, if it were not that what has happened in Georgia has happened in Ohio and Illinois. The race riots in North Carolina were of a piece with the same proceedings in the state of Lincoln. The men who shoot the Negro in Hogansville are blood brothers to those who hang him in Urbana, and the deed is neither better or worse because it happens in one section of the country or the other. The race spirit in the United States is not local but general.[49]

Going further, Dunbar attacks the very forces which placed constraints on his literary career, ironically commenting on what he himself was accused of doing, i.e., perpetuating stereotypes:

> For so long a time the black man believed that he is an American citizen that he will not be easily convinced to the contrary. It will take more than the hangings, the burnings, and the lynchings, both North and South, to prove it to his satisfaction. He is not credulous as he was. He is a different man. The American people cannot turn back the tide of years and make him what he was. And so it was an entirely new people with whom they have to deal. It is an entirely new problem which is presented to them for solution. Why then should it not be met with calmness, justice, breadth and manliness which should characterize a great nation?[50]

It is extremely doubtful that Dunbar's audience would have accepted such a "black" point of view from a writer they assumed would limit himself to entertaining them. The subject itself—lynching—was very controversial, owing much to the rhetoric of one of Dunbar's so-called forerunners, Thomas Nelson Page. On this matter Dunbar and Page are in direct opposition:

> This is borne out by the increase of crime among them, by the increase of superstition, with its black trail of unnamable immorality and vice; by the homicides and murders, and by the

> outbreak and growth of that brutal crime which has chiefly brought about the frightful crime of lynching which stains the good name of the South and has spread northward with the spread of the ravisher. The crime of rape . . . is the fatal product of new conditions. The Negro's passion, always his controlling force, is now, since the new teaching, for the white woman. Lynching is justifiable.[51]

It would be easy to consider Page as merely a "regional" writer with long-standing regional biases, contending logically that his opinions did not affect, or represent, a national constituency. This is just not the case. Page was a very popular writer, primarily responsible (along with his regional contemporaries) for propagandizing retrogressionist beliefs through the nation. As Rayford Logan has documented, "most of the books and volumes of poetry about the Negro that Northerners read were by Southerners."[52] In fact, Dunbar's counter-position can be seen as radical, and certainly nationalistic. Moreover, Dunbar's nonfiction shows he had carefully assessed the situations affecting his community and expressed, in practical resolution of those situations:

> He showed that he had fully absorbed a black point of view. The development of black enterprise, the molding of an ethnic political opinion, the creation of a distinctive black cultural and artistic mode, the need for vehicles of communication in the community, the development of black pride, the involvement of all black institutions in one organ, the creation of black consciousness and the development of self-esteem in individuals, a call for social agitation, and attacks upon white denigrations of the black community—these themes are all rapidly but unmistakably adumbrated in the observations with which Dunbar began his paper.[53]

So it is that "Recession Never" and another article published in *The New York Times* in 1903 stand as testimonials of Dunbar's efforts to "assert and defend the nobility of his people."[54]

By far Dunbar's best article, the essay written about the celebration of Independence Day, illustrates his power to employ prose as a symbolic and ironic weapon in the black struggle for equality. There is also a degree of cynicism, a clearly pessimistic outlook, contained in the piece, not characteristic (or even comparable) to Dunbar's usually optimistic poetry:

> The papers are full of the reports of peonage in Alabama. A new and more dastardly slavery there has arisen to replace the old. For the sake of re-enslaving the Negro, the Constitution has been trampled under feet, the rights of man have been laughed out of court, and the justice of God has been made a jest, and we celebrate. Every wire, no longer in the South alone, brings us news of a new hanging or a new burning, some recent outrage against a helpless people, some fresh degradation of an already degraded race."[55]

The ideas expressed in this article, the last one Dunbar would write, are comparable to the ideas of his contemporary activist counterparts—Du Bois, Douglass, Monroe Trotter, and Martin Delaney. His opinions place him within the context of a collective militancy and in opposition to the accommodationist notions of the "chosen" black spokesman, Booker T. Washington. And yet, and this is significant, since Dunbar's nonfictional prose has remained literally obscure, he has never been situated within this broader, more aggressive, frame.

The Independence Day letter continues in much the same manner—aggressive, assertive, and forceful. In the passages that follow, Dunbar extends his perceptions to areas even more controversial than lynching—racism in the workplace, where the immigrant received favorable treatment and where the black American was regarded as an alien, or stranger:

> Like a dark cloud, pregnant with terror and destruction, disenfranchisement has spread its wings over our brethren of the South. Like the same dark cloud, industrial prejudice glooms above us in the North. We may not work save when the new come foreigner refuses to, and then they, high prized above our sacrificial lives, may shoot us down with impunity. And yet we celebrate.[56]

When considered with "Recession Never," this article reveals an unfamiliar Dunbar, a Dunbar propelled by a singular, sincere commitment to his people, a Dunbar history has denied us. Indeed, an argument can now be made that views Dunbar's journalism as the counterpoint to his career as an imaginative writer, in conflict with some of the "types" critics have accused him of perpetuating. Certainly Dunbar's nonfictional prose is yet another manifestation of his dualism, the "twoness" so definitively articulated by Du Bois. In the case of the "Independence Day" letters, the conflict was moot; Dunbar was verbalizing the ideas of a black writer connected to a larger, national black community, willing to defend that community. In this one instance Paul Laurence Dunbar was a writer clearly conscious of his identity and purpose.

The Institutionalization of Dunbar: Career as Example, Precedent, and Device

George Kent, in an essay titled "Patterns of the Harlem Renaissance," said that Dunbar was a "precursor" to the Harlem Awakening. He also said that Dunbar's works represented an attitude which could be rebelled against by the Harlem writers. Both statements are extremely accurate. But additionally Dunbar's work not only anticipates the Harlem Awakening; his very career, the changes he endured as man, and as writer, tell us much about the black writer in general—struggling to create a viable, vibrant literary tradition while at the same time being forced to rewrite history. Dunbar's success and/or failure depends ultimately on what the reader deems of utmost importance. When one considers the latter obligation, it is possible to conclude that Dunbar's reputation has suffered because he failed to make needed corrections in the historical record. Nevertheless, much can be gained by reexamining the matters affecting the writer that were tangential in Dunbar's day. It is these tangential matters that pose a series of threshold questions begging an answer from contemporary Afro-American scholars.

Dunbar's journalism went overlooked for so long because a reexamination of his ideas—in their totality—would have subsequently impacted his reputation, eventually affecting the employment of his works, the safe ones, in public and private educational institutions. Dunbar is only a safe writer as long as his role as a dialect poet remains perpetually intact; any of his works that contradict the prefixed mold would have to be examined and discussed, resulting in dialogues on lynchings, racism, and other (still controversial) historical topics the public elementary and secondary schools have artfully avoided for decades. Further, previous scholars scrutinized only what was provided for their analyses. Since their professors (in the main) were unaware of Dunbar's nonfictional prose, it follows that their scholarship rests almost exclusively on the premise that Dunbar was "merely" a dialect poet. Generation upon generation of students have been entertained by Dunbar without ever considering the possibility that there was a serious, analytical character to some of his writing.

More importantly, the tangential matters affecting Dunbar's work—categorization (being viewed solely as a dialect poet); criticism (malignant and lionizing in the same breath); individualized isolation (allowing Dunbar fame and success while denying Chesnutt comparable notoriety); and polemical gamesmanship (choosing aspects of Dunbar's work to generalize about the attitudes and behavior of the black masses)—would also affect the work of each successive generation of black writers in the twentieth century.

NOTES

1. Paul Laurence Dunbar's poem, "The Master Player," inspired the title. Moreover, in street vernacular a "master player" is a person who plays the game of life—win or lose—with enthusiasm and specialized knowledge. Dunbar was both vigorous and creative; he just did not realize that as far as black writers are concerned, the game was (and is) fixed.
2. Herbert Gutman, *The Black Family in Slavery and Freedom: 1750–1925* (New York: Vintage Books, 1976), p. 538.
3. Sterling Brown, "The Negro Character as Seen by White Authors," in *Dark Symphony*, ed. James Emmanuel and Theodore Gross (New York: The Free Press, 1968), pp. 139–71.
4. Middleton Harris, *The Black Book* (New York: Random House, 1974), pp. 42–47.
5. Donald Bogle, *Toms, Coons, Mulattoes, Mammies, and Bucks* (New York: Bantam Books, 1973), pp. 7–8.
6. William H. Robinson, *Early Black American Poets* (Dubuque, Iowa: William C. Brown Co., 1969), pp. 22–30.
7. Larzer Ziff, *The American 1890s: Life and Times of a Lost Generation* (New York: The Viking Press, 1966).
8. John Hope Franklin, *From Slavery to Freedom* (New York: Alfred A. Knopf, 1947), p. 43.
9. Adam David Miller, "Some Observations on a Black Aesthetic," in *The Black Aesthetic*, ed. Addison Gayle (New York: Doubleday and Co., Inc., 1971), p. 400.
10. George Kent, "Patterns of the Harlem Renaissance," in *The Harlem Renaissance Remembered*, ed. Arna Bontemps (New York, Dodd, Mead and Co., 1972), pp. 27–28.
11. Addison Gayle, *Oak and Ivy* (New York: Doubleday and Co., 1971), p. 52.
12. Hoyt Fuller, "The New Black Literature: Protest or Affirmation," in *The Black Aesthetic*, ed. Addison Gayle (New York: Doubleday and Co., 1971), p. 353.
13. Gayle, *Oak and Ivy*, p. 31.
14. Ibid., p. 38.

15. See Paul Laurence Dunbar, *Majors and Minors* (Toledo: Hadley Hadley, 1895).
16. Most poets, myself included, make a distinction between works they consider effective in print versus those pieces that gain a greater strength and vitality when read aloud. It is a well-known fact, to laymen and scholars alike, that poetry on the page takes on additional dimensions because readers have the time to pause, reflect, and re-read—a luxury not provided by an oral presentation. Moreover, and this is just as important, an audience that has ventured away from home and paid money to hear "Art" is predisposed to the notion of being entertained, a notion most artists feel uneasy about, though obligated to "perform."
17. Linda Keck Wiggins, *The Life and Works of Paul Laurence Dunbar* (Naperville, Illinois: J. L. Nichols and Co., 1906 (?)), p. 64.
18. Gayle, *Oak and Ivy*, p. 43.
19. William Dean Howells, introd., *Lyrics of Lowly Life*, by Paul Laurence Dunbar (New York: Dodd, Mead and Co., 1896), p. xvi.
20. Howells, Introd., *Lyrics of Lowly Life*, p. xviii.
21. Gayle, *Oak and Ivy*, p. 79.
22. Howells, Introd., *Lyrics of Lowly Life*, p. xviii.
23. Kenny Williams, "The Masking of a Novelist," in A *Singer in the Dawn*, ed. Jay Martin (New York: Dodd, Mead and Co., 1975), pp. 157–58.
24. See Rayford Logan, *The Betrayal of the Negro* (New York: Collier Books, 1965).
25. Franklin, *From Slavery to Freedom*, p. 342.
26. Ibid., p. 410.
27. W. E. B. Du Bois, *The Souls of Black Folk* (New York: New American Library, 1969), p. 45.
28. The successful black artist—that is, successful in the "mainstream"—lives in a rarefied atmosphere. Consequently, he sometimes confuses his own existence with that of the black masses: a totally different reality. Dunbar's case—his acceptance, that is—was unprecedented, and as a result, he had no way of knowing what would be acceptable to his audience. The reception of *The Uncalled*, his first novel, demonstrated how black writers are categorized and limited; they are attacked for being parochial when they deal exclusively with black characters, or deemed insincere, or even worse, inaccurate, when they depict white characters.
29. Addison Gayle, "Literature as Catharsis," in *A Singer in the Dawn*, ed. Jay Martin (New York: Dodd, Mead & Co., 1975), p. 144.
30. Wiggins, *The Life and Works of Paul Laurence Dunbar*, p. 67.
31. *Ibid.*, pp. 67–68.
32. Gayle, in *A Singer in the Dawn*, p. 141.

33. Benjamin Brawley, *Paul Laurence Dunbar. Poet of His People* (Chapel Hill: Univ. of North Carolina Press, 1936), p. 77.
34. Ibid., p. 76.
35. See Ralph Ellison's "King of the Bingo Game" or Richard Wright's *Eight Men*.
36. Wiggins, *The Life and Works of Paul Laurence Dunbar*, p. 83.
37. Gayle, *Oak and Ivy*, p. 89.
38. Brawley, *Paul Laurence Dunbar: Poet of His People*, p. 85.
39. Wiggins, *The Life and Works of Paul Laurence Dunbar*, p. 109.
40. Brawley, *Paul Laurence Dunbar: Poet of His People*, p. 77.
41. Wiggins, *The Life and Works of Paul Laurence Dunbar*, p. 109.
42. Jay Martin and Gossie Hudson, *The Paul Laurence Dunbar Reader* (New York: Dodd, Mead and Co., 1975).
43. Ibid., p. 31.
44. Ibid.
45. Ibid., p. 32.
46. Brawley, *Paul Laurence Dunbar: Poet of His People*, p. 18.
47. Gayle, *Oak and Ivy*, p. 17.
48. Martin and Hudson, *The Paul Laurence Dunbar Reader*, p. 32.
49. Ibid., p. 36.
50. Ibid., p. 39.
51. Gutman, *The Black Family in Slavery and Freedom: 1750–1925*, p. 141.
52. Rayford Logan, *The Betrayal of the Negro* (New York: Collier Books, 1965), 167.
53. Jay Martin, *A Singer in the Dawn* (New York: Dodd, Mead and Co., 1975), p. 23.
54. Ibid.
55. Martin and Hudson, *The Paul Laurence Dunbar Reader*, p. 50.
56. Ibid., p. 51.

RICHARD A. LONG

A Weapon of My Song: The Poetry of James Weldon Johnson

The verse output of James Weldon Johnson falls into four groups: lyrics in standard English, poems in the dialect tradition, folk-inspired free verse, and a long satirical poem. The first two groups are contemporary and were published in the volume *Fifty Years and Other Poems* (Boston, 1917). The prayer and seven Negro sermons of the third group constitute *God's Trombones* (New York, 1927). The last group is represented by the poem "St. Peter Relates An Incident of the Resurrection Day," privately printed in 1930, and republished with a selection of earlier poems in 1935.

The early poetry of Johnson belongs to the late nineteenth century tradition of sentimental poetry in so far as its techniques and verse forms are concerned, seldom rising above the mediocrity characteristic of American poetry in the period 1890–1910, during which it was written for the most part. In purpose, however, Johnson's early verse was a species of propaganda, designed sometimes overtly, sometimes obliquely, to advance to a reading public the merits and the grievances of blacks. In this sense the poetry of Johnson is an integral part of a coherent strain in the poetry of Afro-Americans beginning with Phillis Wheatley:

Remember, Christians, Negroes, black as Cain,
May be refined, and join th' angelic train.
(Phillis Wheatley, "On Being Brought from Africa to America")

More particularly, we may note the relationship of Johnson's early poetry to that of Paul Lawrence Dunbar, his much admired friend and contemporary. Though they were about the same age, Dunbar was by far the more precocious, and his virtuosity had an obvious impact on Johnson, though little of Dunbar's verse bears any obvious burden of racial protest, in spite of the real personal suffering Dunbar underwent because of misunderstanding and neglect that he ascribed to his color.

Another factor of importance in the early verse of Johnson is his composition of verses to be set to music by his brother J. Rosamond Johnson; the search for euphony and piquancy and the use of devices such as internal rhyme betrays the hand of the librettist.

The division of Johnson's poetry into standard lyrics and dialect verse, as in the case of Dunbar's poetry, reflects a self-conscious distinction made by the author himself. Johnson's first collection of his poetry, which appeared eleven years after Dunbar's death, presents forty-eight standard poems, followed by a segregated group of sixteen "Jingles and Croons." The dialect poems reflect of course a literary tradition of their own since in point of fact the themes and forms of such dialect poetry as was written by Dunbar and Johnson and many others reflect no tradition of the folk who used "dialect." In point of fact, it is useful to remember that the dialect poets learned mainly from their predecessors and employ for the most part uniform grammatical and orthographic conventions which suggest that they did not consciously seek to represent any individual or regional dialect. Johnson himself gives a brief account of the dialect literary tradition in his introductions to Dunbar and other dialect poets in *The Book of American Negro Poetry* (New York, 1931).

One of Johnson's dialect poems, because of its popular musical setting, is widely known and thought by many to be a genuine folk-product. The low-key sentimentality of "Sence You Went Away" is nevertheless that of the stage and not of real life. The last stanza will illustrate the point:

Seems lak to me I jes can't he'p but sigh,
Seems lak to me ma th'oat keeps gittin' dry,
Seems lak to me a tear stays in ma eye,
Sence you went away.

The other dialect poems in Johnson's first collection which should be classified among the "croons" are "My Lady's Lips Are Like De Honey," "Nobody's Lookin' But de Owl and de Moon," "You's Sweet to Yo' Mammy Jes de Same," "A Banjo Song." The titles are sufficiently indicative of their range and content. The "jingles" are frequently in the form of dramatic monologue, and while they (partly because of their later publication), have never become platform rivals to Dunbar's monologues, "Tunk (A Lecture on Modern Education)" and "The Rivals" can challenge comparison. The first is an exhortation to a truant schoolboy in which the light duties of white folks in offices are contrasted with the labors of black folks in the fields. The second is an old man's reminiscences of a crucial episode in the courtship of his wife. Both poems are written in long line rhyming couplets, Johnson's preferred verse form for his dialect verse, though a variety of stanza forms and rhyme schemes is employed, some with great versatility as the refrain from "Brer Rabbit, You's de Cutes' of 'Em All" illustrates:

"Brer Wolf am mighty cunnin',
Brer Fox am mighty sly,
Brer Terrapin an' 'Possum—kinder small;
Brer Lion's mighty vicious,
Brer B'ar he's sorter 'spi'cious,
Brer Rabbit, you's de cutes' of 'em all."

Of the standard poems of Johnson collected in *Fifty Years*, at least ten are more and less overtly on the race problem and among these are several of Johnson's most important poems. In contrast, the more generalized poems have hardly more than a passing interest except for a group of six poems "Down by the Carib Sea" in which Johnson treats images from his Latin-American experience as a U.S. consul in Venezuela and Nicaragua. Unfortunately, even here, conventionality of diction vitiates what might have been a poetic expression of enduring interest and value.

The group of ten race poems includes three of the "appeal" genre in which the black poet addresses his white compatriots and invites an improvement in their attitudes toward the blacks. This genre of Afro-American poetry runs from Phillis Wheatley to Gwendolyn Brooks, and may be said to have been already conventional when Johnson essayed it, though the sincerity with which he takes up the form cannot be doubted. In the short poem "To America" he asks:

How would you have us, as we are?
Or sinking 'neath the load we bear?
. . . .

Strong willing sinews in your wings?
Or tightening chain about your feet?

"O Southland" makes the poet implore

O Southland, fair Southland!
Then why do you cling
To an idle age and a musty page,
To a dead and useless thing.

And in "Fragment" he declares

See! In your very midst there dwell
Ten thousand blacks, a wedge
Forged in the furnaces of hell. . . .

The somewhat stern Calvinistic fervor of this poem suggests that the system is foredoomed to divine malediction.

Another genre in the race poems is that of pointing out the virtuous black and inviting sympathy and understanding. "The Black Mammy" and "The Color Sergeant" illustrate this genre. The theme of the Black Mammy who has nursed with tenderness the white child who may someday strike down her own black child has its own kind of immortality, combining as it does the mawkishness of mother love with America's quaint racial customs. "The Color Sergeant" is based on a real incident in the Spanish-American War and may be said to prefigure the Dorie Miller and similar poems of succeeding wars.

A lynching poem is called "Brothers" and is a stilted dramatic exchange between a lynch victim and the mob who burn him alive. The division of objects from the ashes is intended perhaps to recall the casting of lots for Christ's clothes:

"You take that bone, and you this tooth, the chain—
Let us divide its links; this skull, of course,
In fair division, to the leader comes."

Still another poem which I classify as a race poem because of its obvious symbolism and because Johnson places it at the end of that group in the arrangement of the poems in *Fifty Years* could be read simply as a poem of ghostly circumstance. "The White Witch" describes a beauteous apparition who lures young men to their death. The poem's progenitors are the Romantic literary ballads. It is possible that Johnson had heard of the Jamaican ghost legend of the White Witch of Rose Hall, but there is no obvious patterning of his scenario on the legend.

In two of the race poems Johnson addresses black people specifically. One of these is the famous ode to the dead creators of the spirituals, "O Black and Unknown Bards." The harmony and dignity of the poem are fully deserving of the praise it has received. The poet marvels continually:

> There is a wide, wide wonder in it all,
> That from degraded rest and service toil
> The fiery spirit of the seer should call
> These simple children of the sun and soil.

But his conclusion seems timid and apologetic,

> You sang far better than you knew; the songs
> That for your listeners' hungry hearts sufficed
> Still live,—but more than this to you belongs:
> You sang a race from wood and stone to Christ.

The bulk of the poems written by Johnson which fall into the two categories just discussed were written before 1910. The poem which serves as the title poem to his first collection is itself a commemorative poem written in 1912 to mark the fiftieth anniversary of the Emancipation Proclamation. The poem begins with an apostrophe to his fellow blacks:

> O brothers mine, today we stand
> Where half a century sweeps our ken . . . .

He then invokes the scene of the first blacks arriving in Jamestown in 1619. And from these few (aided, as the poet does not note, by the energetic exploitation of the slave trade) have come a race "ten million strong / An upward, onward marching host." He goes on to declare

> This land is ours by right of birth,
> This land is ours by right of toil;
> We helped to turn its virgin earth,
> Our sweat is in its fruitful soil.

He cites the labors of blacks and their frequent defense of the flag. He observes that despite these things blacks are maltreated and persecuted, but he urges

Courage! Look out, beyond, and see
The far horizon's beckoning span!
Faith in your God-known destiny!
We are a part of some great plan.

And the poem closes with expression of faith in God's intentions for the best. The poem is in twenty-six octosyllabic quatrains, rhyming a b a b in *Fifty Years and Other Poems*. Johnson abridged it to twenty stanzas for its appearance in *The Book of American Negro Poetry*. In the 1935 collection it appears as a poem of twenty-four stanzas, with a prefatory note.

One poem, related in tone and character to "Fifty Years," written in 1900, was not included in *Fifty Years and Other Poems*, but was included in the 1935 collection. This is the famous song lyric "Lift Every Voice and Sing," known far and wide as the "Negro National Anthem." Its heroic language, fully sustained by the harmonies of J. Rosamond Johnson, have played a role in the life of black America that no patriotic song could have fulfilled.

We have come over a way that with tears has been watered,
We have come, treading our path through the blood of
  the slaughtered,
Out from the gloomy past,
Till now we stand at last
Where the white gleam of our bright star is cast.

The second decade of the twentieth century was a period of innovation and change in American poetry. The establishment of *Poetry Magazine*, the Imagist manifesto, the appearance of Frost, Masters, Sandburg, Lindsay and Pound all bespeak the new spirit. The annual anthologies of Magazine verse edited by William Stanley Braithwaite beginning in 1913 which were one of the chief forums of the new spirit despite Braithwaite's own conservatism were surely well-perused by his friend James Weldon Johnson. Accordingly, it is not surprising to find a sudden modification in Johnson's poetic practice develop during this decade, for his poem "The Creation" precedes by almost a decade its publication with companion pieces in *God's Trombones* in 1927. He recounts his immediate inspiration for "The Creation" in the Preface to *God's Trombones*:

> . . . He [a rural black preacher] strode the pulpit up and down in what was actually a very rhythmic dance, and he brought into play the full gamut of his wonderful voice. . . . He intoned, he moaned, he pleaded—he blared, he crashed, he thundered. I sat

> fascinated; and more, I was, perhaps against my will, deeply moved; the emotional effect upon me was irresistible. Before he had finished I took a slip of paper and somewhat surreptitiously jotted down some ideas for the first poem, "The Creation."

"The Creation" was conceived, as it were, in the heat of the moment. Only gradually did Johnson develop the series of poems which constitute the seven sermons and the opening prayer of *God's Trombones*. The principles he employed in writing these poems, based closely on the practice of the folk preacher, are explained in the Preface. He explains why he did not write them in dialect (in the sense of an attempted indication of folk speech):

> First, although the dialect is the exact instrument for voicing certain traditional phases of Negro life, it is, and perhaps by that very exactness, a quite limited instrument. Indeed, it is an instrument with but two complete stops, pathos and humor. This limitation is not due to any defect of the dialect as dialect, but to the mould of convention in which Negro dialect in the United States has been set, to the fixing effects of its long association with the Negro only as a happy-go-lucky or a forlorn figure. . . .
>
> The second part of my reason for not writing these poems in dialect is the weightier. The old-time Negro preachers, though they actually used dialect in their ordinary intercourse, stepped out from its narrow confines when they preached. They were all saturated with the sublime phraseology of the Hebrew prophets and steeped in the idioms of King James English, so when they preached and warmed to their work they spoke another language, a language far removed from traditional Negro dialect. It was really a fusion of Negro idioms with Bible English; and in this there may have been, after all, some kinship with the innate grandiloquence of their old African tongues. To place in the mouths of the talented old-time Negro preachers a language that is a literary imitation of Mississippi cotton-field dialect is sheer burlesque.

Johnson says in the Preface that "the old-time Negro preacher is rapidly passing." Nothing could have been further from the truth. "Old-time" Negro preaching is not only fully present in 1971 in large churches as well as in store-front meeting rooms, but its eloquence has dominated political forums and civil rights meetings, sometimes to the exclusion of action. This eloquence underlies much of the prose of Ellison and Baldwin as well as that of many writers of the sixties.

The medium Johnson chose for the sermon poems is a cadenced free verse which very effectively reflects the rhythmical speech of the folk preacher. Johnson uses the dash to indicate "a certain sort of pause that is marked by a quick intaking and an audible expulsion of the breath. The arrangement of prayer and sermons in *God's Trombones* is

Listen, Lord—A Prayer
The Creation
The Prodigal Son
Go Down Death—A Funeral Sermon
Noah Built the Ark
The Crucifixion
Let My People Go
The Judgment Day.

"Listen, Lord," "The Creation," "Go Down Death," and "The Crucifixion" are generally of a more exalted interest than the other pieces, but all of them capture effectively the imagery, the intensity, the sly humor, and the hypnotic grandeur of the black sermon tradition. In "Listen, Lord" the blessing of God is invoked on the preacher in these terms

Put his eye to the telescope of eternity,
And let him look upon the paper walls of time.
Lord, turpentine his imagination,
Put perpetual motion in his arms,
Fill him full of the dynamite of thy power,
Anoint him all over with the oil of thy salvation,
And set his tongue on fire.

The actual events of awful moments are iterated in "The Crucifixion":

Jesus, my lamb-like Jesus,
Shivering as the nails go through his feet.
Jesus, my darling Jesus,
Groaning as the Roman spear plunged in his side;
Jesus, my darling Jesus,
Groaning as the blood came spurting from his wound.
Oh, look how they done my Jesus.

In "Noah Built the Ark" Satan is depicted with familiarity:

> Then pretty soon along came Satan.
> Old Satan came like a snake in the grass
> To try out his tricks on the woman.
> I imagine I can see Old Satan now
> A-sidling up to the woman.
> I imagine the first word Satan said was:
> Eve, you're surely good looking.

After the story of the exodus is told in "Let My People Go" the preacher concludes with a magnificent coda:

> Listen!—Listen!
> All you sons of Pharaoh.
> Who do you think can hold God's people
> When the Lord God himself has said,
> Let my people go?

The general technique developed by Johnson for *God's Trombones* constitutes a giant leap from his archaizing early poetry. Unfortunately the many pressures of his life as a public man and as a cultural mentor prevented him from utilizing his new freedom in a substantial body of work though the continuing popularity of *God's Trombones* since its initial publication and its appeal to a broad stratum of readers have given the slim volume an importance in American poetry enjoyed by few other works of comparable scope.

A special irony of Johnson's creations is that they have often themselves reentered the folk stream they were intended to fix and commemorate, and have in turn sustained through countless recitations the continuation of a living tradition.

While Johnson expressed no overt ideological objectives concerning his verse sermons, it is significant that they were not offered either in the spirit of his early standard verse or of his "jingles and croons." The sermons are an assertion of black pride and black dignity with no reference to perspectives and standards of others.

A further direction in his poetic practice was revealed by Johnson in the long satirical poem "St. Peter Relates an Incident of the Resurrection Day." Johnson describes the genesis of the poem in the third person in his 1935 foreword:

> . . . The title poem of this volume was originally printed in 1930, in an edition of 200 copies for private distribution. In the summer of that year the author was busy on the manuscript of a book. He read one morning in the newspaper that the United States government was sending a contingent of gold-star mothers to France to visit the graves of their soldier sons buried there; and that the Negro gold-star mothers would not be allowed to sail on the same ship with the white gold-star mothers, but would be sent over on a second and second-class vessel. He threw aside the manuscript on which he was working and did not take it up again until he had finished the poem, "Saint Peter Relates an Incident of the Resurrection Day."

The poem, arranged in six sections of varying length, presents St. Peter, long after Resurrection Day, recounting to some of the heavenly host the unburying of the Unknown Soldier. The discovery that the man who had been honored by generations of Americans in his magnificent tomb was black is the O'Henryesque reversal in the poem. The limpidity of Johnson's handling of the theme in quatrains of rhyming couplets, a favorite meter for narration and monologue with him in his earlier verse, is illustrated by his description of the reaction to the Klan's suggestion that the soldier be reburied:

> The scheme involved within the Klan's suggestion
> Gave rise to a rather nice metaphysical question:
> Could he be forced again through deaths dark portal,
> Since now his body and soul were both immortal?

The publication of "St. Peter Relates an Incident of the Resurrection Day" in 1935 provided the occasion for Johnson to issue a new selection of his poems. Thirty-seven poems, including eight in dialect, from *Fifty Years and Other Poems* were reprinted, as well as "Lift Every Voice and Sing." Four additional poems were a sonnet "My City," a celebration of Manhattan, and "If I were Paris," a lyric of twelve lines, both in his earlier manner; a free-verse poem "A Poet to His Baby Son" written in a later colloquial manner; and a translation from the Cuban poet Placido, "Mother, Farewell!" a sonnet which Johnson had published in the 1922 edition of *The Book of American Negro Poetry* and again in the 1931 revised edition. *Fifty Years and Other Poems* had included the translation of another poem of Placido.

An untitled envoy, the last poem in *Fifty Years and Other Poems*, contains the following lines, central to its thought:

> . . . if injustice, brutishness and wrong
> Should make a blasting trumpet of my song;
> O God, give beauty and strength—truth to my words . . . .

Eighteen years later a revised and now titled "Envoy" closes the second and final selection of Johnson poems:

> . . . if injustice, brutishness, and wrong
> Stir me to make a weapon of my song;
> O God, give beauty, truth, strength to my words.

In this revision two important points are presented in capsule. Johnson continued to revise and modify his poems, a fact which should be taken account of in any future study devoted primarily to the texts. The second point is that Johnson's conception of the function of the poet, the black poet particularly, had evolved from the apologetic tradition, in which racial justice is implored and in which an attempt to show the worthiness of blacks is made by showing their conformism, to a militant posture, in which the poet uses his talent as a weapon with concern only for beauty, truth and strength. In both phases, Johnson was a poet who recognized the propriety of propaganda. His earlier concern was with influencing opinion ("a blasting trumpet"); his later concern was asserting the verities, with a willingness "to make a weapon of my song."

GETA J. LESEUR

Claude McKay's Romanticism

Jamaica gave to English and American literature a great poet in Claude McKay. As a Negro writer writing at a time when it was popular to use modern forms, he chose to combine the lilting melody and warm human emotion of the earlier romantics in his writing. He wrote poems of exuberance, sorrow, faithful affection, patriotism, and sturdy independence. In such poems as "The Tropics in New York," "Flame-Heart," "The Spanish Needle," "The Snow Fairy," "Spring in New Hampshire," and "Home-Thoughts," these attitudes are poignantly expressed with allegiance to the native and foreign—Jamaica and the United States—the real and the romantic. McKay never saw any of these as being in conflict; they were always two "natures" completely independent of each other. This, however, was a personal and literary philosophy. His poetry is one which says yes to life—rich, free, passionate, and concerned.

McKay has been referred to from time to time as "Jamaica's Bobbie Burns," which in itself is an interesting but valid comparison. Those who knew him personally and those who only know his poetry constantly made this reference. McKay himself made this statement more precise in his autobiography, *A Long Way From Home*, and in the short article "On Becoming a Catholic":

From *CLA Journal* XXXII, no. 3 (March 1989).

> I had always thought of myself as a pagan. I chose Burns as my model, as he was so strong, sweet and amorous of abundant life, and I was writing in the Jamaican dialect.[1]

The comparison is by no means an accident and seems even more relevant when it is noted that Robert Burns was supposed to visit Jamaica after an unlucky love affair with his Scottish sweetheart. The trip never came to fruition, however. Burns' poetry was only one aspect of British literature that all Jamaicans and British colonials were expected to master. Every school boy and girl was expected to memorize several British lyrics, ballads, and narratives or be whipped for not doing so. It is no accident, therefore, that McKay and his schoolmates knew and admired poets like Burns, Keats, Shelley, and Wordsworth. When McKay says that he used Burns as a model, he is also suggesting a silent rebellion on the part of a West Indian youth. When he wrote poetry in the Jamaican Scottish dialect, he used Burns' Scottish dialect as a model. His first poems published in the dialect were *Songs of Jamaica* (1912) and *Constab Ballads* (1912). This was only the beginning of the sturdy independence and faithful affection he was to exercise throughout his life and writing career.

Allegiances and coalitions were goals visualized by Claude McKay. They are present in his autobiography, as a specific statement of purpose, and in his verse. Although a radical, he was a conservative poet, for his verse forms were traditional. The sonnet was his favorite, and he actually wrote most of his poems on the time-honored subjects of love and nature.[2] Regardless of the fact that the writing tradition adopted by McKay was that of the romantic "movement" from his school days in Jamaica, it was not until he came to the United States in 1912 at age twenty-three that his best poetry-writing began. Max Eastman, his lifelong friend and editor of the *Liberator*, which he coedited, later said this of him:

> It was not until he came to the United States that Claude McKay began to confront the deepest feelings in his heart and realize that a delicate syllabic music could not alone express them. Here his imagination awoke, and the colored imagery that is the language of all deep passion began to appear in his poetry.[3]

And about the poetry written in America, Eastman goes on to say:

> The quality is here in them all—the pure, clear arrow-like transference of his emotion into our breast, without any but the inexitable words—the quality that reminds us of Burns and

> Villion and Cattalus, and all the poets that we call lyric because we love them so much. It is the quality that Keats sought to cherish when he said that "Poetry should be great and unobtrusive, a thing which enters into the soul, and does not startle or amaze with itself, but with its subject . . . It is the poetry of life and not the poet's chamber. It is the poetry which looks upon a thing and sings.[4]

McKay has said that, of the English models and schools of writing he has been associated with, it is the classicists and romantics that he admires, but he owes "allegiance to no master." He adds that he has used only that which he considered to be the best of the poets of all ages. The language used in his poetry was that derived from the Jamaican dialect, archaic words, and figures of speech, which are then reshaped to suit his specific purposes. The introductory pages ("Author's Word") to *Harlem Shadows* has been cited repeatedly by scholars, critics, and McKay's readers to justify or support theories regarding his poetry. The important information given in that short essay is that McKay thinks the traditional should work best on "lawless and revolutionary passions and words, "so as to give the feeling of the "highest degree of spontaneity and freedom." "For me," he says, "there is more quiet delight in 'The golden moon of heaven' than in 'The terra-cotta disc of cloud land.'"[5] The last quoted line here is ironically from a poem by one of the best-known Harlem Renaissance poets, Langston Hughes.

It is no accident that Claude McKay felt uncomfortable with the poetry and lifestyle of the New Negro Movement of the 1920s. He was never really a part of that whole milieu. He disagreed with their involvement with "art for art's sake" and with their being self-appointed messiahs to uplift the privileged few. Theirs was a tightly knit circle which excluded many. Because McKay's tendencies were more akin to the European tradition and experience, he was a misfit at a time when blackness was being celebrated. First, McKay's reading was Byron, Shelley, Keats, and the late Victorians. Secondly, his friends, personal and literary, were the whites in New York's suburbs and its downtown Greenwich Village. Thirdly, he was older than most of the Renaissance writers—Hughes, Cullen, Toomer, and others. And fourthly, he lived in Europe during most of the key Renaissance years. Consequently, for these reasons and more, he was, as Frank Harris of Pearson's Magazine noted, "an oddity. . . . a noble black poet with romantic intentions."[6]

McKay felt a great tension between black content and traditional white form, and this, for him, was perhaps the hardest problem to solve. He grappled with the two as to where the thrust of his writing should be. He had been praised for producing poems which gave no hint of color. James Weldon Johnson, one of the few close black poet friends he had, advised him to do so; and, from the collection *Spring in New Hampshire*, "If We Must Die," perhaps his best-known poem, was left out to retain the "no color" identity. The poem begins:

> If we must die, let it not be like hogs,
> Hunted and penned in an inglorious spot,
> While round us bark the mad and hungry dogs,
> Making their mock at our accursed lot.[7]

The problem became a personal one of how to keep his allegiance to the British models—whose poetry he truly felt and knew well—and be a black poet emotionally. Writing poetry was not difficult for him, but what was difficult was the personae in conflict, the paradox of self which mars some of the poems.

Consequently, while McKay constantly preferred to keep the West Indian identity and the British training, he was conscious that nothing could change the fact that he was a writer who also happened to be a Negro. When told to mask his identity, and when in his novel *Banana Bottom* (1933) certain words were changed into "Britishisms," he became extremely angry and replied to his publishers and friends in this way:

> Of all the poets I admire, major and minor, Byron, Shelley, Keats, Blake, Burns, Whitman, Heine, Baudelaire, Verlaire and Rimbaud and the rest—it seemed to me that when I read them—in their poetry I could feel their race, their class, their roots in the soil, growing into plants, spreading and forming the background against which they were silhouetted. I could not feel the reality of them without that. So likewise I could not realize myself writing without that conviction.[8]

Again, the problem of allegiance and coalition were surfaced to deal with these constant attempts to subjugate color to content. The natural and the creative became problematic also. McKay, regardless of all the places to which he traveled, realized that the artist's faith had to be in his origins, a patriotism as one might find in Whitman's America and in Yeats' Ireland. Furthermore, McKay's best poetry and prose were about Jamaica; as for him, the artist being inseparable from his roots would be an alien thought.

The title of his autobiography, *A Long Way from Home*, is from a Negro spiritual, the opening line of which is, "Sometimes I feel like a motherless child, a long way from home." The title, however, is not coincidental, and even though McKay never returned to Jamaica but chose American citizenship instead, the title is a misnomer because Jamaican memories permeate his best later writings. The poetry looks romantically to Jamaica and prophetically to blackness. His prophecy for Jamaica as an independent, Third World nation, for example, was fulfilled in the last two decades. *Spring in New Hampshire* (1920) and *The Selected Poems* (1953) have in them mostly nostalgic lyrics about Jamaica and songs celebrating nature, and they reflect those themes found in the nineteenth-century Romantics.

McKay's romanticism exhibits itself in several ways but primarily in his writing and lifestyle. His literary heroes were writers of conventional works, the sonnet his favorite mode of expression, but some of his poems are done in freer style. An example of the combination of Jamaican remembrance and celebration of nature in the less conventional style is "Flame-Heart."

> So much I have forgotten in ten years,
> So much in ten brief years! I have forgot
> What time the purple apples come to juice,
> And what month brings the shy forget-me-not.
> I have forgot the special, startling season
> Of the pimento's flowering and fruiting;
> What time of year the ground doves drown the fields
> And fill the noonday with their curious fluting.
> I have forgotten much, but still remember
> The poinsetta's red, blood-red, in warm December.[9]

Many critics have lingered over the meaning of the last line, which also closes stanza II, but the intention here is only to show the poems as examples of the different aspects of McKay's romanticism. He has forgotten the cycles of the seasons, but the emotion of the poem is rich in West Indian images.

In "The Spanish Needle" McKay uses a more conventional pattern to write about a very common and wild weed in Jamaica by the same name. It is a plant much like a dandelion in America, but the language and tone which he uses in the poem make the Spanish needle become a regal plant; thus the common and everyday in the hands of a romantic like McKay becomes uncommon. The following verses of that poem show the endearment which he feels for the ordinary:

> Lovely dainty Spanish needle
> With your yellow flower and white,
> Dew bedecked and softly sweeping,
> Do you think of me to-night?

Shadowed by the spreading mango,
Nodding o'er the rippling stream,
Tell me, dear plant of my childhood,
Do you of the exile dream?

Do you see me by the brook's side
Catching crayfish 'neath the stone,
As you did the day you whispered:
Leave the harmless dears alone?

. . . .

Lovely dainty Spanish needle,
Source to me of sweet delight,
In your far-off sunny southland
Do you dream of me to-night?[10]

This poem is very much in the romantic tradition of Shelley and Keats and is probably one of the few poems by McKay that every Jamaican schoolchild must recite "by heart." "Home-Thoughts" is one of his better poems with the homeland theme:

Oh something just now must be happening there!
That suddenly and quiveringly here,
Amid the city's noises, I must think
Of mangoes leaning o'er the river's brink,
And dexterous Davie climbing high above,
The gold fruits ebon-speckled to remove,
And toss them quickly in the tangled mass
Of wis-wis twisted round the guinea grass;
And Cyril coming through the bramble-track
A Prize bunch of bananas on his back;

. . . .

This is no daytime dream, there's something in it,
Oh something's happening there this very minute![11]

The use of local words like *mango*, *wis-wis*, *guinea grass*, *bramble track*, *purple apple*, *ground dove*, *pimento*, *ping-wing*, *rose apple*, *poinsetta*, and *banana* in "Flame-Heart," "The Spanish Needle," and "Home-Thoughts" are entire images in themselves, and even without notes to explain their meanings and connotations, the mood, tone and theme of the poems are obvious. These poems all go back to the West Indian scene, and in them are found the similar conflicts and opposing attractions which plagued McKay throughout his lifetime. In them, also, joy and sorrow are accepted with the stoic indifference which was part of the romantic passion.

"The Snow Fairy," "Spring in New Hampshire," and "After the Winter" use the same American seasonal landscape as their background. They too are good, have a simplicity of diction and tone, and are full of longing and passion, but they by no means compare with the lilting, spontaneous yet deep emotion of "Tropics in New York." In comparing a few lines from "Spring in New Hampshire" with "The Tropics in New York," one can see that the differences are very obvious, not only because of the subject, but because of McKay's involvement with the places closest to his heart:

> Too green the springing April grass,
> Too blue the silver-speckled sky,
> For me to linger here, alas,
> While happy winds go laughing by,
> Wasting the golden hours indoors,
> Washing windows and scrubbing floors.[12]

The weariness and tedium of scrubbing floors in spring is felt, while outdoors the enjoyment of nature passes. Rather than being happy in nature, there is sorrow because the speaker is physically removed from it but is mentally aware of its presence. He is a prisoner of circumstance. "The Tropics of New York" finds the speaker a prisoner also in a foreign country, but the nostalgia, though sorrowful, is much more lyrical, and he seems closer to this subject, and the poem is richer:

> Bananas ripe and green, and ginger-root,
> Cocoa in pods and alligator pears,
> And tangerines and Mangoes and grape fruit,
> Fit for the highest prize at parish fairs,
>
> Set in the window, bringing memories
> Of fruit-trees laden by low-singing rills,
> And dewy dawns, and mystical blue skies
> In benediction over nun-like hills.
>
> My eyes grew dim, and I could no more gaze;
> A wave of longing through my body swept,
> And, hungry for the old, familiar ways,
> I turned aside and bowed my head and wept.[13]

McKay obviously is the speaker in this poem, although he speaks for the hundreds of West Indians who became exiles away from their homeland primarily because of economic and diplomatic reasons. The poem, therefore, does have a oneness of feeling about it. The alienation felt is one of time and distance, and the consequence and helplessness is clearly felt in the last three lines. The progression is from glorious song to despair. It is one of his most moving poems on this theme, and the experience, as in "If We Must Die," is the universal black experience.

It is not in the poems only that Claude McKay's romantic nature is exhibited, but in his lifestyle and relationship with people and the world. He traveled to Russia, England, Spain, Germany, and Morocco, and he had romances singularly with each of them. The flirting with Communism was short-lived, and in England he was just another West Indian. Both experiences were disappointing because of the romantic notions he held about them. Burns, Keats, Wordsworth, and Shelley were dead, and prejudice was alive. Learning from those two short "romances," he tried to savor the best in all of the other countries which he visited and in which he lived. In Spain it was the romanticism of the bullfight and the world of Hemingway; in Germany and France it was the beautiful art and architecture. The despairing moments were overshadowed by the glorious experiences of the people he met and the new countrysides to sing about. Again, some of McKay's better writings were done in Europe. His best works were not about the New York, Jamaica, or American scenes while he was living in these places but when he was away from them. In Tangiers, Morocco, he felt at home more than at any other time in his life. In a letter to Max Eastman (1 December 1980) he wrote, "There are things in the life of the natives, their customs and superstitions reminiscent of Jamaica." And in another letter (1 September 1932) he stated, "My attachment to Tangiers is sort of a spiritual looking backwards."[14]

McKay, therefore, seemed to have done his best work when he maintained a distance between himself and his subject. This in itself was not true of all romantic writers, but it is true of the romantic spirit for nostalgia, mysticism and fascination. About life McKay wrote to Eastman (28 July 1919):

> . . . life fascinates me in its passions. It may survive when everything else is dead and fused into it. I revere all those spirits who in their little (bit?) way are helping the life force to attain its wonderful and beautiful communication.[15]

In the same letter he says, "I love your life more than your poetry, more than your personality. This is my attitude toward all artists."

It is apparent that McKay believes strongly in the nationality, personal identity, and uniqueness that each writer brings to his art. It is that special uniqueness which makes each one different and reinforces the sturdy independence of each human's nature. It was in Europe and elsewhere that he missed America most and in America that he reminisced about Jamaica consistently.

All poetry, McKay thought, should be judged by its own merits, not by categories of race and nationality. The double standard was something which he opposed, and this too was carried over into his lifestyle. Because he was a "foreign" Negro with white friends, the reality of racial prejudice and the embarrassing moments he experienced from whites and blacks left him torn. He wanted to be accepted, but the pain which nonacceptance brought others plagued him. He was not accepted by the blacks of the Harlem Renaissance group, and his friends were the white literati, not the black "Niggerati," as he called them.[16] It is no wonder, then, that the romantic modes and distances worked best for McKay. Some of the most personal poems are about those experiences such as "To the White Friends" and "The White House."[17] The militancy and anger are there and very uncompromising. Regardless of this, it was the realm of "literary truth" with which McKay was most preoccupied. He spoke of and "defined" it in a letter to Eastman:

> I think that if the intellectual idea of literary truth were analyzed, it would prove at bottom to be nothing more than "a wise saying" or a "beautiful phrase" delivered in a unique and startling manner—an addition to the sum of the universal wisdom of mankind. Such a wisdom exists telling of the passions, the folly and the segacity, success and failure, pain and joy of life. It existed long before modern science and I believe it will continue to exist as vigorous and independent as ever as long as humanity retains the facilities of feeling, thinking—the inexhaustible source of which great and authentic literature springs whether it is cerebral or sentimental, realistic or romantic.[18]

The essence of McKay's romanticism was not only in his poetry, but in the life he lived, the places he visited, and the people and ideas he encountered. His daily vocabulary was very interestingly sprinkled with romantic asides, as was his autobiography, *A Long Way from Home*, and his letters to Max Eastman of *The Liberator*. In *A Long Way from Home*, the Pankhurst secretary is a "romantic middle class woman"; his radical days on *The Liberator* were "rosy with romance"; "The Wondervogel had lost their romantic flavor"; he mentions "D. H. Lawrence's psychic and romantic groping for a way out"; and he comments on the fact that "it was grand and romantic to have a grant to write." It is obvious that McKay was completely immersed in a romantic style of life very similar to that of some of his British models and contemporaries. A vocabulary interspersed with words carrying the romantic notion means that he consciously draws attention to where his allegiances to nature, life, and self lie. All of these coalesced to create poetry which said yes to life by its explicit philosophy.

Claude McKay has been called "Jamaica's Bobbie Burns," although he gave up that citizenship some twenty-eight years later. The land of his birth, Jamaica, about which he wrote his best prose, verse, and lyrics, still claims him as its citizen. The comparison with the Scottish Burns is by no means superficial, however, as there are many similarities in their writing and points-of-view. The romantics—Keats, Shelley, Wordsworth, Whitman, and Yeats—were also his literary heroes, because of the content of their works and the lifestyles which they led. It was, and still is, unusual to have a black man writing in the mode of the romantics, using their themes, subject matter, and meter. The two natures of self and art, of allegiance and coalition, were things for which McKay worked throughout his life and career. Regardless of his thoroughly British orientation, emotionally and literarily he never forgot his blackness. For a modern poet, the sonnet was his favorite form, and he wrote most of his poems on the time-honored subjects of love and nature. The universality of his romanticism and poetry surpasses color or time lines.

Notes

1. Claude McKay, "On Becoming a Catholic," *Phylon*, 25, No. 3 (1964). [Reprint]
2. Wayne Cooper and Robert C. Reiders, "A Black Briton Comes Home," *Race*, 9 (1967).
3. Claude McKay, *Harlem Shadows*, introd. Max Eastman (New York: Harcourt, 1922), p. xiii.
4. *Harlem Shadows*, Introduction, p. xviii.
5. *Harlem Shadows*, "Authors Word," p. xxxi.
6. Claude McKay, *A Long Way from Home* (New York: Harcourt, 1970), p. 14.
7. James R. Giles, *Claude McKay* (Boston: Twayne, 1976), p. 131.
8. Claude McKay, *Selected Poems* (New York: Harcourt, 1953), p. 16.
9. *Harlem Shadows*, p. 9.
10. Claude McKay, *The Selected Poems* (New York: Harcourt, 1953), pp. 24–25.

11. *The Selected Poems*, p. 11.
12. Ibid., p. 40
13. Ibid., p. 8.
14. Claude McKay's Letters to Max Eastman from 1928 to 1934, Indiana University, The Lilly Library. All quotations are from these letters.
15. Ibid.
16. Claude McKay, Letter to Max Eastman, 28 June 1933.
17. Addison Gayle, Jr.'s book, *Claude McKay: The Black Poet at War*, from Broadside Critics (No. 2) goes into a good discussion of McKay's militancy and anger and tells where he stood on the questions of race and black identity.
18. Claude McKay, Letter to Max Eastman, 25 December 1932.

GEORGE B. HUTCHINSON

The Whitman Legacy and the Harlem Renaissance

Whitman's Legacy to the African American literary tradition remains a largely unexplored topic. We know more today about Walt Whitman among the French, the Russians, the Irish, the Japanese, the Germans, and the Argentineans than about Whitman among the African American modernists. Yet "New Negro" authors enthusiastically embraced Whitman, embraced him with an intimacy that defies the codes typical of interracial relations in the United States and exceeds that of most white American modernists. Ironically, perhaps, they read him as the quintessential "democratic" and antiracist poet, whose legacy could be used to break the racist tradition's control over the limits and possibilities of African American literature. This aspect of the response to Whitman, however, is finally less important than the ways in which *Leaves of Grass* affected black poetics and cultural theory. Inspiring modernist breaks with previous African American as well as Anglo-American literary practices and intellectual traditions, Whitman's writing contributed crucially to some of the most fruitful developments in black writing of the twentieth century. Having discussed Whitman's importance to Kelly Miller and Langston Hughes elsewhere, in this essay I will present a bare outline of his legacy to "New Negro" poetic theory, literary language, cultural nationalist ideology, sexuality, and spirituality by tracing the responses to Whitman of Alain Locke, James Weldon Johnson, and Jean Toomer.

Alain Locke

Strains of unconventional politics and religiosity helped form Alain Locke's personality and made him particularly open to Whitman. His father, Pliny, for example, was raised a Hicksite Quaker and was educated in the Hicksite schools of Germantown, Pennsylvania. But his most intimate intellectual and spiritual guide was his mother, Mary Hawkins Locke, a teacher and "disciple of Felix Adler," who sent Alain to the Philadelphia Ethical Culture school in his early years.[1] While the Ethical Society was identified with racial and educational progressivism, it was also intimately intertwined with "Whitmanism" in Philadelphia and Camden. Virtually the entire Whitman circle was active in the group, particularly Horace Traubel, whose magazine, the *Conservator*, reported regularly upon Ethical Culture meetings and Adler's lectures and appearances, in addition to Whitmaniana. Indeed, members of the Philadelphia Ethical Society had been instrumental in spreading Whitman's reputation as a social and religious prophet, believing that his poetry exemplified the principles of the Ethical movement. It would be surprising if Traubel and Mary Hawkins Locke did not know each other, particularly since Traubel was regarded as a "friend" of the black community of Philadelphia and Camden, as a family friend would explain to Alain after the latter had matriculated at Harvard and joined the Ethical Society of Boston.[2] When Traubel broke with the Ethical Society in 1895, he founded the Walt Whitman Fellowship, International, on which the well-known black educator Kelly Miller would serve as a director from 1904 to 1917.[3] Thus, Whitman was identified with the cause of black equality in the Philadelphia area from Locke's earliest years.

Between 1898 and 1900, when Alain was beginning high school, he and his mother moved from Philadelphia to Camden—in fact, to 417 Stevens Street, one block from Whitman's Mickle Street home and seven doors from the row house where Whitman had lived with his brother from 1873 to 1884.[4] Whitman was still a common topic of neighborhood gossip, having been dead only six or seven years. Moreover, one of Mary's friends had been Whitman's next-door neighbor and had given him the "lap-board" on which he wrote his last letters. A 1904 letter Mary wrote to Alain at Harvard, which praises John Burroughs's *Whitman: A Study* and recounts several neighborhood stories about the poet, reveals an apparently longstanding mutual interest in "Whitman anecdotes" and books on Whitman, as well as a familiarity with sculptures and paintings of him:

> I have read "Walt Whitman" by "Burroughs" and enjoyed it. . . . Miss Button [Whitman's next-door neighbor] told an anecdote

> of Whitman, when an army nurse in Washington. He asked a young fellow—what he could get him to eat—(he was almost dying) he said home-made rice pudding—Whitman had no idea where he could get the article, but he rang several doorbells, promiscuously, stated his need of the article, till some kindly disposed person made one—he called for it and took it to the poor fellow. Her mother was sent for, when the artist from England was painting his picture, to come in every day and sit with W—Miss B says—the Artist did not like it very well—and when the sculptor made that famous bust, he made it in the yard and Mrs. B was duly mortified and stood up on some "soap boxes" and looked over the fence—to see him at his work.[5]

This letter suggests that, even as a first-year student at Harvard, Locke was following the literature on Whitman and that his mother knew he would be interested in personal anecdotes about the famous neighborhood personality. When she writes "and when the sculptor made that famous bust," we know that Locke knew what bust she was talking about (Sidney Morse's). He probably knew that the "artist from England" was Herbert Gilchrist. Indeed, it would be surprising if he had not been hearing anecdotes about Whitman ever since he moved to Stevens Street, but the evidence no longer exists because it simply was not written down.

By the time Locke entered Harvard in 1904, Whitman had attracted the attention of the scholars who would most influence the aspiring philosopher's further intellectual development—particularly William James and George Santayana. Both of these men regarded Whitman as the quintessential American poet—Santayana coming to appreciate Whitman precisely during the years that Locke was at Harvard.[6] Perhaps even more important for Locke's personal development, however, were the new readings of Whitman as homosexual, chiefly by his British disciples.

Beginning at least in 1907, when he arrived at Oxford as a Rhodes Scholar, Locke (who was gay) closely followed the work of writers concerned with "sex psychology" and particularly homosexuality. Having found a community of mind and heart among the homosexual intelligentsia of Oxford and London, Locke came along at a time when this community had redefined Whitman in line with their own social and sexual preferences. In Edwardian England, as Eve Kosofsky Sedgwick has pointed out, "*Leaves of Grass* operated . . . as a conduit from one man to another of feelings that had, in many cases, been private or inchoate." Indeed, Whitman had a "profound and decisive" influence on the "crystallization" of a new, "broadly-based Anglo-American definition of male homosexuality."[7] Two of the most important contributors to this redefinition were the Whitman disciples John Addington Symonds and Edward Carpenter, who combined the exploration of "sex psychology" with interests in democratic theory and a burgeoning literary "modernism," in the vague sense that term carried before the ascendancy of Ezra Pound and T. S. Eliot.

As Harold Blodgett noted years ago, Carpenter and Symonds believed Whitman's ideas provided a prophecy of a modern transformation in sexual relations, including the liberation and "ennobling" of homosexual desire. Inspired by Whitman, they expected "comradeship" to "regenerate political life and to cement nations." Same-sex friendship, Symonds argued, may become the engine of genuine intercultural communion, world democracy, and reciprocity between peoples—a contention that Locke's training and interests would have made immensely attractive to him. Similarly, Carpenter, known as the "Walt Whitman of England," dreamed of "bringing the Races of the world together," ending inequality between women and men, and restoring humanity to union with nature. Bolder than Symonds in justifying homosexuality, he speculated that the great prophets of the future would be "Uranians" following in Whitman's footsteps and finally realizing his vision. Both Carpenter and Symonds viewed Whitman's "adhesiveness" and religiosity as intimately intertwined, with a spiritualized homosexual love functioning as the herald of a "new social dispensation."[8]

While Locke's published writing never hints of his homosexuality or his view of Whitman's sexuality, his correspondence reveals that he shared Carpenter's *Iolaus* (1902) with Countee Cullen. Significantly, in this work Carpenter presents Whitman as the prophet of an entirely new stage of homosexual self-realization and human liberation, in effect the harbinger of a new stage in universal history. After reading the book Cullen wrote back gushingly: "I steeped myself in its charming and comprehending atmosphere. It opened up for me soul windows which had been closed; it threw a noble and evident light on what I had begun to believe, because of what the world believes, ignoble and unnatural. I laved myself in it, and thanked you a thousand times as many delightful examples appeared, for recommending it to me."[9] Without doubt, Locke's reading of Whitman through Carpenter helped Locke, Countee Cullen, and perhaps other "New Negro" writers (many of whom were gay) redefine their sexual identities. In the 1920s, Langston Hughes would write Locke prior to meeting him in person: "Do you like Walt Whitman's poetry? His 'Song of the Open Road' and the poems in 'Calamus'? I do very much." As Arnold Rampersad points out, Locke could only have interpreted Hughes's query as a way of feeling him out about his sexual orientation.[10]

On the eve of the Harlem Renaissance, Locke regarded Whitman as the first prophet of the modern age and as the only truly "American" artist, whose example all future American writers must take into account. Locke's description of "the American temperament" in his 1911 essay of that title—one of his first publications—in fact reads like a description of the Whitman persona:

> To such a temperament nothing is really trivial, and the points of contact between things are almost infinite. As soon as one examines this trait on an intellectual plane, one sees what curious laws of association govern the American mind. Its superb eclecticism, its voraciousness, its collector's instinct for facts and details, and its joyous disregard for proportion and an artificial order are still in need of adequate exposition. They impose so many handicaps from an artistic point of view that as yet no literary genius except Whitman has found it possible to accept them all.[11]

For Locke, the implied "poetics" of the American self—embodied in Whitman's linguistic eclecticism and apparent disregard for proportion and "artificial" order—has a social correlative.

Deeply impressed by philosophical pragmatism, Locke argued that despite the contradictoriness of the "American temperament," its protean and "contentless" nature, "at present the pragmatic verdict must prevail: it works quickly, effectively as a bond between men and, under the circumstances, seems to them less tyrannous than a convention of forms." The American personality "claims everything and yet refuses to identify itself with anything"—by which Locke means that it refuses to be "pinned down" to a particular social location. Moreover, "the American temperament is histrionic as the healthy child; its naive individuality is unquestionable, and because it is so plastic it knows no self-contradiction." One of the great advantages of this form of individuality is the quickness with which the subject can shift between different group identities. Thus, despite the "startling divergencies and instinctive antipathies" in American society, a corporate feeling has been achieved without the advantages of either "closely knit and socially compact groups" or racial homogeneity. Such traditional bases of national community—and authoritarianism—have been replaced by "an acute responsiveness, an intellectual sensitiveness, that are born of insatiable curiosity and a surplus of individual energy."[12] Clearly, Locke does not describe "the American temperament" as he knows it in daily interaction so much as he describes what he finds exemplary in Whitman. In doing so, he attempts to conceptualize a "cosmopolitan" selfhood consonant with the theory of cultural pluralism, the theory Horace Kallen had formulated in discussions with Locke during their years together at Oxford and that would inform Locke's whole conception of the Harlem Renaissance.[13]

Locke's views about Whitman are further revealed in his essay on Emile Verhaeren published in 1917, which argues for Verhaeren's importance by association with Whitman's. Verhaeren comes across here as Whitman's European successor, joining the American as the prophet of a new epoch. Rather than advancing a merely technical and formal experiment, each poet's style seems "inevitable," "dictated by the idea." (Locke would later use the same terms to valorize classical African art over European modernism.[14]) "This element more than any other, as with Whitman, gives Verhaeren greatness: defying classification, it puts their poetry above that of the schools. . . . The catholic response vibrating to everything, the rhapsodic fling, the cosmic emotion and exultant vitalism in the poetry of each proclaims a striking spiritual kinship between them, which if rightly interpreted establishes their common paternity in the age."[15] Locke goes on to describe these two poet-prophets as the "fathers" of literary modernism.

But what was the nature of this hard-to-define modernism? The answer to this question bears upon Locke's later hopes for the "Negro renaissance," and it differs from the definitions of modernism to which we are accustomed: "Democracy triumphant, the ethics of fervour, the religion of humanity, the cult of cosmicality, emotional pantheism, Dionysian neo-paganism,—all this and more it has been termed without a really satisfying caption. For Whitman and Verhaeren it was all one living creed—but their followers have had to cast lots and part their garments." Locke's concept of modernism is distinctly associated with a sensuous and "pagan" democratic spirituality. Out of the matrix of Whitman's and Verhaeren's prophetic works have sprung the various "isms" of modern literature, "sectarian" cults that fall short of the vision of the seers. "To Whitman belongs the credit of discovery, the sounding of these new notes; to Verhaeren, their linking up and blending into something of a harmony. The modern dithyramb, like the ancient, has a philosophy of life, a religion, back of it: thus there was always in poetry for Verhaeren [and Whitman] an almost religious and paeanizing strain."[16] True to the views of Whitman he had absorbed from many sources over many years, Locke does not differentiate the "political" from the "religious" or "spiritual" poet. Indeed, he regards Whitman's spirituality as indivisible from his social and aesthetic significance.

By the 1920s, Locke believed the unique role of "the Negro" in American civilization to lie in the development of "indigenous" spiritual and cultural possibilities, complementing the more materialistic contributions of

Anglo-American culture. African Americans would provide what Whitman had emphatically called for in *Democratic Vistas*.[17] Whereas European Americans had been stunted in their spiritual development by "pioneering" and the pursuit of wealth, African Americans—denied both geographic and social mobility—had developed spiritual compensations and incarnated them in the most "indigenous" cultural products of the New World. They were destined to be America's artists. "The Negro's predisposition toward the artistic, promising to culminate in a control and mastery of the spiritual and mystic as contrasted with the mechanical and practical aspects of life, makes him a spiritually needed and culturally desirable factor in American life."[18] The "Negro" would provide exactly what Whitman had looked for from the future American poet.

It is worthwhile to notice the correspondences between the qualities Locke most revered in what he now called the "folk temperament" and the qualities he had earlier found in Whitman's "American temperament"—"a mysticism that is not ascetic and of the cloister, a realism that is not sordid but shot through with homely, appropriate poetry."[19] Locke admired this temperament for "its irresistibly sensuous, spontaneously emotional, affably democratic and naive spirit"—the true promise of "Negro" art and the project of Whitman's. His approval of the strain of "paganism" or "pantheism" in Countee Cullen's work recalls the "neo-paganism" and "Dionysian" quality he praised in Whitman's and Verhaeren's poetry. And in regard to Langston Hughes, Locke emphasized his "ecstatic sense of kinship with even the most common and lowly folk," the poet's ability to discover "the epic quality of collective strength and beauty in the masses."[20] Differentiating Hughes from the "dialect school," Locke noted that "Hughes brings to his portrayal of his folk not the ragged provincialism of a minstrel but the descriptive detachment of a Vachel Lindsay and a Sandburg and promises the democratic sweep and universality of a Whitman." Hughes's approach to folk materials, Locke believed, traded on the Whitman legacy at the same time that it grew from and extended African American expressive traditions. This, indeed, is a point that Hughes's own biography and testimony overwhelmingly confirm.[21]

Clearly, many of the qualities Locke most valued and encouraged in black poetry as the "dean" or "midwife" of the Negro Renaissance he had previously meditated upon in relation to Whitman's work as he developed his own orientation to aesthetics and cultural theory generally—well before he had acknowledged anything worthwhile in the black vernacular tradition. Thus, his ideas about and prescriptions for black literature in the years of the Harlem Renaissance often echo the terms of his concept of Whitman. In "Art or Propaganda" (1928), for example, he urges black writers to remain "self-contained," optimistically proclaiming, "I believe we are at that interesting moment when the prophet becomes the poet and when prophecy becomes the expressive song, the chant of fulfillment."[22] The kind of prophecy characterized here is what Locke responded to during his youth while reading Whitman's self-expressive "chants."

JAMES WELDON JOHNSON

James Weldon Johnson had become increasingly dissatisfied with black "dialect" verse as exemplified by Paul Laurence Dunbar when he came across *Leaves of Grass*. "I was engulfed and submerged by the book, and set floundering," he would write in his autobiography. Whitman made him realize the "artificiality of the conventionalized Negro dialect poetry." Not even Dunbar "had been able to discard [the] stereotyped properties of minstrel-stage dialect."[23] Johnson has been accused unjustly of abandoning "dialect" for "standard English" in a misguided attempt to "elevate the race" in the minds of whites.[24] On the contrary, he accused the dialect poets, unlike the oral "folk" poets, of addressing themselves to an "outside audience" and accepting that audience's discriminations between "levels" of poetic discourse: "The psychological attitude of the poets writing in the dialect and that of the folk artists faced in different directions: because the latter, although working in the dialect, sought only to express themselves to their own group" rather than to cultural "outsiders."[25] Johnson argument was not with the adequacy of black English vernacular. Rather, as Langston Hughes and Sterling Brown would recognize, he was after an idiomatic vernacular poetics, and he recognized that a modernist break with the "dialect" tradition was the only route to a new, more variously self-expressive, black poetry. Indeed, Johnson's break with Dunbar—who was unimpressed with Whitman—helped make possible the experiments of Langston Hughes and Sterling Brown, who could nonetheless appreciate the importance of Dunbar's achievements.

It is interesting that, like Hughes, Johnson tried his hand at Whitmanesque free verse before returning to the black oral tradition, believing that "the Negro poet in the United States, for poetry which he wishes to give a distinctively racial tone and color, needs now an instrument of greater range than dialect."[26] The traditional form of dialect poetry, after all, had been authorized from "above." The problem was not merely that it was associated with the dehumanizing conventions of the minstrel show but that it depended upon an implicit separation between "high" and "low" speech. Hence the strict distinction between the two-thirds of Dunbar's poems in "literary English"—for which he primarily wanted to be known—and the one-third in "dialect" (both "black" and "white" dialect). Furthermore, the distinction between the formally educated "poet" and the "uneducated" dialect speaker is implicitly emphasized in poems fitting, say, an antebellum sermon into conventional meters and rhymes of the English tradition. Langston Hughes and Sterling Brown may have learned a lot from Dunbar, but on the whole their work derives from a different orientation to the "poetic," an orientation arrived at by a swerve like Johnson's from Dunbar and precipitated by their own encounters with *Leaves of Grass*.

Whitman had not depended on an exoticizing orthography to create a "speakerly text"; instead, he had broken down the boundaries between racy contemporary speech and "literature," boundaries essential to genteel "dialect" poetry—indeed, to Johnson's own poetry before his reading of Whitman. Moreover, Johnson noted that black preachers themselves—among the most powerful wordcrafters and image-makers of the "race"—did not employ "dialect" alone in their sermons but rather a more grandiloquent speech that "was really a fusion of Negro idioms with Bible English." "They were all saturated with the sublime phraseology of the Hebrew prophets and steeped in the idioms of King James English."[27] Readers of Whitman should notice some kinship here.

If a stock element of the minstrel show was a travesty of black oratory, ridiculing precisely the sort of syncretic linguistic feats described by Johnson, Whitman undermines such travesty, syncretically merging the colloquial and the sublime (a practice for which he was, likewise, often ridiculed). This is a strategy to which Johnson, Hughes, Toomer, Hurston, and Brown all caught on. Thus, it is only too appropriate that Johnson's first poems after his transformed view of the vernacular would be inspired by a dominant form of oral black religious expression, the sermon—rendered not in traditional meters and rhymes but in a free verse form with each line corresponding to a breath. As C. Carroll Hollis has shown, Whitman strove mightily to develop an "oral" and "speakerly" style with religious and theatrical, even ritualistic, effects. (Portions of "Song of Myself" have even been compared to Haitian vodun ceremonies.)[28] And among the important influences upon Whitman had been both Old Testament prophets and popular preachers, such as Father Taylor of Boston, who used a vernacular style attuned to their working-class audiences. Whitman wanted, like the black preachers Johnson admired, to move his audience to ecstasy.

JEAN TOOMER

The linguistic as well as religious and ecstatic or "mystical" side of Whitman would appeal strongly to Jean Toomer, for whom Whitman was a constant point of reference. When, in about 1919, Toomer began seriously to train himself as a writer, he was deeply under the influence of Whitman's example.[29] From Whitman he shortly turned to Goethe's *Wilhelm Meister*, which confirmed his sense of vocation. Then, wrote Toomer, "I returned to Whitman because he was of America, and I felt he had something to give me in terms of the American world. I spent days in the library reading not only all he had written, but all that had been written about him. The rest of my time I practiced writing."[30] Toomer laved himself in *Leaves of Grass*, *Democratic Vistas*, *An American Primer*, and no doubt studies by Burroughs, Bucke, Traubel, and the other early disciples; then he would go home and write his own leaves.

In a manuscript entitled "Whitman, and the Use of Current Popular Idiom," Toomer uses Whitman's American Primer and "Slang in America!" as "springboards" to an argument about the potential uses of the vernacular in modern literature. He quotes "Slang in America!' at length: "'Slang, profoundly considered, is the lawless germinal element, below all words and sentences, and behind all poetry, and proves a certain perennial rankness and Protestantism in speech.'" "Song of Myself," continues Toomer, makes "deeply creative use" of slang, combining it with elements of traditional "high" culture in a way that jars the reader's expectations and throws cultural hierarchies into question. Significantly, he focuses upon the moment in the poem when Whitman "measures" himself against the "elder religions":

> This poem, it will be noted, does something more than use slang for itself. It is, I believe, inevitably used to express the content and contrast contained in this poem. Granted that Whitman wished to bring into relief his own contemporary position as contrasted with the ancient or historical theologies, how better do this than by juxtaposing such words as Kronos and lithographing, buying drafts and Isis? Here then we have Whitman in a profound use of slang. This characteristic has its negative significance in that it will serve to hold in check a superficial use of slang. And, positively, it channels a creative fusion of popular idiom.[31]

Toomer's work exemplifies his own modernist attempt to fuse slang, vernacular, and "standard" diction to bring into relief a new historical, racial, and religious position. He thought of himself as developing a "classic American prose" in the process of serving the nation's "spiritual ripening." Fascinated by the intercultural urban transformation of language, he resisted the romantic enshrinement of so-called authentic black folk speech. Forfeiting the desire for "pure" racial origins, linguistic or otherwise, he built for the future with all the mismatched materials at hand. And in this bricolage he consciously extended the legacy of Whitman. *Cane* was hailed immediately in *Crisis and Opportunity* as the harbinger of a new movement in African American letters and has been considered by many ever since as the greatest single achievement of that movement, not least for its linguistic experimentation—despite the fact that Toomer apparently never considered himself a "Negro" author.

Toomer's linguistic experiment followed his commitment to American cultural nationalism, for which, again, Whitman was the central icon. He explicitly mentions Whitman in "Box Seat" in a context suggesting the bard's function as a role model for the protagonist. Dan Moore ponders the experience of a sphinxlike former slave in Washington and seeks in his eyes the imprinted image of America's "wound-dresser"/prophet: "He saw Walt—old man, did you see Walt Whitman? Did you see Walt Whitman! Strange force that drew me to him. And I went up to see. . . . I told him to look into the heavens. He did, and smiled. I asked him if he knew what that rumbling is that comes up from the ground." The "rumbling," we know from an earlier passage, is the sound of "a new-world Christ . . . coming up," born of the "powerful underground races."[32]

Unquestionably, Toomer thought of himself as Whitman's successor in the American prophet/healer's role. He felt in 1923 (the year *Cane* was published) that the revolt against puritanism and materialism had run its course and that great creation must move beyond protest and "inspired propaganda" to that "abundance which includes acceptance. . . . When I have made the path easy and in all ways to be desired, what strength will you show then in taking it." If this passage echoes the early Whitman's exhortations to "shoulder your duds" and take to the American road, another echoes the "later Whitman" in prescribing a literary shift from social critique to a "balance and inclusion. . . . Starting from the premise that an adjustment, adjustment in the sense of an acceptance of, and a healthy functioning from the physical environment, and a stirring towards a desired spiritual fulfillment, are fundamental to the life of any nation." The essay calls for writers to follow Whitman's lead.[33]

The influence of theories of "cosmic consciousness" (which appealed to the Waldo Frank circle because they answered the perceived American need for "spiritual ripening"[34]) began to grow upon Toomer even as he was composing *Cane* and came under the influence of A. R. Orage, a chief sidekick of G. I. Gurdjieff who introduced Gurdjieff's ideas to New York intellectuals in the teens and twenties and then recruited Toomer to proselytize among the Harlem intelligentsia. Wrote one observer, "The 'cosmic consciousness' of Walt Whitman was a great theme of his."[35] P. D. Ouspensky's *Tertium Organum*, which influenced both Toomer and Hart Crane, among others, also borrowed from Bucke's theories and his views of Whitman.[36] Certainly, the more mystical passages of *Cane*, as Rudolph Byrd has argued, are compatible with the theories that would shortly monopolize Toomer's attention.[37]

Toomer apparently never stopped identifying with Whitman. At various points in his unpublished autobiography, "Earth-Being," when an event or remembered scene brings up an association with Whitman or a hint of Toomer's destiny, he connects the two. At other points he launches into clumsy Whitmanesque catalogs, blatantly imitative.[38] Indeed, the inspiring figure of Whitman as role model and American prophet is a crucial connecting link between the various phases of Toomer's disjunctive career. Even after he abandoned the "Gurdjieff work," in the final period of his life he would continue his spiritual seeking in Whitman's natal religious denomination—the Society of Friends.

In conclusion, broadly speaking, the "New Negro" authors who saw themselves as descendants of Whitman came to believe that African American culture offered precisely the answer to Whitman's prayers, that it filled the void Whitman's white descendants continually decried in their fulminations against the emotionally desiccated, spiritless America of the puritan and the pioneer, against the yawning chasm between the highbrow and the low. Moreover, this position was also typical of the white authors and critics—many of them Whitman disciples—who were most closely allied to the movement, who read the manuscripts and reviewed the books of black authors, edited the magazines and anthologies through which their work reached an interracial public, and wrote for the black magazines that showcased the Negro Renaissance. In other words, the early canonization of Whitman in the United States and the rise of black literary modernism were intimately interrelated and complementary developments. Moreover, the very advances for which even its critics credit the "New Negro" movement—generally, for advancing a distinctly African American tradition in literature—are developments in which the impact of Whitman was critical.

Hence, if we accept the validity of recent readings of Whitman's texts as fostering a white imperialist self and ideology, complicit with white American hegemony—and I think such readings have merit—then we are left with the paradox that, overall, the effects of his work in the early twentieth century—on African American authors, at least—emphatically contradicted the ideological "message" that recent critics have elucidated. This is as attributable to the interests, needs, and imaginations of his readers and the contexts in which they read him as to the ideological ambiguities of his poetry. James Weldon Johnson recognized the importance of this point when he misquoted Whitman to conclude a eulogy for Julius Rosenwald at Fisk University in 1932:

> All architecture is what you do to it when you look upon it.
> Did you think it was in the white or gray stone?
> Or in the lines of the arches and cornices?
> All music is what awakes from you when you are reminded by the
> instruments.
> It is not the violins and the cornets,
> It is not the oboe nor the beating drums,
> Nor the score of the baritone singer singing his sweet romanza,
> Nor that of the men's chorus,
> Nor that of the women's chorus,
> It is nearer and farther than they.[39]

The power and beauty of the artwork are to be found, Johnson reminds his black collegiate audience, by way of Whitman, in the uses to which one puts it in one's life. To argue for the pervasive impact of Whitman's legacy on the Harlem Renaissance is not, then, to attempt to "save" Whitman from examinations of his racism or to try to contain racial difference within American sameness—but it is to insist on a "mulatto" aspect of American traditions that coexists with and continually revitalizes their multicultural distinctiveness. And it is to demonstrate the need to go beyond ideological interrogation toward diverse historical investigations of the complex, productive, and often ironic or scandalous interrelations between ostensibly separate "racial"/cultural traditions in the United States.

NOTES

1. Michael R. Winston, "Locke, Alain," in Rayford W. Logan and Michael R. Winston, eds., *The Dictionary of American Negro Biography* (New York: Norton, 1982), 398–404; Eugene C. Holmes, "Alain L. Locke and the Adult Education Movement," *Journal of Negro Education* 30 (Winter 1965): 5; Douglas K. Stafford, "Alaine Locke: The Child, the Man, and the People," *Journal of Negro Education* 30 (Winter 1961): 26. Stafford

calls Mary Locke "one of the earliest followers of Felix Adler" and notes that, "aside from the Society of Friends [the Ethical Society] was in many ways the most liberal of the respectable organizations open to the Negro, explicitly providing for his participation in all its projects" (26–27). The research for this article was pursued as part of a larger project entitled "American Cultural Nationalism and the Harlem Renaissance," which was funded in 1989–1990 by a National Endowment for the Humanities fellowship.

2. William C. Bolivar to Alain Locke, February 14, 1909, Alain Locke Correspondence Files, Alain Locke Papers, Moorland–Springarn Research Center, Howard University.
3. See the *Walt Whitman Fellowship Papers* for these years. Miller was a member of the organization from its founding in 1895 and addressed its first meeting with his essay "What Walt Whitman Means to the Negro," which I have discussed in "Whitman and the Black Poet: Kelly Miller's Speech to the Walt Whitman Fellowship," *American Literature* 61 (1989): 46–58.
4. Thanks to Tony Gutwein, librarian at the Camden County Historical Society, for tracing these facts for me.
5. Mary Hawkins Locke to Alain Locke, April 12, 1905, Alain Locke–Mary Hawkins Locke Correspondence Files, Box 2, Alain Locke Papers. The Miss Button referred to in the letter was a painter and art teacher who donated the drawing board that Mary Davis (Whitman's housemate and housekeeper) converted into a tray for Whitman to write on during the last weeks of his life (Elizabeth Leavitt Keller, *Walt Whitman in Mickle Street* [New York: Mitchell Kennerley, 1921], 168). The episode with the artists mentioned in the letter took place in the summer of 1887, when Sidney Morse was working on a bust of the poet and Herbert Gilchrist showed up from England at the same time to do Whitman's portrait. The story is vividly told in Keller (76–81).
6. See Kenneth M. Price, "Imagining Whitman at Harvard," *Whitman and Tradition* (New Haven: Yale University Press, 1990).
7. Eve Kosofsky Sedgwick, *Between Men: English Literature and Male Homosocial Desire* (New York: Columbia University Press, 1985), 205, 203.
8. Harold W. Blodgett, *Walt Whitman in England* (Ithaca: Cornell University Press, 1934), 207.
9. Countee Cullen to Alain Locke, March 3, 1923, Alain Locke Correspondence Files, Alain Locke Papers.
10. Langston Hughes to Alain Locke, n.d. (circa May 1923), Alain Locke Correspondence Files, Alain Locke Papers. Locke's sexual pursuit of

Hughes, in part provoked by this letter, is discussed in Arnold Rampersad, *The Life of Langston Hughes* (New York: Oxford University Press, 1986), 1: 69.

11. Alain Locke, "The American Temperament," in Jeffrey C. Stewart, ed., *The Critical Temper of Alain Locke* (New York: Garland, 1983), 404. The essay was first published in the *North American Review* 194 (August 1911): 262–270.
12. Locke, "The American Temperament," *Critical Temper*, 401, 403.
13. For an account of Kallen's and Locke's interactions vis-à-vis cultural pluralism, see Werner Sollors, "A Critique of Pure Pluralism," in Sacvan Bercovitch, ed., *Reconstructing American Literary History* (Cambridge: Harvard University Press, 1986), 263–273.
14. Locke, "African Art: Classic Style," *Critical Temper*, 151.
15. Locke, "Emile Verhaeren," *Critical Temper*, 37.
16. Ibid.
17. Alain Locke, ed., *The New Negro* (1925; rpt., New York: Atheneum, 1970), 15–16.
18. Locke, "The Negro's Contribution to American Art and Literature" (1928), *Critical Temper*, 448.
19. Locke, "Beauty Instead of Ashes" (1928), *Critical Temper*, 25.
20. Locke, "Color—A Review" (1926), *Critical Temper*, 39–40.
21. Locke, "The Poetry of Negro Life" (1927), *Critical Temper*, 47. George B. Hutchinson, "Langston Hughes and the 'Other' Whitman," in Robert K. Martin, ed., *The Continuing Presence of Walt Whitman: The Life after the Life* (Iowa City: University of Iowa Press, 1992), 16–27.
22. Locke, "Art or Propaganda," *Critical Temper*, 27.
23. James Weldon Johnson, *Along This Way* (New York: Viking, 1933), 158–159. An excellent discussion of the differences between Dunbar and Johnson can be found in Myron Simon, "Dunbar and Dialect Poetry," in Jay Martin, ed., *A Singer in the Dawn: Reinterpretations of Paul Laurence Dunbar* (New York: Dodd, Mead, 1975), 144–154.
24. Perhaps the most influential recent statement of this view is that of Henry Louis Gates Jr., in *Figures in Black: Words, Signs, and the "Racial" Self* (New York: Oxford University Press, 1987), 184.
25. Johnson, *Along This Way*, 158–159.
26. James Weldon Johnson, "Preface," in *God's Trombones: Seven Negro Sermons in Verse* (1927; rpt., New York: Viking, 1942), 8.
27. Johnson, "Preface," 9.
28. C. Carroll Hollis, *Language and Style in Leaves of Grass* (Baton Rouge: Louisiana State University Press, 1983); Robin Magowan, "The Horse of the Gods: Possession in 'Song of Myself,'" *Walt Whitman Review* 15 (1969): 67–76.

29. Just about the time Toomer "discovered" Whitman, his grandfather sold the family home and sent him $600, which Toomer decided to live on, believing he was at a turning point in his life. Toomer quit his job and devoted himself full-time to music and literature. See "Outline of the Story of an Autobiography," 43–44, Box 20, Folder 515, Jean Toomer Papers, Collection of American Literature, Beinecke Rare Book and Manuscript Library, Yale University.
30. Toomer, "Outline," 43–44.
31. Toomer, Typescript, Box 48, Folder 1,009, 1–2, Jean Toomer Papers.
32. Jean Toomer, *Cane*, ed. Darwin T. Turner (New York: Norton, 1988), 68, 65.
33. Ms. fragment, Box 48, Folder 1,010, Jean Toomer Papers. Though the fragment is undated, its emphasis upon the need for fulfillment in American literature and for a movement beyond protest against America indicates that it comes from the period before, during, or immediately after the composition of *Cane*, for Toomer was to abandon interest in such topics by 1924. Moreover, about the time *Cane* came out, he was planning a volume that would follow the lines suggested in the fragment.
34. James Webb, *The Harmonious Circle: The Lives and Work of G. I Gurdjieff, P. D. Ouspensky, and Their Followers* (New York: Putnam, 1980), 275.
35. Gerald Cumberland, *Set Down in Malice* (New York: Brentano's, 1919), 132.
36. One manuscript reader immediately noticed the similarities between Toomer's ideas and those of Bucke. Anonymous rejection letter, Box 17, Folder 472, Jean Toomer Papers.
37. See Rudolph P. Byrd, *Jean Toomer's Years With Gurdjieff: Portrait of an Artist, 1923–1936* (Athens: University of Georgia Press, 1990).
38. See, for example, "Earth-Being," typescript second draft, Book III, 129, 19–20, Box 12, Folder 386, Jean Toomer Papers. Late in his life, when speculating upon how long it might be before the "American" race would come to fruition, he would write, "May be it will befall my vision as it befell Walt Whitman's in that, just as I today can see no large signs of the country developing along his lines, so an individual one hundred years hence may see no large signs of the country having developed along my lines" (Preface 3 to Book X, 9, Jean Toomer Papers).
39. James Weldon Johnson, *The Shining Life* (n.p., 1932).

JOHN S. WRIGHT

The New Negro Poet and the Nachal Man: Sterling Brown's Folk Odyssey

In 1936, the year Sterling Brown and John Lomax joined forces supervising the collection of oral slave narratives for the Federal Writers' Project (see Mangione 257-63), Lomax and his son Alan published the first extended study of an American folksinger. That singer, one Walter Boyd, alias Hudie Ledbetter, alias "Leadbelly," had been the self-proclaimed "King of the Twelve String Guitar Players of the World," as well as the number one man in the number one gang on the number one convict farm in Texas. He had fought his way into prison and had sung his way to freedom, to fleeting fame, and to what would be a pauper's death in Bellevue in 1949. A man of prodigious physical strength, emotional volatility, unpredictable violence, and indisputable creativity, unschooled if not unassuming, he was shaped by record, film, and the printed page into the prototypic national image of the "folk Negro." For the recording industry, his songs were a golden hedge against hard times. For the generation of newly professional folklorists that the Lomaxes represented, he was a "find" that helped buttress the assault of the Depression era folklore radical democrats against the old aristocratic folklore scholarship. For the thinkers and artists of the black world-within-a-world from which he came, however, Leadbelly made concrete an old enigma alternately energizing and embarrassing—and one left largely unplumbed by the outspokenly "folk conscious" New Negro movement of

From *Black American Literature Forum* 23, no. 1 (Spring 1989).

the twenties. Lawbreaker, illiterate, brawler, boozer, womanizer, cotton-picker, and vagrant; singer of prison dirges, work songs, cowboy ballads, children's songs, spirituals, lullabies, and barrel-house blues, Leadbelly was a grinning, gold-toothed incongruity. Vernacular tradition's "nachal man" incarnate, he was in one rough frame the bruised and imbruted "man farthest down" for whom Booker T. Washington and the organizations of racial uplift had lowered their proverbial buckets, *and* he was the voice of that transcendent "Negro genius" which W. E. B. Du Bois and the Talented Tenth had exalted as creator of "the most beautiful expressions of human experience born this side of the seas" (265). In the preceding decade Jean Toomer, Claude McKay, Zora Neale Hurston, and Langston Hughes had all directed their imaginative energies to penetrating the layers of abstraction that created incongruity from the folklife Leadbelly nonetheless had to live. But perhaps nowhere had so clear a perspective emerged for seeing such a man whole as in the work of Sterling Brown.

In 1932 Brown had published *Southern Road*; and with a social realism honed to poetic precision, he had struck through the masks with which minstrelsy, local color, the plantation tradition, and jazz Age primitivism had defaced the folk. Alain Locke, self-professed "literary midwife" of the New Negro movement, in reviewing *Southern Road* hailed Sterling Brown as "The New Negro Folk Poet" and described him as an artist who had revealed better than any of his contemporaries the "racial touch," independent of dialect, which enabled him to catch the deeper "idiom of feeling" (89). Locke had predicted some years earlier that "the soul of the Negro will be discovered in a characteristic way of thinking and in a homely philosophy rather than in a jingling and juggling of broken English" (89). The secret of Sterling Brown's poetic effects was that he had "listened long and carefully to the folk in their intimate hours," talking to themselves, their protective masks dropped. A "more reflective, a closer student of the folk-life. . . . a bolder and more detached observer" than his fellow poets, Sterling Brown had recaptured what was "more profoundly characteristic" than types of metaphors or mannerisms of speech—he had recaptured the philosophic attitudes, material and metaphysical, that lay beneath the surface of folksongs, fables, proverbs, and argot (90). And in giving the folk credit for thinking he had discovered the "poetic divining-rod" for rendering, with Aesopian clarity and Aesopian candor, that ancient common wisdom of the group which promised to bridge the then highly publicized gap between the Old Negro and the New.

Rejecting the Old Negro and the traditional poetry of folk caricature, James Weldon Johnson had advocated a symbolic rather than a phonetic literary mimesis, and had forecast the doom of dialect poetry. But Sterling

Brown perceived that the problem of defining a poetic language for folk portraiture was a problem not so much of materials as of perspective. "Dialect, or the speech of the people," he maintained, "is capable of expressing whatever the people are. And the folk Negro is a great deal more than a buffoon or a plaintive minstrel. Poets more intent upon learning the ways of the folk, their speech, and their character, that is to say, better poets, could have smashed the mold. But first they would have to believe in what they were doing. And this was difficult in a period of conciliation and middle class striving for recognition and respectability" (qtd. in Redmond 227–28). Brown's less conventional strivings provided critical as well as poetic demonstrations of his own unshakable belief in "the validity, the power, and the beauty of folk culture." His was an aesthetic of reorientation, and its achievement rested no less surely on his poems than on the critical paths he cut through the jungle of theory and interpretation, censorship and commercialization, romanticism and mysticism, that engulfed the study of Afro-American folklore between the 1920s and the 1950s.

The twenties, besides hosting the New Negro movement, fostered another phenomenon not unconnected to the black cultural ferment of the time with its artistic focus on, in Locke's terms, "the revaluation of the Negro": After a war decade remarkable for the *accumulation* of major folklore collections in America, the twenties became a decade remarkable for the *publication* of folklore collections. Several decades earlier, in 1888, the American Folklore Society had been founded as a kind of rescue operation to record what were thought to be the "fast vanishing relics" of rural folk groups before their projected disappearance from an urbanizing, industrializing modern culture (Brunvand 9). Though the academic study of folklore would not be established in the United States until the 1940s, an interim throng of avid amateurs and bootlegging scholars trained in other fields—English literature, anthropology, sociology, musicology, history, and languages—began consolidating in the twenties a vast repository of folklore and folksong which by the forties had tapped extensively the traditions of such occupational, regional, ethnic, and racial groups as Western cowboys, Nova Scotian sailors, Midwestern lumberjacks, Pennsylvania Germans, Southwest Mexican-Americans, Utah Mormons, and Ozark mountaineers (Brunvand 9, 19).

In this surge of folklore collecting, studies of Afro-American lore and song loomed large. Such collecting was not new, of course: The first serious collection, *Slave Songs of the United States*, had been made in 1867. Between the end of Reconstruction and the turn of the century, a series of literary figures, beginning with William Wells Brown (*My Southern Home*, 1880) and including Joel Chandler Harris, with his Uncle Remus collections, and

Charles Chesnutt (*The Conjure Woman*, 1899), made literary capital from black folktales and anecdotes. White collectors like C. C. Jones, Jr., and Virginia Boyle transcribed folk myths and devil tales in the Sea Islands Gullah dialect. And during the 1880s and '90s a black folklore group met regularly at Hampton Institute in Virginia and published summaries of papers and the texts of oral lore in the *Southern Workman* (Dorson 110). Interest in the folk, though, had waned enough by the opening years of the new century to lead Booker T. Washington to complain, in his 1904 introduction to Samuel Coleridge-Taylor's *Twenty-Four Negro Melodies*, that the plantation songs were dying out with the generation that had given them birth (Lovell 494).

When the resurgence of Afro-American folklore collecting appeared early in the twenties, it was with the force of a revitalized national interest in native traditions behind it. John Lomax's publication of *Cowboy Songs and Other Frontier Ballads* in 1910 and Cecil Sharp's *English Folksongs from the Southern Appalachians* in 1917 had pioneered a turnabout in American folklore research by revealing living folksong traditions that were not vanishing but instead surviving and in fact being continually reborn. In 1915, amidst a flurry of regional collecting, music critic Henry Krehbiel had directed attention away from the ongoing "ballad wars" and toward the Afro-American folksongs he sought "to bring into the field of scientific observation" (v). Krehbiel had centered his study around the questions of "whether or not the songs were original creations of these native blacks, whether or not they were entitled to be called American, and whether or not they were worthy of consideration as foundation elements for a school of American composition" (vi). Krehbiel had answered all these in the affirmative; and his formulation then of the problems of origins, of methods of composition, and of provenience did much to set the terms of discourse for the new black folklore studies that flowed out into the public arena in the twenties and early thirties.

Those studies revealed a body of Afro-American oral tradition that was massive, vital, and portentous. The published collections included Thomas Talley's *Negro Folk Rhymes* (secular songs and linguistic lore) and Ambrose Gonzales' *With Aesop Along the Black Border* (coastal fables in Gullah dialect) in 1922; Elsie Parson's *Folklore of the Sea Islands* in 1923; Dorothy Scarborough's *On the Trail of Negro Folk-Songs* in 1925; Howard Odum and Guy Johnson's *The Negro and His Songs* and *Negro Workaday Songs* in 1925 and 1926, respectively; James Weldon Johnson's *Book of American Negro Spirituals* and *Second Book . . .* in 1925 and 1926; Newbell Niles Puckett's *Folk Beliefs of the Southern Negro* in 1926; Newman White's *American Negro Folk Songs* in 1928; E. C. L. Adams' *Congaree Sketches and Nigger to Nigger* (coastal jokes and tales) in 1927 and 1928. Howard Odum's novelistic trilogy about travelin' man Left Wing Gordon—*Rainbow Round My Shoulder*, *Wings on My Feet*, and *Cold Blue Moon*—appeared in 1928, 1929, and 1930; Guy Johnson's *Folk Culture on St. Helena Island* in 1930; J. Mason Brewer's slave tale collection *Juneteenth* in 1932; Zora Neale Hurston's *Mules and Men* in 1935; and John and Alan Lomax's *Negro Folk Songs as Sung by Leadbelly* in 1936.

In the face of this expanding repository of traditional art and customs, the prevailing notion that no distinctive Afro-American culture existed, or that such culture as did exist was one of either fossilized African survivals or debased imitations of white models, began to give ground. And the folk ideology so central to the New Negro creed formulated by Alain Locke received a concrete foundation of folk myths, legends, symbols, and character types upon which many of the major black literary achievements of the next two decades would build. Prospects for employing the new folklore studies either for aesthetic purposes or in support of the sociopolitical "literature of racial vindication," however, were vitiated by a trio of conceptual problems and controversies that implicated the whole of folklore research and interpretation at the time.

First, American folklorists, who, as Richard Dorson has noted, were rarely trained in folklore and rarely Americanists, subscribed heavily to Eurocentric theories that (a) predicated the existence of folklore on the presence of a traditional peasantry that did not exist in America, (b) treated folklore genres hierarchically, with the Anglo-Saxon ballad first and foremost, and (c) approached American folk forms generally as corrupted, inherently inferior imitations of Old World originals (Dorson 4–7). Under the disabling influence of these theories, Fisk professor Thomas Talley, for example, in his pioneering study of Afro-American folk rhymes, labored tortuously to force his materials into an elaborate system of ballad classification based on his defensively mystical proposition that "all [Negro] Folk Rhymes are Nature Ballads" with call-and-response structures that somehow "hover ghostlike" over them (250, 285).

Second, nineteenth-century racist ethnology, though under attack in the anthropological work of Franz Boas and his students, remained a potent force in the new folklore research—reinforced by lingering Social Darwinism and the currents of popular nativism and racism. The mystique of racial "gifts," "temperaments," and "geniuses" helped contort the endless debate over the origins of folk forms waged between diffusionists, who believed in a single origin of folk themes with their subsequent spread, and polygeneticists, who argued for the repeated reinvention of similar materials because of similar psychological or historical conditions (Brunvand 11). Their romantic racialism made studies like Odum and Johnson's *The Negro and His Songs*, which presented the earliest extended analysis of the blues, read, as contemporary folklorists have acknowledged, "like a Music of the Darkies with a bit of enlightened sociological body English" (Jackson 7).

Third, the new folklore studies were hampered by the absence of any scientific or humanistic theory of American culture and national character capable of comprehending, as a cultural matrix for folklife, this country's modernity, its radical heterogeneity, and its peculiar blend of social fixedness and fluidity. Moreover, the folkloric enterprise was subject to pressures from popularization, commercialization, and the emerging mass media that were plagued with distortions and fabrications of folk culture that produced the "bankrupt treasuries" Stanley Edgar Hyman lambasted in the mid-forties and that led Richard Dorson eventually to coin the distinction between folklore and the rising tide of "fakelore" (Dorson 5–7).

Into this fray Sterling Brown brought a keen critical intelligence, his convictions about the cultural integrity and aesthetic significance of folklife, and his instincts as a creative writer. Afro-American folklorists were scarce to say the least, and in the quarter-century of folkloric fervor that spanned the Jazz Age, the Great Depression, and the Second World War, Sterling Brown's essays in *Opportunity* and *Phylon*, and his editorial and scholarly work with the Federal Writers' Project Negro Affairs division, filled the void with a wide-ranging folklore critique fully cognizant of the shifting grounds of folklore scholarship yet fixed unerringly on the perspectives of the folk themselves. Brown had spent the years after the publication of *Southern Road* absorbed in Afro-American literary history and the iconography of racial stereotypy—preoccupations fleshed out in his *The Negro in American Fiction* and *Negro Poetry and Drama*. With his appointment to the Federal Writers' Project in the spring of 1936, he turned toward the sociohistorical study of the black folk and urban experience, immersing himself first in the gathering of ex-slave narratives which was then underway and which would be perhaps the Writers' Project's greatest contribution to the study of Afro-American life.

The collection of slave narratives had been begun in 1934 by the Federal Emergency Relief Administration, at the instigation of black historian Lawrence Reddick, who had voiced the growing historical consensus that the story of slavery and Reconstruction could not be complete "until we get the view as presented through the slave himself" (Mangione 257). The Writers' Project had inherited the undertaking; and in 1936, when John Lomax became the Project's first folklore editor, Sterling Brown began guiding the interviewing efforts that would lead finally to the publication of seventeen volumes of manuscripts containing over two thousand slave narratives (Mangione 263). Under Lomax's supervision, and after 1938 under the leadership of Benjamin Botkin, the Project proceeded to collect folk materials on a scale larger than ever previously attempted.

Under Botkin's influence especially, the Project countered the antiquarian orientation of academic folklorists with an emphasis on oral history and "living lore." Sterling Brown, who had contributed poems and critical reviews to Botkin's four-volume regional miscellany *Folk-Say* between 1929 and 1932, found Botkin's proletarian emphasis congenial to his own. "The folk movement must come from below upward rather than from above downward," Botkin contended; "otherwise it may be dismissed as a patronizing gesture, a nostalgic wish, an elegiac complaint, a sporadic and abortive review—on the part of paternalistic aristocrats going slumming, dilettantish provincials going native, defeated sectionalists going back to the soil, and anybody and everybody who cares to going collecting" (Mangione 270). Folk imagination more than folk knowledge became the Project's aim, and the outlook and skills of writers such as Sterling Brown became crucial to capturing it.

For Sterling Brown the aim also was, in his words, to "produce an accurate picture of the Negro in American social history," to reveal him as an integral part of American life and to do so in a way that mediated between the competing chauvinisms of both white and black historians (Mangione 259). The device of correlating folklore with social and ethnic history was the tactic Brown emphasized in his editorial role and in his efforts to have Afro-American materials included in the Project's state guidebooks then being compiled around the country. The publication of *The Negro in Virginia* in 1940 demonstrated the value of this approach. It was produced under the local supervision of black historian Roscoe Lewis, but Brown's role in this field project was considerable. Built upon years of carefully collected oral histories and interviews and on painstaking research that traced neglected materials back to the arrival in Virginia of the first Africans in 1619, *The Negro in Virginia* became a model of documentary research and narrative drama (Mangione 260–61).

In a talk before the Conference on the Character and State of Studies in Folklore in 1946, Brown looked back at his years with the Project: "I became interested in folklore," he recalled, "because of my desire to write poetry and prose fiction. I was first attracted by certain qualities I thought the speech of the people had, and I wanted to get for my own writing a flavor, a color, a pungency of speech. Then later I came to something more important—I wanted to get an understanding of people" ("Approach" 506). Respectful of the scientific approaches to folklore but untroubled by any definitional or procedural obstacles that might block his access to the "living-people-lore" of, for instance, so fascinating a tribe as urban jazzmen, Sterling

Brown had developed a flexible, functionalist approach to folklore. It was an approach that, as Alan Lomax advocated in the same session, rejected views of the folk as ignorant receptacles for traditions and ideas which they do not themselves understand, and which make very little sense until they are pieced together and explained in historical terms by the comparative scholar." Such an approach instead saw folklore as "equipment for living," saw the folklorist as performing not only an archaeological role but one of recording a vigorous human tradition, and it recognized that "the best interpretations of folklore may be obtained in the end from the folk themselves" (Lomax, "Functional Aspects" 507).

In the early forties, the conviction that the folk may be their own best interpreters became one of the trademarks of Sterling Brown's series of articles on black folk expression. His synoptic essay in *The Negro Caravan* in 1941, on the sources and genres of black oral literature, stands even today as the single best introduction to the subject because, in threading its way through all the scholarship and interpretative quandaries of the previous decades, it maintains its balance by never falling victim to the disorienting proposition that, as Newman White had myopically insisted, "the Negro never contemplated his low estate."

"Nigger, your breed ain't metaphysical," one of the voices in Robert Penn Warren's poeticized fable "Pondy Woods" had proclaimed, confronting New Negroes with the old stereotype of the crusading New South. "Cracker, your breed ain't exegetical," Sterling Brown responded dialectically, as he outlined a critique that treated black forms as distillations of communal *mind* and *ethos* (Brown interview). In his essays on the blues in particular, Brown treated the products of folk imagination as *self*-conscious wisdom—tragic, comic, ironic, shrewd, emotionally elastic and attitudinally complex, capable of supporting a variety of stances toward life, and resistant, as such, to ideological straitjacketing or implications of naïveté. Worldly and self-aware, the spirit of the blues, he submitted, is defined by the songs themselves, in lines which assert that "the blues ain't nothin' but a poor man's heart disease" or "the blues ain't nothin' but a good man way, way down" or, more obliquely, "Woke up this morning, blues walking round my bed / Went in to eat my breakfast, blues was all in my bread." The blues fused stoicism in a concrete, *metaphoric metaphysic*: It was a frank Chaucerian *attitude* toward sex and love that kept even the bawdiest authentic blues from being prurient and pornographic. It was "elemental *honesty*," "depth of *insight*," and *sophistication* about human relations that lay behind their appeal across caste lines. It was *imagination* making the love of life and the love of words memorably articulate which turned the best blues into potent lyric poetry.[1]

Brown's reading of the blues tradition did not go uncontested. In a lengthy, two-part essay on the spirit and meaning of black folk expression published in *Phylon* in the early fifties, he acknowledged that "the field of folklore in general is known to be a battle area, and the Negro front is one of the hottest sectors" (Autumn 1950: 319). But he needed no new battlepieces, no defensive ethnic chauvinism. Incorporating the insights of Stith Thompson's then definitive study of the folktale, he found, in the newly revealed patterns of interchange and diffusion characteristic of even Old World African folklore, support for his vision of the underlying unity of the world's and the nation's many cultural traditions. After all, he noted, in the cosmology of black folk traditions themselves, "tales about the origin of the races leave little room for chauvinism about a chosen people. The slaves knew at first hand that the black man had a hard road to travel, and they tell of the mistakes of creation with sardonic fatalism" (Autumn 1950: 325). Looking then at the prospects for the future of folklife, he knew that hard road was all too literal. Black folk culture was breaking up, he thought. In migrating to the city "the folk become a submerged proletariat. Leisurely yarn-spinning, slow paced aphoristic conversation become lost arts; jazzed-up gospel hymns provide a different sort of release from the old spirituals; the blues reflect the distortions of the new way of life. Folk arts are no longer by the folk for the folk; smart businessmen now put them up for sale. Gospel songs often become showpieces for radio-slummers, and the blues become the double talk of the dives." And yet, he interjected, "the vigor of the creative impulse has not been snapped, even in the slums," and the folk roots "show a stubborn vitality" (Winter 1953: 60–61).

Leadbelly was a few years dead then, his pauperized last seasons spent as a resident "living legend" in Greenwich Village coffeehouses. The "blues boom," the "rediscovery" of New Orleans jazz, and the folk revivals of the fifties were taking hold. *Southern Road*, though, was out of print and Sterling Brown's poetry largely unremarked since the thirties by the canonizers of American verse. In his various roles as teacher, scholar, poet, husband, mentor, and self-confessed "Teller of Lies," Brown weathered those years, and the years after, sustained by the same lyric loves he found in the blues—the love of words, the love of life, and the love of all things musical, as he was wont to say, "from Beethoven to the boogie-woogie." And perhaps concluding with this one of Brown's own pointed incongruities makes sense if, blues-like, we "worry" it a bit. Beethoven, save for the tarbrushings that allege him to be quite literally a "soul brother," is a relatively unambiguous reference for defining one aesthetic pole and one kind of hero on the spectrum of "strange legacies" Sterling Brown's work embraces. The boogie-woogie, though, evokes almost as unruly an image as Leadbelly, for the phrase masks onomatopoetically a complex legacy of juxtaposed folk meanings: The boogie-woogie was simultaneously a fast-stepping, Kansas City jazz-influenced piano blues in which the bass figure comes in double time; it was the knee-flexing jitterbug one danced in accompaniment; it was a racial epithet; it was a wartime moniker for enemy aircraft; it was an intransitive vernacular verb connoting the uninhibited pursuit of pleasure; it was a reference to the devil and all the troubles associated with him; and it was, less openly but no less significantly, a Southern euphemism for a case of secondary syphilis. There was a multilayered joke proffered, in other words, in Brown's wry conflation of Beethoven with the boogie-woogie, an irreverent populist riff that counterpointed democratically the classical with the vernacular, the academy with the Southern road, white icons with black reprobates; and that now, in remembrance, binds Brown the scholar/poet with the many-monikered chaingang songster as nachally as a professing Teller of Lies might be to the legend with the gold-toothed grin.

Notes

1. Sterling Brown, "The Blues as Folk Poetry," *Folk-Say*, 4 vols., ed. Benjamin Botkin (Norman: U of Oklahoma P, 1930) 1: 324–39; "Blues, Ballads and Social Songs," *Seventy-five Years of Freedom* (Washington: Library of Congress, 18 December 1940) 17–25; "The Blues," *Phylon* 13 (Autumn 1952): 286–92.

Works Cited

Brown, Sterling. "The Approach of the Creative Artist," *Journal of American Folklore* 59 (Oct. 1946): 506–07.

———. "Folk Literature." *The Negro Caravan*. Ed. Sterling Brown, Arthur Davis, and Ulysses Lee. 1941. New York: Arno and The New York Times, 1970. 412–34.

———. Interview with Sterling Brown. With John Edgar Tidwell and John S. Wright. Washington, 13 July 1980.

———. "Negro Folk Expression." *Phylon* 11 (Autumn 1950): 318–27.

———. "Negro Folk Expression: Spirituals, Seculars, Ballads and Work Songs." *Phylon* 14 (Winter 1953): 45–61.

Brunvand, Jan Harold. *Folklore: A Study and Research Guide*. New York: St. Martin's, 1976.

Dorson, Richard. *American Folklore and the Historian*. Chicago: U of Chicago P, 1971.

Du Bois, W. E. B. *The Souls of Black Folk* (1903). *Three Negro Classics*. Ed. John Hope Franklin. New York: NAL, 1969. 207–389.

Jackson, Bruce. Foreword. *American Negro Folksongs*. By Newman White. 1928. Hatbora, PA: Folklore Associates, 1965.

Krehbiel, Henry. *Afro-American Folksongs: A Study in Racial and National Music*. New York: Schirmer, 1914.

Locke, Alain. "Sterling Brown: The New Negro Folk Poet." *Negro Anthology*. Ed. Nancy Cunard. 1934. New York: Ungar, 1970. 88–92.

Lomax, Alan. "The Functional Aspects of Folklore." *Journal of American Folklore* 59 (Oct. 1946): 507–10.

Lomax, John, and Alan Lomax. *Negro Folk Songs as Sung by Leadbelly*. New York: Macmillan, 1936.

Lovell, John. *Black Songs. The Forge and the Flame*. New York: Macmillan, 1972.

Mangione, Jerre. *The Dream and the Deal. The Federal Writers' Project, 1935–1943*. New York: Avon, 1972.

Redmond, Eugene. *Drumvoices: The Mission of Afro-American Poetry*. Garden City: Anchor, 1976.

Talley, Thomas. *Negro Folk Rhymes. 1922*. Port Washington: Kennikat, 1968.

ANITA PATTERSON

Jazz, Realism, and the Modernist Lyric: The Poetry of Langston Hughes

In 1940 Richard Wright, praising Langston Hughes's contribution to the development of modern American literature, observed that Hughes's "realistic position" had become the "dominant outlook of all those Negro writers who have something to say."[1] Nineteen years later James Baldwin faulted Hughes for failing to follow through consistently on the artistic premises laid out in his early verse. The problem with his unsuccessful poems, Baldwin said, was that they "take refuge, finally, in a fake simplicity in order to avoid the very difficult simplicity of experience." In succumbing to the idiomatic demands of a sociological perspective the pressure, that is, to "hold the experience outside him"—they did not fulfill an essential criterion of Baldwin's realism, namely, the evocation of a point of view that stands "within the experience and outside it at the same time." To argue his point, Baldwin cited the last line of a jazz poem by Hughes called "Dream Boogie," which first appeared as part of *Montage of a Dream Deferred* in 1951. "Hughes," said Baldwin, "knows the bitter truth behind these hieroglyphics, what they are designed to protect, what they are designed to convey. But he has not forced them into the realm of art where their meaning would become clear and overwhelming. 'Hey, pop! / Re-bop! / Mop! conveys much more on Lenox Avenue than it does in this book, which is not the way it ought to be."[2]

From *Modern Language Qaarterly* 61, no.4, (December 2000).

The main criticism Baldwin raises against jazz poems like "Dream Boogie" is that they do not offer a clearly recognizable, accurate record of experience that calls attention to their embeddedness in history. Such summary judgment has hampered further exploration of how Hughes's jazz poetics contributed to twentieth-century realism or to the development of the modernist lyric.

This essay situates Hughes's jazz poetics within the arc of his entire career to show how modernist experiments in poems like "Dream Boogie" are in keeping with his earlier attempts at lyric realism. I will focus on two main ideas. The first is that Hughes's poems challenge the critical distinction between "realism" and the "avant-garde": even his simplest, most documentary, and most historically engaged poems evince a characteristically modernist preoccupation with the figurative implications of form. Second, Hughes's realist approach to the lyric offers a fresh perspective on some central tendencies in transatlantic modernism: his repudiation of racial separatism, his interest in the relationship between poetry and American music, and his experiments with a jazz poetics are, in many ways, comparable to the critique of romantic cultural nationalism undertaken by Ezra Pound, Hart Crane, T. S. Eliot, and other modernists writing in the aftermath of the Great War. The convergence between Hughes's techniques and those of the American avant-garde highlights the importance of metonymic style, and of the historical knowledge that underlies the impulse toward formal experiment and improvisation, as a relatively neglected feature of the modernist lyric.

It is by now almost a commonplace to say that Hughes revised and extended the populist angle of vision explored in the previous decade by Edwin Arlington Robinson, Vachel Lindsay, Carl Sandburg, and others. But we have yet to understand the series of formal experiments he executed within the lyric that show his engagement with questions shared by his high modernist contemporaries.

Realism and Form in Hughes's Poetry

As a rubric, realism has been subject to heated debate and casual dismissal in the history of American criticism. "American realism virtually has no school; its most dominating and influential advocate, William Dean Howells, often seems to ride along in a strange vacuum, nearly unheeded in his continual insistence on the proprieties of the everyday, stable characterization, and moral certainty, while almost every other important author of the period simply refused, on these terms, to become a realist."[3] Whereas in Europe the great period of realism occurred throughout the second half of the nineteenth century, in North America the movement emerged in full force only with Howells's advocacy in the nineties.[4]

Partly in response to Erich Auerbach's *Mimesis*, theoretical descriptions of realism in modern American fiction have proliferated in recent decades.[5] Yet little sustained, systematic analysis has been done on the formal development of realism in the modern lyric.[6] Such neglect may be explained in part by the fact that the realist movement was long excluded from accounts of twentieth-century American poetry, because it was considered formally without interest-a servile, transparent copying of the world.[7] *The New Princeton Encyclopedia of Poetry and Poetics*, for example, defines realism solely in contradistinction to the intensified perception, densely metaphorical style, and artificiality of the lyric and adds that, "in a general sense, realistic poetry may result from any down-to-earth opposition to what seem artificial rules of versification or arbitrary restrictions on matter or diction. . . . The precepts of realism are often considered inimical to the spirit of lyric poetry."[8]

The latent critical bias against realism was memorably addressed by Georg Lukács, who in the late 1950s offered a surprising and useful theoretical reappraisal that paid special attention to formal issues. In *The Meaning of Contemporary Realism* Lukács arrived at a description of literary realism that helped readers bracket ideological content and focus instead on innovations in language and method. One objection he raised to current critical approaches to realism was that the political message of literature was fast becoming the overriding preoccupation of reviewers; as a result, literary standards were falling precipitously.[9] Another pressing concern was that modernist tastes in the 1920s had led critics to neglect works that exhibited the traditional mimetic techniques of realism. Criticism, according to Lukács, was hindered by the unexamined belief that realism was always, by definition, antithetical to modernism:

> Let us begin by examining two prejudices. The first is typical of much present-day bourgeois criticism. It is contained in the proposition that the literature of "modernism," of the *avant-garde*, is the essentially modern literature. The traditional techniques of realism, these critics assert, are inadequate, because too superficial, to deal with the realities of our age. (13)

Hughes's poems raise questions about stultifying critical binarisms that for years have pitted modern realism against modernist antirealism, tradition against the avant-garde, political content against artistic form. As a poet, Hughes constantly tries to illustrate how formal qualities may assist an act of engaged social criticism. Instead of using words that deceive us into seeing only their "transparency" and make us believe that we are taking an unmediated look through a windowpane to a world outside the poem, Hughes offers historical knowledge by directing our attention to his careful arrangement of words on the page. His style often dramatizes how language shapes the poem's social perspectives.

"Flight," which first appeared in the June 1930 issue of *Opportunity*, demonstrates how Hughes's realist poetics meets modernist formal expectations. The poem is set in a swamp, during the postemancipation period: a black man, accused of raping a white woman, is trying to escape from a lynch mob. The pursuit of hounds recalls the history of slavery and suggests that rituals of racial violence in the South continued, and even escalated, after emancipation. Hughes's speaker assumes two points of view: observer and victim. The poem begins by giving the victim, who initially occupies the same position as the reader, the impossible task of stepping in mud without leaving tracks:

> Plant your toes in the cool swamp mud.
> Step and leave no track.
> Hurry, sweating runner!
> The hounds are at your back.
>
> *No I didn't touch her*
> *Whiteflesh ain't for me.*
>
> Hurry! Black boy, hurry!
> They'll swing you to a tree.[10]

In "Flight" Hughes uses a short lyric form to present a splintered aspect of a reality too vast and horrifying to comprehend in its entirety. Instead the speaker describes, analyzes, and orders a tragic, swiftly unfolding moment. The lyric evokes a tension between Hughes's artistic suspension of time and the time-bound social realities that are the subject of his poem. But despite his reliance on the temporal restrictions of the genre, Hughes refuses to rest content with the familiar consolations of lyric transcendence and disengagement. Distrustful of such forced integrities and closures, he builds in a narrative structure that implies a larger, sociohistorical context, giving disquieting openness to the exigencies that lend the poem shape and significance.

The reign of terror in the wake of emancipation generated the special conditions in which modern African American poetry emerged. In the postbellum South slavery was replaced by other forms of racial subjection: indentured servitude, black codes, the contract system, vagrancy statutes, and lynching.[11] Between 1900 and 1930 massive numbers of African Americans fled the rural South and traveled to northern cities like Chicago, Detroit, and New York. During the time that Hughes wrote, many of his contemporaries started the long process of coming to grips with his lyric's main subject, namely, the violent causes of this exodus, now known as the "Great Migration."[12] "Flight" documents how, for many southern freedmen, migration had become more than a necessary socioeconomic resource; it was a way of life, a means of preserving their safety, sanity, and dignity.

In "Flight," however, realist verisimilitude coexists with modernist formal innovation. In this respect Hughes's style fits an essential criterion that Hugo Friedrich proposes for the modernist lyric.[13] The preoccupation with expressive freedom makes sense inasmuch as the plight of the lynched man described in "Flight" forces us to question a fundamental tenet of nineteenth-century realism: that a realist work should depict a form of social life in which the individual can act with "autonomous motivation" (Preminger and Brogan, 1016).

The guiding metaphor in the poem's title also works to correct popular misconceptions of the causes of the Great Migration, misconceptions exacerbated by the constant use of the trope in journalistic analyses by Hughes's black contemporaries. In *Opportunity*, the same journal in which Hughes's poem appeared, Charles S. Johnson asked, "How much is migration a flight from persecution?"[14] Black public intellectuals such as Alain Locke, portraying the social formation of the "New Negro" in 1925, tried to play down the violent causes of migration by using the image of "deliberate flight" to suggest that African Americans were engaged in a mythic, quintessentially American quest for opportunity.[15]

Lynching was, in certain respects, similar to the experience that the Great War offered transatlantic modernists, since its moral horrors spurred Hughes and other African American poets to discover formalist freedoms that were wholly new. But although Hughes's passion for freedom resembles that of the avant-garde, his practices as a modern lyricist are distinctive insofar as they dramatize his effort to bridge a cultural divide between a folkloric African American tradition that is largely oral and the privileged arena of "literature." Thus the lyric's opening line may be read as an apt allegory of Hughes's predicament as a modern African American poet. It compares his effort to fashion enduring metrical feet that fit the rhythms of an oral tradition with a fleeing man's attempt to "plant" his "toes" in the mud.

Because self-referentiality penetrates a privileged arena, there is also the suggestion of trespass: the poet's act is described in terms that bring to mind a man in flight, a man accused of rape. Hughes's exhilarating discovery of freedom through formal modes of expression—metaphors rich in ambiguity, the distancing effects and pleasures of rhyme and writerly italicization, the metrical swing of his verse—is counterpointed by an awareness that such freedom implicates him in the history he relates. Hughes's use of italics, for example, makes the victim's words echo, as if lifted from a realist novel about a lynching that was written for a mass audience.[16] The device reminds us that, by adopting the lyric as his preferred genre, Hughes has aligned himself with other avant-garde artists in refusing to satisfy the raging market demand for sensationalist fiction that exacerbated a mass audience's tendency toward escapism. Even as his poem resists such a flight from reality, however, Hughes also insists on his freedom as an artist: the freedom, that is, to work continually at formal experimentation and to transcend the all-determining, muddy historical contingencies that fatally distort perception.

Hughes's gesture toward modernist innovation—his veiled reference to an avant-garde flight from verisimilitude—ultimately serves the ends of his realism, insofar as it raises the reader's awareness of the postemancipation context of the lyric. The violent historical developments that caused the Great Migration and spurred Hughes's engagement with formal questions are linked to the rhythmic cadences of "Flight" by the verb swing, at the end of the poem: the neat succession of rhythms that fall ("Hurry! Black boy, hurry!") and rise again ("They'll swing you to a tree") ominously dramatizes the swinging motion of the hanged man's body.

"Flight" questions familiar definitions of literary realism, as well as the idea that Hughes's realist commitments foreclose the possibility of modernism. At the same time that he tries to document the violent conditions that shaped the emergence of modern African American poetry, Hughes also invites us to consider how, and why, the poet's manipulation of his medium expresses artistic freedom from the contingencies he depicts. In the end he shows us that the nineteenth-century realist goal of transparent verisimilitude is unattainable in the modern lyric. Such figurative complexity highlights a modernist tendency in Hughes's realism.

"The Weary Blues": Hughes's Critique of Black Cultural Nationalism

To confer shape on what Eliot described as the "immense panorama of futility and anarchy which is contemporary history," Hughes turned not to classical myths but to a poetics of migration that had been used to impose order on and give significance to the traumatic postemancipation experience of African Americans, and that figured in many ballads, reels, and blues and ragtime songs Hughes remembered hearing during his childhood in Lawrence, Kansas.[17] A great deal has already been said about the "modernity" of African American music and, in particular, about the centrality of the blues to Hughes's lyric practice.[18] Arnold Rampersad's suggestion that the blues poems in *Fine Clothes to the Jew* are some of Hughes's most important works has prompted a critical reassessment of his project and legacy.[19] There is, however, much to be learned about how his blues and jazz poetics fit in the development of the modernist lyric, both in the United States and in Europe, and, conversely, how his engagement with modernism contributed to his technique as a realist poet.

In his autobiography Hughes, appealing to the strength, humor, and "rooted power" of the blues, tries to change the derogatory view of folk culture that prevailed among the African American middle class and Euro-Americans.[20] Ralph Ellison once described the blues as a "chronicle of personal catastrophe expressed lyrically," a mode of remembrance that keeps the experience alive and also transcends it, "not by the consolations of philosophy, but by squeezing from it a near-tragic, near-comic lyricism."[21] The artistic possibilities of traditional blues are examined in "Red Clay Blues," a poem Hughes wrote in collaboration with Richard Wright. The lyric states, with eloquent simplicity, a near-tragic vision of history that is tempered by a strong belief in the sanctity of knowledge. The first premise of the opening stanza is that "knowing" history means knowing what it feels like to long for the red clay of Georgia:

> I miss that red clay, Lawd, I
> Need to feel it in my shoes.
> Says miss that red clay, Lawd, I
> Need to feel it in my shoes.
> I want to get to Georgia cause I
> Got them red clay blues.
> (*CP*, 212)

These lines suggest, with remarkable precision, the transition from spiritual to blues, and from sacred to secular idioms, that took place during the late nineteenth century. For instance, the syntax subsumes the act of praying in an ornamental cadence ("Lawd") designed to enhance the expression of personal, daily needs. Despite the starkly conventional form, the lyric's style affirms the individuality of both speaker and poet. The line breaks rhythmically emphasize the importance of human desire and possession ("miss," "need," "want," "got"), Hughes's unabashed embrace of the oral tradition and a vernacular blues syntax ("Says miss that red clay"), and the metrical freedom discovered through repeated pronominal self-naming ("I").

Hughes broke new ground in his poetry, partly because he saw that his engagement with canonical texts and his interest in traditional English and American prosody would provide a much-needed, clarifying distance from the rich but potentially formulaic idioms he borrowed from African American folk culture. Ellison made a comment that seems to encapsulate Hughes's efforts to establish a critical, intellectual perspective on the folk tradition as a poetic resource:

> The Negro American writer is also an heir of the human experience which is literature, and this might well be more important to him than his living folk tradition. For me, at least . . . the stability of the Negro American folk tradition became precious as a result of an act of literary discovery. . . . For those who are able to translate its meanings into wider, more precise vocabularies it has much to offer indeed.[22]

Hughes was well aware that, as a poet, he needed to come to terms with the fundamental difference between blues language and poetic language. Despite his devotion to the traditional African American folk idiom, in a number of poems written during the 1920s he took a serious look at the artistic costs and devastating emotional consequences of the strict expressive constraints imposed by the blues.

In "The Weary Blues," first published in 1925, Hughes expresses his desire to encounter the idiomatic options raised by the blues as possibilities that he was free to choose, not as habitual motions that he was compelled to reiterate. The blues song has been framed by the mediating perspective of the lyric speaker, who describes the "moan" of the "poor piano." In contrast to the speaker, who tries to put the meaning of the music into words, the blues player conveys his feelings not so much with words as with the "lazy sway" of his body:[23]

> Droning a drowsy syncopated tune,
> Rocking back and forth to a mellow croon,
>   I heard a Negro play.
> Down on Lenox Avenue the other night
> By the pale dull pallor of an old gas light
>   He did a lazy sway . . . .

He did a lazy sway . . . .
To the tune o' those Weary Blues.
With his ebony hands on each ivory key
He made that poor piano moan with melody.
O Blues!
Swaying to and fro on his rickety stool
He played that sad raggy tune like a musical fool.
Sweet Blues!
Coming from a black man's soul.
. . . .
Thump, thump, thump, went his foot on the floor.
He played a few chords then he sang some more—
"I got the Weary Blues
And I can't be satisfied.
Got the Weary Blues
And can't be satisfied—
I ain't happy no mo'
And I wish that I had died."
And far into the night he crooned that tune.
The stars went out and so did the moon.
The singer stopped playing and went to bed
While the Weary Blues echoed through his head.
He slept like a rock or a man that's dead.
(*CP*, 50)

Hughes expected many readers to think that poems such as "The Weary Blues" were not about anything more than a piano player playing blues. In fact, he often invited and validated such interpretations.[24] The poem may be seen to enact, however, a renunciation of metaphor—a despairing gesture suggesting that imaginative dreamlike escapes from the "outer" world do nothing to change social conditions. In another poem the romantic images of the stars and moon going out would be richly evocative and metaphorical, signifying unfulfilled desire or desolation over a dream deferred. But here their figurative weight is offset by a context that leads us to believe that Hughes merely wants to indicate the passage of time. The latent metaphorical meaning of his idiom is suppressed. Whereas in "Flight" Hughes acknowledges his passion for figuration as a mode of transcendence, in this lyric he dramatizes how having the blues may undermine a poet's belief in the modernist freedom to trope. The stars and moon going out and the player going to bed illustrate the action of lulling metaphorical language to the dead sleep of verisimilitude.

In "The Weary Blues" Hughes implies that the conventional blues idiom is so compelling, and so limited, as to threaten his imaginative freedom. In addition, the mechanical objects that occupy the poem's setting—the gas light, the rickety stool, the piano parts, and so on—evoke another modern development that imperils artistic freedom. Like many of his contemporaries, both in the United States and abroad, Hughes was aware of the cultural crisis caused by mechanization. In 1933 F. R. Leavis, quoting H. G. Wells, would vividly condemn the "vast and increasing inattention" resulting from new forms of mechanical reproduction: "The machine . . . has brought about changes in habit and the circumstances of life at a rate for which we have no parallel. . . . When we consider, for instance, the processes of mass-production and standardisation in the form represented by the Press, it becomes obviously of sinister significance that they should be accompanied by a process of levelling-down." Two years before Hughes published "The Weary Blues," Eliot warned against the insidious effects of gramophones, motorcars, loudspeakers, and cinemas in which the mind was "lulled by continuous senseless music and continuous action too rapid . . . to act upon."[25]

Hughes's concern about the leveling-down effects of technology, which are barely hinted at in "The Weary Blues," becomes a point of focus in "Summer Night," which first appeared in the December 1925 issue of *Crisis*. Like the typist in Eliot's *Waste Land*, who paces about her room, her brain allowing only a "half-formed thought," and who "smoothes her hair with automatic hand" as she puts a record on the gramophone, Hughes's lyric speaker is left virtually without words once the player piano, the Victrola, and the other "sounds" of Harlem fall silent in the still night.[26] He can only toss restlessly, muttering ineffective generalities:

> The sounds
> Of the Harlem night
> Drop one by one into stillness.
> The last player-piano is closed.
> The last victrola ceases with the
> "Jazz-Boy Blues."
> The last crying baby sleeps
> And the night becomes
> Still as a whispering heartbeat.
> I toss
> Without rest in the darkness,
> Weary as the tired night,
> My soul

Empty as the silence,
Empty with a vague,
Aching emptiness,
Desiring,
Needing someone,
Something. (*CP*, 59)

The passage demonstrates the high stakes of Hughes's project as a poet who deals in words, and it implies his effort, as Pound might say, to "modernize" his perspective by distancing himself from the nonverbal expressiveness of the blues.

Together, "Summer Night" and "The Weary Blues" scrutinize the view that the blues is an essentially "black" musical emotion that can never be individuated for Euro-American readers. By raising this question, Hughes anticipates Paul Gilroy's proposition, in his recent study of music and the black diaspora, that a "topos of unsayability"—a habitual invocation of truths that cannot be put into words—lies at the heart of black musical culture.[27]

Gilroy's discussion follows in large part from W. E. B. DuBois's analysis of African American spirituals in *The Souls of Black Folk*. DuBois was one of the first to notice that many things were conventionally left unsaid in the folk lyrics. Such "omissions and silences," and the lack of reference to social conditions, testify to the violent subjugation of enslavement and reflect the "shadow of fear" that hung over the slaves. DuBois concludes that, in this crucial respect, the folk idiom imposed constraints on "allowable thought" and confined poetry "for the most part to single or double lines":

> Over the inner thoughts of the slaves and their relations one with another the shadow of fear ever hung, so that we get but glimpses here and there, and also with them, eloquent omissions and silences. Mother and child are sung, but seldom father; fugitive and weary wanderer call for pity and affection, but there is little of wooing and wedding; the rocks and the mountains are well known, but home is unknown. . . . Of deep successful love there is ominous silence. . . . [The] rhythm of the songs, and the limitations of allowable thought, confined the poetry for the most part to single or double lines, and they seldom were expanded to quatrains or longer tales.[28]

Gilroy argues that the "topos of unsayability" is an outgrowth of the experience of slavery, and no doubt DuBois and Hughes would agree. But whereas Gilroy celebrates this topos, which can be used "to challenge the privileged conceptions of both language and writing as preeminent expressions of human consciousness" (74), Hughes considered it part of the debilitating legacy of slavery and was deeply concerned about the "silences" that structure thought and expression in the blues. True, in the short lyric "Hey!" Hughes jokes about the curious effects of unsayability by drawing our attention to the alluring ambiguity of the blues singer's sustained note, "hey":

> Sun's a settin',
> This is what I'm gonna sing.
> Sun's a settin',
> This is what I'm gonna sing:
> I feels de blues a comin',
> Wonder what de blues'll bring?
> (*CP*, 112)

But Hughes also understood how severely limiting such a convention was. In "The Weary Blues" he suggests that unsayability cannot be a topos so long as it is forced on African Americans by the memory of "racial terror" (Gilroy, 74).

As we have seen, the stylistic complexity of many of the poems Hughes wrote during the 1920s and early 1930s creates a clarifying perspective on the folk tradition and distances him from racial separatist explanations of culture.[29] Although Hughes was noted as one of the first poets to celebrate the beauty of the blues as an American art form, he was not a "black nationalist," in Amiri Baraka's sense of the term.[30] In *Blues People: Negro Music in White America* (1963) Baraka began to advance a separatist line of argument:

> Blues as an autonomous music had been in a sense inviolable. There was no clear way into it . . . except as concomitant with what seems to me to be the peculiar social, cultural, economic, and emotional experience of a black man in America. . . . The materials of blues were not available to the white American. . . . It was as if these materials were secret and obscure, and blues a kind of ethno-historic rite as basic as blood.[31]

Forty years before the Black Arts movement Hughes was writing poems that examined the tragic implications of racial separatist logic. As "The Weary Blues" shows, it would have been impossible for him to write completely in accordance with the verbal constraints of the folk tradition: to do so would have resulted in an endlessly mechanical recapitulation of the racial terror of slavery. Viewed in these terms, Hughes's repudiation of racialist ideas about culture in poems written during the 1920s anticipates the positions he explored in his so-called radical poetry, written between 1932 and 1938.[32]

HUGHES AND THE MODERNIST CRITIQUE OF ROMANTIC NATIONALISM

Hughes's resistance to separatist descriptions of African American culture is, in certain respects, strikingly similar to the critique of romantic nationalism undertaken by many of his modernist contemporaries, both in the United States and in Europe. D. H. Lawrence, T. S. Eliot, Ezra Pound, Wallace Stevens, Hart Crane, and others wrote poems in which they tried to come to terms with the difficult necessity of cross-cultural identification. Many of these poems centered on the changing nature of musical experience and the devastating, far-reaching consequences of European nationalism that culminated in the Great War.

An early draft of Lawrence's "Piano," which first appeared in *New Poems* in 1918, explores how the speaker's response to Hungarian music reflects the historical causes of the war. Like Hughes, Lawrence tried to show how traces of history were ceaselessly echoed in nineteenth-century musical forms. But whereas Hughes was primarily concerned with illustrating the American legacy of racial violence that shaped musical forms such as swing and the blues, Lawrence confronted the legacy of romanticism in Europe:

> Somewhere beneath that piano's superb sleek black
> Must hide my mother's piano, little and brown, with the back
> That stood close to the wall, and the front's faded silk, both torn,
> And the keys with little hollows, that my mother's fingers had worn.
>
> Softly, in the shadows, a woman is singing to me
> Quietly, through the years I have crept back to see
> A child sitting under the piano, in the boom of the shaking strings
> Pressing the little poised feet of the mother who smiles as she sings.
>
> The full throated woman has chosen a winning, living song
> And surely the heart that is in me must belong
> To the old Sunday evenings, when darkness wandered outside
> And hymns gleamed on our warm lips, as we watched mother's
> fingers glide.

Or this is my sister at home in the old front room
Singing love's first surprised gladness, alone in the gloom.
She will start when she sees me, and blushing, spread out her hands
To cover my mouth's raillery, till I'm bound in her shame's heart-
spun bands.

A woman is singing me a wild Hungarian air
And her arms, and her bosom, and the whole of her soul is bare,
And the great black piano is clamouring as my mother's never could
clamour
And my mother's tunes are devoured of this music's ravaging
glamour.[33]

"Piano" is as much about the creative hunger to absorb different cultural influences, and the threat it poses to the cherished individuality of regions, as it is about the fateful vying for dominance among the major European powers in the decades preceding the Great War. The "wild Hungarian air" (a phrase Lawrence omitted in the final version of the poem) recalls the intensification of European nationalist rivalries during this period.[34] The poem is built on a perceived contrast between, on the one hand, the speaker's present experience of the "clamouring" sound of a sleek black concert hall piano and a song that bares a woman's soul to the public; and, on the other, his secretly erotic childhood memories of his mother and sister performing hymns and love songs at home. By searching for hidden continuities between the raging, devouring glamour associated with Hungarian music and the speaker's fond memories of British middle-class musical culture, Lawrence discloses the speaker's painful ambivalence toward the sentiment awakened in him by the song.[35]

"Piano" also refers, more broadly, to the changing of European musical experience and sensibility from the early nineteenth to the early twentieth century. Concert life and musical tastes were dramatically transformed in the Allied countries during and after the Great War. Fewer keyboard battle pieces, for example, were written then than at the height of romantic nationalism during the nineteenth century, and composers began to turn their attention to serious vocal and orchestral laments. In the Allied countries there was a growing tendency to ban concert performances of German music; in England, France, and America musicians were encouraged to perform the works of "native" composers.[36] In the first half of the nineteenth century chamber music had gradually been moved out of domestic spaces and salons into public performance halls. "Personality," observes James H. Johnson, "thrust itself to center stage in the romantic decades."[37]

Lawrence and Hughes both questioned popular notions of racial authenticity in music. Like Hughes's "Weary Blues," Lawrence's "Piano" expresses ambivalence toward the expressive and perceptual constraints of the "polarization" of peoples in "particular localit[ies]."[38] Hughes was concerned to stand, as it were, both inside and outside the blues and figuratively to imply his own motives for moving away from the rich but ultimately constraining formulas of traditional blues lyrics. Lawrence's stance is similar, insofar as his speaker affirms, with great affection, the distinctive musical heritages of nations while he conveys the horrifying irony that such seemingly benign cultural distinctions would, in the end, be used as a justification for war. By upholding both the distinctiveness and the universality of musical experience, both poets suggest that music, in the words of Theodor Adorno, "more than any other artistic medium, expresses the national principle's antinomies" (quoted in Gilroy, 72).

Hughes's technically self-conscious approach to realism in the lyric, his prosodic resistance to separatist paradigms, and his interest in the history and irreducible hybridity of African American culture are aspects of his lyric practice that he shared with his American modernist contemporaries. Pound's 1920 poem *Hugh Selwyn Mauberley*, for example, may be said to anticipate Hughes's "Weary Blues," since it also confronts the problem of realism in the lyric. Although Pound keeps references to social setting and details to a bare minimum in the poem, his interest in finding a modern poetic equivalent to Henry James's realism is evident in a 1922 letter to Felix Schelling, in which Pound calls his poem "an attempt to condense the James novel."[39] Moreover, like Hughes, Pound uses the image of a piano to explore how modern art has come dangerously close to the mass-produced conformity, planned obsolescence, and rapid replacement associated with fashion. The pianola metonymically represents the forces of mass production:

> The tea-rose tea-gown, etc.
> supplants the mousseline of Cos,
> The pianola "replaces"
> Sappho's barbitos.[40]

Another American modernist, Hart Crane, examined how the violent history that gave rise to African American music ultimately shaped the imagery and cadence of his own idiom:

> "what do you want? getting weak on the links?
> fandaddle daddy don't ask for change—IS THIS

FOURTEENTH? it's half past six she said—if
you don't like my gate why did you
swing on it, why *didja*
swing on it
anyhow—"

And somehow anyhow swing—

The phonographs of hades in the brain
Are tunnels that re-wind themselves, and love
A burnt match skating in a urinal—
Somewhere above Fourteenth TAKE THE EXPRESS
To brush some new presentiment of pain—[41]

In 1948, in *The Auroras of Autumn*, Wallace Stevens vividly probed the sources of his ambivalent love of and animosity toward primitivist decadence: the mind's eye first summons up a festive scene of "negresses" dancing and then suddenly becomes cruelly analytic, mocking the whole party for their brutish disorderliness:

The father fetches negresses to dance,
Among the children, like curious ripenesses
Of pattern in the dance's ripening.

For these the musicians make insidious tones,
Clawing the sing-song of their instruments.
The children laugh and jangle a tinny time.

. . . .
What festival? This loud, disordered mooch?
These hospitaliers? These brute-like guests?[42]

Of Hughes's modernist contemporaries, however, the poet whose interest in realism, racial cross-identification, and American music comes closest to his own is not Pound, Crane, or Stevens but Eliot. In many of the early poems collected in the leather-bound notebook begun in 1909—some, such as "Opera," "First Caprice in North Cambridge," and "The Burnt Dancer," which were unpublished until 1996, and others, such as "Rhapsody on a Windy Night" and "Portrait of a Lady," which appeared in *Prufrock and Other Observations* in 1917—Eliot shares Hughes's preoccupation with realism and the analogy between musical and poetic forms.[43] But whereas Hughes's poems more often than not call attention to the African American folk origins of the blues as an American musical form, Eliot takes the occasion of these early poems to explore the hybrid European origins of modern American music by adapting the idea of the "caprice" or the "rhapsody": pieces that were written out, not improvised, most likely for the piano.

In *The Dialect of Modernism* Michael North offers a groundbreaking, provocative analysis of how Eliot adapted techniques such as linguistic mimicry and racial masquerade to make the language new and to resist institutional forces of standardization. In 1921 Eliot "was laboring to put his knowledge of black music to work in *The Waste Land*, which contained at one time references to a number of rag and minstrel songs."[44] The musical allusions cut from the final text are of particular interest, since many of them—for example, Eliot's reference to a song ("I'm proud of all the Irish blood that's in me") from a musical play called *Fifty Miles from Boston* and his adaptation of lines from minstrel shows ("By the Watermelon Vine," "My Evaline," and "The Cubanola Glide")—cryptically encode the composite regional landscapes and irreducibly hybrid cultures evoked by American popular music.[45]

Eliot's fascination with ragtime is best understood in light of his effort to understand the idea of "purity" in poetry, that is, the peculiar effect of works that direct the reader's attention primarily to style and virtually exclude consideration of their subject matter. In "From Poe to Valéry," for example, he discusses poems in which words have been chosen for the right sounds while the poet has been deliberately "irresponsible" toward their meaning.[46] In "The Music of Poetry" Eliot singles out Edward Lear's "non-sense verse," whose reader is moved by the music and enjoys, again, a "feeling of irresponsibility towards the sense." In these instances, however, the source of enjoyment is not a "vacuity of sense," or the poet's total escape from meaningful representation. Rather, Lear's "non-sense . . . is a parody of sense, and that is the sense of it."[47]

In *The Waste Land* Eliot illustrates the rich senses of nonsense by alluding to a popular ragtime song that hit the charts in 1912, called "That Shakespearian Rag":

> That Shakespearian rag,—
> Most intelligent, very elegant,
> That old classical drag,
> Has the proper stuff, the line "Lay on Macduff,"
> Desdemona was the colored pet,
> Romeo loved his Juliet—
> And they were some lovers, you can bet, and yet,
> I know if they were here today,

They'd Grizzly Bear in a diff'rent way,
And you'd hear old Hamlet say,
"To be or not to be,"
That Shakespearian Rag.[48]

Eliot adapted lines from the original chorus by adding the "O O O O" and a syncopated syllable in "Shakespeherian" (McElderry, 185–6):

O O O O that Shakespeherian Rag—
It's so elegant
So intelligent
"What shall I do now? What shall I do?"
(*WL*, 57)

The poem's miming of ragtime gives both the speaker and the reader a brief reprieve from the burdensome duty to convey meaning truthfully. But the "vacuity of sense" brought about by the repetition of the apostrophe "O"—a repetition that reduces the trope, quite literally, to a series of zeroes on the page—also signals the tragic lack of continuity, as well as a tragic lack of engagement with the sense of Shakespeare's vibrant words, evidenced by American popular music. Eliot's allusion to ragtime, followed by the listless, bored, near-hysterical line "What shall I do now? What shall I do?" evokes apocalyptic dread. The passage implies that, taken to an extreme, such fleeting moments of enjoyable irresponsibility toward sense may promote an increasingly automated, vast inattention in American society. By pursuing the analogies between music and poetry in *The Waste Land*, Eliot's "Shakespeherian Rag" responds stylistically to conditions that imperiled artistic freedom and anticipated Hughes's experiments with a jazz poetics.[49]

The Waste Land calls attention to the danger of popular ragtime songs, in which words have been torn away from their traditional contexts. In "The Music of Poetry," however, Eliot proposes that nonsense verse also has profoundly restorative powers, as in Lear's work. "*The Jumblies*," for example, "is a poem of adventure, and of nostalgia for the romance of foreign voyage and exploration; *The Yongy-Bongy Bo* and *The Dong with a Luminous Nose* are poems of unrequited passion—'blues' in fact. We enjoy the music, which is of a high order, and we enjoy the feeling of irresponsibility towards the sense" (*PP*, 21). In "Fragment of an Agon," part of the unfinished jazz play *Sweeney Agonistes*, Eliot illustrates the poetic vitality and beauty of nonsense. The poem includes the following text, adapted from a popular song written by the African American poet James Weldon Johnson, called "Under the Bamboo Tree":

Under the bamboo
Bamboo bamboo
Under the bamboo tree
Two live as one
One live as two
Two live as three
Under the bam
Under the boo
Under the bamboo tree.

Where the breadfruit fall
And the penguin call
And the sound is the sound of the sea
Under the bam
Under the boo
Under the bamboo tree.

Where the Gauguin maids
In the banyan shades
Wear palmleaf drapery
Under the bam
Under the boo
Under the bamboo tree.[50]

That the other personages in the play are ludicrous, materialistic, and superficial does not suggest that Eliot's allusion to Johnson's lyric "imprisons the song once again in the minstrel tradition" (North, 88).[51] The sense of adventure and the nostalgia for exotic romance that Eliot identifies in Lear's poems are beautifully highlighted in the passage he borrows from Johnson's artful rendering of the African American vernacular.[52] The enjoyable irresponsibility toward sense that the poem dramatizes enhances the meaning: it is a poem of "unrequited passion—'blues' in fact." The provocatively playful nonsense of "Two live as one / One live as two / Two live as three" expresses the speaker's yearning to transform the social fragmentation of American society and hints at Eliot's deeper motive for incorporating Johnson's lyric. Two poets—one Euro-American, the other African American—in effect "live as one" in Eliot's poem and intimately share a sensibility embodied by the blues. The poem's outlook is hopeful and forward-looking: after all, as Eliot has shown, the hope of perpetuating any given culture lies in the creative action of exchanging ideas and influences with others.[53]

Conclusion: Jazz and Modern Realism

Many, if not all, of Hughes's late jazz poems highlight the freedom of improvisation and formal innovation. In "The Trumpet Player: 57th Street," published in 1947, the freedom of choice Hughes himself exercises in creating a metonymic style opens new expressive possibilities.[54] The lyric not only educates the reader to hear his writing as trumpetlike, an instrument with voiced inflection and phrasing. It also dramatically illustrates the advantages of metonymy:

> The Negro
> With the trumpet at his lips
> Has dark moons of weariness
> Beneath his eyes
> Where the smoldering memory
> Of slave ships
> Blazed to the crack of whips
> About his thighs.
> . . . .
> The music
> From the trumpet at his lips
> Is honey
> Mixed with liquid fire.
> The rhythm
> From the trumpet at his lips
> Is ecstasy
> Distilled from old desire—
>
> The Negro
> With the trumpet at his lips
> Whose jacket
> Has a fine one-button roll,
> Does not know
> Upon what riff the music slips
> Its hypodermic needle
> To his soul. (*CP*, 338)

Even as the lyric speaker refers to the uses of metaphor in describing the "ecstasy / Distilled from old desire" expressed in the trumpet's rhythm, he ends up showing us the profound artistic satisfactions and referential range of metonymy, the depiction of the body's surface and the temporal and spatial relatedness of everyday objects in the room. As an expression of weariness, traces of a personal and collective history of oppression, the "thump, thump, thump" of "The Weary Blues" is here inscribed on the body as "dark moons of weariness" beneath the trumpet player's eyes. The relatively obscure meaning of the moon going out as an image of thwarted desire and a dream deferred in "The Weary Blues" is considered and then freely cast off in "The Trumpet Player" in favor of hybrid tropes that hover somewhere between metonymy and metaphor:

> Desire
> That is longing for the moon
> Where the moonlight's but a spotlight
> In his eyes,
> Desire
> That is longing for the sea
> Where the sea's a bar-glass
> Sucker size. (*CP*, 338)

Like a held chord, the romantic, sentimental idiom of "longing for the moon" is sustained and, at the same time, transmuted into a "spotlight / In his eyes." As an evocation of desire, the sea is condensed into a "barglass, / Sucker size."

Insofar as Hughes's later poems mime the improvisatory action of jazz to discover emancipatory techniques, they are stylistically similar to works written by the American avant-gardes of the interwar period. In *Spring and All*, for example, William Carlos Williams praises the freedoms of improvisation, while he laments the dangers of incomprehensibility:

> The Improvisations—coming at a time when I was trying to re-
> main firm
> at great cost—I had recourse to the expedient of letting life go
> completely in order to live in the world of my choice. . . .
>
> The virtue of the improvisations is their placement in a world
> of new values—
> their fault is their dislocation of
> sense, often complete.[55]

The convergence between Hughes's techniques and those of Williams, Eliot, and others discloses the historical knowledge that informs the impulse toward formal experiment and improvisation in the modernist lyric.

At the beginning of this essay we saw Baldwin criticize Hughes's late jazz poem, "Dream Boogie," for falling short of the standards of realism. I want to conclude by suggesting that, Baldwin's criticisms notwithstanding, the spirit of formal innovation in "Dream Boogie" is entirely in keeping with Hughes's earlier realism in poems such as "Flight."

"Dream Boogie" is far more modernist than "Flight," since it manifests a sustained, figurative effort to move away from the realist duties of verisimilitude. It avoids familiar reference to historical contexts; it twists away from language toward abstract sequences of sound; and it brings us into a discursive world in which speech and perception have been broken down into fragments. Insofar as the speaker touches on realities, his treatment of them is almost wholly nondescriptive:

> Good morning, daddy!
> Ain't you heard
> The boogie-woogie rumble
> Of a dream deferred?
>
> Listen closely:
> You'll hear their feet
> Beating out and beating out a—
>
> *You think*
> *It's a happy beat?*
>
> Listen to it closely:
> Ain't you heard
> something underneath
> like a—
>
> *What did I say?*
>
> Sure,
> I'm happy!
> Take it away!
>
> *Hey, pop!*
> *Re-bop!*
> *Mop!*
>
> *Ye-a-h!* (*CP*, 388)

Like many works written by his avant-garde contemporaries, Hughes's poem is not designed to meet our interpretive expectations; it contains no meaning that, as Eliot says, would readily satisfy a "habit" of the reader (*UP*, 151). According to Eliot, modern poems are sometimes intended primarily to amplify the reader's experience of the intensity of feeling that results from the poet's movement toward ideas at the "frontiers of consciousness," where meanings have not yet been put into words. In "The Music of Poetry" he writes: "We can be deeply stirred by hearing the recitation of a poem in a language of which we understand no word. . . . If, as we are aware, only a part of the meaning can be conveyed by paraphrase, that is because the poet is occupied with frontiers of consciousness beyond which words fail, though meanings still exist" (*PP*, 22).

In "Dream Boogie" Hughes's idiom is modernist in Eliot's sense: the lyric's form embodies an effort to move beyond the frontiers of social consciousness and expression. The line breaks; the arrangement of words on the page, flush left and flush right; and the use of italics are stylistic elements that show the ambivalence and animosity of an African American speaker trying to explain the meaning of the music to a Euro-American listener. The rhetorical question "*You think / It's a happy beat*?" has the visual effect of stretching, tonally inflecting, and thereby extending the meaning of the trope to include its own correct response. The poem pauses, calling attention to its own act of figuration and to the poet's act of writing. Hughes's modernist predilection for experimental forms that allegorize the struggle for and against verisimilitude, and his constant awareness of the constraints of language as an artistic medium, is central to his practice as a realist poet.

Although "Dream Boogie" is modernist insofar as it illustrates an effort to escape from historical referentiality and refuses to state explicitly the bitter social truths encoded in what Baldwin calls the "hieroglyphics" of African American music, it also remains anchored in the particularities of its own time and place, since it is essentially about the dangers posed to American society as a whole when these truths are not brought to light in the realm of art. The speaker's ambivalence toward the project of meaningful representation makes sense only when we realize that the poem takes on a subject that Adorno systematically elaborated in his celebrated diatribe against the popular culture industry: the poem figuratively suggests a deplorable lack of conscious perception on the part of many Euro-Americans who considered themselves avid jazz fans.

Like Adorno, Hughes in "Dream Boogie" suggests that too many people who listened to jazz did not hear the seriousness of its emotional message and were not aware of the violent historical conditions out of which the impulse to formal innovation emerged. Instead many Americans regarded jazz merely as a pleasant background for conversation or a happy accompaniment to dancing.[56] The italicized question addressed to the Euro-American reader marks a crucial transition from the lyric's effort to mime violence (that is, from its performance of a nonrepresentational, violent motion of beating measured feet) to an all-out confrontation with meanings on the verge of verbal explicitness. The italics themselves highlight the social and emotional pressure exerted on the speaker when he tries to say that the historical implications of jazz as an art form—a form rooted in the traumatic postemancipation history of lynching and migration—were anything but happy; they express the speaker's frustration at the listener's inability to hear the social and emotional truths conveyed by the music.[57]

Hughes's experiments with realism in the lyric help us question the distinction between realism and the avant-garde in accounts of transatlantic modernism. Like Eliot, Crane, Stevens, and other twentieth-century American poets, Hughes demonstrated that certain modernist styles were created in response to historical conditions and addressed the danger posed by modernity to artistic freedom. Leo Bersani once said that "the realistic novel gives us an image of social fragmentation contained within the order of significant form—and it thereby suggests that the chaotic fragments are somehow socially viable and morally redeemable" (quoted in Anesko, 83), and this claim also seems an apt description of Hughes's poetic evocation of jazz. Insofar as his lyrics transcend frontiers of consciousness and culture, they fulfill a cherished criterion of modernism, and this modernism, in turn, serves the moral ends of realism by allowing him to encompass, order, and preserve fragments of history.

Notes

1 Wright, "The Big Sea," in *Langston Hughes: Biblical Perspectives Past and Present*, ed. Henry Louis Gates Jr. and K. A. Appiah (New York: Amistad, 1993), 21. Comparing Hughes to Theodore Dreiser, Wright observed that both writers undertook the crucial task of "freeing American literary expression from the restrictions of Puritanism" (21).

2. Baldwin, "Sermons and Blues," review of *Selected Poems*, by Langston Hughes, *New York Times Book Review*, 29 March 1959, 6.

3. Eric J. Sundquist, ed., *American Realism: New Essays* (Baltimore, Md.: Johns Hopkins University Press, 1982), 4.

4. Louis Budd, "The American Background," in *The Cambridge Companion to American Realism and Naturalism: Howells to London*, ed. Donald Pizer (Cambridge: Cambridge University Press, 1995), 21–46. The concept of realism surfaced again in the 1920s, when a generation of journalists—

H. L. Mencken, John Macy, Van Wyck Brooks, Ludwig Lewisohn, Lewis Mumford, and Randolph Bourne, to name a few—probed the social purpose of literature and lavished praise on previously neglected artists, such as Mark Twain, Stephen Crane, and the late Howells, who had been critical of America's social and economic values. In 1930 Vernon Louis Parrington published *The Beginnings of Critical Realism in America: 1860–1920*, an influential analysis that roundly criticized writers who were too committed to narrowly "belletristic" aspects of literature. Parrington was, in turn, condemned to obscurity by critics like Lionel Trilling, who sharply criticized his literary nationalism and his insistence that literature should appeal to a popular constituency. More recently, at least since the publication of Warner Berthoff's *Ferment of Realism: American Literature, 1884–1919* in 1965, a number of revisionary studies have explored the social construction of American realism: Sundquist; Amy Kaplan, *The Social Construction of American Realism* (Chicago: University of Chicago Press, 1988); and Michael Anesko, "Recent Critical Approaches," in Pizer, 77–94.

5. Auerbach, *Mimesis: The Representation of Reality in Western Literature*, trans. Willard R. Trask (Princeton, N.J.: Princeton University Press, 1953). Auerbach's helpful, systematic account of the emergence of modern realist fiction identifies four criteria of realism as a literary method: detailed description of everyday occurrences; serious treatment of "socially inferior groups" as subject matter for existential representation (491); belief in the capacity of language to reveal truths about the phenomenal world; and portrayal of the individual's destiny in both a particular social hierarchy and a broader historical context.
6. In a useful account of the diverse approaches undertaken by modern American poets, Cary Nelson discusses "partly forgotten poetry—including black poetry, poetry by women, the poetry of popular song, and the poetry of social mass movements—thereby giving those texts new connotations appropriate to our time" (*Repression and Recovery: Modern American Poetry and the Politics of Cultural Memory, 1910–1945* [Madison: University of Wisconsin Press, 1989], 22–3). But his study is primarily historical: he gives no extended formal analyses and—aside from remarking that "traditional forms continued to do vital cultural work" throughout the modern period (23)—tells us little about the poetics of realism.
7. See Jonathan Arac, "Rhetoric and Realism; or, Marxism, Deconstruction, and the Novel," in *Criticism without Boundaries: Directions and Crosscurrents in Postmodern Critical Theory*, ed. Joseph A. Buttigieg (Notre Dame, Ind.: University of Notre Dame Press, 1987), 161.

8. Alex Preminger and T. V. F. Brogan, eds., *The New Princeton Encyclopedia of Poetry and Poetics* (Princeton, N.J.: Princeton University Press, 1993), 1016.
9. "If every mediocre product of socialist realism is to be hailed as a masterpiece," Lukács writes, "confusion will be worse confounded. My *tertium datur* is an objective critical appraisal of the very real innovations which we owe to socialist realism. In exposing literary mediocrity, and criticizing theoretical dogmatism, I am trying to ensure that the creative aspects of this new realism will be more clearly understood" (*The Meaning of Contemporary Realism*, trans. John Mander and Necke Mander [London: Merlin, 1963], 11).
10. *The Collected Poems of Langston Hughes*, ed. Arnold Rampersad and David Roessel (New York: Knopf, 1994), 127; hereafter cited as *CP*.
11. See Saidiya V. Hartman, *Scenes of Subjection: Terror Slavery, and Self-Making in Nineteenth-Century America* (New York: Oxford University Press, 1997).
12. See, e.g., W. E. B. DuBois, *The Philadelphia Negro: A Social Study* (1899; rpt. New York: Schocken, 1967); Carter G. Woodson, *A Century of Negro Migration* (1918; rpt. New York: Russell and Russell, 1969); Emmett J. Scott, *Negro Migration during the War* (1920; rpt. New York: Arno, 1969); Louise Kennedy, *The Negro Peasant Turns Cityward: Effects of Recent Migrations to Northern Cities* (New York: Columbia University Press; London: King and Son, 1930); E. Franklin Frazier, *The Negro Family in Chicago* (Chicago: University of Chicago Press, 1932); St. Clair Drake and Horace R. Cayton, *Black Metropolis: A Study of Negro Life in a Northern City* (1945; rpt. New York: Harcourt, Brace and World, 1962); and Gunnar Myrdal, *An American Dilemma: The Negro Problem and Modern Democracy*, 2 Vols. (1945; rpt. New York: Harper and Row, 1962). For a useful overview of the vast literature on the Great Migration see Joe Trotter, "Black Migration in Historical Perspective: A Review of the Literature," in *The Great Migration in Historical Perspective: New Dimensions of Race, Class, and Gender*, ed. Joe William Trotter Jr. (Bloomington: Indiana University Press, 191), 1–21.
13. Friedrich argues, on the evidence of poems by Baudelaire, Rimbaud, Mallarmé, and others, that "modern poetry, in its dissonances, is obeying a law of its style. And this law . . . is, in turn, obeying the historical situation of the modern mind, which, because of the excessive imperiling of its freedom, has an excessive passion for freedom" (*The Structure of Modern Poetry: From the Mid-Nineteenth to the Mid-Twentieth Century*, trans. Joachim Neugroschel [Evanston, Ill.: Northwestern University Press, 1974], 168). Cf. Paul de Man's claim that a definitively "modern"

poet must reject the burdensome assumption that artists convey meaning, since it poses a limit on expressive freedom and denies "the conception of language as the act of an autonomous self ("Lyric and Modernity," in *Blindness and Insight: Essays in the Rhetoric of Contemporary Criticism* [Minneapolis: University of Minnesota Press, 1971], 171).

14. Johnson, "How Much Is Migration a Flight from Persecution?" *Opportunity*, September 1923, 272–5.
15. Whereas in 1930 Hughes used the image of flight ironically, juxtaposing the poem's title with the closing image of a hanged black man swinging in a tree, in 1925 Locke had used a similar image to mythologize the modernizing effects of migration: "The wash and rush of this human tide on the beach line of the northern city centers is to be explained primarily in terms of a new vision of opportunity, of social and economic freedom. . . . With each successive wave of it, the movement of the Negro becomes more and more a mass movement toward the larger and the more democratic chance—in the Negro's case a deliberate flight not only from countryside to city, but from medieval America to modern" ("The New Negro," in *The New Negro* [New York: Atheneum, 1992], 6).
16. Hughes did not use these italics until 1949, when the poem appeared in the collection *One-Way Ticket*. But he did use quotation marks in 1931, when it was published in *Dear Lovely Death*.
17. "'Ulysses,' Order, and Myth," in *Selected Prose of T. S. Eliot*, ed. Frank Kermode (New York: Harcourt Brace Jovanovich, 1975), 177. For a discussion of Hughes's early exposure to black music see Steven Tracy, "To the Tune of Those Weary Blues," in Gates, 69–93. Tracy observes that during his childhood (from about 1902 to 1915) Hughes would have heard ballads, reels, and the "crude blues" of an older man like Henry Thomas; that the blues shouter Big Joe Turner led blues singers through the streets of Kansas City during the late 1910s and early 1920s; and that, although early blues was often accompanied by crude homemade instruments, orchestral-type blues was already emerging during the 1910s.
18. For a discussion of Hughes's folk sources and references to blues structure, themes, and imagery, and for a useful bibliography on jazz and blues, see Steven Tracy, *Langston Hughes and the Blues* (Urbana: University of Illinois Press, 1988). For other insights into Hughes's use of the blues idiom see Patricia E. Bonner, "Cryin' the Jazzy Blues and Livin' Blue Jazz: Analyzing the Blues and Jazz Poetry of Langston Hughes," *West Georgia College Review* 20 (1990): 15–28; Patricia Johns and Walter Farrell, "How Langston Hughes Used the Blues," *Melus* 6

(1979): 55–63; and Edward E. Waldron, "The Blues Poetry of Langston Hughes," *Negro American Literature Forum* 5 (1971): 140–9

19. Rampersad insists that we take a revisionary look at Hughes's aesthetic as having been shaped by his recognition of a link between poetry and black music; he claims that *Fine Clothes to the Jew*, Hughes's least successful volume, marks the height of his creative originality ("Hughes's *Fine Clothes to the Jew*," in Gates, 54). Rampersad's monumental biography of Hughes, as well as his and Roessel's recent edition of the *Collected Poems*, has also contributed to the renewed interest in Hughes's poetry. For an illuminating review of the *Collected Poems* that characterizes Hughes's poems in light of four main attributes—his poetics of "announced . . . [but] cryptic reciprocity," his "idiosyncrasy of personal identity," his inveterate sociality, and his humorous irony—see Helen Vendler, "The Unweary Blues," *New Republic*, 6 March 1995, 37–42.
20. "I tried," Hughes observes, "to write poems like the songs they sang on Seventh Street—gay songs, because you had to be gay or die; sad songs, because you couldn't help being sad sometimes. But gay or sad, you kept on living and you kept on going. . . . Like the waves of the sea coming one after another, always one after another, like the earth moving around the sun, night, day—night, day-night, day—forever, so is the undertow of Black music with its rhythm that never betrays you, its strength like the beat of the human heart, its humor, and its rooted power" (*The Big Sea*, 2d ed. [New York: Hill and Wang, 1993], 215).
21. Quoted in Shelby Steele, "The Content of His Character," *New Republic*, 1 March 1999, 30.
22. Ellison, *Shadow and Act* (New York: Vintage, 1995), 58–9.
23. R. Baxter Miller argues that the blues performance in "The Weary Blues" dramatizes several actions, including black self-affirmation, a remaking of the black self-image, and Hughes's transcendence of racial stereotypes through lyric discourse (*The Art and Imagination of Langston Hughes* [Lexington: University Press of Kentucky, 1989], 55). My discussion suggests, on the contrary, that the figurative complexity of Hughes's poem helps him arrive at a clarifying, critical perspective on the folk tradition.
24. Hughes remarked that "it was a poem about a working man who sang the blues all night and then went to bed and slept like a rock. That was all" (*Big Sea*, 215).
25. Leavis, "Mass Civilization and Minority Culture," in *For Continuity* (Cambridge: Minority, 1933), 16–8; Eliot, "Marie Lloyd," in *Selected Essays* (New York: Harcourt, Brace and World, 1960), 407. "In an

interesting essay in the volume of *Essays on the Depopulation of Melanesia*," Eliot writes, "the psychologist W. H. R. Rivers adduced evidence which has led him to believe that the natives of that unfortunate archipelago are dying out principally for the reason that 'Civilization' forced upon them has deprived them of all interest in life. They are dying from pure boredom. When every theatre has been replaced by 100 cinemas, when every musical instrument has been replaced by 100 gramophones, when every horse has been replaced by 100 cheap motor cars, when electrical ingenuity has made it possible for every child to hear its bedtime stories from a loud-speaker, when applied science has done everything possible with the materials on this earth to make life as interesting as possible, it will not be surprising if the population of the entire civilized world rapidly follows the fate of the Melanesians" (407–8)

26. Eliot, *The Waste Land*, in *Collected Poems, 1909–1962* (New York: Harcourt Brace, 1963), 62; hereafter cited as *WL*.
27. "The question of racial terror," Gilroy suggests, "always remains in view when these modernisms are discussed because their imaginative proximity to terror is their inaugural experience. . . . Though they were unspeakable, these terrors were not inexpressible, and . . . residual traces of their necessarily painful expression still contribute to historical memories inscribed and incorporated into the volatile core of Afro-Atlantic cultural creation. . . . The topos of unsayability produced from the slaves' experiences of racial terror . . . can be used to challenge the privileged conceptions of both language and writing as preeminent expressions of human consciousness" (*The Black Atlantic: Modernity and Double Consciousness* [Cambridge, Mass.: Harvard University Press, 1993], 73–4).
28. DuBois, *The Souls of Black Folk*, in *Writings*, ed. Nathan Huggins (New York: Library of America, 1986), 542–3.
29. In "The Negro Artist and the Racial Mountain," a polemical essay published in the *Nation* in 1926, Hughes emphasizes his "racial individuality" as a poet. But even here he implies that knowledge of traditional prosody would have helped him acquire an interpretive, distanced perspective on folk resources: the African American artist, he says, must learn to "interest himself in *interpreting* the beauty of his own people" (*Within the Circle: An Anthology of African American Literary Criticism from the Harlem Renaissance to the Present*, ed. Angelyn Mitchell [Durham, N.C.: Duke University Press, 1994], 55–6).
30. In the 1960s Baraka advocated a racial separatist approach to African American music. Many of his essays written in 1965, for example, affirm nineteenth-century racialist ideas of black manifest destiny and propose

the formation of a black nation through a cultural consciousness flowing from the soul of the artist: "The Black Man must realize himself as Black. And idealize and aspire to that. . . . The Black Artist's role in America is to aid the destruction of America as we know it" (*Home: Social Essays* [New York: Morrow, 1966], 248, 252).

31. Although at this point in his career Baraka's position is not entirely separatist, insofar as he concedes that the blues can be "appreciated" by non-African Americans, what comes across here is the inaccessibility of the blues to a Euro-American audience (*The Leroi Jones/Amiri Baraka Reader*, ed. William J. Harris [New York: Thunder's Mouth, 1991], 37).
32. For a discussion of Hughes's repudiation of racial separatist accounts of African American culture during the 1930s see Anthony Dawahare, "Langston Hughes's Radical Poetry and the End of Race," *Melus* 23, no. 3 (1998): 21–41.
33. Lawrence, *Complete Poems*, ed. Vivian de Sola Pinto and Warren Roberts (New York: Penguin, 1994), 943.
34. For a discussion of the themes and figurative resources used to remember, mythologize, and represent the war see Paul Fussell, *The Great War and Modern Memory* (New York: Oxford University Press, 1975).
35. In the final, frequently anthologized version of the poem, the speaker recognizes that the sentiments inspired by the "insidious mastery" of music betray him even as he helplessly yields to them, "till the heart of me weeps to belong / To the old Sunday evenings at home" (Lawrence, *Complete Poems*, 148).
36. Ben Arnold, *Music and War: A Research and Information Guide* (New York: Garland, 1993), 135. Arnold writes that "the concert life naturally changed, particularly in the Allied countries, where German music had been so widespread. In Great Britain, all German music was at first banned outright. . . . Musicians performed more music by native composers in France, England, and America than before the war" (135). See also Barbara L. Tischler, "World War I and the Challenge of 100% Americanism," in *An American Music: The Search for an American Musical Identity* (New York: Oxford University Press, 1986), 68–91.
37. Johnson, *Listening in Paris: A Cultural History* (Berkeley: University of California Press, 1995), 267.
38. Lawrence's statement sheds some light on "Piano": "Every people is polarized in some particular locality, which is home, the homeland. . . . The Island of Great Britain had a wonderful terrestrial magnetism or polarity of its own, which made the British people. For the moment, this polarity seems to be breaking. Can England die? And what if England

dies?" (*Studies in Classic American Literature* [New York; Doubleday, 1953], 16).

39. *The Letters of Ezra Pound, 1907–1941*, ed. D. D. Paige (New York: Harcourt Brace, 1950), 180.
40. Pound, *Diptych Rome–London* (New York: New Directions, 1994), 40.
41. *The Bridge*, in *The Complete Poems of Hart Crane*, ed. Marc Simon (New York: Liveright, 1993), 98–9.
42. *The Auroras of Autumn*, in *The Collected Poems of Wallace Stevens* (New York: Vintage, 1982), 415. Helen Vendler suggests that "the source of the disgust for the father-impresario seems to be Stevens' revulsion against that deliberate primitivism of his own . . . which sets itself to conjure up negresses, guitarists, and the 'unherded herds' of oxlike freed men, all in a vain attempt to reproduce on an ignorant and one-stringed instrument the sophisticated chaos of the self" (*On Extended Wings: Wallace Stevens' Longer Poems* [Cambridge, Mass.: Harvard University Press, 1969]1, 252).
43. Eliot, *Inventions of the March Hare: Poems*, 1909–1917, ed. Christopher Ricks (New York: Harcourt Brace, 1996), 13, 17, 62.
44. North, *The Dialect of Modernism: Race, Language, and Twentieth-Century Literature* (New York: Oxford University Press, 1994), 10.
45. Eliot, *The Waste Land: A Facsimile and Transcript of the Original Drafts Including the Annotations of Ezra Pound*, ed. Valerie Eliot (San Diego: Harcourt Brace, 1994), 125, nn. 2–3.
46. Eliot, "*From Poe to Valéry*," in *To Criticize the Critic, and Other Writings* (London: Faber and Faber, 1965), 32.
47. Eliot, "*The Music of Poetry*," in *On Poetry and Poets* (New York: Farrar, Straus and Cudahy, 1957), 21: hereafter cited as *PP*.
48. Quoted in Bruce McElderry, "Eliot's Shakespeherian Rag," *American Quarterly* 9 (1957): 185.
49. For a discussion of Eliot's pursuit of analogies between musical and poetic procedures, which situates his engagement with symbolism within the context of Stravinsky's *Shakespeare Songs* and works by other twentieth-century composers, see James Anderson Winn, *Unsuspected Eloquence: A History of the Relations between Poetry and Music* (New Haven, Conn.: Yale University Press, 1981), 295–9.
50. Eliot, "Fragment of an Agon," in *Collected Poems, 1909–1962*, 119–20.
51. Referring to the nature of his "experiment" in writing *Sweeney Agonistes*, Eliot recalled: "I once designed, and drafted a couple of scenes, of a verse play. My intention was to have one character whose sensibility and intelligence should be on the plane of the most sensitive and intelligent members of the audience; his speeches should be addressed to them as

much as the other personages in the play—or rather, should be addressed to the latter, who were to be material, literal-minded and visionless, with the consciousness of being overheard by the former. There was to be an understanding between this protagonist and a small number of the audience, while the rest of the audience would share the responses of the other characters in the play. Perhaps this is all too deliberate, but one must experiment as one can" (*The Use of Poetry and the Use of Criticism: Studies in the Relation of Criticism to Poetry in England* [London: Faber and Faber, 1933], 153–4; hereafter cited as *UP*).

52. Henry Louis Gates Jr. observes, "We are forced to wonder aloud where in dialect poetry, with the notable exception of Sterling Brown, a black poet used his medium as effectively as did Eliot in *Sweeney Agonistes*" (*Figures in Black: Words, Signs, and the "Racial" Self* [New York: Oxford University Press, 1987], 289 n. 17).
53. See, e.g., Eliot, *Notes towards the Definition of Culture* (London: Faber and Faber, 1948), 121; and Eliot, "The Social Function of Poetry," in *PP*, 13.
54. In *Allegories of Reading: Figural Language in Rousseau, Nietzsche, Rilke, and Proust* (New Haven, Conn.: Yale University Press, 1979), Paul de Man argues that the link between metonymy and its referent is contingent and accidental; thus reliance on metonymic fragments of social reality is problematic. Although Hughes is aware that the reader may not understand the historical context of the trope, his poems repeatedly affirm that the meaning of African American experience, in certain instances, may be shared by readers from different social worlds and cultural backgrounds. His insistence on metonymy as a mainstay of his realist poetics is an assertion of his right to creative freedom of expression, even at the risk of incomprehensibility.
55. *Spring and All*, in *The Collected Poems of William Carlos Williams*, ed. A. Walton Litz and Christopher MacGowan, vol. 1 (New York: New Directions, 1986), 203.
56. Theodor Adorno, "Fetish Character in Music and Regression of Listening," in *The Essential Frankfurt School Reader*, ed. Andrew Arato and Eike Gebhardt (New York: Continuum, 1982), 288.
57. Babette Deutsch wrote that the poems in *Montage of a Dream Deferred* suffered "from a will to shock the reader, who is apt to respond coldly to such obvious devices" ("Waste Land of Harlem," *New York Times Book Review*, 6 May 1951, 23).

PETER POWERS

"The Singing Man Who Must Be Reckoned With": Private Desire and Public Responsibility in the Poetry of Countée Cullen

> His lyric gift was incontestable and, indeed, exceptional. But his poetry has none of McKay's fiery virility, and the treasures it encloses are, rather, those of a soul that at times indulged in an excess of sensibility and preferred to express itself in the half-tones and nuances of a high scrupulousness. (Wagner 283)

> Cullen's creative work is often effetely comfortable and self-consciously vulnerable. (Hill et al. 909)

> No other Negro writer of the 1920s was more anxious to use primitive and atavistic motifs than the poet Countee Cullen. It is a bit ironic, because none of the Harlem writers was more formally schooled, none more genteel in inclination and taste, none indeed more prissy than Cullen. (Huggins 161)

In working up to writing about Countée Cullen, I found it difficult to read very far into the scholarship without noticing a drumbeat of *sotto voce* criticisms, often eloquently stated but revealing themselves as variants of the schoolyard taunts directed toward boys who never quite manage to throw a spiral, who make the mistake of squealing or giggling too often, or whose

From *African American Review* 34, no. 4. © 2000 Peter Powers.

step across the blacktop may mince a bit too much.[1] "MY GOD!" the critics seem to agree, "HE WRITES LIKE A GIRL!" Most often this dismissal of the poetry coincides with a dismissal of the man. For Jean Wagner, Cullen lacks McKay's virility, and for the editors of the *Riverside Anthology of the African American Literary Tradition*, he has exhausted whatever virility he may have had and is simply effete—perhaps a more politically palatable term than "effeminate." For Darwin Turner he is "childishly petulant" and given to "self-pitying despair" (74). Nathan Huggins thinks he's prissy. For David Levering Lewis, the combination of Cullen's suspect masculinity and his overwhelming popularity among Talented Tenth Harlemites signifies the general failings of the Renaissance as a whole. He grants literary Harlem some manly discernment by hoping speculatively that "Cullen must have set even Harlem's teeth on edge with *Crisis* throwaways lisping of a 'daisy-decked' Spring with her 'flute and silver lute'" (77). But Lewis's general dismay at the failures of the black bourgeoisie comes quickly to the fore as he notes, "Harlem loved Langston Hughes, Cullen's only serious rival. . ., but it revered Countee Cullen. With his high-pitched voice, nervous courtliness, and large Phi Beta Kappa key gleaming on the chain across a vested, roly-poly middle, he was the proper poet with proper credentials" (77).

Alas, poor Cullen! Fat, highpitched and lisping, childish writer of effete verses. Not a candidate, according to the critics, for man of the year.

To some degree these gendered interpretations echo the masculine anxieties of an Ezra Pound or a T. S. Eliot decrying the effeminate line of the Amygists. It's not my purpose here to defend Cullen from the manly modernist critical tradition by suggesting that Cullen's poetry really is virile after all. What that could mean, I'm not entirely sure. Rather, it seems to me that the critical attention given to Cullen's supposedly flaccid masculinity is responding to a crisis over the nature of black masculinity that Cullen's poetry everywhere embodies. This crisis turns fundamentally on the unresolved tensions it displays over the relationship among blackness, homoeroticism, and Christian ethics, especially given that Cullen is living in a predominantly white, heterosexual, and increasingly secularized cultural milieu. Given the popularity of Cullen's work at the time, it seems possible to hypothesize that Cullen's work was not only popular because of his Phi Beta Kappa key but also because the tensions and contradictions that drive his work embody the tensions and contradictions of his cultural context, particularly as they revolve around the definitions of masculinity, race, and religion.

During the period that gave birth to the Harlem Renaissance, masculine anxiety coursed like a fever through the veins of Americans both black and white. In the first thirty years of the century the Boy Scouts flourished, as did the Men and Religion Forward Movement, the YMCA, men's lodges and social clubs, and the National Park Service—conceived by Teddy Roosevelt to help combat what he perceived as the effeminacy of overly civilized boys and men. The strenuous life was to save not only the male body and character; it would save the nation. So thought Roosevelt.[2] So, in fact, thought Countée Cullen's foster father, who devoted a chapter of his spiritual autobiography to the moral and racial uplift that athletics could provide (F. A. Cullen 102–105). *Birth of a Nation*, a wildly popular racist film on the development of the Klan, dramatized the anxieties of white Southern manhood facing both Northern political dominance and a newly assertive black masculine presence.

While often birthed among white Americans, most of these cultural institutions and discourses had close cousins among African Americans. As early as 1903, Du Bois had proclaimed that the "history of the American Negro is the history of this strife—this longing to attain self-conscious manhood. . ." (102). In 1923, when Cullen is writing the poems that would establish his reputation, Reverend Reverdy Ransom gave forth on the nature of black manhood:

HE IS NEW, he is old as the forests primeval.
Stark in their nakedness of limb,
His forebears roamed the jungle and led the chase.
Crystalized by the heat of Oriental suns,
God made him a rock of undecaying power,
To become at last the nation's corner stone.
Rough hewn from the jungle and the desert's sands,
Slavery was the chisel that fashioned him to form,
And gave him all the arts and sciences had won.
The lyncher, mob, and stake have been his emery wheel.
TO MAKE A POLISHED MAN of strength and power.
In him, the latest birth of freedom,

God hath again made all things new.
Europe and Asia with ebbing tides recede,
America's unfinished arch of freedom waits,
Till he, the comer stone of strength,
Is lifted into place and power.
Behold him! dauntless and unafraid he stands.
He comes with laden arms,
Bearing rich gifts to science, religion, poetry and song.
Labor and capital through him shall find

The equal heritage of common brotherhood,
And statesmanship shall keep the stewardship
Of justice with equal rights and privileges for all.
HE KNOWS HIS PLACE to keep it
As a sacred trust and heritage for all.
To wear God's image in the ranks of men
And walk as princes of the royal blood divine,
ON EQUAL FOOTING everywhere with all mankind.
With ever-fading color on these shores,
    The Oriental sunshine in his blood
Shall give the warming touch of brotherhood
And love, to all the fused races in our land,
He is the last reserve of God on earth,
Who, in the godly fellowship of love,
Will rule the world with peace. (Spencer 453–54)

Registering the same links among athletics, morality, and racial uplift that animated Frederick Cullen's ministry, Ransom saw this messianic figure embodied as early as 1910 in Jack Johnson, a man whose symbolic championing of black manhood in the boxing ring spanned the years of Cullen's childhood.[3] Gerald Early notes that Johnson symbolized the preoccupations of the Renaissance with masculine self-realization. "This became the basic idea of the New Negro—the black who asserted his rights and his manhood, who wanted to best the white, who was 'reckless, independent, bold, and superior in the face of whites'" (26).[4] When, in "The City of Refuge," Rudolph Fisher's protagonist gawks at a black policeman ordering about white motorists, he is looking wide-eyed into the dawning of a form of black male self-assertion not previously thought possible in the face of white racism.

Black male self-assertion, the perception of economic insecurity attendant upon industrialization and massive immigration, and the toxic psychology of most Southern whites coming out of Reconstruction proved a volatile brew. Of the 3,513 lynchings of African Americans in the years between 1882 and 1927, two-thirds occurred after 1903, the year of Cullen's birth. Ninety-seven percent of these victims were men (Harris 7). This says nothing of the various race riots, beatings, and other forms of humiliation attendant upon mythologies of maleness. The psychological and ideological threads that provoked such atrocities also wove themselves into the cultural and intellectual tapestry of white Americans. Spengler's work on the decline of Western civilization—wildly popular in many parts of educated white America—is fraught with a masculinist vision of the declining male potency of the West, which is giving way before the sexualized hordes of the colored world. Similarly, as David Levering Lewis points out, even sympathetic and concerned whites of the twenties romanticized the black male as a sexual and spiritual dynamo. Indeed, Ransom's poem above could easily have been endorsed by any number of white aficionados of blackness, such as Carl Van Vechten. Lewis quotes Malcolm Cowley: "'One heard it said . . . that the Negroes had retained a direct virility that the whites had lost through being overeducated'" (91).[5]

While the black bourgeoisie was aware of such stereotyping and its potentially pernicious implications, they seemed to agree with the general assumption that racial and even national salvation lay in a clearly articulated masculine style.[6] Ransom's rhapsody on the black male is only one good example. But what that style should be was a point of some debate. The gaudy military plumage of the Garveyites? Or perhaps the crisp Victorianism of W. E. B. Du Bois with his cane, his moustache modeled after Germany's Wilhelm II, and his general air of urbane sophistication? Or perhaps the traditionally patriotic sharp lines of the 15th regiment on Fifth Avenue? The "primitivist" hedonism of the working-class clubs and cabarets celebrated by Langston Hughes and Claude McKay? Or perhaps even the proper Christian gentleman, of whom Cullen's adoptive father, Frederick Asbury Cullen, was one of the prime exemplars? All these embodied different masculine styles and indeed suggested different conceptions of blackness that African American men embraced or rejected in the quest for a route out from under the thumb of white America. Thus, much of the aesthetic work of the Harlem Renaissance turned not simply on the question of race but around the nexus of race and gender. From the sharp disagreements between Cullen and Hughes on the proper subject matter for poetry, to the late arguments between Hurston and Wright, the politics of race was also the politics of gender and sexuality. The cultural explosion of the twenties, which Cullen embodied for many African Americans, explores the tricky terrain in which the achievement of manhood is seen to be an achievement of racial self-realization.

Perhaps no poet was more vexed by the dilemma of his masculinity than Countée Cullen. Adopted out of an impoverished childhood, and perhaps illegitimacy, into the upper reaches of Harlem society by a Methodist minister, living a barely concealed gay life while still marrying Yolande Du Bois, Cullen embodied the contradictory social significance of varying masculine styles in his one body. Critics have documented Cullen's anguished bifurcation as a black man dedicated to a dream of Africa and to the intellectual traditions that he imbibed at Clinton DeWitt High School,

NYU, and Harvard. In the balance of this essay, I suggest that the crucial and finally insurmountable problem of Cullen's poetry is found not simply in this intellectual problem, but in the problem of his male body, centered as it is at the nexus of several contradictory masculine styles. Because these styles provoked what must have seemed to Cullen to be mutually exclusive desires, none could be affirmed save at the expense of self-mutilation. The most critical of these styles—which I would describe loosely as that of the Christian public servant and the gay lover—brought Cullen's desire for public service, approbation, and racial leadership into conflict with his desire for love and sexual fulfillment.

To some degree, Cullen was aware of all this, as his oft-quoted statement that he could not resolve a Christian upbringing with a pagan inclination makes clear. However, the implications of this conflict for Cullen's quandaries concerning masculine sexuality and race have yet to be fully explored. Critics often note the conflict between Cullen's Africanist longings and his attachment to white traditions, but no one has noted that in Cullen's work "paganism" stands primarily as a marker for erotic desire, a movement toward an object of love or erotic experience rather than a search for origins. For Cullen this "inclination" or desire was primarily gay.[7] We can thus see the irony of Cullen's position as a man with longings for other men who would become an exemplar of the race by writing poetry. This poetry often evokes an eroticism associated with blackness, which must have often evoked in Cullen his private homoerotic desires, desires which did not clearly fit the heroic black male image embodied by Jack Johnson and the soldiers of the 15th regiment, or even of the Christian public servant embodied by his father and Reverdy Ransom. All of this at least implies that the assertion of blackness and maleness, for Cullen, must potentially have asserted homoerotic desire, the frank revelation and indulgence of which could only have served to diminish his position as a poet laureate. "What is Africa to me?" Indeed.

On this score, Cullen was not simply conflicted among allegiance to Africa, African Americans, and white cultural forms—different forms of cultural/public expression, we might say. Rather this cultural conflict was also a coded conflict between the public persona with its own very real longing and public displays of the body (one thinks of the dangling Phi Beta Kappa key at which Lewis smirks and the rather uncomfortable suits which Cullen always seems to be wearing in publicity photographs) and the private longings of the lover. Indeed, if we follow Houston Baker, Jr., and notice that the predominant motive of Cullen's romantic poetry is love, it seems appropriate to say that his private and illicit desires were the occasion for the lyric poetry that made him famous, that made his public and proper self-display possible at all (53). Cullen embraced a particular form of public "blackness" in his position as poet, but that very public position, which he eagerly wished to maintain, conflicted with a very different form of "blackness" embodied in his private desires for black men. The tension between these different modes of being produced the creative tension out of which much of Cullen's poetry was born.

This split in the body between public face and private desire is, of course, relatively typical to Victorian masculinity in general, figured predominantly in someone like Dr. Jekyll and Mr. Hyde, all manner of vampire novels, even Dimmesdale lashing himself mercilessly/masochistically in the privacy of his closet while his sadistic counterpart, Roger Chillingsworth, leers at the spectacle from the crack in the door. It found a different but related psychological expression among African Americans in the many works associated with the problems of passing or of having to "wear the mask" in a hostile racial environment. This split in Cullen was perhaps inevitable given his homosexual inclinations, since few men of any stripe were openly and assertively gay at this particular point in American history. While Bruce Nugent may have written a short story that openly displayed homosexual desire and behavior, and while Claude McKay may have included a homosexual character in *Home to Harlem*, these few drops of public literary homosexuality seem meager indeed when compared to the rivers of desire that seem to have flowed among many of the Harlem Renaissance literary masters—Alain Locke, McKay, Cullen, Nugent, and Langston Hughes, to name only a few.[8] DuBois's scathing denunciations of literary works that depicted bohemian sexual practices—he reviewed or spoke negatively of McKay, Van Vechten's *Nigger Heaven*, and the anthology *Fire*, which contained Nugent's short story—suggest the degree to which the cultural leadership of the Renaissance subscribed to traditional bourgeois social values, at least as a matter of public discourse.[9]

The split between public and private was all the more inevitable for Cullen given his situation in his adoptive home. Rumor has it that Frederick Asbury Cullen modeled this kind of split for his son, serving both as exemplary Christian leader of the race and as seducer of choir boys (Lewis 76). Perhaps more pertinent for my purposes is Reverend Cullen's model of responsible Christian maleness, "responsibility" in this case turning on one's public activity on behalf of the race. Reverend Cullen's autobiography is replete with the values of Christian self-renunciation in service to God and others. The elder Cullen transformed Salem Methodist Episcopal from a tiny, struggling mission church to one of the most powerful African American churches of the twenties, with more than three thousand members, large property holdings, and a plethora of ministries to the tidal wave of immigrants from the South. While much has been made of Reverend Cullen's criticisms of the cabaret and club life, as well as the prostitution and sexual peccadillos that his adopted son found alluring, Cullen was far from a simple-minded moralist. Indeed, some of his most important work included public action on issues attendant to the assertion of black maleness in the world. He served as president in the local chapter of the NAACP and helped to organize a protest of the race riot in Brownsville, Texas. He helped send W. E. B. Du Bois to the League of Nations, helped organize the Silent Parade, and helped found the Urban League. Among his most important ministries at Salem was a commitment to the YMCA, through which he hoped to rescue Harlem boys from gang activity in the streets (Ferguson 20–21; Sernett 134). Whatever the limitations of such activism proved to be, it can hardly be said that Reverend Cullen's Christianity encouraged racial self-hatred. Indeed, in many ways, Reverend Cullen stood as an exemplar of that icon of racial leadership, the black preacher, noted by Du Bois as a man at "the centre of a group of men, now twenty, now a thousand in number" (199).

Whatever Reverend Cullen's private sexual proclivities, it seems clear that he encouraged his son to replicate his belief in the importance of public leadership and proper public deportment. The younger Cullen's notorious complaint against the lowlife depictions of some Harlem Renaissance work surely reflects his father's moralism. But as his father's position is more complicated, so too is the son's. While not entering the ministry, the young poet was drawn to positions of leadership within his own vocation, serving as editor of journals and anthologies from his days as a school boy until the days he ceased most professional activity as a writer. While Cullen has been critiqued for not having followed an editorial policy more clearly focused on folk traditions when he brought out his anthology *Carolina Dusk*, he clearly conceived of the project as a form of racial promotion—a way of putting the best foot forward, as it were. Houston Baker has suggested that Cullen's poetic project was "celebrated by black people because he demonstrated authentic, poetical achievement to appreciative whites" (47). I would go a bit further and say that it demonstrated such achievement to any number of appreciative members of the black bourgeoisie as well.

What is significant to me here is the public and quasi-political role Cullen knew his role as poet was serving. Commenting on his former classmate, Martin Russak notes that Cullen served as a significant intellectual leader even among some white Americans at NYU, something that in small represented the kind of political and cultural power to which many African Americans aspired in the Harlem Renaissance (Tuttleton 130–31). Little wonder then that many saw in the soon-to-be-disastrous marriage of the daughter of W. E. B. Du Bois and the son of Frederick Asbury Cullen the marriage of a new Adam and a new Eve, exemplars of a New Negro race to be. Even according to the editors of the Norton Anthology of African American Literature, Cullen "was probably the figure from the Harlem Renaissance who most closely corresponded to Alain Locke's idea of the New Negro" (Gates and McKay 1303). Locke seems to have affirmed this in private correspondence with the poet, saying that "you and one or two more very much represent the younger generation as far as my hopes and interests go."[10]

Seen in this light, Cullen's plaintive longing to be taken as only a poet, not a Negro poet, seems less simply like self-alienation and racial self-hatred than a desperate attempt to mitigate the consequences of being seen as "THE New Negro," a particular mode of blackness that he felt called upon to embrace, and indeed wanted to embrace. But that embrace made his own longstanding and deeply personal embrace of men like Harold Jackman—a man to whom most of his poetry is dedicated in one form or another—excruciatingly complicated indeed, since the public forums where he wished to be taken seriously made little or no room for unconventional sexual practices.[11] Cullen himself seemed aware of the significance of public approbation and the costs of public ridicule, and that the public character of his poetry was of paramount importance. In a letter to Harold Jackman, he accuses himself of playing to the public too readily: "'There is actually no excuse for enjoying the plaudits of the populace as I do. I fairly revel in public commendation. Perhaps I am the one living poet who will confess that he doesn't write for his own amusement, and that what others think of his work can affect him'" (qtd. in Shucard 10). Still, Cullen seems to have been torn by the public significance of his work. When Alain Locke argued that "the present day Negro poet regards his racial heritage as a more precious endowment than his own personal genius, and to the common legacy of his art adds the peculiar experiences and emotions of his folk," Cullen wrote a disturbed rejoinder that argued for the importance of the personal (Shucard 20). Indeed, even Cullen's famous repudiation of the more bohemian school of Hughes and McKay, while clearly concerned with the reception of a white audience, is also simply riven with anxieties about hidden and private things becoming exposed:

> There is no more childish untruth than the axiom that the truth will set you free; in many cases it will merely free one from the concealment of facts which will later bind you hand and foot in ridicule and mockery. Let art portray things as they are no matter what the consequences, no matter who is hurt, is a blind bit of

> philosophy. There are some things, some truths of Negro life and thought, of Negro inhibitions, that all Negroes know, but take no pride in. ("Dark Tower" 171)

Cullen is parroting the aesthetic assumptions of someone like Du Bois, and whatever the degree of racial self-hatred present in Cullen's life, he also seems primarily to be arguing for a particular mode of blackness, a definition of what a Negro is or ought to be, as well as for the freedom not to revel in or reveal the sexuality that threatened his public face.[12] Crucial here is less racial hatred than a mind riven by fears of discovery, particularly fears of falling short of what a Negro ought to be—at least in his own mind and in the mind of the black bourgeoisie. The quotation moves from a general statement of the imprisoning effects of social ridicule, to a general sense that there are any number of things that Negroes know about but would rather not discuss in public. Only after this does Cullen move to an explicit statement that the receptiveness of white audiences should be taken into account. Cullen is fearful of the consequences of his desires being uncovered as a general principle, not simply out of a slavish devotion to the prerogatives of white people—all of which suggests that desire is never a purely personal matter, at least for the person desiring a public voice.

This bifurcation between public responsibility and private desire is evident throughout "Heritage," a poem that is, of course, about the problematic status of Africa in Cullen's imagination and in the Harlem Renaissance in general, and about the sense of split between a pagan self and a Christian or civilized self. Without denying these readings, I wish to point out that this poem is also clearly about the conflicted desire of the poet's own body, particularly a desire directed toward the male body. The narrator of the poem lies, apparently in bed and alone, meditating on the nature of his own body. In this body he feels "the unremittant beat / Made by cruel padded feet / Walking through my body's street. / Up and down they go, and back, / Treading out a jungle track" (106). The beat alluded to in the first line is a figure for bodily desire in the poem, though Cullen separates this from the body itself and figures his desire as something walking on him cruelly, as if dominating and beating down his body in some all but unbearable manner. A similar linking of anguish and desire occupies the next lines, as the body is no longer simply trod upon by desire but writhes in response:

> I can never rest at all
> When the rain begins to fall;
> Like a soul gone mad with pain
> I must match its weird refrain;

Ever must I twist and squirm,
Writhing like a baited worm,
While its primal measures drip
Through my body, crying, "Strip!
Doff this new exuberance.
Come and dance the Lover's Dance!"
In an old remembered way
Rain works on me night and day. (106)

The evident anguish here replicates that caused by the cruel padded feet of the earlier line. However, here the poet's body responds by twisting, squirming, and writhing, movements easily seen as sexual passion, but a sexual passion identified with entrapment. Rather than imagining sexual ecstasy as a form of self-fulfillment, the narrator feels himself a baited worm, a body trapped by desires beyond his ability to control, desires in fact that are imperious and demanding, calling for the narrator to "strip" and to "dance," verbs used in the imperative voice.[13] Desire calls the poet to reveal himself fully and to cease lying; that is, to get up and act on his sexual desires but also to give up his duplicitous, double life, and reveal himself for who he is as a desiring being. The linking of erotic desire and enslavement is not an unusual combination in the romantic literary tradition. In the context of Cullen's growing awareness of himself as a public figure embodying the hopes and longings of other people, the bifurcation takes on particular resonances. The poem is dedicated to Harold Jackman, Cullen's male lover of longest standing. Given that, it is intriguing that the opening segments of the poem evoke images of sexuality that are clearly heterosexual and/or reproductive in character. The "Strong bronzed men, or regal black / Women from whose loins I sprang" and the "Jungle boys and girls in love" are fairly commonplace images of Africa for the time. However, these strong images of heterosexual racial pride are associated with an Africa toward which the narrator has an ambivalent attitude, an identification he can only make through a cerebral engagement with books. More important is the drumbeat within his own blood, the desires that would call him to "strip" and cast aside his bookish images of Africa in favor of the dance. For Cullen, of course, such book learning was one of the most important sources of his public authority. Moreover, the clothes he is called upon to leave behind symbolize the public face of respectability, the outward symbol of a civilized, educated, and clearly heterosexual Christian gentleman who, writhing on his bed at night, has desires for something which a civilized, educated, and clearly heterosexual Christian gentleman ought not to desire. Thus the dream, or desire, is always deferred. As a black gay man expected to perform in a number of publicly prescribed ways, the narrator here feels the necessity of keeping his desiring black body safely in the closet—or, in Cullen's case, safely encased within his ill-fitting suits and Phi Beta Kappa Key—unstripped, unrevealed, and writhing on his bed of lies.

That Cullen concludes the poem with an imagined prayer to Christ partially replicates this more general effort to protect the body. But at the end of "Heritage," Cullen is attempting desperately to reconcile his reasonable desire for safety with his longing to express his erotic desire for black men, and attempting to reconcile all of this with a desire to assert a black masculinity that will be taken to be fully manly even if it happens to be gay. Thus an angry and erotically compelling black Christ is a "dark god" that Cullen "fashions" so that he can have a black male with whom he can identify. This Christ has "Dark despairing features" that are "Crowned with dark rebellious hair," figures that suggest sexual vitality as well as Cullen's resentment at perpetually deferred sexual self-revelation. Nevertheless, even after fashioning such a Christ, Cullen withdraws from what he takes as an impetuous act of creation, begging forgiveness of the Lord because his "need" or desire "Sometimes shapes a human creed." Thus, in the poem's conclusion, the narrator follows not the imperative to "strip," as called for by his hot desire, but the imperative of self-renunciation: "All day long and all night through, / One thing only must I do: / Quench my pride and cool my blood, / Lest I perish in the flood." Whereas his days and nights at the beginning and in middle of the poem have been wracked by desire and the imperative to act, even by the imperative to shape a black god who could fill his "need," the poem concludes with an assertion of the need for self-protection.

The rejection of the Black Christ is peculiar on any number of scales. While much has been made of the embrace of a white Jesus throughout much of African American Christianity at the time, Cullen's longing that "he I served were black" is hardly novel to Cullen or to the Black Theology movement of the 1960s. Among the educated and middle-class ministerial circles in which Cullen moved, assertions of a Black Christ were relatively common (Douglas 9–34). Such images also had broad popular appeal in Harlem. In direct appeals to the masses, Garveyites incorporated the notion of a Black Christ, a Black God, and a Black Madonna into their quasi-religious ritualism, and the Cullen household had been known to take the Garveyites seriously.[14] Thus, proclaiming a Black Christ was not a radical notion, though the depiction of a highly eroticized Black Christ was. However mildly heterodox the notion of a Black Christ might have been, what is truly unique and potentially disturbing to middle-class Afro-Christians or white readers is the depiction of an eroticized Christ whom the male narrator finds attractive. When the narrator wishes for a Black Christ so that his heart would not lack "Precedence of pain to guide it," the pain to be recalled within the poem itself is primarily that of the illicit and "unChristian" sexual desire that pierces his body like a hook. Indeed, the narrator reinscribes the problematic public–private split that is complicating Cullen's erotic desires when he wants the Black Christ to be able to feel his pain, "Let who would or might deride it" (107). The narrator longs for an acceptably public male object of desire, one who would release him from the pain of public censure, dismissing those who would deride him. One thinks here of the snickering nubile girls that Lewis evokes in his description of Cullen's social position in the Renaissance (76). In the predominantly Christian environs of Harlem, what could be more publicly acceptable than Christ himself? The problem, then, is not simply the blackness of Christ, but a black Christ who can experience the pain of desire. While the former was well within the realm of acceptable speculative possibility, the latter could have been scandalous to the predominantly heterosexual Harlemites as well as the proper white folks to whom Cullen's verses appealed, supportive readers who may have indulged the sexual failings of one of their leading lights but could hardly have accepted having those sexual failings baptized in the image of Christ.

So it is not surprising that at the end of "Heritage" the narrator chooses survival. If his heart and head—his private longings, thoughts, and desires—have not yet realized they are civilized, he at least must guard against the destructive flood their publicity might entail. He seeks to cool his blood, an image of the death of his desire that avoids the social death that his stripping might occasion. Indeed, perhaps it is not accidental that in the collection *Color*, Cullen chose to follow "Heritage" with "For a Poet," wherein he imagines his dreams wrapped in a silken cloth and buried in a coffin-like box, a form of psychic death that purchases a form of public freedom.[15]

"Heritage" is often taken to be Cullen's best poem. In many ways it foreshadows the obsessions that mark Cullen's poetry throughout the rest of his career, particularly an obsession with the need to sacrifice individual desire for some greater good, often but not exclusively associated with Christianity. In "Judas Iscariot," the clearly homosocial and suggestively homoerotic bond between Judas and Jesus is broken when Jesus asks Judas to betray him to fulfill God's work of salvation.

> Then Judas in his hot desire
>   Said, "Give me what you will."
> Christ spoke to him with words of fire,
>   "Then, Judas, you must kill

> One whom you love, One who loves you
> As only God's son can:
> This is the work for you to do
> To save the creature man." (126)

In this reading, Judas is the most faithful disciple to his friend/lover Christ. He gives the "young Christ heart, soul, and limb / and all the love he had" (128), but he gives that love precisely by giving up Jesus as the object of his "hot desire" for the higher purpose of the people's salvation. In "The Ballad of the Brown Girl," the doubting "Lord Tom" gives up on the true object of his desire in order to marry a "nut-brown maid" with riches and social standing.

Many of the poems that appear in *Copper Sun* and in *The Black Christ* deal with the problem of lost love, failed love, the failure to love—too many to analyze individually. While some of this can be attached to his failing marriage with Yolande Du Bois, it also seems clear that Cullen is crestfallen at his decision to leave behind male lovers for a publicly acceptable marriage, men whom he cast in the role of poetic muses. During this period Cullen writes Alain Locke, complaining not only of his sexual failures in marriage but of his loss of social contact with male associates who have since been identified as gay (Reimonenq 150). Further, in the dedicatory poem for *The Black Christ*, Harold Jackman and two others are described as three who have not bowed the knee to "grasp a lock / Of Mammon's hair." Instead, they are those "Who have not bent / The idolatrous knee, / Nor worship lent to modern rites . . . / Three to whom Pan is no mere myth / But a singing Man / To be reckoned with" (180). Pan, as Gerald Early points out, is a mythological figure noted not only for his singing abilities but also for his sexual prowess, a predilection often directed toward young males (180). For the poet, Jackman appreciates the powers of a highly sexualized singing man. If Cullen's marriage to Yolande Du Bois was a way of sealing his position in acceptable social circles, it seems that Cullen's lamentations of the lost loves and desires of his youth have less to do with Yolande than with the losses required to achieve social acceptance.

Ultimately, Cullen begins to associate the loss of private desire with the loss of poetry itself. The tensions and creative interactions among sexual desire, creative production or "singing," and the temptations of social acceptance form the central conflict of much of "The Black Christ." Its inability to resolve these conflicts marks the dying fall of Cullen's poetic project. "The Black Christ" makes explicit what remains lurking just beneath the surface of "Heritage": that the realization of illicit forms of desire results in death, a death Cullen is finally unwilling to undergo.

Whereas the drama of desire and self-renunciation in "Heritage" is figured as a split within the one body of the narrator, in "The Black Christ" these are divided into various characters: the mother who becomes the feminine figure of Christian patience and forbearance; the white mobs who embody the threats that remain mostly felt but not seen in "Heritage"; the rebellious brother Jim who represents both sexual desire and to some degree the inspiring spirit of lyric poetry; and, of course, the narrator, who in the end represents nothing so much as the poetics of self-renunciation. The poem, in fact, opens with an act of self-renunciation similar to that which concludes "Heritage," as the narrator pleads to God for forgiveness, partially because he believed God would not act on his behalf. The burden of his guilt is something that the poet will carry with him to eternity, and his only response can be to sing "For all men's healing." His poetry must serve a public social purpose nobler than the failures of his individual soul which is "of flaws Composed" (207).

Thus we already know before things get started what the appropriate mode of masculine behavior is to be: that of repentance and self-renunciation. Whereas the combination of desires in "Heritage" at least makes the narrator "writhe" with both ecstasy and indecision, creating a dramatic tension that needs to be resolved, in "The Black Christ" the plea for forgiveness and the enunciation of social purpose dissolve all dramatic tension from the outset. Ironically, the poet goes on to ask a few lines later why no powerful manifestations of masculine presence can be found in the present:

> We cry for angels; yet wherefore,
> Who raise no Jacobs any more? . . .
> No men with eyes quick to perceive
> The Shining Thing, clutch at its sleeve,
> Against the strength of heaven try
> The valiant force of men who die;
> With heaving heart where courage sings
> Strive with a mist of Light and Wings,
> And wrestle all night long, though pressed
> Be rib to rib and back to breast,
> Till in the end the lofty guest
> Pant, "Conquering human, be thou blest." (208)

Despite the sublimated suggestion of homoerotic desire in bodies that "wrestle all night long, though pressed / Be rib to rib and back to breast," the poem's opening lines clearly indicate that all the wrestling that needs to be done has been in the past. Rather than wrestling blessings from angels, the narrator needs somehow to wrestle a pardon from God that he will not receive until the last day.

This effort to erase desire before it can ever really be articulated structures the entire poem. In the second stanza, the conflict is set between the desiring Jim and his mother, whose voice emphasizes stasis, rootedness, and acceptance over the writhing and dissatisfied activity of the desiring body:

> I count it little being barred
> From those who undervalue me.
> I have my own soul's ecstasy.
> Men may not bind the summer sea,
> Nor set a limit to the stars;
> The sun seeps through all iron bars;
> The moon is ever manifest.
> These things my heart always possessed.
> And more than this (and here's the crown)
> No man, my son, can batter down
> The star-flung ramparts of the mind.
> So much for flesh; I am resigned,
> Whom God has made shall He not guide? (211)

The mother's voice resists the very masculine striving that the narrator purports to long for in the figure of the athletic Jacob. Her feminine counsel to patience and forbearance implicitly opposes the longings of Jim's body, insisting that the beauty of creation amply compensates for the exclusion and imprisonment of the body. While awaiting a heavenly kingdom, she provisionally accepts the prison bars that immobilize and hide the body.

The mother's image is complicated in that, besides being a sign of Christian pacification, she is also clearly presented as an origin of black identity, whether linguistic or biological. The father is dead. The mother is presented in nearly mythical terms as an ur-mother, the black Southern woman at one with the earth, a figure of the Southern roots of authentic black culture common to such works as Du Bois's *The Souls of Black Folk*, Toomer's *Cane*, and Hurston's *Their Eyes Were Watching God*. She is the source of language, conveying a form of black cultural heritage to her rebellious sons through "legends" of an enslaved people whom God saves after a long and arduous patience (212). In passing on these stories to her sons she is the figure of intergenerational connection, indeed the figure of generations, of blackness itself. She also seems to represent the fount of language itself, the mother tongue that makes it possible to articulate desire at all. While of a different class and geographical location, she symbolizes a mode of blackness with which Cullen would have been quite familiar, one marked by Christian longsuffering. But she is also the source of the Christian stories which framed much of black public and private discourse, stories which shaped a great deal of Cullen's poetry.

Thus, the mother provides the narrator with the languages necessary for poetry, but the contours of that language conflict with the realization of male desire. This is not to say that personal concerns and desire are necessarily opposed to racial solidarity, as Jim's anger at the world is often provoked by the death or humiliation of other black men. But within the ideological framework of Cullen's perception of Christianity, Jim's desiring and desirable body, with its seemingly inexorable thrust toward sexual consummation, presents the central problem for Christian longsuffering. Thus the body is in a conflicted relationship with the available language that can bring its desire to linguistic expression. Throughout the poem, the mother constantly attempts to quell and quiet Jim's desire, reading that desire as potentially self-destructive.

Nevertheless, this body is constantly threatening to break out beyond the mother's words that seek to control it through "sorely doubted litanies." Indeed, we first see Jim lying abed, not unlike the protagonist of "Heritage": "Jim with a puzzled, questioning air, / Would kick the covers back and stare." Jim's language at this stage of the poem is primarily interrogative, a linguistic marker of his desire since the question moves toward its future answer rather than accepting the mother's hortatory litanies that refuse to assault the "ramparts" of God's mind and will. Jim kicks back the covers, exposing his body to the air, not unlike the writhing lover of "Heritage." His body contains an "Aetna" that seethes with passion and fury. His bones reveal themselves through the skin of his hands "like white scars" when he is enraged at the death of some other black man. He imagines himself speeding "one life-divesting blow / Into some granite face of snow." If the mother's words speak of spirit, Jim seems to be all body, naked and exposed. His physical expressions of rage are immediately "covered" by the mother's words.

When such hot venom curled his lips
And anger snapped like sudden whips
Of lightning in his eyes, her words—
Slow, gentle as the fall of birds
That having strained to win aloft
Spread out their wings and slowly waft

> Regretfully back to earth—
> Would challenge him to name the worth
> Contained in any seed of hate.
> Ever the same soft words would mate.
> Upon her lips: love, trust, and wait. (214)

Here a disembodied language is opposed to desire, using language to cool the blood rather than inflame it, to deflect and blunt desire. Although Cullen attaches a sexual metaphor to the mother's words, the mating that occurs is of "soft words" and words that call for sèlf-renunciation and the deferral of desire: "love, trust, and wait."

Jim's early but still restrained questioning and anger are linked to his gradual revelation as an erotically attractive male. As with "Heritage" the body of a young male is the only desiring and desirable body in the poem. A few lines after "hot venom" curls his lips, Jim is "handsome Jim" who, something of a cavalier, sets out to present his sexuality in the most overt and provocative ways possible:

> But Jim was not just one more fly,
> For he was handsome in a way
> Night is after a long, hot day.
> If blood flows on from heart to heart,
> and strong men leave their counterpart
> In vice and virtue in their seed,
> Jim's bearing spoke his imperial breed.
> I was an offshoot, crude, inclined
> More to the earth; he was the kind
> Whose every graceful movement said,
> As blood must say, by turn of head,
> By twist of wrist and glance of eye,
> "Good blood flows here, and it runs high.
> He had an ease of limb, a raw,
> Clean hilly stride that women saw
> With quickened throbbings of the breast.
> There was a show of wings; the nest
> Was too confined: Jim needed space
> To loop and dip and interlace;
> for he had passed the stripling stage,
> And stood a man, ripe for the wage
> A man extorts of life; his gage
> Was down. (215)

The language here is clearly akin to that of "Heritage." Desire is figured in the blood—in this case, "high" blood. Moreover, his high blood provokes restless movement as Jim has a "clean hilly stride." He "needed space / To loop and dip"—language reminiscent of the command to dance the lover's dance in "Heritage."

Unlike the narrator in "Heritage," Jim doesn't hesitate to express desire. However, desire still throws him into conflict with the social world. While the narrator of "Heritage" struggles against the expression of desire, finally killing it to preserve the body, Jim expresses his desire openly and defiantly. Sexual expression becomes a means of challenge, of throwing down his "gage." He is lynched in short order.[16] As I indicated in my opening, the ritual of lynching is centered on the white obsession with and fear of black male sexual desire. We might say that lynching is the public evocation of black male sexual desire on the part of white Americans so that it might more securely be controlled or cut off from public expression. On the one hand, that Cullen focuses on a lynching scene makes him part of a long literary tradition that includes Baldwin, Morrison, Wright, and others. Nevertheless, that this lynching takes place within a poem that is obsessed with and unnerved by black male desire leaves Cullen's rendering of the lynching and its aftermath deeply troublesome. First, just as the lynch mob erases Jim's body for his sexual and social transgressions against white Americans in the Jim Crow South, the narrator's language gradually erases Jim's physicality. After first attempting to hide the body away in a closet, the narrator turns to discover Jim miraculously reappearing before the mob itself, as if offering himself in sacrifice for the life of his family:

> Each with bewilderment unfeigned
> Stared hard to see against the wall
> The hunted boy stand slim and tall;
> Dream-born, it seemed, with just a trace
> Of weariness upon his face,
> He stood as if evolved from air;
> As if always he had stood there . . . .
> What blew the torches' feeble flare
> To such a soaring fury now
> Each hand went up to fend each brow,
> Save his; he and the light were one,
> A man by night clad with the sun. (227)

This is the first of two subtle but important transformations in Jim's body. The language here gradually removes the threatening sexuality that had characterized Jim only a few lines earlier in the poem. Earlier a man in full bloom whose "gage" is down, here he is a "hunted boy" who is "slim and tall." Earlier characterized by movement, here he simply stands "As if always he had stood there," the desire signified by movement apparently drained from the now undesiring body. He is "evolved from air" and "Dream born" rather than being the product of the sexual relations of the mother and the absent father who is elsewhere in the poem described as a "dandy." Finally, of course, he is described as a "night clad with the sun," a phrase which echoes an earlier description of the mother as a sun lightening a dark sky. If we understand the mother as an unmoving and desexualized bearer of Christian light to her angry children, then whatever Jim was before the moment of the lynching, he is now gradually being covered or "clad" by the mother's vision—static, patient, and deferring every personal desire.

Gerald Early and James Smylie have both suggested that the resurrection actually inverts the traditional Christian emphasis on self-renunciation by having God approve of and embrace the life of the rebellious Jim, just as the resurrection in the Christian gospels is taken to be the seal of God's approval on the perfect obedience of Jesus. By this accounting, Jim would become the fully realized, rebellious, and desiring Black Christ that is desperately longed for at the end of "Heritage." However, this analysis fails to recognize the dramatic shift in Jim's persona at the resurrection scene. Just as "Heritage" concludes with an imperative to self-renunciation that rejects all that had made that poem most interesting, Cullen resurrects a Jim divested of all that had made him a desirable and powerful character in the first place. While the lynching is occurring, the narrator laments his brother as "My Lycidas . . . My Jonathan, my Patrocles," saying, "For with his death there perished these" (232–33). Lycidas and Jonathan are common traditional figures of homoerotic desire, while Lycidas is linked with the production of poetry and Patrocles with warfare against the enemies of Greece. If these died with Jim, one might have thought they would be resurrected with Jim as well, but this is clearly not the case. Although the narrator insists that Jim's "vital self" has been resurrected, that the vision is of the "Live body of the dead," we in fact get the barest glimpse of that body. The narrator approaches his resurrected brother like a doubting Thomas and for the briefest moment passes his fingers "down his slim / Sides, down his breathing length of limb" (233). This all-too-brief moment of physical intimacy may be manifesting Cullen's homoeroticism, but the narrator immediately withdraws and says, "No more." He cries, "this is too much / For one mad brain to stagger through." This repudiation is strikingly similar to the repudiation of the sexualized black Christ at the end of "Heritage."

Jim's resurrection has an ironic effect on the narrator; rather than confirming Jim's life and the image of sexual desire and rebellion that he embodied, the resurrection provokes the narrator to confirm the mother's vision that men should not assault the ramparts of God's mind. Indeed, despite Jim's reappearance, it is as if even his physical presence is too much for the poem itself, and he disappears without explanation. In the last 100 lines of the poem, the narrator moves away from touching Jim's resurrected body to strong assertions of Christian orthodoxy. The disturbing and exciting aspects of the poem that the tension between the mother's language and Jim's body had provoked are dissolved. The anger and desire to which Jim had given voice are trumped by his mother's disembodied patience, as there is now "No sound then in the sacred gloom / That blessed the shrine that was our room / Except the steady rise of praise / To Him who shapes all nights and days / Into one final burst of sun" (234).

Given the association of the mother's Christianity with a sun that blots out the blackness of Jim's night, and with soft words that quiet Jim's angry, questioning desire, these lines suggest that Jim's resurrection has killed the possibility of a poetry of individual desire and love, a poetry that Cullen at one time sought to preserve. Such private desire is replaced with the publicly accessible music of hymn and prayer. There are no sounds, no individual voices, only the collective sounds of Christian hymns repeating the longing for heaven that the mother's earlier legends and litanies evoked. Romance, eroticism, human love—the stuff of lyric poetry associated with a figure like Lycidas are as effectively dead now as they were at the culmination of the lynching and, indeed, as they have been from the very beginning of the poem—perhaps more securely so because the narrator has interpreted Jim's death and resurrection not as a compelling call to follow in the footsteps of Jim's rebellion, but as a call to erase his desire in accepting the public responsibilities of Christian behavior.

As the poem concludes, in fact, Jim disappears entirely, and we see the narrator united in the stasis with which the poem began, united not with Jim or anything that looks like him, but with his mother in self-renunciation:

> While I who mouthed my blasphemies,
> Recalling now His agonies,
> Am found forever on my knees,
> Ever to praise her Christ with her,
> Knowing He can at will confer
> Magic on miracle to prove
> And try me when I doubt His love. (235)

Intriguing at this juncture is that the narrator praises "her Christ with her." So strong is the element of self-renunciation that the narrator does not even own the substance of his own praise by singing to "my Christ" or to "our Christ." The structure of prayer and praise at the end of the poem is dependent on the same renunciation of desire that Cullen felt compelled to invoke at the end of "Heritage." The difference between "Heritage" and "The Black Christ" is that in the latter poem Cullen sought to write poetry that negates desire from the beginning, in order to affirm a publicly acceptable form of masculine presence, one that urges him to repeat the legends and litanies of the people of Israel that he has inherited from his stepmother and father. "The Black Christ" makes clearer that Cullen is not simplistically denying a readily given "blackness" in favor of the approbation of white audiences. Rather he is acceding to a particular mode of blackness in the public face of the New Negro. In doing so he gives up the poetry of private desire that cannot find its way out of the closet. Or rather, it could only find its way out of the closet at the expense of a social death Cullen was not willing to endure.

To some degree Cullen's quandary reflects the quandary of any black man of the Harlem Renaissance who felt he must put aside, or at least hide, personal desires in the name of racial leadership and responsibility. Certainly Du Bois reflected this split in different ways, maintaining the façade of a happy marriage while pursuing a variety of love affairs. Langston Hughes kept his sexuality under such tight wraps that as late as the 1980s Arnold Rampersad refused to say definitively that Hughes had homosexual lovers. The encompassing realities of racism exacerbated the kinds of splits required of such public leaders, but it would seem that Hughes and Du Bois managed this tension with more energy and aplomb than Cullen could muster—perhaps in part because neither Hughes nor Du Bois took the specifics of Christian belief with such seriousness. The irony of Cullen's position is that, in giving up on his desires in the name of a publicly acceptable poetry more akin to hymns than homoerotic lyricism, he also seemed to give up on poetry altogether and lived off the public reputation he had already established by the time "The Black Christ" was published. Mostly Cullen turned to prose works for children and, interestingly, to the publicly responsible position of teaching.

In choosing the poetry of Christian ethics, Cullen gradually gave up on being the sexualized Pan who is the "singing Man to be reckoned with." But in doing so, he complicated the reading of a man who was a failure to his race. Indeed, what is clearest in this reading of public responsibility versus private desire is that Cullen was a poet who—when he could not find a way to reconcile his private desires—tried to sacrifice them in order to be the public "Voice of the Harlem Renaissance." Rather than abandoning race, in

"The Black Christ," he abandons desire and embraces a particular notion of race in the figure of the mother who tells the legends and litanies of the people, a figure of heterosexual reproduction that Cullen tried briefly to embody in his marriage to Yolande Du Bois, a figure of generational passage and biological inheritance upon which notions of race must in some fundamental sense rely. In embracing his role as "THE New Negro," Cullen tried, in the complicated and sometimes noble tradition of Christian self-renunciation, to sacrifice desire in order to be canonized as a saint.

Notes

1. I'd like to thank the many readers of early versions of this manuscript, especially my colleague Julia Kasdorf and the respondents in panels at MLA (Toronto, 1997) and MELUS (Howard University, 1998). Their insights and criticisms have been invaluable.
2. For a good overview of issues surrounding American masculinity, particularly but not exclusively among white Americans, see Kimmel 117–56 and 191–222.
3. Said Ransom on the eve of Johnson's fight with Jim Jeffries, "What Jack Johnson seeks to do to Jeffries in the roped arena will be more the ambition of Negroes in every domain of human endeavor" (qtd. in Early 26).
4. The connection among athleticism, spirituality, and racial deliverance has a long history worthy of a paper of its own, only one important instance being Muhammad Ali's relationship with Malcolm X and the Nation of Islam. See Wilson Moses 155–82 for the most significant investigation of this relationship to date.
5. This fascination with the supposedly superior virility of the African American male is, of course, not restricted to the Harlem Renaissance. Writers as various as James Baldwin and Amiri Baraka have analyzed it, and white writers such as Norman Podhoretz in "My Negro Problem—And Ours" and Norman Mailer in "The White Negro" were stating this fascination bluntly in the 1960s. For a brief survey of the place that black men occupy in the minds and imaginations of white men, see hooks 74–75.
6. As with white romanticizing of the black male, the equation in African American political and cultural rhetoric of blackness with maleness, and indeed even with a virulent form of heterosexual masculinism, is longstanding. Books such as Michelle Wallace's *Black Macho and the Myth of the Superwoman*, bell hooks's *Ain't I a Woman*, and the anthology *But*

Some of Us are Brave have clearly chronicled this tendency. For a brief overview of the tendency in black nationalist thinking to link racial uplift with a forcefully articulated heterosexual black manhood, see hooks 76–88.

7. The choice of terminology here is difficult. Strictly speaking, *gay* is anachronistic, and the term *homosexual* was of relatively recent provenance, used in psychological and psychoanalytic circles to indicate a sexual pathology rather than a form of sexual identity. Indeed, for Cullen the obsessive gay narrative of sexual self-revelation is only useful in a limited sense, since the idea of having a positive gay "identity" is a relatively recent phenomenon. I have chosen most often to use the words *gay* and *homosexual* since they will serve as the best shorthand description for the practices and desires familiar to a contemporary audience. I have also chosen to use the phrase *gay desire* or other words indicating desire rather than phrases indicating identity. This choice avoids the somewhat anachronistic question of whether or not Cullen had a "gay identity." What seems to be clearly the case is that he periodically desired various attractive women. He also seems to have more regularly desired attractive men, desires which came into conflict with his public role as poet laureate, so much so that he seems to have been willing to make a bad marriage to Yolande Du Bois. For a good reading of the complications surrounding homosexual narrative, see Allen. For a thorough biographical description of the various sexual relationships that Cullen developed with men throughout his life, see Reimonenq.
8. See Eric Garber for a description of the gay and lesbian subculture in Harlem.
9. The degree to which homosexuality was accepted within the African American community prior to the 1960s has been a matter of some debate. Marion Ross makes the persuasive argument that homosexuality was far more visible and acceptable within the African American community than the white community at least up until the 1970s. Nevertheless, even Ross seems to suggest that the tolerance of homosexuality was a matter of degree that fell somewhat short of endorsement. As he puts it, "How could the white homosexual understand that black society's embracing of their homosexual sons was not the same as black society's embracing of homosexuality itself." (201) Henry Louis Gates points out that the organizing force behind the March on Washington, Bayard Rustin, was not named director of the March because he was a homosexual. The example of Rustin is particularly telling for my purposes since it suggests that the limit of

homosexual acceptance turned on the public face of African American political and cultural activity. So while some in Harlem may have been aware of Cullen's sexual preferences and didn't run him out of town with baseball bats, Cullen apparently was concerned enough about the relationship of his sexual practices to his public image to keep them well-hidden from cultural leaders like Du Bois, upon whom his position as a "poet laureate" partially depended.

10. For a description of the symbolic characteristics of the Cullen–Du Bois wedding, see Huggins 306. For a fuller description of Cullen as a public representative of the Harlem Renaissance, see Shucard 118–20.
11. Cullen wasn't the only poet to deal with this dilemma. De Jongh points out that, while one Atlantic City church invited Hughes to read his poetry, the pastor threatened to remove Hughes from the pulpit if he read "any more blues" (24). While the blues would not necessarily signify homosexuality, they did evoke the illicit sexuality that many members of the Afro-Christian bourgeoisie saw as unacceptable and demeaning to the race. The championing of jazz and blues as a "natural" expression of the best of blackness in the work of someone like Amiri Baraka would seem to be primarily a phenomenon of the last two-thirds of the twentieth century, a phenomenon that Hughes was instrumental in constructing.
12. See Baker (61–63) for a description of Cullen's commitment to artistic freedom for African Americans over and against the prescriptions of a white discourse or what he took to be somewhat faddish indulgence in low-life Harlem among other poets of the era.
13. My colleague Samuel Smith has suggested that the worm upon the hook is a medieval image of the Christian doctrine of the atonement, wherein the worm is the physical body of Jesus designed to lure Satan into a trap set for him by God. Whether Cullen had this image in mind is impossible to say, but to follow out the analogy, the divine action of God in the medieval image becomes the sexual passion of the hook in Cullen's poem. The possibility is intriguing here given that Cullen goes on in the poem to portray a highly sexualized Christ and to long for that sexualized Christ so that he can identify with Cullen's suffering. The link is also suggestive in that Christ's suffering is typically referred to as his "passion." But from what I have been able to discover thus far, such a reading would have to remain within the realm of speculation.
14. From Rev. Cullen's autobiography: "While sight seeing we met Mr. and Mrs. Marcus Garvey, my old friend, who had been forced out of the United States for his aggressive race loving spirit" (90).

15. I'm much indebted to Amitai F. Avi-ram's study of Cullen, though he is far more interested in the specifics of poetic form than am I. Avi-ram reads the coffin/box of "For a Poet" as the homosexual closet in which Cullen hides his sexual identity. The only aspect of Avi-ram's otherwise excellent formalist reading that troubles me is the tendency to rely too uncritically on a late-twentieth-century notion of Cullen's sexual "identity." See n6 above.
16. The political connotations of sexual activity are inevitably troubled in the racial climate that the United States is only slowly overcoming. Given that so much of the ritual brutalization of African American men focused on sexuality, it is perhaps not surprising that the display of sexual prowess has been seen to have political connotations in some quarters, notably in the work of someone like Eldridge Cleaver, who at one point equated rape with a revolutionary act, or in the work of some contemporary rap groups. For the pernicious effects upon women of such forms of black nationalist consciousness, see hooks.

Works Cited

Allen, Dennis W. "Homosexuality and Narrative." *Modern Fiction Studies.* 41.3–4 (1995): 609–34.

Avi-Ram, Amitai F. "The Unreadable Black Body: 'Conventional' Poetic Form in the Harlem Renaissance." *Genders* 7 (1990): 32–46.

Baker, Houston A., Jr. *Afro-American Poetics: Revisions of Harlem and the Black Aesthetic.* Madison: U of Wisconsin P, 1996.

Cullen, Countée. "The Dark Tower." 1928. *Black Writers Interpret the Harlem Renaissance.* Ed. Cary D. Wintz. New York: Garland, 1996. 171.

———. *My Soul's High Song: The Collected Writings of Countee Cullen, Voice of the Harlem Renaissance.* Ed. Gerald Early. New York: Anchor, 1991.

Cullen, Rev. Frederick Asbury. *From Barefoot Town to Jerusalem.* N.p.: n.p., 1924.

De Jongh, James. *Vicious Modernism: Black Harlem and the Literary Imagination.* Cambridge: Cambridge UP, 1990.

Douglas, Kelly Brown. *The Black Christ.* Maryknoll: Orbis, 1994.

Du Bois, W. E. B. *The Oxford W. E. B. Du Bois Reader.* Ed. Eric J. Sundquist. New York: Oxford UP, 1996.

Early, Gerald. "Introduction." Cullen, *My Soul's High Song* 1–73.

Ferguson, Blanche E. *Countee Cullen and the Negro Renaissance*. New York: Dodd, 1966.

Garber, Eric. "A Spectacle in Color: The Lesbian and Gay Subculture of Jazz Age Harlem." *Hidden from History. Reclaiming the Gay and Lesbian Past*. Ed. Martin Bauml Duberman, Martha Civinus, and George Chauncey, Jr. New York: Penguin/NAL, 1989. 318–31.

Gates, Henry Louis. "Blacklash?" *English Server*. 8 July 1993. Carnegie Mellon. 1 Aug. 1998. <http://eserver.org/race/blacklash.txt>

Gates, Henry Louis, and Nellie Y. McKay, eds. *The Norton Anthology of African American Literature*. New York: Norton, 1997.

Harris, Trudier. *Exorcising Blackness: Historical and Literary Lynching and Burning Rituals*. Bloomington: Indiana UP, 1984.

Hill, Patricia Liggins, et al., eds. *Call and Response: The Riverside Anthology of the African American Literary Tradition*. Boston: Houghton, 1998.

hooks, bell. "Reconstructing Black Masculinity." *The Masculine Masquerade: Masculinity and Representation*. Ed. Andrew Perchuk and Helaine Posner. Cambridge: MIT P, 1995. 69–88.

Huggins, Nathan. *Harlem Renaissance*. New York: Oxford UP, 1971.

Kimmel, Michael. *Manhood in America: A Cultural History*. New York: Free P, 1996.

Lewis, David Levering. *When Harlem Was in Vogue*. New York: Oxford UP, 1979.

Locke, Alain. Letter to Countée Cullen. 16 Nov. 1922. Amistad Research Center, New Orleans.

Moses, Wilson Jeremiah. *Black Messiahs and Uncle Toms: Social and Literary Manipulations of a Religious Myth*. Rev. ed. University Park: Pennsylvania State UP, 1993.

Reimonenq, Alden. "Countee Cullen's Uranian Soul Windows." *Critical Essays: Gay and Lesbian Writers of Color*. Ed. Emmanuel S. Nelson. Binghamton: Haworth P, 1993. 143–65.

Ross, Marlon B. "Some Glances at the Black Fag: Race, Same-Sex Desire, and Cultural Belonging." *Canadian Review of Comparative Literature/Revue Canadienne de Litterature Comparée* 21.1–2 (1994): 193–219.

Sernett, Milton C. *Bound for the Promised Land: African American Religion and the Great Migration*. Durham: Duke UP, 1997.

Shucard, Alan R. *Countee Cullen*. Boston: Twayne, 1984.

Smylie, James H. "Countee Cullen's 'The Black Christ.'" *Theology Today* 38 (July 1981): 160–73.

Spencer, Jon Michael. "The Black Church and the Harlem Renaissance." *African American Review* 30 (1996): 453–60.

Tuttleton, James W. "Countee Cullen at 'The Heights.'" *The Harlem Renaissance: Revaluations*. Ed. Amritjit Singh, William S. Shiver, and Stanley Brodwin. New York: Garland, 1989. 101–38.

Wagner, Jean. *Black Poets of the United States: From Paul Laurence Dunbar to Langston Hughes*. Trans. Kenneth Douglas. Urbana: U of Illinois P, 1973.

RONALD E. SHEASBY

Dual Reality: Echoes of Blake's Tiger in Cullen's Heritage

What is Africa to me?
—*Countee Cullen*

Did he who made the lamb make thee?
—*William Blake*

Many critics have pointed out that Countee Cullen's poetry was written largely in traditional English forms, such as the sonnet, and was heavily influenced by the romantic poets, most of all John Keats. However, no one has yet suggested that Cullen's "Heritage," his best and most famous work, may owe a debt to William Blake's "The Tiger." This paper will.

That a black American of the twentieth century should adopt a style popular among white Englishmen of the previous one offends some people and fills others with pride and pleasure. Those who like it see a black man expressing racial and nonracial themes in traditional and beautiful ways; those who do not like it see a slavish imitation which weakens the antiracist poetry and dilutes the rest.

Gerald Early is one of the latter, calling Cullen's use of traditional forms "quaint and old fashioned."[1] Cullen uses the clause "so I lie" so often in

From *CLA Journal* XXXIX, no. 2 (December 1995).

"Heritage" that Early thinks he may be also lying when he says that Africa is important to him (59–60). Early is not certain, but Darwin T. Turner is: he calls Cullen a liar who fakes an African heritage, though being neither particularly black nor militant; his conventional poetic devices mask his pretense.[2] Harvey Curtis Webster agrees,[3] and Blyden Jackson adds the condemnation that Countee was black but had a white outlook.[4]

In *Silence to the Drums*, Margaret Perry sees Cullen's romantic heritage as a mixed blessing, both inspiring and hampering him,[5] elsewhere comparing him favorably to John Keats.[6] Houston A. Baker, Jr., is also ambivalent: Countee has to use traditional forms to please the white audience and African themes to satisfy the black one;[7] it is perhaps because of this that he is simply "a minor poet" who never achieves the "Vision Splendid."[8]

Alan R. Shucard is unequivocal in his praise: Countee Cullen is an "absolute master of conventional structures and language." Writing with a true lyric gift, Cullen produces pretty poems such as "Heritage."[9] Ronald Primeau sees the Keatsian influence as positive: the imagery and theme of "Heritage" shows traces of the Englishman.[10] Gary Smith adds that Cullen chooses sonnets because those forms lend themselves rather well to syllogistic reasoning, an approach that is used in the racial poems,[11] and Richard Lederer agrees[12] (219–23). And, finally, Baker quotes James Weldon Johnson:

> Cullen is a fine and sensitive lyric poet, belonging to the classical line. . . . All of his work is laid within the lines of the long-approved English patterns, and by that very gauge a measure of his gifts and powers as a poet may be taken. The old forms come from his hands filled with a fresh beauty. A high test for a poet.[13]

And so, whether or not Countee "sold out" or heightened his themes by the use of traditional romantic forms, all agree that he did, indeed, use those forms. Let us turn to the poem itself.

"Heritage" first appeared in the 1 March 1925 *Survey*.[14] Since the poem was published well before Cullen's Harvard matriculation (where, incidentally, his studies led him to produce "the first rime royal in America," according to Robert Hillyer[15]), we must turn to his NYU days for a time of composition and possible influences. Apart from school magazines, there is no record of a published poem by Countee Cullen before NYU.

Cullen did not study at NYU under a Blake scholar but he did take most of his courses from a traditionalist—a Keats specialist and a collector of ballads named Hyder Rollins—including a course entitled English Poetry of the Nineteenth Century. Tuttleleton says that Rollins had written books on both Keats and ballads, and adds that "there is no doubt that for Hyder Rollins the English tradition from the Middle Ages onward was the right foundation for a poet."[16] It would not take much of an imagination to picture that somewhere in the above-mentioned two-semester poetry survey course was an analysis of William Blake's "The Tiger." Young Countee's mind must have been like a sponge, incorporating everything he studied—and if he did study Blake's poem, it would not be too much of a surprise to find it reappearing, considerably altered, to be sure, but reappearing nonetheless, in the body of Cullen's poetry! Let us look at both poems in question.

William Blake's "The Tiger" is written in either iambic tetrameter truncated or trochaic tetrameter catalectic. The last stanza exactly repeats the first:

> Tiger, Tiger, burning bright,
> In the forests of the night,
> What immortal hand or eye
> Could frame thy fearful symmetry?[17]

The second couplet is characterized by a half rhyme—*eye* and *symmetry*, and ends with a question; indeed, every stanza in the poem ends with a question which either announces or repeats the theme: "Did he who made the Lamb make thee?" The capitalized "Lamb" evokes "the Lamb of God who taketh away the sins of the world," Jesus Christ. According to Robert Hillyer, this poem was a companion piece for "The Lamb," which overtly Christianizes lambs:[18] "He is called by thy name / For he calls himself a lamb."

"The Tiger" asks if the creator who made Jesus also made the big cat, suggesting a pagan, non-Christian and lower-case god similar to those described in William Ernest Henley's "Invictus," a god who made the tiger while another lamb-like Christian God made the lamb and the Lamb. How could one deity make both?

Imagery of fire dominates the poem until almost the end. The tiger's eyes are "burning bright," with references to their fire: "What the hand dare seize the fire?" is asked, then "In what furnace was thy brain?" Soon, however, the imagery shifts to water. Stars throw "Down their spears," then water "Heaven with their tears." Having briefly digressed from fire to water, Blake returns to his furnace: "Tiger, tiger, burning bright. . . ." Blake's imagery thus comes full circle, from fire to water and back to fire.

Countee Cullen's "Heritage" is written in either iambic tetrameter truncated or trochaic tetrameter catalectic. He repeats his thematic question "What is Africa to me?" several times, word for word and in variations such as "What's your nakedness to me?" or "What is last year's snow to me?" And he twice repeats an italicized chorus that echoes Blake's opening and closing stanza syllable for syllable, beat for beat:

> *One three centuries removed*
> *From the scenes his fathers loved,*
> *Spicy grove, cinnamon tree,*
> *What is Africa to me?*[19]

And just as Blake half rhymes "eye" and "symmetry," Cullen half rhymes "removed" and "loved."

The echoes extend far beyond meter and rhyme. As Blake's theme is announced by answering "Did he who made the Lamb make thee?" Cullen answers "What is Africa to me?"

> Jesus of the twice-turned cheek,
> *Lamb of God* although I speak
> With my mouth thus, in my heart
> Do I play a double part. . . .
> Wishing He I serve were black. . . . (Italics mine)

The black narrator trying to relate to a white god is a contradiction at least as striking as a God (or gods) who makes tigers and lambs (or Lambs). The poet is Christian but black; Africa calls to him with the burning eyes of a tiger hidden in the deep, lush, green jungle. There is no release

> From the unremittent beat
> Made by cruel padded feet
> Walking through my body's street.
> Up and down they go, and back,
> Treading out a jungle track.

Now the tiger, or at least a near relative, is stalking through Cullen's poem and body!

Some tiger-like animals appear elsewhere in this poem: cats crouch

> . . . in the river reeds,
> Stalking gentle flesh that feeds
> By the river brink; no more
> Does the bugle throated roar
> Cry that monarch claws have leapt
> From the scabbards where they slept.

The "monarch claws" suggest lions rather than tigers, but they are both predatory cats—and described as making circles "through the night," not unlike Blake's tiger, eyes aflame in "the forests of the night."

And Blake's "forests of the night" are composed of trees like this:

> . . . The tree
> Budding yearly must forget
> How its past arose and set. . . .

or these:

> *Spicy grove, cinnamon tree,*
> *What is Africa to me?*

Water imagery dominates "Heritage," until almost the very end, when it shifts to fire, somewhat the opposite of "The Tiger," which goes from fire to water and back to fire.

> So I lie, whose fount of pride,
> Dear distress, and joy allied,
> Is my somber flesh and skin,
> With the dark blood damned within
> Like great pulsing tides of wine
> That, I fear, must burst the fine
> Channels of the chafing net
> Where they surge and foam and fret.

The links with Christianity once established ("fount" and "wine"), he continues with water:

> So I lie, who never quite
> Safely sleep from rain at night—
> I can never rest at all
> When the rain begins to fall:
> ....
> While its primal measures drip
> Through my body, crying, "Strip!
> Come and dance the Lover's Dance!"
> In an old remembered way
> Rain works on me night and day.

The poet says that he must "*Quench my pride and cool my blood, / Lest I perish in the flood.*" He then switches images, just as does Blake, and continues:

> *Lest a hidden ember set*
> *Timber that I thought was wet*
> *Burning like the dryest flax,*
> *Melting like the merest flax,*

and five lines later, concludes his poem.

The narrator's dilemma is that he is neither lamb nor tiger, pagan nor Christian, native African nor inheritor and modifier of the romantic tradition—and it is in this very dichotomy that "Heritage" most resembles "The Tiger." What sort of world is it, both poets ask, that has meek lambs and barbaric tigers, the Christian God and pagan gods, poets who write out of the romantic tradition but whose ancestors come from darkest Africa? It is the same question which Countee Cullen asks in "Yet Do I Marvel": What sort of God would "make a poet black and bid him sing"? Caucasian William Blake had no such concern—but still in all, he saw the world divided into two parts, and so did Countee Cullen.

There are other differences, as well. Blake's work is much shorter, only twenty-four lines, asking fourteen questions. "Heritage" asks six questions and takes 129 lines to do it. However, Cullen deliberately modeled "The Ballad of the Brown Girl" after an old English source that was either ten or fifteen lines long, depending on the source book.[20] Cullen's ballad is very nearly exactly as much longer than its model as "Heritage" is longer than "The Tiger"!

Cullen's poem, despite its structural similarities to Blake's, flows more rhythmically, pulsing in a manner more evocative of jungle drums, somewhat reminiscent of Vachel Lindsay's "The Congo." A reader of "The Tiger" sees feline eyes glowing in the dark; a reader of "Heritage" hears "Great drums throbbing through the air."

And finally, Blake writes of a tiger, Cullen about a man. However, that highlights the difference between plagiarism and the sort of modeling (or at least unconscious influence) that I am suggesting. Cullen took bits and pieces—meter, rhyme scheme, symbolism, theme—from Blake and echoed them in his own poem, about his own experiences, in ultimately his own way.

So there are identical meters and rhyme schemes, the repetition of thematically significant questions in both poems. There is a similar dichotomy in both, the Lamb of God versus paganism, and the appearance of predatory felines, as well as the trees of the jungle—and water turning into fire, which turns into water. And, of course, there are all those critics agreeing that Countee Cullen was heavily influenced by traditional English sources.

Are such echoes deliberate, as Cullen's work with ballads was? I do not know—nor do I think anybody does, at least until further evidence appears. They are at the very least unconscious, and it may be that some overt modeling took place, as well. Did he model "Heritage" after "The Tiger"? Perhaps. Was Cullen's poem influenced by Blake's? It seems likely. Did Cullen even *read* "The Tiger?" Almost certainly, but I can not prove it.

Geniuses such as Countee Cullen are readers before they are poets or novelists—and after they start writing, they continue to read. Almost all writers read voraciously, and many, if not all, write in occasional imitation of those writers they most admire. Sometimes this is deliberate, sometimes unconscious. It is not important whether or not they occasionally mirror their sources (Need I mention more than Shakespeare?) as it is how well they execute their designs, how well the finished product flows organically. Poetry is meant to be enjoyed, with or without a knowledge of the influences that might have helped shape it. And "Heritage" is a poem that people have enjoyed reading for over two thirds of the twentieth century! It seems petty to criticize its creator for using language more germane to the nineteenth.

Notes

1. Gerald Early, introd., *My Soul's High Song*, by Countee Cullen (New York: Doubleday, 1991) 6. Hereafter cited parenthetically in the text.
2. Darwin T. Turner, "Countee Cullen: The Lost Ariel," *In a Minor Chord: Three Afro-American Writers and Their Search for Identity* (Carbondale: Southern Illinois UP, 1971) 63.
3. Harvey Curtis Webster, "A Difficult Career," *Poetry* 30 (1947): 222–26.
4. Blyden Jackson, "Largo for Adonis," *The Waiting Years: Essays on American Negro Literature* (Baton Rouge: Louisiana State UP, 1976) 42–65.
5. Margaret Perry, *Silence to the Drums: A Survey of the Literature of the Harlem Renaissance* (Westport, Conn.: Greenwood, 1971) 54–59. Hereafter cited parenthetically in the text.
6. Margaret Perry, *A Bio-Bibliography of Countee P. Cullen: 1903–1946* (Westport, Conn.: Greenwood, 1971) xxiii.
7. Houston A. Baker, Jr., *Modernism and the Harlem Renaissance* (Chicago: U of Chicago P, 1987) 86.
8. Houston A. Baker, Jr., *A Many-Colored Coat of Dreams: The Poetry of Countée Cullen* (Detroit: Broadside, 1974) 52.

9. Alan R. Shucard, *Countee Cullen* (Boston: Twayne, 1984) 52.
10. Ronald Primeau, "Countee Cullen and Keats's 'Vale of Soul-making,'" *Papers on Language and Literature* 12 (1976): 84–85.
11. Gary Smith, "The Black Protest Sonnet," *American Poetry* 2.1 (1984): 2–5.
12. Richard Lederer, "The Didactic and the Literary in Four Harlem Renaissance Sonnets," *English Journal* 62 (1973): 219–23.
13. Baker, *Many* 52.
14. Perry, *Bio* 82.
15. Robert Hillyer, *In Pursuit of Poetry* (New York: McGraw, 1966) 70.
16. James W. Tuttleton, "Countee Cullen at the Heights," *The Harlem Renaissance: Revaluations*, ed. Amritjit Singh, William S. Shiver, and Stanley Brodwin (New York: Garland, 1989) 123–33.
17. William Blake, "The Tiger," *The Norton Introduction to Literature*, 4th ed., ed. C. E. Baïn, J. Beaty, and J. P. Hunter (New York: Norton, 1988).
18. Hillyer, 147–48.
19. Countee Cullen, "Heritage," *The Norton Anthology of Modern Poetry*, 2nd ed., ed. Richard Ellman and Robert O'Clair (New York: Norton, 1988).
20. Tuttleton 128.

MARIANN B. RUSSELL

Evolution of Style in the Poetry of Melvin B. Tolson

The consideration of Melvin Tolson's evolving style concerns the maturation of his thought. Here I concentrate on his epic form and his developing perspective. I shall first generalize about his worldview and then trace the development of the hero figure, for both processes set into relief the stylistic growth. The examination includes less the discussion of metrics and figurative language than the concern for poetics in the deepest sense.

Tolson writes: "A great preacher is a great artist. Words are his tubes of paint. Verse, his brush."[1] These sentences go far to explain the poetics of the speaker. He does not belong to that stream of Anglo-American poetry which is purely lyric, expressing directly and mellifluously the poet's own emotions. He concerns himself, on the contrary, with social issues as the barebones of life. His style comes closer to oratorical rhetoric than to song, and his poem is generally public rather than confessional.

The son of a "fighting preacher"—"I used to watch my Dad in the pulpit and feel proud. . ."[2]—Tolson was himself a great speaker and debate coach as well as a director of theater. Concerned with the underdog in general and with the Black underdog in particular, he saw words as weapons in the war against social ills. Closely linked to the Afro-American oral tradition and the personal commitment to fighting injustice, he shaped a

Christo-Marxist worldview.[3] As in the poetry of others during the thirties, his lyric encompassed a social, metaphysical, and communal burden.

Over the years he had four books of poetry published. The first, written about 1934, was brought out posthumously. *A Gallery of Harlem Portraits*,[4] as it was called, contained verses about Harlemites. His next book was *Rendezvous with America* (1944),[5] a collection somewhat influenced by World War II; his third volume, *Libretto for the Republic of Liberia* (1953),[6] was written after he had been chosen the poet-laureate of the country so named. In "academic" style the booklength ode celebrates the African nation. His final volume, *Harlem Gallery* (1965),[7] was another booklength ode, intended as the beginning of an epic about the American Black.

Before undertaking any discussion of the first book, it would be helpful to outline Tolson's cultural theory. His poetry begins with his life experience, which he mulls over, talks over, and subsumes into his phenomenally eclectic reading. Then he transmutes the whole into verse. For the talented and intellectually probing college professor in the Southwest and West from 1923 to 1965, racial discrimination and prejudice were abiding concerns. A Jim Crow existence provoked direct protest and probing into human nature. The Marxist interpretation became a focal point of his thought.[8]

Tolson's epic intention persists in varying forms. In a world that is class-divided and economically determined, the exploited masses become crucial. The underdog, the despised, the poor appear heroic now and foreshadow even greater heroism after the establishment of a new society. Tolson, sometimes ironically, celebrates the human potential embodied in the voiceless majority of the underprivileged.

The masses, in their human potential, become an abstract ideal, a generic hero. But Tolson finds individual nations such as America and Liberia heroic in the present promise and in the future apocalypse. Individual characters who are heroic include persons like Crispus Attucks and Paul Bunyan as well as the poet-prophet, the "ape of God." In one way or another, such various heroes inform his epics.

But Tolson is not merely an epic poet looking for an epic hero. His perspective encourages the epic search, since he proposes the great man theory of history. In his newspaper columns he asserts that geniuses improve humanity's lot. He cites poets, prophets, and scholars as specific types through whose efforts humankind comes to understand and ultimately reform its condition. His early books portray many political and social reformers as well as folk heroes as appropriate instruments. In the last book, he shifts to the poet-prophet, the true artist in any mode, as the necessary means to social equality.

The first book, *Portraits*, responds to the remark by a fellow student, himself German-American: "Say, we've never had a Negro epic."[9] Tolson finds precedent for the genre in the Anglo-American literary heritage. His models are, among others, Longfellow, Whittier, Milton, Tennyson, and Poe.[10] His Tennyson is not the melancholy lyricist, but the poet who envisages "the Parliament of man." Tolson emphasizes the Donne of "no man is an island" rather than the metaphysical poet. Edwin Markham and Langston Hughes, mentors and friends, embody the American populist tradition in white and Black. Literature as well as life fostered his epic intention.

The immediate model for *Portraits* is the *Spoon River Anthology* volume, which attempts to tell "the story of an American country town so as to make it the story of the world."[11] Tolson wants to fashion the story of Harlem into a metaphor for the Afro-American. The technique, an extended synecdoche, "gives . . . Negro America its comedy and tragedy in prismatic epitome" ("Notebooks"). His Harlem becomes metonymically the "mecca," "city of refuse," "Nigger-Heaven," "City of Refuge," and "Capital of the Negro world."[12]

When Tolson presents in *Portraits* approximately two hundred characters significant of the Black community, his worldview becomes clear. The tragicomic tone emanates from the assumption that "the basis of racial prejudice in the United States is economic" (*Caviar and Cabbage*, p. 83). He sees the Harlem community, with its great variety of types, classes, and colors, not as the exotic area of "jungle-bunny" fame but as the subject of an "earthy, unromantic and sociological literature."[13] Throughout the book, indirectly and sometimes directly, Tolson advocates the union of the masses, poor white and poor Black, as the solution to racial and class discrimination. The final goal of proletarian unity is an apocalyptic democracy—classless, multiracial, multicultural—an attainable utopia.

The hero of *Portraits* is the "underdog," who might some day understand and assume his own destiny. Those Harlemites who already have such knowledge are more directly heroic. The group includes Big Jim Casey and Zip Lightner, proletarian heroes who live for the union of Black and white workers. But the particularly flawed hero is Vergil Ragsdale who, as his name suggests, is the poet of the people. He shares their exploited condition. Though there are more effective artists, he appears at greatest length. His perspective may most approximate Tolson's view then:

> "Harlem, O Harlem,
> City of the Big Niggers,
> Graveyard of the Dark Masses,
> Soapbox of the Red Apocalypse. . . ."
>
> (*Portraits*, p. 4)

Sustained by gin and cocaine, Vergil, the dishwasher at Manto's cafe, dreams of completing his epic poem to Harlem.[14] Although he truly foresees his own pathetic death from tuberculosis, he does not predict the real tragedy: an ignorant landlady will burn the poem, his raison d'être, as trash. Still, this character articulates and represents his people's condition as well as imagines their retribution. His life is ambiguous, as is his heroism.

The style of these poems suits Tolson's epic intention. Characters, presented in short vignettes of about a page, represent the great variety of Harlem humanity, from Peg Leg Snelson to Mrs. Alpha Devine to the Black Moses. As with the poems in *Spoon River*, each of these short ones ends with a climax, a dramatic event, a revelation, a statement, or, in many instances, a blues verse. Tolson, influenced by the imagists, relies on presentation more than on commentary. The larger poetic structure of the entire book, however, lacks variety as poem after poem is introduced mechanically. The diction characterizes occasionally the people in dialect and blues, but the larger voice is the narrator's. The latter speaks of the "little man" as victim but assumes an appreciative tone. The poem presents nobly the techniques of survival in a blues style.

Tolson's next book, *Rendezvous with America*, continues the epic intention in a different vein. As the author broadens his thematic concerns from Harlem to various places in America and to the world at large, the social concerns deepen. The subject here is man—Black and white—as revealed through economics, sociology, and psychology. But the heroes are still political and artistic. Such poets as Sandburg and Whitman set precedents for Tolson's celebration of human potential, despite the actual corruption, inequality, and injustice in still flawed America. Democracy, true justice, and multiculture continue to engage him: "These States breed freedom in and in my bone: / I hymn their virtues and their sins atone" (*Rendezvous*, p. 33).

The epic strain here is less obvious than in *Portraits*. Under the impetus of World Ward II,[15] Tolson sees good and evil written large in human affairs. Celebration of American promise and human potential go hand in hand with the praise of such historical figures as Nat Turner, Frederick Douglass, and Harriet Tubman. The book is replete with heroic figures (and some villains) who become symbolic in the literary context—Daniel Boone, Joe Dimaggio, Thomas Paine, Abraham Lincoln, and many more.

How then do these hymns to America and humanity differ from the art in Rockefeller Center during the 1930s or from Fourth of July oratory? Although the poetry emphasizes American ideals, it escapes from being merely patriotic encomia. The poetry is skillfully grounded in realistic observation. In many poems from "Ex-Judge at the Bar" to "Vesuvius,"

Tolson illustrates the "idols of the tribe"[16]—those deliberately fostered myths of race, caste, and class that separate mankind. His optimism takes root in the faith that the masses will eventually see through the snares, shams, and hypocrisies to a republican ideal. His ironic—sometimes satiric—tone works against any blind faith in the American dream; he reveals frequently through incident, character, or animal imagery the gulf between the dream and reality.

By now he has worked out for himself a poetic ideal. He refers to the "'3 S's of Parnassus'—Sight, Sound, and Sense."[17] Sight concerns the look of a poem on a page. He experiments frequently with centered placement, especially of short lines, to emphasize his point. At other times he works a short line against a longer one for visual effect. His second "S" refers to sound. Sensitive to the ear, he writes poetry to be read aloud—he seldom uses an eye-rhyme. His frequent use of parallelism encompasses both sound and sight. The last "S" means "sense," meaning and imagination—chiefly the use of figurative language. Tolson's tropes depend on often startling associations or similarities, frequently using personifications and synecdoche to link seemingly opposed realities in a kind of imaginative dialectic.

Some examples of Tolson's figurative language appear in the long title poem, "Rendezvous with America": "his bat cuts a vacuum," "surfed in white acclaim," "scaling the Alpine ranges of drama with the staff of song," "blue-printing the cabala of the airways," "imprisoning the magic of symphonies with a baton," "enwombing the multiple soul of the New World" (pp. 6–7). Although some of these metaphors are not entirely satisfactory, they do illustrate the quality and kind of Tolson's imagery.

To see the effect of this aesthetic ideal—the sight, sound, meaning, and language of a poem beautifully meshed—I shall consider another of *Rendezvous'* long poems, "Dark Symphony," in detail. On the surface, Tolson's theme merely transforms the cliché of the melting pot into the onomatopoeia of symphonic movement. Called on ode by Joy Flasch (p. 63), the poem has six sections, each with a different musical direction. The first part, three quatrains long, *Allegro Moderato*, moves visually down the page like a series of "s's." The long line, the short line to the left, and the long line, short line to the right, play against each other. While the metric scheme has the long lines in each stanza and the short lines rhyming, the initial line of each stanza does not do so. There is some alliteration.

In such a poem the names Crispus Attucks and Patrick Henry are expected but not so the lines, "the vertical / Transmitting cry," and "No Banquo's ghost can rise / Against us now" (p. 37). Such obvious metaphors as "the juggernauts of despotism" and "hobnailed Man" and "thorns of greed / On Labor's brow" (p. 37) are offset by "dust is purged to create brotherhood"

(p. 37). The stanzas are controlled through their parallel structure and by the musical movement.

The next section, "*Lento Grave*," details the pathos of those who perform spirituals emblematic of their condition:

Black slaves singing *One More River to Cross*
In the torture tombs of slave-ships,
Black slaves singing *Steal Away to Jesus*
In jungle swamps. (p. 38)

Here again Tolson controls rhythm through the musical direction and the parallel structure, as one line of each couplet, the "Black slaves," ends with the title of a spiritual; the following line indicates the symbolic place where it is sung.

The third section, "*Andante Sostenuto*," counterpoints the previous stanza's slave songs to Psalm 136 (137 in Protestant bibles), which calls to mind the Jewish Babylonian captivity. Each of the three stanzas opens and closes with a repetend, the first two with "They tell us to forget," and the third with "Oh, how can we forget?" Here the expected indictment of racial discrimination in America occurs, but the effective Biblical echo and analogue transcend mere cliché; "They who have shackled us / Require of us a song" recalls Psalm 136. The climactic, "Oh, how can we forget" recalls the Psalmist's "How could we sing a song of the Lord in a foreign land?"

The fourth part, with the direction "*Tempo Primo*," turns to the New Negro, "Hard-muscled, Fascist-hating, Democracy ensouled," who becomes an ideal of Democracy through his identification with Afro-American heroes. This generic Black signifies his race's contribution by referring to the work done by the slave and free Black masses throughout American history. Their contributions appear in the parallel structure which controls the Whitmanesque categories of Black labor. The section ends with the inevitable stanza showing the New Negro's striding toward the Promised Land of Tomorrow (p. 40).[18]

"*Larghetto*," the fifth section, returns to the first section's satire on white lip service to Democracy. The repetend in each of the four sestets exempts Blacks from particular hypocrisies: "None in the Land can say / To us black men Today" (p. 40).

The final section's *March Tempo* works well through the stanzas of iambic tetrameter and the oft-repeated short line, "We advance!" (p. 43) recalling "The Underdog" (*Portraits*) in the call to unite. In "Dark Symphony," with the irregular rhyme schemes, varied meters, repetitions, and word placements on the page, Tolson illuminates the stock subjects, at least for Black poets during the twenties and thirties. For him, such topics shape themselves into the art epic.

Throughout *Rendezvous*, with few exceptions (there are very few private poems), Tolson practices oratorical rhetoric and evinces social concern. Here the reader encounters a variety of styles in the four long poems, "Rendezvous with America," "Dark Symphony," "Of Men and Cities," and "Tapestries of Time." There is still greater experimentation in the short poems grouped in sections including free verse, Shakespearean sonnet, ballad, and ballade. One poem in iambic monometer, "Song for Myself," is a poetic tour de force, as the diversity in poetic forms increases.

Even where there may be a dramatic incident, or a striking character in the short poems, it has a parabolic effect in building to a climax. The effective "Ballad of the Rattlesnake" is framed by another poem which portrays Black and white sharecroppers. Although they extend now beyond the specific Harlem community, Tolson's concerns remain now in the deeper structure, the same as those in *Portraits* earlier, but they take shape in both conventional and unconventional metrics. In the long and more complex poems, he uses devices that are both poetic and oratorical, including repetition with variation, striking metaphors, and wide-ranging allusions. He subsumes the Black sermon into the artistic voice, and it readdresses the cultural concern. The rhetorical triangle which binds the folk source, the independent imagination, and the appreciative audience continues unbroken.

Besides the American promise and the proletarian expectation, there is another heroic element. Here appears the figure of the bard. "The Poet" portrays a generalized figure who, though largely disregarded in his time, looks uncaringly into the nature of things:

> An Ishmaelite
> He breaks the icons of the Old and New
> . . . .
> The poet's lien exempts the Many nor the Few

and

> A champion of the People versus Kings—
> His only martyrdom is poetry:
> A hater of the hierarchy of things—
> Freedom's need is his necessity.
> (*Rendezvous*, p. 29)

The proud "Ishmaelite" and "anchoret" intuits a "bright new world." Heroic in insight, he dedicates himself to the communication of his vision, which penetrates custom. He reincarnates the Vergil Ragsdale figure, but without the same locale and pathetic circumstances. In *Rendezvous* the Ethiopian Bard of Addis Ababa is equally a kind of prophet. From insight into contemporaneity, he foresees the "bright new world." Lyric vision and social celebration merge.

> His name is an emblem of justice
> Greater than lumot of priest
>
> . . . .
>
> The seven league boots of his images
> Stir the palace and marketplace.
>
> (*Rendezvous*, p. 84)

These two, poet and prophet, fuse in Tolson's great man or genius. Tolson saw heroes and villains as representative of human potential for greatness and evil. To serve this social vision, his style evolved with many of the characteristics of oratorical rhetoric.

During his time spent at Columbia University (1931–32) and Greenwich Village (1930s), Tolson became acquainted with the first wave of the moderns represented by Sandburg, Hughes, and Masters. On his own he discovered Eliot's *The Waste Land* and later Crane's *The Bridge* which, according to Mrs. Tolson, "showed her husband that he was 'on the wrong road.'"[19] He therefore set out, still on his own, to come to terms with this academic style:

> Imitation must be in technique only. We have a rich heritage of folklore and history. We are a part of America. We are a part of the world. Our native symbols must be lifted into the universal. Yes, we must study the techniques of Robert Lowell, Dylan Thomas, Carlos Williams, Ezra Pound, Karl Shapiro, W. H. Auden. The greatest revolution has not been in science but in poetry. We must study such magazines as *Partisan Review*, the *Sewanee Review*, *Accent*, the *Virginia Quarterly*. We must read such critics as Crowe Ransom, Allen Tate, Stephen Spender, George Dillon and Kenneth Burke. (Flasch, *Tolson*, p. 70)[20]

In the period between the publication of *Rendezvous* and the writing of *Libretto*, Tolson included in his eclectic reading the moderns who set the tone of the two decades between the world wars. The reading and the public occasion of Liberia's centenary resulted in the style and content of *Libretto*. In the poem packed with Eliotic notes, we have Tolson's venture in a style aimed at the literary caviar.[21]

Here his view extends from Liberia and Africa to the world. The hero is, symbolically, Liberia, one of only two uncolonized nations in Africa then. Tolson reflects on this historical fact,[22] on Liberia's contribution to Allied efforts in World War II, and on the history of this republic founded by American Blacks freed from slavery; he therefore celebrates its national identity. The epic qualities from *Portraits* and *Rendezvous* reappear here in a different context. Liberia, historically exploited by France and England, aids these two countries by supplying rubber and providing airports during the war. The campaign against "fascists" becomes almost a holy war. Liberia, the name and motto signifying freedom, emerges as both real and symbolic. Transcending racial and economic biases, it foreshadows Africa's triumph in the world. Tolson thus fuses epic material and "academic" style.[23]

The poem is either an ode or a series of eight odes.[24] The titles of metrically varying sections range the diatonic scale from "Do" to "Do." The sections are thematically and symbolically interconnected in the ode form:

> Metrically, the term ode usually implies considerable freedom in the introduction of varied rhythmic movements and irregularities of verse-length and rhyme-distribution. There is something "oratorical" about a true ode; and its irregularities may be con-ceived of as produced by its adaptation to choric rendition or to public declamation, either actual or imagined. . . . Primarily, it [ode] refers to the content and spirit of a poem, implying a certain largeness of thought, continuity of theme, and exalted feeling.[25]

Tolson, faced with the problem of writing an occasional poem about a little-known nation, turns deliberately to the ancient form.

Besides the real and symbolic Liberia, there is a lesser heroic image in the poet-visionary. Because for Tolson man complexly fuses the biological, the sociological, and the psychological, only the Ishmaelite poet knows him deeply. Knowing humanity, historical and contemporary, the poet-prophet discerns the future. Tolson embodies human history in the ferris wheel symbol, which subsumes empires and nations. They rise and fall, alternating decadence and "bright new beginnings." To escape the cyclic nature of power, Tolson asserts through the protagonist[26] that humankind must advance teleologically to a classless utopia. Liberia therefore marks the vanguard, the poet-prophet being instrumental to the movement.

The style reveals a formal polish and philosophical weight in a broad reference which requires pages of notes.[27] Some elements descend directly from earlier techniques, such as Tolson's love of word play, his use of neologism, and his extensive allusions.[28] Once more he uses parallel structure to control the verse. Such elements, all subject to the "3 S's," mark the Tolsonian style.

The first and final "Do" illuminate the manner. The first sets out the principal themes in the attempt to define the meaning of Liberia. A centered question, "Liberia?" highlights the dominant image. In each eight-line stanza, there follows a negation of some cliché: "micro-footnote," "barker's bio-accident," "pimple on the chin of Africa," "caricature with a mimic flag," and "wasteland" (Europe) or "destooled elite" (Africa). After a denial, the fifth line in each stanza recenters the definition around the repetend "You are." In regular rhyme-schemes the metrically irregular verses relate Liberia to Europe as lightning rod and Canaan's key and "The rope across the abyss. . . ." Images abound as definition proceeds; Liberia is a metonym spatially to "The Orient of Colors everywhere," philosophically to "*Liberatas* flayed and naked by the road," mythically to "Black Lazarus risen from the White Man's grave," and nationally to "American genius uncrowned in Europe's charnel-house." The final two lines indicate how the nation eludes logical definition: "Liberia and not Liberia, / A moment of the conscience of mankind!" (pp. 13–15).[29]

The poem, unlike earlier ones, minimizes direct, hortatory rhetoric. Allusions help structure and codify meanings. Here the tagends of quotation as well as infusions from different languages including Spanish, French, German, Italian, Latin, Russian, Greek, Turkish, and Hebrew, complicate a line already abstruse. So do the African languages. Symbols like the *Hohere*, the ferris wheel, the merry-go-round, and the tiny republic enrich the verse.

The first section reveals the tone and many of the poetic devices which recur throughout the verse. Liberia has survived the exploitation of Western colonizers. Although its freedom is "flayed and naked," the ideal lives on in promise. "Liberia and not Liberia," the dialectic, the tension of opposites plays throughout the ode. It leads from the initial poem of definition through those which describe the nation's founding ("Mi," "Sol," "La,") to the relationship to France, Britain, and the United States ("Fa," "Ti"). Finally, it widens to classic African civilization ("Re") and the masses everywhere ("Ti" and *passim*). Tolson resolves the tension in "Africa-To-Be" (second "Do" and *passim*).

In the long last section ("Do"), Tolson crafts languages and symbols into a vision of Africa's bright future. Through the metaphors of the automobile, train, and ship, as well as the airplane, he aesthetically transports Liberia,

Africa, and the world to an apocalyptic Pluralism. Africa saves itself (p. 53) as well as Europe, America, and Australia. Africa achieves the cosmopolis, *Hobere*, through the United African Nations' cooperation in "polygenetic metropolises polychromatic." The Parliament of African Peoples[30] redeems both the elite and the masses.

The final "Do" sums up the significance of the Liberian experience. It evokes the future in verse that changes from sestet through staggered unrhymed couplets, to centered patterns (p. 47, ll. 555–57) and finally to prose poetry (pp. 48–55, ll. 575–770). The final "Do" thickens with fragments in different languages, references to African as well as European and American thought. Why does the ode, despite the chillingly simple poem, "Fa" (ominous in its simplicity), end in prose paragraphs? Possibly, oratory and Tolson's notion of climax[31] coincide here.

The entire ode moves to a climax as each of the eight sections achieves a minor affirmation. While the first "Do" climaxes in the symbolic definition ("A moment of the conscience of mankind"), the final "Do" declares a new beginning ("the Rosh Hashana of the Africa calends"). And it silences doubters: "'*Honi soit qui mal y pense!*'" Yet Tolson does not deny the corruption in society and the individual. While "profit" and "avarice" continue, the masses are on a merry-go-round of the "unparadised" who have nowhere to go. The gorged snake, the bird of prey, and the tiger wait in a false peace to strike again. And African nations still wear "Nessus shirts from Europe on their backs" (p. 38).

Tolson's last book of poetry, *Harlem Gallery*, fuses the early subject matter of *Portraits* with his later techniques. Although he presents mechanically more than two hundred Harlemites in *Portraits*, he abandons the strategy here in favor of a much more dynamic one. A number of poems are thematically integrated into the one irregular ode. A different letter of the Greek alphabet labels each of the twenty-four poems in order, just as the names of notes mark *Libretto*. Both poems work toward a signed and structured climax.

The ode incorporates Tolson's epic principle. He has viewed *Harlem Gallery: Book I, the Curator* as the first of five works that would delineate Afro-American history from the African origins to the contemporary world. He has intended to "analogize the history of the Hebrew people in the episodes of the Old Testament as regards persons, places, and events. The dominant idea of the *Harlem Gallery* will be manifest" ("Notebooks"). According to the plan, Book II, Egypt Land, is to be an analogue for the Slave Trade and Southern Bondage; Book III, the Red Sea, an analogue for the Civil War; Book IV, The Wilderness, an analogue for Reconstruction, and Book V, The Promised Land, an analogue for the race's present existence: "a gallery of highbrows and middlebrows and lowbrows against the ethnological panorama of contemporary America" ("Notebooks").

In *Portraits* the once-mentioned Curator places the book's characters on his gallery walls. His voice is unheard throughout the book. The protagonist in *Libretto* (p. 76 n. to l. 554) speaks in the two "Do's" and possibly throughout the entire ode, but the primary text does not develop him.[32] In *Harlem Gallery* the Curator is continually present. Here, too, he has his gallery, though his paintings do not represent the characters in the ode.

While the protagonist in *Libretto* is undramatized throughout the ode, the Curator is a real persona, appearing in significant places like the Zulu Club, meditating on art and life, and interacting with various others. His gallery, though symbolic, is real with regents, gallery-goers, pictures on the four walls, and real curators. The last ones include himself and his alter-ego, Dr. Obi Nkomo. Tolson combines the Curator in *Portraits*, a speaker who is scarcely even a framing device, and the protagonist in *Libretto*, possibly the consciousness through which the poem is played. This evolution marks the current curator.

The Harlem Gallery is a firmer and more centralized metaphor than was Liberia. Harlem appears less now through representation than through evocation. As with Liberia and America in the earlier books, the area is both place and symbol. It maintains historicity but assumes a larger meaning. Although the numbers of characters are fewer, major figures are more deeply probed. Harlem the social place becomes Harlem the human type.

The figures of Vergil Ragsdale (*Portraits*), the poet, Good Grey Bard (*Rendezvous*), and the Bard of Timbuktu (*Libretto*) become fused and enlarged here. The artists evoke both their personal and public lives. The division between private failure and public assurance in the aesthetic vocation, evident even in Ragsdale, appears uniquely human. Harlem, a nexus of Afro-American artist-heroes, shares the inhabitants' ambivalent and tragicomic blues. The inhabitants suit well the modern epic:

> in this race, at this time, in this place,
>   to be a Negro artist is to be
> a flower of the gods, whose growth
>   is dwarfed at an early stage—
>   a Brazilian owl moth,
> a giant among his own in an acreage
>   dark with the darkman's designs,
> where the milieu moves back downward like the sloth.
>
> (*Harlem Gallery*, p. 153)

Tolson even maintains the abstract hero and symbolizes Art itself, but the hero no longer strides with the masses toward an apocalyptic new earth. Tolson has his concept or an economically determined world transmuted by true art. The true artist foreshadows the new world not as the "Futurafrique" (*Libretto*), but as the "dusk of dawn." The artistic subsumes the political. Art, like John Laugart's "Black Bourgeoisie," so long as authentic, becomes sanative.

The style of the ode is more dynamic than that in *Libretto*. The new mode, with allusiveness and complexity of metaphor, image and symbol, excludes verbiage. Here emerge greater mastery and flexibility.[33] The poems project their themes through a flux of character, interaction, and talk. The peripatetic Curator goes to Laugart's apartment, Aunt Grindle's Chitterling Shop, the Harlem Gallery, and the Zulu Club. He hears or knows about the happenings at the police station, the Haha Club, and the Angelus Funeral Home. His wanderings focus the geography of Harlem. His thoughts about the characters, life, and art are projected in both discursive and narrative cantos. At once a dramatic persona and an undramatized prophet like Eliot's Tiresias, he represents the consciousness through which the ode is played. In a sense he "makes" the "autobio-fragment"—the ode itself—literally humanize intellect and oratory. The poem ends then with the achievement of the metonym:

> The allegro of the Harlem Gallery
>   is not a chippy fire,
> for here, in focus, are paintings that chronicle
>   a people's New World odyssey
>   from chattel to Esquire!
>
> (*Harlem Gallery*, p. 173)

Some indication of how Tolson's poem works can be seen in the first canto. In "Alpha," one hears the voice of the Cutrator for the first time. The basic symbols appear in the first two lines (p. 19):

> The Harlem Gallery, an Afric pepper bird,
>   awakes me at a people's dusk of dawn.

The Harlem Gallery, like the pepper bird native to Africa, stirs the Curator to action. He must envision the ode, the "autobio-fragment," at a people's dusk of dawn,[34] the transition between night and morning symbolically figuring a new socioeconomic age. Here the Afro-American will attain his full stature. The ode itself will both prophetically and aesthetically help to usher this in.

Then the poem evokes some Third World challenges to the "Great White World," the former being the social equivalent to the Curator's craft. Introspectively, the Curator turns to himself, faces the task, and sees himself as flawed, being comic where seriousness is called for, being serious when comedy is required. He shares humankind's meandering approach to the necessary search for true freedom. He envisions the task again, now hearing "a dry husk-of-locust" blues asking "Black Boy, O Black Boy, / is the port worth the cruise?" Inhibitions based on self-doubt harden the task; to maintain the integrity of self, humanity, and race proves nearly too much. The "clockbird's jackass laughter" haunts his effort. Challenged by the pepper bird, but mocked by the clockbird, he reveals the spirit of transitional man in a transitional world.

As in "Alpha" the entire ode centers in irregular rhyme, internal rhyme, alliteration, assonance, and consonance. Major symbols in the ode, such as Harlem Gallery, African pepper bird, Dusk of Dawn, and clockbird, recur now. The Buridan's ass and "the gaffing *To ti*" have appeared earlier in different genres, but images of the Hambletonian gathering for a leap, the apples of Cain, and barrel cactus are fresh. Here closes the decade long evolution in his worldview as an Afro-American, for his craft subsumes and perfects his oratory.

But with an epic intention, why does he abandon the folk model for the academic one? Why, if so committed to the Black and white masses, does he write in the style of the literary elite?

Perhaps *Harlem Gallery* is not exclusively for the elite. Here one reads and enjoys with persistence more than with erudition. Or, maybe Tolson regards the style as a criterion of excellence. Perhaps he wants to master the technique but to maintain his Afro-American experience. A final answer comes from Tolson, himself one of the "crafty masters of social conscience"[35]:

Today
The Few
Yield Poets
Their due;
tomorrow
The Mass
Judgment
Shall Pass.
(*Rendezvous*, p. 50)

NOTES

1. *Caviar and Cabbage: Selected Columns by Melvin B. Tolson from the Washington Tribune, 1937–1944* by Robert M. Farnsworth (Columbia: Univ. of Missouri Press, 1982), 29. Hereafter cited in the notes as *C. and C.* Quotations by permission of the Univ. of Missouri Press; Copyright 1980 by the Curators of the Univ. of Missouri.
2. Ibid., 53: "At his best, the old preacher had the poetry of words and motion. . . ."
3. Farnsworth sees a melding of Christianity and Radicalism in Tolson; see ibid., Introduction, 5–6 and Sec. I.
4. Melvin B. Tolson, *A Gallery of Harlem Portraits*, ed. Robert M. Farnsworth (Columbia: Univ. of Missouri Press, 1979). Hereafter cited as *Portraits*. Quotations by permission of the Univ. of Missouri Press; copyright 1979 by the Curators of the Univ. of Missouri.
5. Melvin B. Tolson, *Rendezvous with America* (New York: Dodd, Mead, 1944). Hereafter cited as *Rendezvous.*
6. Melvin B. Tolson, *Libretto for the Republic of Liberia* (London: Collier-Macmillan, 1970). Hereafter cited as *Libretto.*
7. Melvin B. Tolson, *Harlem Gallery: Book I, the Curator* (New York: Twayne, 1965). Hereafter cited in the notes as *H.G.*
8. Tolson pursued many of these ideas in his newspaper columns and in unpublished novels and plays. One can find essentially the same ideas in different genres.
9. A concept that Tolson pursued in "The Ape of God" in which he explicates the characteristics and functions of the artist-visionary. Material will be found in Tolson's unpublished Notebooks and Papers in the Manuscript Room, Library of Congress. Hereafter cited as "Notebooks."
10. Frost, Whitman, Hughes, Wright, and Sterling Brown are also part of the American literary tradition celebrating the "common man." Tolson had a familiarity with these authors.
11. Babette Deutsch, *Poetry in Our Time: A Critical Survey of Poetry in the English-Speaking World 1900 to 1960* 2d ed. (New York: Doubleday, 1963), 48.
12. Tolson uses all these names in one version of the opening poem in *Portraits*; "Harlem," *The Arts Quarterly*, I (April–June 1937), 27.
13. Melvin B. Tolson, "The Harlem Group of Negro Writers," master's thesis, Columbia Univ., 1940, p. 121.
14. Thus constituting an epic within an epic as Tolson was later to do in "Upsilon," *H.G.*, in which the smaller poem complements the larger one.

15. Tolson was originally much opposed to American entry into World War II but later changed his opinion. See *C. and C.* and *passim*.
16. "Idols of the Tribe," a term derived from Francis Bacon's *Novum Organum*, is a metaphor that becomes symbolic in Tolson's treatment.
17. The three S's of Parnassus were first developed as an ideal for his poetry in the 1930s. See Joy Flasch, *Melvin R. Tolson* (New York: Twayne, 1972), 48 and *passim*. Hereafter cited as Flasch, *Tolson*.
18. Such an ending, looking to the future, is typical of Tolson.
19. Interview with Mrs. Ruth Tolson, Washington, D.C., 23 Oct. 1974.
20. See also Tolson in "A Poet's Odyssey," *Anger and Beyond: The Negro Writer in the United States*, ed. Herbert Hill (New York: Harper and Row, 1966), 195. Besides Eliot, Yeats, Baudelaire, and Pasternak, Tolson studied "all the great moderns."
21. Tolson remarked about his "The Man Inside": "It was not written for you, like 'Caviar and Cabbage.' It was written about you. It speaks to those super-intellectuals who whoop it up for democracy," *C. and C.*, 229. This illustrates his conscious preparation of form to accommodate different audiences.
22. Tolson in "Notebooks" states: "Start horizontally from fact to metaphor: then the idea moves vertically from metaphor to symbol at the apex of the language."
23. Since the *Libretto* jacket blurb calls the poem an "African Odyssey" and "this epic masterpiece," there is some indication of Tolson's intention.
24. See Flasch, *Tolson*, p. 75: "The *Libretto* is a long ode consisting of eight sections. . ."; see also Jon Woodson, "A Critical Analysis of the Poetry of Melvin B. Tolson," doctoral diss., Brown Univ., 1978: "the poem, consisting of eight Pindaric odes. . ." 110. This same difference of opinion occurs about *H.G.*, called an ode by Flasch. "*Harlem Gallery* is structured so that there is an ode for each letter of the ancient Greek alphabet . . ." Woodson, 195.
25. J. F. A. Pyre, "A Short Introduction to English Versification," Appendix, *English Poetry of the Nineteenth Century*, ed. Oscar Campbell and J. F. A. Pyre (New York: Appleton-Century-Crofts, 1929), 754.
26. Woodson points out the existence of the protagonist: "Note 367 contains, besides note 554, the only direct assertion that the poem, consisting of eight Pindaric odes—thus presumably spoken by someone—contains a protagonist. Tolson's protagonist, in contrast to Eliot's identification of the seer Tiresias as 'a mere spectator and not indeed a "character" . . . is not anywhere named. . . . The reader of the *Libretto* is provided no key as to whom the protagonist might be' (pp. 110–11). See entire discussion, pp. 110–13.

27. Tolson's notes, like Eliot's, still leave much of the work of deciphering the poem to the reader.
28. Tolson's reading habits were essentially eclectic: "The worst thing you can do if you expect to get through a college or university is to pattern your reading after mine. I have reading sprees. I may get to thinking about snakes and spend weeks studying rattlers, cobras, pythons, Gilas, and chameleons. . . . Or I may start on a reading spree that covers the history of undertakers," *C. and C.*, 166.
29. Tolson here builds on his earlier poetry in his use of the technique of repetition with a twist and/or reversal in the final repetend.
30. "The poet Tennyson dreamed of a Parliament of Man, a Federation of the World. I cast my vote for that," *C. and C.*, 127. See also Tennyson, "Locksley Hall."
31. See discussion of "climax," Flasch, *Tolson*, p. 76 and Tate, *Libretto*, p. 10.
32. For full discussion of protagonist and his relationship to the content of poem, see Woodson, ch. 3.
33. All the poems in *H.G.* are centered.
34. "Dusk of Dawn" is the title of W. E. B. Du Bois' autobiography. For a longer discussion see Mariann Russell, *Melvin R. Tolson's Harlem Gallery: A Literary Analysis* (Columbia: Univ. of Missouri Press, 1980), 54, 67.
35. Jane Kramer, "In the Garrison," *New York Review of Books* (2 Dec. 1982), 8.

GARY SMITH

A Hamlet Rives Us: The Sonnets of Melvin B. Tolson

> I am an optimist. I believe a better world is coming by and by. I believe that human nature can be converted, changed, reconditioned. I do not believe man is born to be selfish, poverty-stricken, ignorant, unthinking.
>
> —*Melvin B. Tolson*[1]

One of the more interesting but heretofore unexplored aspects of Melvin B. Tolson's poetic career is his work as a sonneteer. Although there appears to be good justification for this critical oversight, it might be explained by two related reasons. First, early in his career, Tolson was convinced by a fellow graduate student at Columbia University that the sonnet was not big or lusty enough to contain the epic of Afro-American life that he wanted to write.[2] Tolson subsequently regarded the sonnet as a form of dead classicism in literature. He not only ignored the sonnet; he also dramatically fashioned his poetic style in the direction of Modernistic poetry with its emphasis on free verse, literary allusion, imagistic compression, and temporal and spatial dislocation. The Modernist epic that Tolson actually wrote, *Harlem Gallery: Book I, The Curator* (1965), provoked such an outcry against its obtuse literary references, arcane style, and elliptical images that critics suggested he had

From *CLA Journal* XXIX, no. 3 (March 1986).

succeeded in outpounding Pound.[3] For this reason, critics tend to draw a narrow circle of interest around his poetry. They begin with his widely anthologized early poems, "Rendezvous with America" and "Dark Symphony," and end with his controversial Harlem Gallery.

Nonetheless, as Tolson's sonnets clearly indicate, his poetry offers a much wider range of interest and achievement, thereby ranking him with the few distinguished black poets who wrote during the post-renaissance period of Afro-American literature.[4] All twelve of Tolson's published sonnets appear in his first work, *Rendezvous with America* (1944).[5] As its Whitmanesque title suggests, Tolson's overriding theme in the book is America as a burgeoning land of opportunity. Tolson consciously celebrates the unique mixture of the heroic and commonplace in American life. But he differs from Walt Whitman, Carl Sandburg, and Vachel Lindsay—other poets of America's *democratic vistas*—in his profoundly ambivalent attitude toward American socioeconomic life. Much like Gwendolyn Brooks and Robert Hayden, two other poets from the poet-renaissance, Tolson's poetic vision is tempered by the paradoxes of racism and socioeconomic injustice that exist within the American Dream. If the poems in *Rendezvous with America* herald America's limitless future, they also decry the limitations of its past and present. For Tolson, America's democratic ideals fail to the precise extent that black Americans are denied the social liberties and economic opportunities enjoyed by whites.

The traditional sonnet, with its paradoxical questions and syllogistic structure, gave Tolson the ideal form to articulate his personal ambivalence. Like Claude McKay and Countee Cullen, New Negro poets from the Harlem Renaissance, Tolson realized that if the sonnet was too limited for the epic expression of Afro-American life, it could be transformed into a devastating instrument of social protest. As an outsider to the largely genteel, European sonnet tradition, Tolson's mastery of the form proved his credentials as a poet and simultaneously revealed his vision of the racial injustice within American society. Moreover, the sonnet's strict formal and metrical discipline served to control the prosaic, Whitmanesque tendencies in his early poetic style.

Unlike the New Negro poets, Tolson's approach to the sonnet was hardly mimetic. While he consistently used the Shakespearean form, his sonnets do not argue the merits of love as much as they narrate the ironies, ambiguities, and paradoxes of modern life. They contrast the ideals of truth and honesty with the harsh realities that threaten these ideals. Stylistically, by adding the inherent characteristics of the folk tale—short narration, dialogue, and an explicit moral[6]—to the form of the Shakespearean sonnet, he creates what might be called the sonnet-fable or the sonnet-parable, in which he effectively yokes the dramatic and the philosophical. His sonnet-parables satirize the universal condition of mankind while moralizing about the issues of racism and socioeconomic injustice.

II

One of the more traditional of Tolson's sonnets is "If You Should Lie to Me." Structurally, it conforms to the Shakespearean sonnet in its use of iambic pentameter and alternating rhyme scheme. As the title suggests, its theme is unrequited love. In the opening quatrain, the persona addresses by implication the paradoxical question: how can true love countenance deceit?

> If you should lie to me and I should find
> My soul webbed in the calculus of a lie,
> Of snares in hell and earth the most unkind,
> This snare would bleed the core of affection dry.

The speaker's initial appeal is emotional; he argues that a lie would "web" his soul and "bleed the core of affection dry." This personal appeal is then transformed, in the next two quatrains, into an argument for the truth of their love:

> We vowed our constancy without ado
> And let love's flat merge the fiefs of heart.
> If to this truth, then, you and I are true,
> Nothing or none can rend our lives apart.

The final couplet returns to the persona's emotional appeal and further suggests the emptiness that deceit would create within him:

> The seven deadly sins I can abide:
> A lie? That kills the *raison d'être* inside!

The most interesting aspect of this ostensibly conventional sonnet is the metaphysical wit that the speaker uses to create the emotional distance separating him from his lover. In the first quatrain, he uses mathematics and geophysical language: "webbed in the calculus of a lie" and "snares in hell and earth"; in the second quatrain, the speaker turns to parliamentary language: "And let love's fiat merge the fiefs of heart"; and, finally, he evokes Iago to underline the insidious nature of deception: "A fraud, a kiss of guile, a hidden knife— / These for Iago." These incongruent metaphors obviously play into the complexity of the persona's emotional ordeal.

While "If You Would Lie to Me" is conventional in its form, three other sonnets, "Dictionary of the Wolf," "A Legend of Versailles," and "Inevitability" present radical shifts in theme and style. First, the poems are unconventional in their manipulation of the sonnet's syllogistic structure. Rather than a paradoxical question addressed through metaphorical conceits, a major and minor premise, and a conclusion, these sonnets adopt the dramatic elements of the fable. The *dramatis personae* are not human lovers but wolves, tigers, and politicians, who narrate conflicts between instinct and rational behavior. The drama within these poems lies in the attempt to negotiate the logical and aesthetic differences between universal democratic ideals and topical social realities.

In the sonnet "A Legend of Versailles," Tolson creates a dialogue between the political leaders of the First World War and a tiger. Ironically, the tiger becomes a symbol of rational thought, while the human beings—Lloyd George, Woodrow Wilson, and Georges Clemenceau—are befuddled statesmen seeking an end to war. In the octave, however, the tiger questions the seriousness of their quest for peace:

> Lloyd George and Woodrow Wilson and Clemenceau—
> The Big Three: England, America, and France—
> Met at Versailles. The Tiger ached to know
> About the myth to end war's dominance.
>
> "One moment, gentlemen," the Tiger said,
> "Do you really want a lasting peace?" And then
> Lloyd George assented with his shaggy head
> And Woodrow Wilson, nodding, chafed his chin.

Here, the simple irony lies in the meagre human response to the tiger's pointed question: "Lloyd George assented with his shaggy head" and "Woodrow Wilson, nodding, chafed his chin."

This ironic mockery continues in the third quatrain when the tiger reveals his own peace proposal:

> "The price of such a peace is great. We must give
> Up secret cartels, spheres of power and trade;
> Tear down our tariff walls; let lesser breeds live
> As equals; scrap the empires we have made."

The Western leaders' reaction to this revolutionary proposal is predictable: "The gentlemen protested, 'You go too far.'" They object to the tiger's solution to war, since it calls for a socialist reordering of Western economic and social life. More importantly, however, the tiger's peace proposal exposes the incongruities between the statesmen's ideals and their actual values. Thus, in the final line, the tiger roars to their objection: "You don't mean peace, but war!"

The *dramatis personae* of "The Dictionary of the Wolf" are Abraham Lincoln and a grizzled axman. Like the tiger of the previous sonnet, Lincoln moralizes about the disparity between words and reality. The poem begins *in medias res* with Lincoln's observation that the word "liberty" means "all sorts of things," including its antithesis:

> "We all declare for liberty," Lincoln said.
> "We use the word and mean all sorts of things:
> *In the sweat of thy face shalt thou eat bread.*
> *Rifle the basket that thy neighbor brings.*"

The implications of this Biblical pun is further stressed in the third quatrain with a parable:

> "The wolf tears at the sheep's throat: and the sheep
> Extols the shepherd for cudgeling tyranny;
> The wolf, convulsed with indignation deep,
> Accuses the shepherd of murdering liberty.

The wolf, shepherd, and sheep—archetypal symbols for instinct, reason, and innocence—are ensnared in a web of meanings associated with the words "liberty" and "tyranny." For the wolf, liberty means the right to "tear at the sheep's throat"; but for the sheep and, by implication, the shepherd, liberty is the right to exist without tyranny. Lincoln's parable thus infers the treachery of those who use words to justify their actions. This difficulty is reinforced by the moral that closes the poem:

> "But the dictionary of the wolf is writ
> In words the rats of time chew bit by bit."

The "dictionary of the wolf" is an image of tyranny masked in words, while the "rats of time" recalls the ominous grizzled axman of the second quatrain. Together, the images condemn the use of words which mask their users' heinous social deeds.

"Inevitability" also uses the wolf as a symbol of tyranny. In the previous sonnets, the tiger and Abraham Lincoln represent standards for peace and liberty, but "Inevitability" noticeably lacks a moral center. The initial quatrain foreshadows this absence through its wasteland imagery:

> The mausoleum of a winter's day
> Entombs a cosmic waste of hill and vale.
> Yon cannibal pack of wolves tears at its prey,
> Like villains fabled in a Norseman's tale.

Ironically, the death of the tyrannical king, who "bought a reign of terror to man and beast," does not signal the start of social democracy; instead, the king's subjects celebrate his death by "feasting on his carcass" and emulating his tyrannical rule:

> Thus decorated toadies ape the king,
> Goosestep his thoughts and trumpet his success;
> But when his toppled pomp goes glimmering,
> The eunuched underlings deepen his distress.

The speaker suggests that the roles of oppressed and oppressor are interchangeable. However, his word choices and viewpoint imply a moral standard. By labeling the king's subjects as "decorated toadies" and "eunuched underlings," he condemns their unenlightened and hypocritical behavior. In the final lines, this condemnation extends to the hope that, once the king's subjects realize his "counterfeit greatness," they will no longer "ape" his tyrannical behavior.

The personae in the final two sonnets, "The Braggart" and "The Blindness of Scorn," explore the tyranny of white supremacy. The sonnets examine racism as a barrier to human understanding. Like the cultural blindness of the Western leaders in "A Legend of Versailles," racism is a blindness that undermines the ideals of social democracy.

In "The Braggart," white racism becomes a part of "nature's plan," wherein lesser breeds are relegated to inferior, roles in the great chain of being:

> "The eagle kings of the realm of birds," he said;
> "The lion monarchs the jungle; the world of trees
> Kneels to the redwood; Everest's imperial head
> Outdazzles the peaks; the Pacific queens the seas.

"Elite and mongrel! That is Nature's plan,
A ladder-scheme and not a level-hood.
The Nordic is the zenith rung of Man,
And envy sires the lesser breeds no good."

Of course, the arrogance of this world view mocks itself. More importantly, in the first quatrain, the narrator undercuts the white racist's authority by describing his ethics as "dog-eat-dog" and isolating his "blond magnificence" outside the larger human community:

His blond magnificence keyed his vanity,
As snowdrifts moored us at the cabined hearth.
His dog-eat-dog ethics appalled, and we
Were sea fish caught within the damming garth.

Like snowdrifts, the white racist represents a peril to the human community; he is, in fact, an aberration rather than the norm.

"The Blindness of Scorn" further explores white supremacy by showing its inevitable consequence. In this poem, the "lesser breed" is a Malaysian guide who is charged with leading an "alien white" through a jungle. As in the previous poem, the white racist is isolated outside the natural order:

The jungle huddled in like dungeon walls:
Green catacombs of shrub, vague dinosaurs
Of sweating trunks, hanging gardens of palls,
And potter's fields of weeds and pollinars.
The Malay guide, in loin cloth, walked ahead
Along the corkscrew trail, with ear and eye
Alert; behind him, bronzed and helmeted,
The alien White came, cursing earth and sky.

Dressed in a loincloth, the Malaysian merges his identity with nature; he walks ahead of the white man "with ear and eye alert." On the other hand, the alien white, "bronzed and helmeted," curses earth and sky.

The poem's greater irony, though, lies in the white racist's blindness to the Malaysian's humanity. By insisting on a servant–master relationship, the racist is vulnerable to the perils of the jungle as well as the Malaysian's treachery:

"Sahib!" the Malay cried. "Sahib!" He bowed
And dropped his goatskin pack. "Stinkbug of hell!"

The master raged. The guide, with fear endowed,
Shoved violently the White. The python fell.

The Malaysian's treachery is not directed at the alien white as much as it is toward his blindness. The poem implicitly condemns the tyranny of white racism and its social oppression. Its moral, therefore, celebrates the triumph of righteous anger over complacent scorn:

The Malay said, as the coils piled high and dense:
"Sahib, the blindness of scorn provokes offense."

III

There are three major stylistic differences between Tolson's sonnet-fable and his sonnet-parable. In the sonnet-parable, human beings now replace personified animals as the *dramatis personae*. Accordingly, the paradoxical dilemmas of the parables exist on a higher, more complex ethical plane. Finally, whereas the moral statement of the fable structure is closer to the dramatic surface of the sonnet, here the moral is woven within the parable's narrative. Thematically, the overriding concern of the sonnet-parable is the inherent conflicts within the human heart. As opposed to racial or political tyranny, the personae are beset by the tyranny of human emotions. Love, empathy, and self-sacrifice struggle against hate, scorn, and indifference. Moreover, these struggles are not resolved through the simple triumph of good over evil, but rather in a closer understanding of the complex nature of the human heart. In short, if Tolson's sonnet-fable protests the tyranny of political and social perversions that reduce human beings to "lesser breeds," his sonnet-parable explores the emotional conflicts and demands of the human heart.

In the first of the sonnets, "The Big Game Hunter," Tolson examines the complex relationship between fear and courage. In the octave, the narrator tells of a perplexing encounter between a Zulu tribe and a lion:

All day the Zulu hunters and their chief
Tracked in the bushland. Then a sudden roar
Cleaved forests, and with naked unbelief
The warriors watched the charging carnivore.

The giant chief saw that his rooted band
Would be wiped out. Though terror iced his heart,
He charged the jungle kind; the fisted hand
Shot into the cavern mouth like an ebony dart.

The implied paradoxical question is why the Zulu chief, surrounded by fear, would charge the lion and face certain death. As the narrator makes clear, the chief is as fearful as his "rooted band." On the simplest level, then, his courageous action reveals pride of leadership: "The giant chief saw that his rooted band would be wiped out." However, as the narrator's hyperbolic language indicates, individual pride does not entirely explain the chief's self-sacrifice: "the fisted hand / Shot into the cavern mouth like an ebony dart."

The final quatrain offers a partial explanation for the chief's courageous act:

> The brave are blind to danger; the courageous see
> And feel and know. Wise Latins placed the seat
> Of courage in the heart, where it should be,
> That naught may ape its grandeur, none may cheat.

Now, the chief's action is raised to the level of human valor. The chief is courageous because he sees, feels, and knows the imminent danger of the lion but still instinctively and fearlessly acts. The eulogistic conclusion underscores the humanity of his deed: "The Flower of sacrifice blooms the lunar year, / And conscience serves as pallbearers of fear."

Like the previous sonnet, "The Gallows" is a study of personal heroism. But as its macabre title suggests, its focus is upon the ironic relationship between self-sacrifice and human apathy. Throughout the initial two quatrains, the protagonist, a teacher, is portrayed as a Christ-like figure who miraculously transforms the dormant lives of his students:

> He was my teacher a continent of years ago;
> Yet bright as blood is the red-letter day he came
> Into the drouth of the class, with his wits aflow,
> To freshen the sesame in each alien name.
>
> Month after month, the pan of his alchemy
> Found nuggets of gold where others found alloy.
> And the miracle of his integrity
> Put bone and blood and soul into girl and boy.

As the conceits suggest, the teacher succeeds largely because he works within the potential value of his students' lives. His presence is water that flows into the "drouth of the class" and freshens the "sesame in each alien name." Indeed, his teaching is the alchemist's pan wherein base metal is turned to gold; and his exemplary behavior restores the spiritual health of his students.

However, in the climactic third quatrain, when the teacher probes the subsoil of intellectual and spiritual poverty, his actions become antagonistic:

> He dumped the debris of customs on the refuse heap,
> He tore down fences propped with a great Amen,
> He set apart the huddling goats and sheep,
> He let the oxygens of the freedoms in.

The teacher attempts to establish a new social consciousness not only in the classroom but also in the town. His dramatic development, therefore, is from an outsider, to an esteemed teacher, and finally to a revolutionary. Moreover, as the teacher's social roles change, his relationship with his students also changes. They are no longer girls and boys but rather sheep and goats. Implicitly, then, the "oxygen of freedoms" refers to the life-sustaining chemical element as well as the teacher's libertarian socio-politics. Finally, the moral conclusion indicates the dedicated teacher's ironic fate:

> The lame, the halt, the blind-these struck him down;
> Then the gallows of ignorance hanged the little town.

The final two sonnets, "The Note" and "A Hamlet Rives Us," are narrated from the first person singular. Each poem focuses upon the psychological barriers that thwart a full comprehension—if not understanding—of the depths of human emotions. The protagonists, identified only as "I," experience a perplexing encounter with death. But unlike the teacher's personal tragedy, which is closely identified with specific social actions, the human motives in these poems lack social or political correlatives. Their dramas do not move outward into the realm of social action but rather inward into the complex realm of psychology.

In the first poem, "The Note," the persona tells of a clandestine love affair he has had with a poor store clerk. However, the romantic elements within the sonnet noticeably lack concrete details. In the octave, the speaker admits that, although he did not love the woman, "A soul compulsion drew me to her side":

> I saw her in a cluttered basement store,
> Across a counter frivolous with toys.
> Her alien face held griefs that haunt the poor,
> As she wrapped up the trinkets for the boys.

I met her often, though I loved her not:
A soul compulsion drew me to her side.
On holidays in an untraveled spot,
We talked and dreamed and watched the combing tide.

Here, the store counter with its clutter of toys and trinkets not only connotes the triviality of the love affair, but it also suggests the psychological barriers between the lovers. While the persona carefully avoids self-description, the woman's identity is inseparable from the toys and trinkets. "The untraveled spots" and "combing tide," which are conventional romantic images, further suggest the stale, unsuccessful attempts to provoke an emotional and aesthetic response in their affair.

The final quatrain reveals little about the lovers' failure to consummate their love. Instead, it focuses on the woman s fateful decision:

This note is all she left to tell me why
She swam out to that fatal rendezvous.
Again I read . . . again: "It's best to die,
When there is nothing else for one to do."

The note, like the earlier toys and trinkets, reinforces the chilling equation the speaker makes between his feelings for the woman and her suicide. Nonetheless, the elipsis and redundancy emphasize how deeply disturbed he is by her action. His bafflement continues into the conclusion when he offers a partial explanation for his perplexed emotions:

And now I know that pity's worse than scorn
And love roots deepest when of pity born.

The key words "roots" and "born" reveal the fatal attachment he has to the woman and, perhaps, a closeness that, only after her death, he fully understands.

"A Hamlet Rives Us" is again a groping effort to empathize with the suffering of others. The emphasis is upon the superficial emotional attachments that belie more profound psychological motives. The poem begins in the same ominous manner as the previous sonnet:

I saw him faltering toward me in the street:
His eyes emptied of living, his grief unshed.
Pain pitted my heart and meshed my doubtful feet,
As memory's alcove revealed his loved one dead.

Our sorrows mated then, for I had lost
The next of kin in the fogland of the year.
And yet a Hamlet rives us when the frost
Of death comes like a specter buccaneer.

The psychological distance between the speaker and his secret sharer is insurmountable. Even though both have confronted grief in the form of a dead loved one, they are unable to transact their separate but identical emotions. The "Hamlet" and "specter buccaneer" refer to Hamlet's emotional paralysis; but these literary answers fail to explain completely the conundrum of each man's isolation in his emotional grief.

The final quatrain dramatizes the emotional paralysis that afflicts the persona:

I must console him in this awful hour.
It is the wise and decent thing to do.
Embarrassed, helpless, I was thieved of power
To utter the tags tragedy ordained untrue.

The conflicting emotions render the speaker helpless. On the one hand, his sincerity is unmistakeable: "It is the wise and decent thing to do"; yet the word "thieved" is as tentative an explanation of his emotional paralysis as the earlier reference to "Hamlet." Finally, the moral conclusion provides yet another insight into this ordeal:

My friend passed by, unseeing in his grief,
And the lash of conscience gave me sweet relief.

Ironically, the secret sharer is as helpless in his grief as the speaker; he, too, fails to connect the common thread of emotion that binds him to another human being. Thus, the "lash of conscience" relieves the persona of his guilt feelings; he is comforted by his awareness that his fellow sufferer is equally paralyzed by grief.

As Tolson's sonnets ably demonstrate, his best work is a fusion of art, philosophy, and socio-politics. Like the New Negro poets, he realized the value of art as an instrument for social change. His sonnets contain unmistakable racial consciousness, but his most persistent theme is the tyranny of social distance that blinds mankind to its essential oneness. This theme is found not only in his political fables but also in his social parables. In both, Tolson suggests that social democracy, when unfettered by race and class, is an attainable ideal. Yet, on a psychological level, as his personae grope toward an understanding of themselves, they almost invariably find their griefs and frustrations reflected in the lives of others. Thus, the vitality of Tolson's poetry lies in the tension between an imagined, ideal world of social democracy and humanistic empathy and the real world of racial discrimination, political tyranny, and aberration. If Tolson's fables and parables describe mankind's inability to attain an ideal world, their morals are blueprints for change.

Notes

1. Melvin B. Tolson, "Every Negro in the United States Is Important," *New Letters*, 47 (Summer 1981), 117.
2. Melvin B. Tolson, "The Odyssey of a Manuscript," *New Letters*, 48 (Fall 1981), 8–9.
3. Ronald Lee Cansler, "The White and Not-White Dichotomy of Melvin B. Tolson's Poetry," *Negro American Literature Forum*, 7 (Winter 1973), 115.
4. By "post-renaissance," I mean the period in Afro-American literature that succeeded the Harlem Renaissance of the 1920s and '30s but ended with the onset of the Black Arts Movement of the 1960s. For a more precise definition of this time period, see C. W. E. Bigsby, *The Second Black Renaissance* (Westport, Connecticut: Greenwood Press, 1980), p. 3.
5. Melvin B. Tolson, *Rendezvous with America* (New York: Dodd, 1944), pp. 59–70. All subsequent quotations of Tolson's sonnets come from this source.
6. See Karen Kennerly, Introd., *Hesitant Wolf and Scrupulous Fox: Fables Selected from World Literature* (New York: Random House, 1973), pp. 3–9.

Works by the Poets

Phillis Wheatley (1753-1784)

Poems of Phillis Wheatley: A Native African and a Slave. Bedford, Mass.: Applewood Books, 1995.

Mason, Julian D., Jr., ed. *The Poems of Phillis Wheatley*, rev. and enl. ed. Chapel Hill: University of North Carolina Press, 1989.

Frances Ellen Watkins Harper (1825-1911)

Foster, Frances Smith, ed. *A Brighter Day Coming: A Frances Ellen Watkins Harper Reader.* New York: Feminist Press at the City University of New York, 1990.

Graham, Maryemma, ed. *Complete Poems of Frances E.W. Harper.* New York: Oxford University Press, 1988.

Paul Laurence Dunbar (1872-1906)

Howells, W.D., ed. *The Complete Poems of Paul Laurence Dunbar, With an Introduction to "Lyrics of Lowly Life."* New York: Dodd, Mead & Co., 1967.

James Weldon Johnson (1871-1938)

Wilson, Sondra Kathryn, ed. *Saint Peter Relates an Incident: Selected Poems.* New York: Penguin Books, 1993.

Claude McKay (1890-1948)

Dewey, John and Max Eastman, eds. *Selected Poems of Claude McKay*. New York: Bookman Associates, 1993.
Cooper, Wayne F., ed. *The Passion of Claude McKay: Selected Poetry and Prose.* New York: Schocken Books, 1973.

Jean Toomer (1894-1967)

Jones, Robert B. and Margery Toomer Latimer, eds. *The Collected Poems of Jean Toomer*. Chapel Hill: University of North Carolina Press, 1988.

Sterling A. Brown (1901-1989)

Harper, Michael S. *The Collected Poems of Sterling A. Brown*. Evanston, IL: Another Chicago Press, 1989.

Langston Hughes (1902-1967)

Rampersad, Arnold and David Roessel, eds. *The Collected Poems of Langston Hughes*. New York: A.A. Knopf: distributed by Random House, 1994.
Roessel, David E, ed. *Langston Hughes: Poems*. New York: Knopf, 1999.

Countee Cullen (1903-1946)

Caroling Dusk: An Anthology of Verse by Black Poets of the Twenties. Secaucus, N.J.: Carol Publishing Group, 1993.
On These I Stand: An Anthology of the Best Poems of Countee Cullen. New York: Harper & Row, 1966.

Melvin Beaunorus Tolson (1898-1966)

Nelson, Raymond, ed. *"Harlem Gallery" and Other Poems of Melvin B. Tolson.* Charlottesville: University Press of Virginia, 1999.

Works about the Poets

Baker, Houston A. *A Many-Coloured Coat of Dreams: The Poetry of Countee Cullen*. Detroit: Broadside Press, 1974.

Benson, Bryan Joseph and Mabel Mayle Dillard. *Jean Toomer*. Boston: Twayne Publishers, 1980.

Boyd, Melba Joyce. *Discarded Legacy: Politics and Poetics in the Life of Frances E. W. Harper, 1825-1911*. Detroit, Mich.: Wayne State University Press, 1994.

Brawley, Benjamin Griffith. *Paul Laurence Dunbar: A Poet of His People*. Port Washington, N.Y.: Kennikat Press, 1967.

Brunner, Edward. *Cold War Poetry*. Urbana: University of Illinois Press, 2001.

Cooper, Wayne F. *Claude McKay: Rebel Sojourner in the Harlem Renaissance: A Biography* Baton Rouge: Louisiana State University Press, 1996, 1987.

Cunningham, Virginia. *Paul Laurence Dunbar and His Song*. New York: Dodd, Mead, 1947.

Davis, Arthur P. "The Alien-and-Exile Theme in Countee Cullen's Racial Poems." *Phylon* 14 (Fourth Quarter 1953): pp. 390-400.

Dorsey, David F. "Countee Cullen's Use of Greek Mythology." *College Language Association Journal* 13, 1970: pp. 68-77.

Faber, Genevieve and Michel Feith, eds. *Jean Toomer and the Harlem Renaissance*. New Brunswick, NJ: Rutgers University Press, 2001.

Farnsworth, Robert M. *Melvin B. Tolson, 1898-1966: Plain Talk and Poetic Prophecy*. Columbia: University of Missouri Press, 1984.

Ferguson, Blanche E. *Countee Cullen and the Negro Renaissance*. New York: Dodd, Mead, 1966.

Flasch, Joy. *Melvin B. Tolson*. New York: Twayne, 1972.

Fleming, Robert E. *James Weldon Johnson*. Boston: Twayne Publishers, 1987.

Gabbin, Joanne V., ed. *The Furious Flowering of African American Poetry*. Charlottesville, Va.: University of Virginia Press, 1999.

———. *Sterling Brown: Building the Black Aesthetic Tradition*. Westport, Conn.: Greenwood Press, 1985.

Gayle, Jr., Addison. *Oak and Ivy: A Biography of Paul Laurence Dunbar*. Garden City: Doubleday, 1971.

———. *Claude McKay: The Black Poet at War*. Detroit, Mich.: Broadside Press, 1972.

Gibson, Donald B. *Modern Black Poets: A Collection of Critical Essays*. Englewood Cliffs, N.J.: Prentice-Hall, 1973.

Guterl, Matthew Pratt. *The Color of Race in America, 1900-1940*. Cambridge, Mass.: Harvard University Press, 2001.

Houston, A. Baker, Jr. *A Many-Colored Coat of Dreams: The Poetry of Countee Cullen*. Detroit: Broadside Press, 1974.

Huggins, Nathan Irvin. *Harlem Renaissance*. London, Oxford and New York: Oxford University Press, 1971.

Jackson, Blyden and Louis D. Rubin, Jr. *Black Poetry in America*. Baton Rouge: Louisiana State University Press, 1974, pp.: 58-62.

Jones, Robert B. *Jean Toomer and the Prison-House of Thought: A Phenomenology of the Spirit*. Amherst: University of Massachusetts, 1993.

Kaplan, Sidney. "Phillis Wheatley," in *The Black Presence in the Era of the American Revolution, 1770-1800*. Greenwich, Conn.: New York Graphic Society, 1973.

Kerman, Cynthia Earl. *The Lives of Jean Toomer: A Hunger for Wholeness*. Baton Rouge: Louisiana State University Press, 1987.

Lawson, Victor. *Dunbar Critically Examined*. Washington: The Associated Publishers, 1941.

Locke, Alain. *Four Negro Poets*. New York: A. & C. Boni, 1925.

Loewenberg, Bert James and Ruth Bogin. *Black Women in Nineteenth Century American Life, Their Words, Their Thoughts, Their Feelings*. University Park: Pennsylvania State University Press, 1976: pp. 38-44.

Martin, Jay, ed. *A Singer in the Dawn: Reinterpretations of Paul Laurence Dunbar*. New York: Dodd, Mead, 1975.

McKay, Nellie Y. *Jean Toomer, Artist: A Study of his Literary Life and Work, 1894-1936*. New York: Simon & Schuster, 1984.

Nielsen, Aldon Lynn, ed. *Reading Race in American Poetry*. Urbana: University of Illinois Press, 2000.

O'Daniel, Therman B. *Jean Toomer: A Critical Evaluation*. Washington, D.C.: Howard University Press, 1988.

Perry, Margaret. *Silence to the Drums: A Survey of the Literature of the Harlem Renaissance*. Westport, Conn.: Greenwood Press, 1976, pp.: 142-48.

Price, Kenneth M. and Lawrence J. Oliver, eds. *Critical Essays on James Weldon Johnson*. New York: London: G.K. Hall: Prenctice-Hall International, 1997.

Redding, J. Saunders. *To Make a Poet Black*. Chapel Hill: University of North Carolina Press, 1939.

Redmond, Eugene B. *Drumvoices: The Mission of Afro-American Poetry*. Garden City: Anchor/Doubleday, 1976, pp. 179-185.

Revell, Paul. *Paul Laurence Dunbar*. Boston: Twayne, 1979.

Robinson, William H., ed. *Critical Essays on Phillis Wheatley*. Boston: G. K. Hall, 1982.

———. "Phillis Wheatley in London." *CLA Journal* 21 (December 1977): 187-201.

———. *Phillis Wheatley: A Bio-Bibliography*. Boston: G.K. Hall, 1981.

Russell, Mariann. *Melvin B. Tolson's Gallery*. Columbia: University of Missouri Press, 1980.

Sanders, Mark A. *Afro-Modernist Aesthetics and the Poetry of Sterling A. Brown*. Athens, Ga.: University of Georgia Press, 1999.

Sherman, Joan R. *Invisible Poets: Afro-Americans of the Nineteenth Century*. Urbana: University of Illinois, 1974, pp. 62-74.

Shucard, Alan R. *Countee Cullen*. Boston: Twayne Publishers, 1984.

Silverman, Kenneth. "Four New Letters by Phillis Wheatley." *Early American Literature* 8 (Winter 1974): 257-271.

Sistrunk, Albertha. "Phillis Wheatley: An Eighteenth Century-Century Black American Poet Revisited." *CLA Journal* 23 (June 1980): 391-98.

Tidwell, John Edgar and John S. Wright, introductions to "Sterling Brown, Afro-American Poet: A Special Edition." *Callaloo: A Black South Journal of Arts and Letters* (February-May 1982): pp. 11-105.

Tillery, Tyrone. *Claude McKay: A Black Poet's Struggle for Identity*. Amherst: University of Massachusetts Press, 1992.

Turner, Darwin T. *In a Minor Chord*. Carbondale and Edwardsville: Southern Illinois University Press, 1971.

Wagner, Jean. *Black Poets of the United States From Paul Laurence Dunbar to Langston Hughes*, trans. by Kenneth Douglas. Urbana, Chicago and London: University of Illinois Press, 1973, pp. 283-347.

Winston, James. *A Fierce Hatred of Injustice: Claude McKay's Jamaica and His Poetry of Rebellion*. London and New York: Verso, 2000.

Woodson, Jon. *To Make a new Race: Gurdjieff; Toomer and the Harlem Renaissance*. Jackson: University Press of Mississippi, 1999.

Biographical Notes

PHILLIS WHEATLEY (1753-1784)

Phillis Wheatley was the first African American, the first slave, and the third woman in the United States to publish a book of poems. Wheatley was born, probably in 1753, in the Gambia, West Africa and later kidnapped and transported aboard a slave ship. She arrived in Boston in 1761, where she was purchased by John Wheatley as a servant for his wife, Susannah, who became very fond of her. Susannah Wheatley recognized both her obvious intelligence and poor health and, thus, Phillis was never trained to be a domestic but instead encouraged by the Wheatleys to study theology along with English, Latin and Greek classics. Phillis Wheatley published her first poem in 1767, and six years later, she published a book entitled *Poems on Various Subjects*. The book was published the same year that John Wheatley emancipated her. She achieved international renown, traveling to London to promote her book and being called upon as well as received by noted social and political figures of the day — including George Washington, to whom she wrote a poem of praise at the beginning of the war, and Voltaire, who commented on her "very good English verse." Her poem, *On Being Brought From Africa to America* (1773) is remarkable for its honesty in speaking about racial prejudice among white Christians. Wheatley had written the original version of this poem in 1768, seven years after she had come to America as a seven-year-old child and African slave. In 1773, *Poems on Various Subjects, Religious and Moral* appeared. She had also become the first African American—and the second American woman—to publish a book. Wheatley traveled to England to oversee the book's publication, but the trip served other purposes as well. She met many British dignitaries and intellectuals, all of whom celebrated her literary ability, including Benjamin Franklin. Shortly after her trip, her owners decided to free her—according to Wheatley, "at the desire of my friends in England." Phillis Wheatley lived in poverty after her 1778 marriage to John Peters, a free black Bostonian. Her short marriage was unhappy, and marred by the deaths in infancy of her first two children. On December 5, 1784, Wheatley died in childbirth along with her third child. At the time of her death, Wheatley was living in poverty and obscurity on the outskirts of Boston, but her memory and her extraordinary achievements was strong enough that her obituary was printed in the Boston papers. Although Phillis Wheatley advertised for subscriptions to a second volume of poems and letters, she died before she was able to secure a publisher. Her final manuscript was never found.

Frances Ellen Watkins Harper (1825-1911)

Frances Ellen Watkins Harper was, by far, the most popular poet of her time. Born on September 24, 1825 to free parents, Frances Ellen Watkins Harper nevertheless suffered from the oppressive slave laws and rampant discrimination of the time. Upon her mother's death, Frances Harper was orphaned at the age of three, and fell into the care of her aunt and uncle. Until the age of thirteen, Harper attended the free school for colored children in which her uncle, Rev. William Watkins, taught. Her formal education came to an end when she took a job as a nursemaid. Yet, despite the many trials and tribulations she endured, interest in and her gift for writing earned her distinction from her peers. Harper's first publication was a collection of poetry and prose entitled *Forest Leaves*, published in 1845. One of the essays in the volume was on Christianity, a subject which remained important to her throughout her lifetime. During her early adult life, Harper moved within the free states of Ohio and Pennsylvania where she worked as a teacher. She became active as lecturer in the Anti-Slavery movement of the 1850's, at one time making her home in Philadelphia "at the station of the Underground Rail Road, where she frequently saw passengers and heard their anguished tales of suffering and wrong. Her work during the Emancipation Proclamation and Lincoln's assassination is further evidence of her eloquence in expressing her hopes and disappointments for her people. with the progress of the fight for equality. In 1860, Harper married the love of her life, Fenton Harper. Advocating women's rights as well as abolition, Harper lectured at the 1869 meeting of the Equal Rights Association. Frances Harper continued her work on behalf of black women, founding the National Association of Colored Women and serving as its vice president until her death in Philadelphia on February 22, 1911.

Paul Laurence Dunbar (1872-1906)

Born on June 27 in Dayton, Ohio, Dunbar was among the first black Americans to achieve national fame and become nationally known among people of his own race for his poetry. He also had the special distinction of being the first black writer whose work was published in establishment magazines and mainstream publishing houses. Dunbar was a prolific writer in several genres, but first established himself through his poetry. He was the son of Joshua and Mathilda, freed slaves who had found their way north from Kentucky. While at Central High, he established the *Dayton Tattler*, a paper "for the colored people of Ohio," and was assisted by Wilbur and Orville Wright (who later became famous for their pioneering endeavors in aviation). At an early stage in his life, Dunbar was an avid reader of the classic English and American poets. His poetry consists of simple love poems, pastorals, meditative poems and a homey philosophy, placing Dunbar within the mainstream of such poets as Longfellow, Tennyson and Keats. During the period of 1896-1897, Dunbar met Booker T. Washington and W.E.B. DuBois, with whom he often appeared on public platforms, and his work reflects the opposing perspective of these two very different writers. It was also during this time that Dunbar met the talented Alice Ruth Moore, a New Orleans writer and teacher of Creole background. The couple was married on March 6, 1898. Dunbar's final years, however, were troublesome and unhappy ones. His health had been steadily declining and his marriage was failing. Dunbar died on February 9, 1906 at the age of thirty-three. Though his literary reputation suffered in the 1940's and 1950's, a reappraisal began in the 1970's with the publication of much previously uncollected work in *The Paul Laurence Dunbar Reader* in 1975, along with the developing critical interest in black studies.

James Weldon Johnson (1871-1938)

Born in Jacksonville, Florida on June 17, 1871 James Weldon Johnson (originally James William Johnson) was a respected poet, composer, lawyer, diplomat, and anthologist of black culture in the United States with a long and impressive list of achievements. In his early years, his schoolteacher mother trained young James in music and other subjects. In 1894 he earned an A.B. degree from Atlanta University, after which he served as the principal of the black high school in Jacksonville, Florida. During this time, he studied law, and in 1897 he became the first African American admitted to the Florida bar. In 1901 James Weldon moved with his brother, composer John Rosamond Johnson, to New York City where the two worked together as songwriters. The songwriting team found success in several Broadway musicals and collaborated on over 200 songs. While in New York, James

Weldon earned his M.A. degree from Columbia University in 1904. It was also during his time in New York that James Weldon befriended Charles Anderson, a black Republican leader and confidant of Booker T. Washington. In 1906, Johnson was appointed by President Theodore Roosevelt to serve as U.S. consul to Puerto Cabello, Venezuela and then in 1909 he became consul in Corinto, Nicaragua. During this time, Johnson worked on the novel, *Autobiography of an Ex-Coloured Man* (published anonymously in 1912). From 1916 to 1920, Johnson served as field secretary of the NAACP, and in 1920 he became their first African-American executive secretary. In 1917 he published his first volume of poetry *Fifty Years and Other Poems* and in 1927 he published his second volume, *God's Trombones*. While his duties as executive secretary seem to have limited his creative output, Johnson assembled three influential anthologies: *The Book of American Negro Poetry* (1922), *The Book of American Negro Spirituals* (1925), and *The Second Book of Negro Spirituals* (1926). Johnson held his position with the NAACP until 1930, after which he wrote three more books: *Black Manhattan* (1930), *Along This Way* (1933), and *Negro Americans, What Now?* (1934). James Weldon Johnson died on June 26, 1938, in Wiscasset, Maine.

Claude McKay (1890-1948)

A man of contradictions, Claude McKay is considered one of the great poets of the Harlem Renaissance of the 1920s. In addition to social and political concerns, McKay wrote on a variety of subjects, from his Jamaican homeland to romantic love, with a use of passionate language. Born in Jamaica in 1890, McKay moved to Harlem in 1915 to join the burgeoning literary scene and contributed articles to Garvey's *Negro World*. Educated by his older brother, who possessed a library of English novels, poetry, and scientific texts, McKay published a book of verse called *Songs of Jamaica*, recording his impressions of black life in Jamaica in dialect at the age of twenty. In 1912, he travelled to the United States to attend Tuskegee Institute, but remained there only a few months, leaving to study agriculture at Kansas State University. In 1917, he published two sonnets, "The Harlem Dancer" and "Invocation," and would later use the same poetic form to record his reactionary views on the injustices of black life in America. During the twenties, he developed an interest in Communism and travelled to Russia and then to France where he met Edna St. Vincent Millay and Sinclair Lewis. With the publication of his *Harlem Shadows* in 1921, McKay became known as the most fiery black poet of the day, whose work was honest and blunt. In 1934, McKay moved back to the United States and lived in Harlem, New York. When he lost faith in Communism, he turned his attention to the teachings of various spiritual and political leaders in Harlem, most notably Marcus Garvey's Black Nationalist movement and, eventually, converted to Catholicism in the late 1920s.

McKay's viewpoints and poetic achievements in the earlier part of the twentieth century set the tone for the Harlem Renaissance and gained the deep respect of younger black poets of the time, including Langston Hughes. He died in 1948.

JEAN TOOMER (1894-1967)

Jean Toomer is best known for his book, *Cane* (1923), a three-part work comprised of short stories, sketches, poems and a play, in which the simple images of rural blacks are contrasted with and analyzed by the urban black sensibility that was evolving in 1920's New York City. Born on December 26 in Washington, D.C., the son of Nathan Eugene Toomer, a Georgia planter, and Nina Pinchback Toomer, he spent most of his early life in Washington at the home of his maternal grandparents after his father deserted in 1896. His grandfather, Pinckney Benton Stewart Pinchback had been a powerful politician associated with the Louisiana governor's office during the Reconstruction era. The Pinchbacks were a racially mixed family, and Jean could not be readily identified as black. In fact, until 1906, he lived in a wealthy white neighborhood until his family's financial status suffered a severe setback in 1910. He attended the M Street High School in Washington, a black high school, and in 1914 he enrolled at the University of Wisconsin, Madison, where he intended to major in agriculture. He changed his mind shortly thereafter and, during the next four years, changed colleges and majors several times, but never stayed long enough to earn a degree. While at the City College of New York in 1917, Toomer began to read such influential writers as George Bernard Shaw, Henrik Ibsen, Walt Whitman and Johann Wolfgang von Goethe.

STERLING A. BROWN (1901-1989)

Hailed as a highly adroit and eloquent poet during the Harlem Renaissance, Sterling Brown also had a distinguished career as a teacher and scholar of African-American folk culture and written literature. Born in Washington, D.C. in May, 1901, Brown was never a resident of New York and his association with the Harlem Renaissance sensibility can be characterized as a more generalized identification with the "New Negro" movement. In an essay written in 1955, entitled "The New Negro," Brown saw Harlem as a place where African-American writing was published, not produced, and that the sophisticated writers of the movement were not truly representative of ordinary black people. As a result of his abiding interest in learning and collecting folklore, Brown absorbed the wit and wisdom of Mrs. Bibby, Calvin "Big Boy" Davis, Slim Greer, and many more actual persons who are refashioned into the many memorable folk characters of his poetry. Sterling Brown's father, the Reverend Sterling Nelson Brown, had been born into slavery but managed to attend Fisk University and Oberlin College and, further on, became a professor of religion at Howard University. Having received a good academic background from Dunbar High School, Sterling went on to Williams College in 1918, and earned a master's degree in English from Harvard in 1923. Brown was greatly influence by his reading of Louis Untermeyer's *Modern American Poetry* which introduced him to such canonical poets as Edward Arlington Robinson, Robert Frost, Carl Sandburg and Vachel Lindsay. While teaching at Virginia Seminary between 1926 and 1928, Sterling met and married Daisy Turnbull in 1927. The couple had one child. Thereafter, Sterling Brown taught briefly at Fisk, Lincoln University and Atlanta University, and in 1929 joined the faculty at Howard University where he remained until retirement. Brown's first book, *Outline for the Study of the Poetry of American Negroes*, published in 1931, was a supplement to James Weldon Johnson's Book of American Negro Poetry. In 1932, Brown published a collection of poetry, *Southern Road*, which had previously appeared in newspapers and magazines. It won critical acclaim, among them Alain Locke, a major theorist of the "New Negro" movement, but it did not sell widely. Motivated by the civil rights movement in the 1960's, Sterling Brown conducted lectures and poetry readings that brought him into national focus. He died in Takoma Park, Maryland in 1989.

LANGSTON HUGHES (1902-1967)

Born in Joplin, Missouri on February 1, 1902 into an abolitionist family, the grandson of James Mercer Langston, the first Black American to be elected to public office in 1855, Hughes had a long and distinguished writing career and inspired the work of countless other African American writers. Hughes graduated from Central High School in 1920 in Cleveland, Ohio, but began writing poetry in the eighth grade, where he was selected as Class Poet. However, his father did not believe that his son would be able to earn a living as a writer, and encouraged him to pursue a more practical career. Thus, Hughes began his higher education at Columbia University, his father promising to pay his tuition if he studied engineering. Nevertheless, he dropped out of the program with a B+ average in 1922, all the while continuing to write poetry. His first published poem was also one of his most famous, "The Negro Speaks of Rivers," which appeared in *Brownie's Book*. Later on, his poems, short plays, essays, and short stories would appear in the NAACP publication *Crisis Magazine* and in *Opportunity Magazine* and other publications. One of Hughes' finest essays appeared in the *Nation* in 1926, entitled "The Negro Artist and the Racial Mountain," states that "[w]e younger Negro artists now intend to express our individual dark-skinned selves without fear or shame." In 1923, Hughes traveled abroad on a freighter to the Senegal, Nigeria, the Cameroons, Belgium Congo, Angola, and Guinea in Africa, and later to Italy and France, Russia and Spain. Throughout all his travels, and at home in New York, one of his favorite pastimes was sitting in the clubs listening to blues, jazz and writing poetry. Through these experiences a new rhythm emerged in his writing, and a series of poems such as "The Weary Blues" were penned. He returned to Harlem in 1924, during the period known as the Harlem Renaissance. In 1925, he won first prize in poetry in *Opportunity* magazine and met the writer Carl Van Vechten, who assisted Hughes in securing a book contract with publisher Alfred A. Knopf. He also enjoyed the acclaim he received from the poet Vachel Lindsay. Hughes received a scholarship to Lincoln University, in Pennsylvania, where he received his B.A. degree in 1929. In 1943, he was awarded an honorary Litt.D by his alma mater, a Guggenheim Fellowship in 1935 and a Rosenwald Fellowship in 1940. Langston Hughes died on May 22, 1967. His residence at 20 East 127th Street in Harlem, has been given landmark status by the New York City Preservation Commission and the street on which he lived has been renamed "Langston Hughes Place."

COUNTEE CULLEN (1903-1946)

As a black, middle-class New Yorker associated with the Harlem Renaissance school, Countee Cullen was faced with the dilemma of wanting to be a traditional poet while, at the same time, remaining faithful to his responsibility for articulating the black experience. As a poet, Countee Cullen was conservative. While he did not ignore racial themes, he based his works on the models of 19th-century Romantic poets, especially Keats, and often used the traditional sonnet form. Born in 1903 in Louisville, Kentucky or Baltimore, Maryland, Cullen was raised by a woman who was probably his paternal grandmother. His real mother did not contact him until he became famous in the 1920s. At about the age of fifteen, Countee Cullen was adopted by the Reverend F.A. Cullen of Salem M.E. Church, one of the largest congregations in Harlem. Later on, Reverend Cullen became the head of the Harlem chapter of the NAACP. As a schoolboy in New York City, Countee won a citywide poetry contest. He also had the advantage of being able to travel in Europe. He earned a Phi Beta Kappa at New York University where he also published his first collection of poems, *Color* (1925) before receiving a B.A. in 1925. He earned an M.A. from Harvard in 1926 and worked as assistant editor for *Opportunity* magazine, where his column, 'The Dark

Tower,' increased his literary reputation. He prefaced his anthology of black poetry, *Caroling Dusk* (1927), by stating the forms of English poetry, not transcriptions of black dialects, were the proper artistic tools. The book was an important document for the Harlem Renaissance poets. His Guggenheim Fellowship of 1928 enabled him to study and write abroad and between the years 1928 and 1934 Cullen travelled back and forth between France and the United States. Unfortunately, his first marriage, to Nina Yolande DuBois, daughter of W.E.B. DuBois, did not succeed and they divorced in 1930. Cullen' second marriage was to Ida Mae Robertson. While he is recognized for his talent as a traditional poet, he worked hard to bring black themes to the awareness of white readers. Cullen died on January 9, 1946.

MELVIN BEAUNORUS TOLSON (1898-1966)

During a propitious year spent in New York in 1930-31, where he was enrolled as a masters degree student at Columbia University, Tolson wrote his first poetry, a group of short narratives, loosely allied with the free verse of Edgar Lee Masters's *Spoon River Anthology.* A few of the poems from that manuscript were published from 1937 to 1939, but the whole work would await printing until the late 1970s when Robert M. Farnsworth presented it as *A Gallery of Harlem Portraits.* Some elements, a few character-types, and the urban setting in these early poems all reappear in Tolson's final published work, *Harlem Gallery* (1965), a long poem in several sections (each with the letter of the Greek alphabet), subtitled *The Curator*, and the first of a projected series of long poems on African-American life. Tolson was born in Moberly, Missouri on February 6, 1898. In 1922, he married Ruth Southall and in 1924 he graduated with honors from Lincoln University. Thereafter, from 1924 until 1947 he taught at Wiley College in Marshall, Texas, taking a year's leave in 1930 to pursue a master's degree from Columbia, where his thesis project centered on interviewing members of the Harlem Renaissance. From 1947 onward he taught at Langston University in Langston, Oklahoma (where he also served three terms, from 1954 to 1960, as Mayor). Tolson's interest, in the 1930s, was in capturing the black vernacular, and in presenting black experience. Excerpts from songs, usually in a black dialect, appear scattered through the texts. In this poetry, Harlem is a viable community, held together by individuals both good and bad, both self-destructive and willing to help others. In contrast to his work during this period, Tolson's *Harlem Gallery*, published in 1965, is written in an artificial and highly intellectualized discourse that he began to develop in the postwar years, a combination of colorful slang and intellectual allusions. Tolson died on August 29, 1966 in Dallas, Texas.

Contributors

HAROLD BLOOM is Sterling Professor of the Humanities at Yale University and Henry W. and Albert A. Berg Professor of English at the New York University Graduate School. He is the author of over 20 books, including *Shelly's Mythmaking* (1959), *The Visionary Company* (1961), *Blake's Apocalypse* (1963), *Yeats* (1970), *A Map of Misreading* (1975), *Kabbalah and Criticism* (1975), *Agon: Toward a Theory of Revisionism* (1982), *The American Religion* (1992), *The Western Canon* (1994), and *Omens of Millennium: The Gnosis of Angels, Dreams, and Resurrection* (1996). *The Anxiety of Influence* (1973) sets forth Professor Bloom's provocative theory of the literary relationships between the great writers and their predecessors. His most recent books include *Shakespeare: The Invention of the Human*, a 1998 National Book Award finalist, and *How to Read and Why*, which was published in 2000. In 1999, Professor Bloom received the prestigious American Academy of Arts and Letters Gold Medal for Criticism.

MARCELLUS BLOUNT is Associate Professor of English and Comparative Literature at Columbia University. He is a contributing editor of *Representing Black Men* (1996).

LEO HAMALIAN is Professor of English at the City College of New York. He is the author of *As Others See Us: The Armenian Image in Literature* (1980), and co-editor of *Lost Plays of the Harlem Renaissance: 1920-1940* (1996) and *Roots of African-American Drama: An Anthology of Early Plays – 1858-1938* (1991).

Patricia Liggins Hill teaches at the University of San Francisco. She is an editor of *Call and Response: The Riverside Anthology of the African-American Literary Tradition* (1998).

George B. Hutchinson is Associate Professor and Chair of the American Studies Program at the University of Tennessee, Knoxville. He is the author of *The Ecstatic Whitman: Literary Shamanism and the Crisis of the Union* (1986).

John Keeling teaches English at Virginia Polytechnic Institute and State University. He is the author of "The Moment Unravels: Reading John Ashberry's 'Litany'" (1992).

Geta J. LeSeur teaches English in the Department of Afro-American Studies at the University of California at Berkeley. She is the author of *Not All Okies are White: The Lives of Black Cotton Pickers in Arizona* (2000) and *Ten is the Age of Darkness: The Black Bildungsroman* (1995).

Richard A. Long is a faculty member in the Department of English at Atlanta University, Atlanta, Georgia. He is the author of *The Black Tradition in American Dance* (1989) and *Grown Deep: Essays on the Harlem Renaissance* (1998).

Julian D. Mason is Professor of English emeritus at the University of North Carolina at Charlotte. He is the author of "'Ocean': A New Poem by Phillis Wheatley" (1999) and "Charles Dickens in the Land We Love" (1987).

Sondra O'Neale has been Professor of English at Wayne State University. She is the author of *Jupiter Hammon and the Biblical Beginnings of African-American Literature* (1993) and an editor of *Keepers of the Flame: Power, Myth and Cultural Consciousness in Ethnic Female Identity* (1998).

Anita Patterson is Assistant Professor of English at Boston University. She is the author of *From Emerson to King: Democracy, Race, and the Politics of Protest* (1997) and "Jazz, Realism and the Modernist Lyric: The Poetry of Langston Hughes" (2000).

Peter Powers is Assistant Professor of English at Messiah College, Grantham, Pennsylvania. He is the author of *Recalling Religions: Resistance, Memory and Cultural Revision in Ethnic Women's Literature* (2001).

Mariann B. Russell is one of the pioneering scholars of Melvin B. Tolson. She is the author of *Melvin B. Tolson's Harlem Gallery: A Literary Analysis* (1980).

Ronald E. Sheasby holds a teaching assistantship at Northern Illinois University. His short stories have been published in three periodicals: *HMGS Dispatch*, *Just a Moment* and the *Elysian Fields Quarterly*.

Gary Smith is Assistant Professor of English at Southern Illinois University-Carbondale. He is the author of *Songs for My Father: Poems* (1984) and co-editor of *A Life Distilled: Gwendolyn Brooks, Her Poetry and Fiction* (1989).

Ralph Story is a specialist in Afro-American literature and teaches at the University of Michigan in Ann Arbor. He is the author of "An Excursion into the Black World: The 'Seven Days' in Toni Morrison's *Song of Solomon*" (1989).

John S. Wright is Associate Professor of English at the University of Minnesota. He is co-editor of *A Stronger Soul Within a Finer Frame: Portraying African-Americans in the Black Renaissance* (1990) and an editor of a special issue of *The Carleton Miscellany* devoted to the works of Ralph Ellison.

Acknowledgments

"The Preacherly Text: African American Poetry and Vernacular Performance" by Marcellus Blount from *PMLA*, vol. 107, no. 3 (May 1992): pp. 582-93. Reprinted with Permission.

"D.H. Lawrence and Black Writers" by Leo Hamalian. From *Journal of Modern Literature*, vol. 16, no. 4 (Spring 1990): pp. 579–596. © 1990 by the Indiana University Press. Reprinted with Permission.

"Introduction" by Julian D. Mason, Jr. from *The Poems of Phillis Wheatley* edited and with an introduction by Julian D. Mason Jr. pp. 1–22. © 1966 by the University of North Carolina Press, renewed 1989. Used by permission of the publisher.

"A Slave's Subtle War: Phillis Wheatley's Use of Biblical Myth and Symbol" by Sondra O'Neale. From *Early American Literature*, vol. 21, no. 2 (Fall 1986): pp. 144-65. ©1986 by the Department of English at the University of North Carolina, Chapel Hill. Used by permission of the University of North Carolina Press.

"Let Me Make the Songs for the People": A Study of Frances Watkins Harper's Poetry by Patricia Liggins Hill. From *Black American Literature Forum*, vol. 15, no. 2 (Summer 1981): pp. 60-65. © 1981 Indiana State University. Reprinted with Permission.

"Paul Dunbar and the Mask of Dialect" by John Keeling. From *The Southern Literary Journal*, vol. XXV, no. 2 (Spring, 1993): pp. 24-38. © 1993 by the Department of English of the University of North Carolina at

Chapel Hill. Used by permission of the University of North Carolina Press.

"Paul Lawrence Dunbar: Master Player in a Fixed Game" by Ralph Story. From *CLA Journal* XXVII, no. 1 (September 1983): pp. 30-55. © 1983 by the College Language Association. Reprinted with Permission.

"A Weapon of My Song: The Poetry of James Weldon Johnson" by Richard A. Long from *Phylon* vol. XXXII, no. 4 (1971): 374-82. Reprinted with Permission.

"Claude McKay's Romanticism" by Geta J. LeSeur. From *CLA Journal* XXXII, no. 3 (March 1989): pp. 296-308. © 1989 by the College Language Association. Reprinted with Permission.

"The Whitman Legacy and the Harlem Renaissance" by George B. Hutchinson. From *Walt Whitman: The Centennial Essays*, Ed Folsom, editor. (Iowa City: University of Iowa Press 1994): pp. 201-16.© 1994 University of Iowa Press. Reprinted with Permission.

The New Negro Poet and the Nachal Man: Sterling Brown's Folk Odyssey by John S. Wright. From *Black American Literature Forum* 23, no. 1 (Spring 1989): pp. 95-105. © 1989 Indiana State University. Reprinted with Permission.

"Jazz, Realism, and the Modernist Lyric: The Poetry of Langston Hughes" by Anita Patterson from *Modern Language Quarterly* 61, no. 4 (December 2000): pp. 651-682. Reprinted with Permission.

"'The Singing Man Who Must be Reckoned With': Private Desire and Public Responsibility in the Poetry of Countée Cullen" by Peter Powers. From *African American Review*, vol. 34, no. 4 (2000): pp. 661-78. Reprinted with Permission.

Dual Reality: Echoes of Blake's Tiger in Cullen's Heritage by Ronald E. Sheasby from *CLA Journal* XXXIX, no. 2 (December 1995): pp. 219-27. © 1995 by the College Language Association. Reprinted with Permission.

Reprinted by permission of The University of Tennessee Press. Mariann B. Russell, "Evolution of Style in the Poetry of Melvin B. Tolson" from *Black American Poets Between Worlds, 1940-1960*, edited by R. Baxter Miller, Tennessee Studies in Literature, volume 30. © 1986 by The University of Tennessee Press.

"A Hamlet Rives Us: The Sonnets of Melvin B. Tolson" by Gary Smith. From *CLA Journal* XXIX, no. 3 (March 1986): pp. 261-75. © 1986 by the College Language Association. Reprinted with Permission.

Index

DATE DUE
